Why Governments and Parties Manipulate Elections
Theory, Practice, and Implications

Why Governments and Parties Manipulate Elections advances a general theory about the motives that drive electoral manipulation and tests some of the theory's main observable implications using a variety of empirical sources. Alberto Simpser argues that there is often substantially more at stake in manipulating elections than simply winning. The central idea is that electoral manipulation can convey information of relevance to the choices and behavior of bureaucrats, politicians, unions, businesspeople, citizens, and other political and social actors. By utilizing electoral manipulation to appear strong, therefore, a party can align actors' incentives with its own, increasing, for example, its bargaining power, reducing demands from out-of-power groups, and mitigating future political challenges. This perspective is able to account for the otherwise puzzling fact that electoral manipulation is frequently utilized excessively and perpetrated blatantly, even when manipulating in this manner cannot contribute to winning. In addition to its theoretical contributions, the book provides an empirical snapshot of the patterns and correlates of electoral manipulation around the world in recent decades.

Alberto Simpser is Assistant Professor of Political Science at the University of Chicago. He has been Research Fellow at the Center for Globalization and Governance at Princeton University and National Fellow at the Hoover Institution at Stanford University. Professor Simpser received his B.Sc. from Harvard College and his Ph.D. in Political Science and M.A. in Economics from Stanford University.

D0840520

A mis padres y abuelos, y a mi bisabuela

Political Economy of Institutions and Decisions

Series Editors

Stephen Ansolabehere, *Harvard University*
Jeffry Frieden, *Harvard University*

Founding Editors

James E. Alt, *Harvard University*
Douglass C. North, *Washington University of St. Louis*

Other books in the series

Why Governments and Parties Manipulate Elections

Theory, Practice, and Implications

ALBERTO SIMPSER

University of Chicago

CAMBRIDGE
UNIVERSITY PRESS

32 Avenue of the Americas, New York NY 10013-2473, USA

Cambridge University Press is part of the University of Cambridge.

It furthers the University's mission by disseminating knowledge in the pursuit of
education, learning and research at the highest international levels of excellence.

www.cambridge.org
Information on this title: www.cambridge.org/9781107448681

© Alberto Simpser 2013

First published 2013
First paperback edition 2014

A catalogue record for this publication is available from the British Library

Library of Congress Cataloguing in Publication data

Simpser, Alberto, 1971–
Why governments and parties manipulate elections : theory, practice, and implications / Alberto
Simpser.
    pages cm. – (Political economy of institutions and decisions)
Includes bibliographical references and index.
ISBN 978-1-107-03054-1
1. Elections – Corrupt practices.   2. Political corruption.   I. Title.
JF1083.S56   2013
364.1′323–dc23   2012036772

ISBN 978-1-107-03054-1 Hardback
ISBN 978-1-107-44868-1 Paperback

Contents

List of Figures

List of Tables

Preface

More than Winning

The initial spark for this study was the observation that there is a mismatch between actual patterns of electoral manipulation and the idea that parties manipulate with the goal of winning: quite frequently, parties assured of victory nevertheless manipulate heavily, and they do so blatantly. The residual, the part that is not accounted for by the idea of manipulating for winning, constitutes the "dark matter" of electoral manipulation: its excessive and blatant use.

Motivated by that mismatch, this book develops a theory of electoral manipulation. The key idea is that electoral manipulation is about more than meets the eye. Beyond its role in helping to accumulate more votes than the next contender, electoral manipulation can provide information to the public about the power of the manipulating party. Manipulating elections excessively and blatantly can make the manipulating party appear strong, while failing to manipulate in this manner can convey weakness. A party that is perceived to be powerful and resourceful will enjoy greater bargaining power, ampler scope for governing, a lesser need to share rents and to compromise in policy, and fewer challenges to its hold on office, than a party that is perceived to be weak and vulnerable. This set of ideas constitutes the gist of the *more than winning* theory of electoral manipulation.

Once the informational properties of electoral manipulation are recognized, the common practice of excessive and blatant electoral manipulation begins to make sense: cheaters do not stop at winning not because they err or miscalculate, but rather because their goal is something other than simply reaching the victory threshold. Under this view, we cease to expect that only unpopular leaders will cheat in elections. Instead, popular leaders with a strong record and a large reservoir of goodwill and legitimacy will often choose to manipulate elections substantially too. In addition, we cease to expect that electoral manipulation will be the discreet, hushed-up affair that it is supposed to be: showing that one can cheat with impunity can make one appear stronger in the public eye. Finally, the *more than winning* perspective implies that even when cheating big leads to a loss in popularity or legitimacy, this need not result in net harm for the manipulator: an unpopular ruling party may nevertheless command considerable deference if it is perceived to be strong.

Attempts at excessive and/or blatant electoral manipulation do not always succeed, but many do. Examples abound and include Mexico's PRI in its heyday, Putin's Russia, and Mugabe's Zimbabwe up until the late 1990s. This practice can form part of a self-sustaining dynamic in which a powerful ruling party further empowers itself via excessive and blatant manipulation, in turn expanding possibilities for subsequently manipulating excessively and blatantly. For this reason, the *more than winning* perspective implies that policies that render electoral manipulation more difficult, or more competitive, can have salutary effects even if they do not manage to fully prevent parties from manipulating or stealing elections. When excess and blatancy are curtailed, manipulation's informational role is undermined: a cheating party that wins with 55 percent of the vote will certainly appear weaker than one that obtains 75 percent, for example, with positive consequences for the vigor of political competition and for the relative balance of power between different social and political forces.

Alberto Simpser
Chicago
August 2012

Acknowledgments

I wrote most of this book at the University of Chicago's Department of Political Science, an extraordinary intellectual community from which this project, and I personally, have benefited enormously. For this I thank all my colleagues. I am especially grateful to Dan Slater for his ongoing, enthusiastic, and reliably insightful advice and support; to Lisa Wedeen, for finding, even as department Chair, the time to carefully read and to comment on a full draft of my manuscript; to Bernard Harcourt for his guidance and support; to Dali Yang for his confidence in this project from its early stages; to John Mark Hansen, former Dean of Social Sciences, for supporting my research and data collection efforts; and to Elisabeth Clemens, who in her capacity as Master of the Social Science Collegiate Division found the occasion to read an earlier version of this book. For their comments and guidance I am also grateful to John Brehm, Cathy Cohen, Julie Cooper, Michael Dawson, Gary Herrigel, Will Howell, John McCormick, John Mearsheimer, Sankar Muthu, Eric Oliver, John Padgett, Jennifer Pitts, Gerald Rosenberg, Betsy Sinclair, Duncan Snidal, and Steven Wilkinson. My cohort of faculty – Julie Cooper, Stan Markus, Jong-Hee Park, Betsy Sinclair, and Paul Staniland – provided advice and levity at key times. Last but not least, a nod to my candy-run companions Dan, Betsy, and Steven, without whom I would have foraged for mind fuel on my own.

This project has also been enriched by the larger community of scholars at the University of Chicago. I thank Milena Ang, Daniel Berger, Chris Berry, Ethan Bueno de Mesquita, Chris Haid, Milton Harris, José Antonio Hernández Company, Juan Fernando Ibarra, Julene Iriarte, Friedrich Katz, Pablo Montagnes, Roger Myerson, Luis Rayo, Jesse Shapiro, Boris Shor, Felicity Vabulas, and Beth Wellman for helpful conversations and for commenting on various pieces of the manuscript.

This book grew out of my doctoral work at the Department of Political Science at Stanford University. I am grateful to the members of my dissertation committee: Alberto Díaz-Cayeros, James Fearon, Stephen Haber, and Norman Nie, for invaluable guidance. I also thank Larry Diamond, Simon Jackman, David Laitin, Isabela Mares, Douglas Rivers, Kenneth Schultz, Michael Tomz, and Jeremy Weinstein for providing feedback and advice. I am especially grateful to James Fearon for providing advice and support from the early stages of this project.

Helen Milner, and the Princeton Center for Globalization and Governance (now the Niehaus Center), where she is Director, sponsored and hosted a book conference devoted to my manuscript in 2010. I am grateful for their generosity. I am also grateful to Steven Levitsky, James Snyder, Carles Boix, and Daniel Posner for being part of the conference and for providing outstanding suggestions, from which the book undoubtedly profited. A Research Fellowship from the Center, which I held in 2005–6, supported work that fed into this book project. I thank Rebecca Morton and the New York University Department of Politics for hosting me in 2005–6 as a courtesy Visiting Scholar. I also thank the Hoover Institution at Stanford University, where I was a National Fellow in 2011, for generously hosting me as I worked on the final stages of this project.

For helpful comments and conversations at different stages of this project I also thank John Aldrich, James Alt, R. Michael Alvarez, Alexandra Benham, Lee Benham, Henry Brady, Bruce Bueno de Mesquita, Gary Cox, Alexandre Debs, Desiree Desierto, Jorge Domínguez, Daniela Donno, Thad Dunning, Jonathan Fox, Adele Frankel, Sebastián Galiani, Miriam Golden, Susan Hyde, Stathis Kalyvas, Phil Keefer, Andrew Little, Peter Lorentzen, Skip Lupia, Ellen Lust-Okar, Nikolay Marinov, James McCann, Juan Molinar, Marusia Musacchio, Rohini Pande, Esteban Rossi-Hansberg, Nasos Roussias, Andreas Schedler, Mary Shirley, Susan Stokes, Milan Svolik, and Joshua Tucker. Special thanks go to Kenneth Greene for providing detailed comments on various chapter drafts; to Michael Bratton and Adrienne LeBas for carefully reading and commenting on the Zimbabwe case study; to Sergey Shpilkin for commenting on the Russia case study, for granting me an interview, and for ongoing conversations about Russian elections; to Alexander Kynev for granting me an interview; to Sergey Sanovich for comments and excellent research assistance; to Maria Yudkevich for logistical support while in Moscow; to Scott Gehlbach for guidance and helpful conversations; to Susan Hyde, for her early and ongoing support of this project; to Dara Kay Cohen for feedback on various iterations of this book; to Daniel Ziblatt for commenting on a chapter draft; to Aldo Musacchio for useful advice and comments; to Mariela Szwarcberg for providing suggestions on various chapters; and to John Nye for helpful insights and suggestions.

I also received useful comments from seminar participants at the University of Chicago, the Harris School of Public Policy, Stanford University, Princeton University, the University of Wisconsin at Madison, Yale University, the University of California at Los Angeles, the Public Choice Seminar at George Mason University, the David Rockefeller Center for Latin American Studies at

Harvard University, the Harvard-MIT Political Economy Seminar, the University of Texas at Austin, the Department of Political Science at Northwestern University, the Northwestern University Law School, the Ronald Coase Institute workshop, the Empirical Implications of Theoretical Models workshop, and the Political Economy in the Chicago Area meetings.

The Social Sciences Division at the University of Chicago provided several grants to fund the data collection reflected in this book, as did the University of Chicago Center for Latin American Studies under its directors, Dain Borges and Mauricio Tenorio, and associate director, Josh Beck. For valuable research assistantship I thank Steven Aaberg, Bushra Asif, Adam Bilinski, Avital Datskovsky, Zach Dorfman, Julene Iriarte, Dylan Silva, Beth Wellman, and Petar Yanakiev.

I thank Eric Crahan, editor for political science and history at Cambridge University Press, for overseeing most of this book's publication process with great professionalism; Lewis Bateman, senior editor for political science and history at Cambridge University Press, for setting the publication process in motion and for seeing it through its final stages; and Robert Dreesen, senior commissioning editor for the social sciences and humanities, and Abigail Zorbaugh, senior editorial assistant, for their support with the production of the book. I also thank Stephen Ansolabehere and Jeffry Frieden, coeditors of the Cambridge Series on the Political Economy of Institutions and Decisions, for including my manuscript in the series. The drawing on the cover is the work of the Mexican artist Celia Camarena. I apologize in advance to anyone I may have forgotten to acknowledge.

Finally, for their love and support, I thank my parents, grandparents, siblings, siblings-in-law, my uncles and cousins, my partner Erica, and my fun and beloved nieces and nephews Gabriel, Max, Alexis, Valeria, and Daniela.

I

Introduction and Overview

1.1 OVERVIEW OF THE ARGUMENT AND FINDINGS

More countries today call themselves democratic than ever before in history, but the elections they hold are often marred by electoral manipulation. Electoral manipulation – the set of practices that includes, among other things, stuffing ballot boxes, buying votes, and intimidating voters or candidates – violates basic political freedoms, undermines the function of elections as mechanisms of accountability, destroys confidence in electoral and democratic institutions, and can lead to social strife, to list only a few of its damaging effects. And electoral manipulation is widespread: according to my estimates, about one in four country-level executive elections in the past two decades were substantially manipulated. To place the issue in historical perspective, more elections were manipulated in 2000 than there were democracies in 1950. Despite the prevalence and the important consequences of electoral manipulation, our empirical and theoretical understanding of its causes is still limited and, crucially, cannot account for some of electoral manipulation's most common, and most pernicious, manifestations.

The central question animating this study is: why do parties, candidates, and governments utilize electoral manipulation? On an obvious level, politicians use manipulation to win, as a final push to bring their vote totals past the post. This perspective is widely held in the scholarly literature and in policy circles; but, as I show in this book, it leaves fundamental puzzles unaddressed. First, electoral manipulation is often utilized when it is patently unnecessary for victory. Second, even when electoral manipulation is needed to win, it is frequently perpetrated far beyond the victory threshold and in excess of any plausible safety margin. Third, electoral manipulation is often perpetrated blatantly, a practice that does not directly contribute to victory and goes against the intuition that, as with any cheating, the perpetrator stands only to lose if his or her activities become known. These three observations constitute what I shall call the puzzle of excessive and blatant electoral manipulation.

One recent example of this puzzle is furnished by the Russian presidential election of 2004. With levels of popularity and job approval that would make almost any Western leader envious, incumbent president Vladimir Putin was by all accounts certain to win. Nevertheless, his government grossly manipulated the election – by some estimates adding close to 10 million votes, or more than one-fifth of Putin's total – and Putin won by an enormous margin of victory, with 49 million votes against 9 million for his strongest opponent. In this case, large-scale electoral manipulation was utilized where a clean vote would have sufficed not only to win, but to win overwhelmingly.[1] The 2009 election in Iran, arguably rigged by the government on a massive scale, also resulted in an impressive margin of victory in favor of the government's candidate, of more than one-fourth the size of the electorate, or about 11 million votes.[2] Many other examples of excessive and blatant manipulation are found in the electoral histories of a range of otherwise diverse countries, and in various time periods, including present-day Belarus, Kazakhstan, Nigeria, Zambia, Zimbabwe, and Yemen, as well as in Mexico under the PRI, and Paraguay under Stroessner, to name a few.

The prevailing set of ideas about the goals and logic of electoral manipulation – to which I subsequently refer as the "prevailing wisdom" on electoral manipulation – holds that the aim of manipulation is to help win the election at hand, and that it is therefore likely to arise in tight races, where a few stolen votes can determine the difference between victory and defeat, and to yield small margins of victory. As one of Joseph Kennedy's sons said about his father, "he was willing to buy as many votes as necessary to win, but he was damned if he would buy a single extra one."[3] The prevailing wisdom also understands electoral manipulation as an activity that ought to be carried out secretly. A recent review piece, for example, concludes that "manifestly fraudulent behaviors... are things that only its victims want publicized" (Lehoucq 2003). The logic of frugality and secrecy rests on the notion that electoral manipulation is a costly and risky political strategy.[4]

The prevailing wisdom about electoral manipulation, while intuitive and widely espoused, nevertheless leaves in its wake a core puzzle: the practice of electoral manipulation in much of the world today is simply at odds with

---

[1] The estimate of the number of votes obtained via manipulation is from Myagkov, Ordeshook, and Shakin (2009). I discuss electoral manipulation in post-Soviet Russia in greater detail in Chapter 6.

[2] As in the Russian example, the Iranian incumbent would likely have won without manipulation (Ansari et al. 2009; Beber and Scacco 2009).

[3] Quoted in Argersinger 1985, 672.

[4] Electoral manipulation generally requires substantial resources, personnel, and planning, and entails the risk of eliciting punishment, inviting international criticism and reprisals, or sparking domestic unrest. I further discuss the costs and the risks of electoral manipulation in Chapter 5.

it. As the examples of Russia and Iran suggest, great effort, expense, and risk are routinely incurred to perpetrate electoral manipulation in situations when it does not – and cannot – contribute to victory, for example when victory could be secured with substantially less manipulation or with none at all. Moreover, electoral manipulation is often pursued in full view of the public – elections in Nigeria and Zimbabwe since independence, for example, have been characterized by blatant methods of electoral manipulation such as voter intimidation; and in Mexico before the 1990s, friends and neighbors could often observe those who were being visited by operatives of the ruling party to buy their votes.[5] In sum, there are many cases for which the prevailing wisdom has analytical purchase, but many others for which it does not. In other words, the literature has not explained, nor has it documented, the considerable heterogeneity in patterns of electoral manipulation.[6]

The Argument in Brief: Electoral Manipulation and Information

To understand such heterogeneity, it is necessary to expand our understanding of the causes of electoral manipulation beyond the confines of the prevailing wisdom. I develop a novel theory about the incentives of political parties and governments to engage in electoral manipulation. My theory calls into question the idea that the sole aim of electoral manipulation is immediate electoral victory; instead, my theory proposes the argument that *electoral manipulation can potentially yield substantially more than simply winning the election at hand.* Specifically, excessive and blatant manipulation has a series of intended effects that include, among other things: to discourage opposition supporters from turning out to vote or to protest; to convince bureaucrats to remain loyal to the government; to persuade potential financial backers of parties and candidates to avoid supporting the manipulator's opponents (and/or to support the incumbent candidate); to deter political elites from opposing the ruling party or from even entering the political fray; to increase the manipulator's post-electoral bargaining power vis-à-vis other political and social groups such as labor unions and other political parties; to reduce the need to share the rents and spoils of government with elites and organizations; and to enhance the career prospects of politicians at subnational levels of government. Overall, these and similar effects reduce the strength of opposition and expand the incumbent's freedom of action and bargaining power. In other words, I argue that electoral manipulation ought to be understood not merely as a marginal

---

[5] See Jason 2003 for the case of Nigeria. Elections in post-independence Zimbabwe are discussed in Chapter 6; Mexican elections in Chapter 7.

[6] A second "conventional wisdom" has developed around the study of single-party elections in highly authoritarian systems. I discuss this later in this chapter, as well as in Chapter 3. Simpser (2005) is an earlier effort to document and explain heterogeneity in patterns of electoral manipulation.

vote-getting technique, but also as an important tool for consolidating and monopolizing political power.

At its core, my theory casts elections not only as contests for office, but also as occasions for the *transmission or distortion of information*. Information about the *strength of incumbents and their rivals* is a key ingredient in political decision-making, and electoral manipulation can be strategically deployed to influence such information and, ultimately, the decisions and behaviors of a broad range of actors including politicians, activists, donors, bureaucrats, organizations, and voters, among others.[7] The informational consequences of electoral manipulation can be so strong as to motivate very substantial manipulation efforts even by parties whose victory is a foregone conclusion.

To elaborate, my theory proposes that electoral manipulation gives rise to two categories of effects. The *direct effects* of electoral manipulation refer, loosely speaking, to its contribution to *winning the election at hand*.[8] In addition, electoral manipulation can have *indirect effects*, which refer to the *influence of electoral manipulation on the subsequent choices and behavior of a wide range of political actors*.[9] The items enumerated in the previous paragraph constitute some of the main kinds of indirect effects of electoral manipulation.

As those items suggest, indirect effects can be quite beneficial to the manipulator. More generally, the potential for electoral manipulation to elicit indirect effects raises the stakes of choices by parties and governments about whether, how, and to what extent to manipulate. In addition to possibly influencing who wins the election at hand, electoral manipulation can, via its indirect effects, have consequences for the *value of office-holding*, and for the *future likelihood of holding office*.[10] Politicians presumably care not only about holding office,

---

[7] The *strength* of a political party depends on a variety of attributes of the party, including its ability to circumvent the law, its access to resources, and its willingness to utilize public resources for partisan ends. It also depends on the likely behavior of the public, including elites and citizens. Importantly, *popularity* may contribute to strength, but it is neither necessary nor sufficient for it: unpopular incumbent parties are sometimes perceived as strong (e.g., as being the "only game in town"). Therefore, my theory implies that electoral manipulation can be informative about the manipulator's strength *even if the public knows that the manipulation took place*. In such a scenario, the public would know that electoral results do not reflect the manipulator's popularity, but could still perceive the manipulator as strong – e.g., as able to circumvent the law and access resources for partisan goals. (I discuss these issues further later in this chapter and in Chapter 4).

[8] The text is accurate for the case of a winner-takes-all election under plurality rule. I provide a more general definition of direct effects, encompassing other electoral rules as well as legislative elections, in the Appendix to Chapter 4.

[9] In prior work (Simpser 2003, 2005, and 2008) I referred to these as the *informational effects* of electoral manipulation. I use the term "indirect effects" in the present work to emphasize the fact that the causal chain does not end with information itself, but instead with the effects of such information on behavior.

[10] Accordingly, indirect effects can be categorized as *electoral* and *non-electoral*, depending on whether they are relevant to the manipulating party's chances of holding office in the future, or to that party's scope for action while in office (the two categories overlap).

but also about how far they can advance their goals while they govern – by implementing the policies they prefer, appropriating rents for personal or partisan purposes, or otherwise making use of the machinery of government in the service of their objectives. To illustrate the potential effect of electoral manipulation on the value of office, consider the demands for policy concessions, or for sharing rents, that a business organization or a labor union might make on a ruling party. The use of electoral manipulation by the ruling party to obtain overwhelming electoral victories could effectively restrain such demands, by showing that no one actor is indispensable for the ruling party's hold on power. Overwhelming victories obtained via electoral manipulation can also influence a ruling party's grip on office – for example, by deterring bureaucrats from supporting rivals, or discouraging opposition supporters from turning out to vote.[11] On the flip side, the failure of a manipulating party to obtain an overwhelming electoral victory, for example, could convey weakness, potentially emboldening social and political actors to step up demands and political challenges, and in consequence reduce the party's scope for action while in office, as well as its ability to retain power in the future. In other words, the informational properties of electoral manipulation, which underlie manipulation's indirect effects, imply that the stakes of manipulating are often substantially higher than previously recognized.

The prevailing wisdom and literature on electoral manipulation pays heed mostly to direct effects.[12] I propose and show, in contrast, that electoral manipulation can be, and often is, motivated by its potential for indirect effects. Putin's Kremlin, and Mexico's PRI in its heyday, utilized electoral manipulation not to reach a majority or a plurality of the vote, but to deter and preempt potential challenges to their rule – to nip opposition in the bud, so to speak – and to increase their freedom to act while in office. In sum, I argue that electoral manipulation has an entirely different purpose from (in addition to) its intuitive role as a short-term, marginal vote-getting tactic, a purpose that has been insufficiently appreciated: to shape the behavior of political and social actors in ways that benefit the perpetrator and enhance its political power, potentially over longer time frames than the election at hand. In terms of incentives to manipulate, these motivations have proved to be just as powerful, if not more so, than the drive to reach the victory threshold in the election of the moment.

How exactly does electoral manipulation lead to indirect effects? The core of the mechanism has to do with *information*, and it can be loosely described

---

[11] Of course, electoral manipulation could simultaneously have effects on the manipulator's (and the other parties') chances of holding office, and on the value of holding office for the ruling party.

[12] I discuss the important contributions of the literatures on electoral authoritarianism (e.g., Geddes 2006; Magaloni 2006; Greene 2007; Wedeen 2008) and on single-party regimes later in this chapter.

in two simple steps. First, under the right conditions (on which more is provided later in this chapter), the consequences to individual citizens, politicians, bureaucrats, and organizations of their political choices and actions today depend strongly on which party ends up holding power tomorrow, and on how powerful such a party turns out to be. Second, electoral manipulation conveys information to the aforementioned actors precisely on these points. In Putin's Russia, for example, the perception that Putin and his associates had an unassailable hold on the Kremlin was largely fostered through the systematic use of excessive electoral manipulation since 2000, and it disciplined the whole political class for at least a decade. In contrast, in Boris Yeltsin's Russia, the widespread perception that Yeltsin's hold on office was tenuous emboldened many bureaucrats, regional officials, and other politicians to either fail to work on his behalf, or to actively support his opponents. To take another example, in Mexico in the 1990s, a history of manipulated elections by the PRI convinced citizens who sympathized with the opposition that casting a vote would at best result in frustration, if not in reprisals, and opposition turnout suffered accordingly.[13]

As these two examples illustrate, electoral manipulation can convey information about two matters that are of central relevance to the choices of actors, such as bureaucrats and citizens, among others. Such actors care about *attributes and capacities of the manipulator*: an incumbent party, for instance, that shows itself able to manipulate an election excessively and blatantly is also likely to have the resources, capacities, and inclinations to overcome or punish opponents, reward supporters, and circumvent the law. In addition, actors care about *how fellow actors are likely to behave*. For example, a citizen who supports an opposition party, yet expects that his or her fellow opposition supporters will stay at home on election day or will sell their vote in exchange for a bribe, is likely to be discouraged from turning out to vote. Insofar as electoral manipulation provides information about attributes of the perpetrator, it functions as a *costly signal*. When it provides information about the likely behavior of other actors, it works as a *coordination device*.[14]

My theory suggests the following distinctions, which I shall utilize throughout the book. Concerning the goals motivating the use of electoral manipulation, it is possible to speak of *manipulation for winning* versus *manipulation for more than winning*. The former is associated with electoral manipulation's direct effects, and the latter with its indirect ones. Concerning the outcomes of electoral manipulation, I shall term electoral manipulation yielding small margins of victory *marginal*, and that which yields large margins *excessive*.[15]

---

[13] A seminal study of political behavior along these lines in Mexico is Domínguez and McCann 1996 (see also Almond and Verba 1963).

[14] These two informational roles of electoral manipulation can coexist and reinforce each other. In Chapter 4 I develop these ideas further with the aid of simple formal models.

[15] I discuss the operationalization of these concepts in Chapter 3.

Bearing in mind that goals and outcomes are conceptually distinct, for simplicity I shall nevertheless sometimes refer to electoral manipulation aimed at winning as marginal, and to that aimed at more than winning as excessive and/or blatant, hoping that it will be clear from the context whether goals or outcomes are meant.[16] Additionally, it is worth emphasizing that the marginal versus excessive dimension of electoral manipulation does not fully overlap with the question of scale or extent: while excessive electoral manipulation is generally associated with large-scale manipulation, the marginal kind can result either from a low amount of manipulation (e.g., in a tight race) or from a large amount (e.g., when the manipulating party initially lags its rival by a substantial amount, or when two parties' manipulation efforts partially neutralize each other).

The theory advanced in this book covers, in one same framework, a variety of empirical patterns or species of electoral manipulation, including the marginal kind, described by the prevailing wisdom, as well as others that have not been systematically theorized – most importantly the excessive and/or blatant kind. Under what conditions is electoral manipulation likely to be marginal versus excessive or blatant? My theory provides insight into the proximate causes of different patterns of electoral manipulation. Generally speaking, political systems where *power is initially disproportionately concentrated* in the hands of the party in government, and where constraints on the *discretion* of government action – whether domestic or external in origin – are relatively weak, constitute fertile ground for excessive and blatant electoral manipulation. As elections have spread to increasingly diverse institutional and socioeconomic settings in the past few decades, such conditions have come to characterize many electoral systems. Contemporary examples of countries where power and resources are substantially concentrated in the hands of the party in office, and where government discretion is at best moderately constrained by the rule of law, include Nigeria, Zambia, Russia, Georgia, Belarus, Armenia, Iran, and Yemen, among many others. In contrast, where these conditions do not hold – for example, where there exist multiple competing centers of political power and resources – electoral manipulation is likely to exhibit a marginal pattern: it will be associated with tight races and slim margins of victory. Examples of the marginal pattern of manipulation include many elections in the United States historically (Campbell 2005), in Costa Rica in the first half of the twentieth century (Lehoucq and Molina 2002), and in the Philippines in the 1950s (Teehankee 2002). The theory offered here, therefore, describes a relationship

---

[16] In practice, the goals and outcomes of manipulation should often correspond, although the possibility of miscalculation – stemming, for example, from unusually high levels of uncertainty (e.g., about how much manipulation effort is needed to attain a given goal) – implies that this will not always be the case. By and large, however, uncertainty high enough to drive a substantial wedge between goals and outcomes would appear to be rare (for further discussion of this issue and its empirical evidence, see Section 5.4 in Chapter 5).

of sequential causation, where the distribution of power and resources shapes *contemporaneous* incentives to, and possibilities for, electoral manipulation; in turn, electoral manipulation influences the *subsequent* distribution of power and resources.[17] For example, at independence in 1980, Zimbabwe's government inherited a powerful state from its former colonizers, which rendered excessive and blatant manipulation both feasible and attractive for the ruling party ZANU. In turn, excessive manipulation in early elections (e.g., in 1985) further consolidated and increased ZANU's power, bolstering its capacity and its motivation to manipulate excessively and blatantly in subsequent elections (e.g., in 1990).[18]

In sum, I provide an information-based theory of the incentives underlying electoral manipulation. My argument proposes that elections are, at root, not only occasions for deciding who is to hold office, but also processes through which parties might shape public information with the potential to influence the subsequent behavior of social and political actors. In this context, electoral manipulation emerges as an instrument of political control.

Empirical Findings

In addition to the theoretical contribution sketched in the previous paragraphs, this book accomplishes two empirical goals. First, it provides a *systematic, global picture of electoral manipulation*. To aid in constructing this picture, I have collected an original dataset of electoral manipulation and related variables covering more than 800 multiparty, country-level elections around the world from 1990 through 2007.[19] The data yield some remarkable findings. For example, of all executive elections that were substantially manipulated in roughly the past two decades, more than two in five were won by the manipulating party by a margin of victory exceeding 40 percent of the vote, suggesting that excessive electoral manipulation is quite common.[20]

Second, the book *assesses some of my theory's main empirical implications* in light of quantitative and qualitative evidence from a variety of sources. The major pieces of qualitative evidence are two in-depth case studies (or "cases"), of post-Soviet Russia (1991–2008) and of Zimbabwe (1980–2008), presented in Chapter 6. The cases accomplish a number of tasks: first, they

---

[17] In the language of dynamic programming, the distribution of power and resources is a state variable, and the extent and blatancy of electoral manipulation are control (i.e., choice) variables. The distribution of power in period t shapes choices about electoral manipulation in the same period t, and such choices, in turn, influence the distribution of power in period $t + 1$.

[18] This account of events in Zimbabwe is simplified for illustrative purposes; the case is discussed in detail in Chapter 6.

[19] Countries with fewer than 1 million inhabitants are excluded.

[20] The margin of victory is the difference in the percentage of the vote obtained by the winner and the first runner-up according to official results. Further details provided in Chapter 2 and Chapter 3.

establish that electoral manipulation was used far in excess of what winning or retaining office would have warranted, and that it was perpetrated in a very public manner. Second, the cases show that excessive and blatant electoral manipulation was pursued for its indirect effects – that is, to influence the behavior of opposition politicians, party leaders, their financial backers, regional notables and bosses, voters, and organizations in ways that enhanced the perpetrator's political strength, discretion, and bargaining power. In the case of Zimbabwe, the rationale for excessive and blatant manipulation was explicitly articulated by the president. Third, the cases show how largely exogenous variation in background conditions – specifically, in the power and discretion of the ruling party – gave rise to variation in the patterns of manipulation as predicted by my theory, and that this relationship (between background conditions and patterns of manipulation) played out in similar ways in countries as different as Russia and Zimbabwe. Fourth, the cases indicate how different patterns of manipulation in turn contributed to eliciting different kinds of behavior from social and political actors – a link about which my theory, elaborated in Chapters 4 and 5, makes specific predictions. Fifth, the cases permit the assessment of some alternative explanations for excessive manipulation, supplementing the discussion of alternative explanations at the end of Chapter 5. In addition to these in-depth cases, I provide two briefer discussions of the indirect effects of electoral manipulation. The first mini-case focuses on the effect of electoral manipulation on the bargaining power of the government with respect to labor unions in Mexico, and the second mini-case on the relationship between electoral manipulation and the behavior of bureaucrats in Belarus. These are presented early in Chapter 4.

The quantitative evidence, contained in Chapter 7, continues the exploration of the indirect effects of electoral manipulation. The first two pieces of quantitative analysis focus on a specific actor: the citizen as voter. A major reason for this is data availability. I was able to locate "large N" datasets with information of relevance to my hypotheses for citizens (i.e., information about voting behavior and perceptions of electoral manipulation), but not for other categories of actors such as party elites, bureaucrats, organizations, and donors (these and other categories of actors are covered in the case studies). The first two analyses in Chapter 7 explore the indirect effects of electoral manipulation on voter behavior. The first analysis utilizes survey data for sixty-two elections in fifty-six countries to study the relationship between perceptions about electoral manipulation and the propensity of an individual citizen to cast a vote. The analysis supports an empirical implication of the theory that illustrates the central role of information: citizens – especially opposition supporters – who perceive elections to be manipulated are less likely to turn out to vote.

The second piece of quantitative analysis uses a different source of evidence to study the indirect effects of electoral manipulation on voting behavior. It makes use of the fact that Mexico undertook deep electoral reforms at the national level in the 1990s to construct a quasi-experimental estimate of the indirect effects of excessive electoral manipulation on voter participation. The analysis compares over-time changes in electoral manipulation and voter participation across the different states of Mexico. The main finding is that excessive and blatant electoral manipulation in Mexico before the 1990s substantially depressed voter participation rates, consistent with the survey findings and with the proposition that such manipulation was pursued by the PRI for its indirect effects.[21]

The final piece of analysis focuses on one of the most general empirical implications of the theory: ultimately, if excessive electoral manipulation yields tangible benefits – as I have argued – it should be associated with a longer duration in office.[22] I test this "reduced-form" idea through a duration analysis based on my original dataset. The analysis shows that excessive electoral manipulation is strongly associated with duration in office, measured either as party duration or leader duration, after controlling for a number of potential confounders.

Overall, the evidence provides strong support for the theory's central ideas. Taken together, the case studies and the quantitative analyses cover a substantial range of the observable implications of the theory. In addition, and throughout this book, I provide evidence, based on my data, about other observable implications of the theory as the discussion calls for it. Nevertheless, the theory is rich enough that future research should be able to identify and to test additional observable implications.

Sometimes, however, a single piece of evidence can be as suggestive as extensive testing of observable implications. One such piece comes from Ukraine, from a set of clandestine recordings in the 1990s of the conversations of then-president Leonid Kuchma. These recordings, known as the Melnychenko tapes, became available in 2000. The tapes contain hundreds of hours of conversations between Kuchma and other prominent figures. They were obtained via a recording device secretly installed in the president's office.[23] The tapes became most famous for linking the president to the murder of a journalist, but they cover a wide range of topics, including the 1999 presidential election.[24] In the

---

[21] The analysis in that chapter draws a distinction between voter participation elicited by electoral manipulation – e.g., through vote buying or intimidation – and participation choices not directly induced by such tactics.

[22] The empirical implication tested in this analysis, therefore, concerns the *electoral* subcategory of indirect effects – i.e., those with the potential to influence the manipulating party's future chances of retaining office.

[23] The authorities disputed the authenticity of the tapes, claiming that they were a cut-and-paste job of the president's voice. Forensic experts have concluded that it is not possible, on the basis of the available evidence, to prove or disprove the authorities' claim (because only a digital rendering of the original analogue recording is available). There are, however, at least two reasons that make the authorities' claim highly unlikely. First, the tapes contain hundreds of hours of conversations, so any falsification job would have been a monumental task. Second, the conversations in the tape – for example, on the topics of Chechnya and on the conduct of elections – correspond closely to the facts and events of the time (see Arel 2001).

[24] The murder is covered in detail in Koshiw 2003.

following excerpt, Kuchma provides directives to the interior minister Yuri Kravchenko regarding the conduct of that election. Specifically, Kuchma asks Kravchenko to convey the following message:

... tell them: guys, if you don't f-ing give as much as necessary, then tomorrow you will be where you should be – yes ... those f-ing central oblasts they should be clear, we are not gonna play f-ing games with them anymore ... we must win with a formidable margin ... when they say two or three per cent, it is not a victory ... not a f-ing place can say that it's protesting [that is, voting against the authorities].[25]

In other words, Kuchma plainly asks his lieutenants to utilize electoral manipulation not to win, but to obtain "a formidable margin," so as to preclude any semblance of a challenge to the government's rule.[26] This conversation is remarkable in that it provides a rare and candid glimpse into a manipulator's motives. It suggests, first, that the patterns of manipulation that we observe, whether marginal, excessive, or otherwise, are the result of purposeful choice by the manipulating party or parties (as well as of their capacities and limitations, of course). Second, it provides a rare unmediated glimpse into the rationale for manipulating excessively as articulated by a head of government. Third, the zeal of the president's urging suggests the importance of the underlying goal – to project, maintain, and enhance the ruling party's power. Later in the book, I document a similar episode in which Zimbabwe's Mugabe, in a public speech, expressed his desire for an overwhelming victory to "frighten away" an already weak opposition (Chapter 6).[27]

1.2 RAMIFICATIONS OF THE ARGUMENT AND RELATION TO OTHER BODIES OF WORK

Electoral manipulation is a recurrent theme at the center of a number of literatures in political science. Having described the book's core theoretical and empirical contributions, in the rest of this chapter I situate these within the scholarly literature, and briefly explore their connections to a number of areas of inquiry and practice. In the process, I take the opportunity to further elaborate various aspects of my argument. Specifically, I pursue the following six tasks. First, I highlight the main similarities and differences between my

[25] This translation is from Wilson 2005, 81; italics added.

[26] Overall, Kuchma was unable to fully consolidate his authoritarian rule, and his capacity to enact his intentions, even in the realm of manipulation, was limited (he won the 1999 presidential election with a margin of victory of 12% in the first round, not 2 or 3% but still shy of the overwhelming margins observed in many other manipulated elections; moreover various "north-central" oblasts voted in majority for Kuchma's rival Symonenko). This was the consequence of a variety of factors, among them the existence of important alternative centers of power, wealth, and institutional autonomy that he was not able to tame (Arel 2001; Way 2005a, 2005b, 2006; see also Birch 2000; Barrington and Herron 2004).

[27] As in much social science research, of course, direct evidence on motive is exceedingly difficult to obtain beyond a handful of serendipitous instances.

arguments about electoral manipulation and those that are found in the literature on elections in authoritarian regimes. Second, I explore the relationship between regime type and patterns of manipulation, drawing out the major theoretical and empirical links between the concepts of electoral authoritarianism, competitive authoritarianism, party dominance, and single-party regimes, on the one hand, and this book's analysis and findings about the practice and patterns of electoral manipulation, on the other. Third, I briefly consider the relationship between electoral manipulation and post-electoral protests. Fourth, I discuss the choice of rulers as to whether to hold elections, and the relationship of that choice to the analysis presented here. Fifth, I discuss the question of tactics or "tools" of electoral manipulation and the choice among these. Finally, I briefly consider the connections of this book's arguments with the literatures on election forensics and electoral-system reform.

Electoral manipulation encompasses a variety of tactics with the capacity to influence elections, and different literatures and individual works of scholarship engage with different subsets of such tactics. I defer a detailed discussion of the concept of electoral manipulation to the next chapter. Nevertheless, for present purposes it is helpful to highlight some relevant distinctions. Although usage varies, "electoral fraud" often refers to the subset of tactics of electoral manipulation that are utilized in temporal proximity to the election itself, such as stuffing ballot boxes or tampering with the vote count. "Vote buying" is often deemed to be different from electoral fraud, even though it is often pursued on election day (it can also be pursued in anticipation of the election).[28] Usage of the term "patronage" also varies: in some cases, it refers to the exchange of public employment for electoral support, while in others it refers more broadly to the utilization of public resources for electoral purposes in ways that may, but need not, involve government jobs as well as vote buying and other pre-electoral exchanges of goods.[29] For purposes of this book, on a conceptual level I use the term "electoral manipulation" broadly, to refer to the gamut of normatively unacceptable tactics that can be utilized for potentially influencing elections. For empirical purposes, I use a more restrictive operationalization of electoral manipulation, which nevertheless still encompasses electoral fraud and vote buying – on or before the election (and which therefore overlaps with the notion of patronage, in its broader sense).[30]

The Logic of Electoral Manipulation in Authoritarian Systems

By casting electoral manipulation as a tool to enhance, concentrate, and monopolize power over time – effectively, to shrink the space for the contestation of

---

[28] Some authors, however, implicitly include vote buying within the broader category of election fraud (e.g., Cox and Kousser 1981, 656–657).

[29] For an example of the broader usage see Greene (2007). The narrower usage is often associated with discussions of machine politics (see Stokes 2007).

[30] For further details see Chapter 2.

political rule – and not just to marginally flip electoral outcomes in tight races, I am highlighting its role as a tool of authoritarianism. This subsection considers how my arguments about electoral manipulation connect to the burgeoning literature on authoritarianism, and in particular on authoritarian regimes that hold elections.

I begin by noting that in terms of scope, this book's central ideas are simultaneously more focused and more general than the literature on authoritarian elections. They are more focused in that they center squarely on electoral manipulation, and therefore do not attempt to fully explain authoritarian regime dynamics. This book demonstrates that electoral manipulation can be harnessed as an important and effective tool of authoritarian control, but electoral manipulation is not the only such tool. At the same time, the book is broader in scope than the literature on authoritarianism because it considers electoral manipulation as it happens in electoral systems in general, not only in authoritarian ones.

In what follows, I consider two issue areas discussed both in the literature and in this book: the logic of electoral fraud and the role of electoral supermajorities.[31] With respect to the first issue, I show that much of the literature on authoritarian elections reflects the view that the main purpose of electoral fraud is to win the election at hand. I argue that this view, while correct in a subset of the cases, is conceptually incomplete and unable to account for the fact that election fraud is often utilized extensively in situations where it cannot reasonably hope to further enhance the cheater's winning chances. Regarding the second issue, I consider the idea, advanced in a handful of important studies of dominant-party authoritarian regimes, that by obtaining electoral supermajorities, parties can deter challenges from political elites and from militaries. Although that deterrence logic resembles my notion of indirect effects, it differs on a crucial point: the literature explicitly precludes the possibility that electoral manipulation might contribute to such deterrence. Instead, the literature argues, to be effective, the supermajorities must be honestly obtained, not fabricated through electoral manipulation. I argue, in contrast, that electoral supermajorities produced via electoral manipulation can effectively deter elite challenges (as well as other kinds of challenges not addressed in that literature), even if it is publicly known that the supermajoritarian result is dishonest – that is, the product of cheating.

My arguments can be understood as contributing to the growing body of scholarship that shows that seemingly democratic institutions and practices, when adopted in authoritarian regimes (also called "dictatorial" or "dominant-party" by different authors), often play roles that differ markedly from their traditional democratic purposes. As Jennifer Gandhi writes: "nominally democratic institutions under dictatorship do matter but in ways that differ from

---

[31] Electoral fraud is a subset of the broader concept of electoral manipulation, as discussed earlier in this section (on this matter see also Chapter 2).

their counterparts in democracies" (2008, xxiv).[32] Such a reexamination and updating of assumptions about the role of nominally democratic institutions and practices has produced important insights on questions such as why elections are held and what function legislatures and political parties fulfill.[33] The present book entails a similar reexamination of the practice of electoral manipulation. I show that, under authoritarianism, electoral manipulation often (but, importantly, not always) plays a role quite different from its function in more competitive or democratic systems.

Consider, for example, the practice of election fraud (a subcategory of the broader concept of electoral manipulation). Contemporary scholarship on

[32] With the so-called third wave of democratization since the 1970s, a large literature on democratic transitions has emerged. Initial optimism about the end point of such transitions eventually gave way to the sobering realizations that regime trajectories would vary, and that elections – even regular, multiparty elections – do not make a democracy (see Sartori 1993; Carothers 1997; Joseph 1997; Bunce 2000; Linz 2000; Diamond 2002; Levitsky and Way 2002; Schedler 2002; Lindberg 2006a, 2006b, among many others). This led to the reexamination of assumptions about the function of democratic forms in nondemocratic settings described in the text.

[33] Gandhi (2008) argues that legislatures and political parties are utilized by authoritarian rulers to "organize concessions" to their opponents; along similar lines, Przeworski and Gandhi (2001, 2007) suggest that dictators create legislative institutions as a way to credibly commit to giving up some control over policy to opponents. Lust-Okar (2006) suggests that the function of legislatures in authoritarian regimes is to distribute patronage to constituents. Blaydes (2008, 2010) also considers the function of elections and legislatures under authoritarianism, arguing that they play key roles in the distribution of rents and promotions among the elite, among other important functions. Boix and Svolik (2007, 2009) emphasize the role of parties and legislatures in mitigating informational asymmetries between the ruler and his allies. Specifically, they argue that such institutions render transparent the size of available rents to the ruler's allies, and thereby allay suspicions that the ruler might be stealing from them. Cox (2009) emphasizes a different kind of informational asymmetry. He argues that authoritarian rulers hold elections to learn about the military strength of their rivals and thereby avoid violent overthrow. Magaloni (2006) argues that authoritarian regimes hold elections to deter challenges from regime insiders. Geddes (2006) argues that authoritarian regimes create political parties and hold elections to deter challenges from the military. Brownlee (2007) argues that robust political parties increase regime durability. In his account, however, strong parties do not stem from acts of choice by rulers; instead, party strength depends on the success with which elite struggles are resolved at the moment that the regime is founded. Gandhi and Lust-Okar (2009) is an excellent review of this literature. Levitsky and Way (2010) focus on a slightly different question – they ask why some competitive authoritarian regimes in the post-Cold War period democratized, others remained stable, and yet others experienced turnovers without democratizing. They argue that competitive authoritarian regimes remained stable when their links to the West were relatively weak (to be precise, they speak of low "linkage," which they define in chapter 2 of their manuscript), and state and party organizations were strong. Strong parties contribute to stability in various ways, of which three are of particular relevance in the context of this discussion: they help to steal elections, they help to mobilize support for the regime, and they make it unlikely that potential defections by insiders will succeed (thereby decreasing incentives to defect). For empirical evidence on the role of co-optation in an authoritarian legislature see Malesky and Schuler (2006). For a discussion of the distinction between institutions of decision-making and institutions of implementation (and, analogously, between despotic and infrastructural power) see Slater (2003).

authoritarianism has rightly noted that electoral fraud is common in authoritarian electoral systems.[34] By and large, however, that scholarship has continued to reflect the view – consistent with that which emerges from the study of competitive or democratic political systems – that the aim of electoral fraud is to help to win the election at hand.[35] Competitive political systems are those characterized by approximate parity among two (or more) main parties in terms of resources, political power, and institutional advantages. Many such systems arose from early intra-elite divisions that eventually translated into vigorous party competition for office.[36] Examples of competitive political systems whose elections have historically exhibited electoral fraud (among other forms of electoral manipulation) include the United States, Chile in the late nineteenth and early twentieth centuries, and nineteenth-century Colombia. In cases of this sort, electoral fraud is generally aimed at winning – it seeks to tilt the balance of votes to just over the victory threshold – and it is marginal in terms of its outcome (i.e., it yields a small margin of victory). The overall scale of electoral manipulation varies from the small (e.g., contemporary United States) to the very large (e.g., the Philippines in the 1950s); but, in general, the two main contending parties are comparably equipped to campaign, to appeal to the electorate, and to manipulate elections in a variety of ways that range from buying votes to stuffing ballot boxes to intimidating opponents.[37] Under these conditions, races are often tight and efforts at election fraud are competitive, similar to arms races, with both parties seeking to tip the vote balance in their favor and neither party wanting to fall behind the other's fraud efforts. In other words, the clear purpose of election fraud in settings of this sort is victory in the election at hand. The logic of election fraud in competitive systems is intuitive and it is implicitly or explicitly echoed in many studies of elections in such systems.[38]

Scholarship on authoritarianism has generally continued to assume that the only effects of electoral fraud are its direct effects (to use my terminology). To

[34] See for instance Levitsky and Way (2002; 2010), Schedler (2002; 2006), and Diamond (2002).

[35] Some scholars of authoritarianism have noted that certain other tactics of electoral manipulation, such as "clientelism," have effects resembling what I call indirect effects; I discuss that work later in this section

[36] Bunce 2000 is an excellent critical review of the literature on democratization and the role of elites.

[37] Even tactics such as patronage (including the exchange of government jobs for electoral support) and redistricting can and have been pursued competitively where competing parties control different subnational regions and different parts of government (for example, historically in the United States; see Campbell 2005).

[38] On United States elections, see Cox and Kousser 1981; Argersinger 1985; Bensel 2004; Campbell 2005; specifically on political machines see Erie 1988; on Costa Rica see Lehoucq and Molina 2002; on Britain see Scott 1972, O'Gorman 1989; on various Latin American countries in the nineteenth century see Posada-Carbó 2000; on the Philippines see Wurfel 1963. For a review of the literature see Lehoucq 2003. For an excellent discussion of competitiveness, and of the relationship between competitive elections and a competitive regime or system, see Sartori 2005, especially chapter 7.

illustrate this point, consider the treatment of electoral fraud in recent work on dominant-party authoritarian regimes. Work on dominant-party regimes takes the view that the value of election fraud lies in its contribution to winning the election at hand. In his excellent study of dominant party success and decline, Greene expects that a dominant party will use election fraud only when "elections are predicted to be close" or, put differently, "in elections it might actually lose" (2007, 14 and 43). My argument differs from this perspective: I argue – and show empirically – that *election fraud contributes to authoritarian survival even when it does not make a difference between losing and winning* (for instance, when victory is assured). Similarly, in her important study of Mexico, Magaloni argues that "electoral fraud is... a relevant factor for authoritarian survival only inasmuch as it can make a difference between the hegemonic party's losing or winning" (2006, 21). Levitsky and Way, in their formidable analysis of the trajectories of "competitive authoritarian" regimes (i.e., authoritarian regimes that hold regular elections) around the world, note that elections in such regimes "are often hard fought contests" and winning them can require fraud (2009, chapter 2, 42). When discussing the contributions of political parties to regime survival, they emphasize that parties "help to *steal* votes" (ibid., emphasis original). In other words, the role that they implicitly accord to electoral fraud is very much along the lines of the prevailing wisdom: it contributes to victory in tight races. Birch's (2012) analysis of the causes of electoral malpractice (a concept that encompasses electoral fraud) asserts that "leaders popular enough to be relatively sure of getting re-elected on the basis of their track record alone will in most cases seek to do so," that is, they will only manipulate elections when they are not popular enough to win without doing so (57).[39] The insightful pieces by Geddes (2006) and Cox (2009) implicitly espouse similar perspectives. In recent work by Chacón (2009) and Magaloni (2010), electoral fraud in authoritarian elections is similarly assumed to function solely as a means to winning the election being contested.

In sum, the literature on authoritarian elections, similar to that on democratic elections, consistently views the goal of winning the election at hand as the main motivation behind electoral fraud. In practice, however, electoral fraud is quite often utilized *excessively*, that is, far beyond the point where it might reasonably contribute to the manipulator's winning chances. My data, for example, indicate that in almost 50 percent of the 132 countries covered by my data, electoral fraud was used excessively at some point in the 1990–2007

---

[39] Birch's argument explicitly applies to electoral authoritarian regimes. To elaborate, she argues that the central tradeoff with respect to electoral malpractice for a political leader is one between the need to cheat to win and the potential loss of legitimacy associated with cheating (e.g., p. 56). Legitimacy is implicitly defined by Birch as an umbrella concept encompassing "procedural legitimacy," reflecting the degree to which the public approves of the conduct of elections, and "performance legitimacy," which pertains to the economic track record of the leader.

period.[40] Existing arguments about election fraud cannot account for this fact, nor can they account for the related observation that fraud is often perpetrated blatantly. My work complements the scholarship on authoritarian regime practices by showing that there exist additional motives driving election fraud (and electoral manipulation more generally) and that such motives are especially likely to operate in authoritarian settings.[41]

I now turn to the issue of electoral supermajorities. Various authors writing on authoritarian elections have independently articulated the idea that electoral supermajorities can indicate high levels of popular support, which in turn deters certain kinds of challenges to the ruler – challenges from regional notables (Boix and Svolik 2007), regime insiders (Magaloni 2006), or the military (Geddes 2006).[42] This idea is similar in spirit to this book's notion of indirect effects, but critically different upon closer scrutiny. To establish this difference I first characterize the ideas in the existing literature and then show how they differ from this book's arguments. The crux of the matter is the claim, in the existing literature, that supermajorities obtained via electoral manipulation cannot deter challenges because they do not signal popular support. The issue is best captured by Geddes' phrase: "honest super majorities" (2006, 21). Geddes argues that unless supermajorities are "honest" – that is, obtained without electoral manipulation – they cannot effectively deter military challenges.[43] For the case of Mexico, Magaloni writes that "electoral victories obtained simply by stuffing the ballots were insufficient to convince powerful politicians within the ruling party of the regime's might" (2006, 9). What is needed instead is "cheering crowds at rallies, TV coverage of adoring supporters, and massive numbers of real voters," writes Geddes (2006, 21). Similarly, Cox argues that electoral manipulation cannot be used by a government to signal power; but attendance at rallies is informative about government power (2009, 12–13) – an idea that echoes Geddes' notion of the honest supermajority. In a study of the role of legislatures and elections in authoritarian regimes, Boix and Svolik (2007) argue that a spoils-sharing bargain between a dictator and his local notables is key to a regime's stability and longevity. In order for the dictator to be willing to share spoils with a specific notable, however, he must be able to

---

[40] On the basis of my country-level data described in Chapter 2. An election counts as excessively fraudulent if it is highly fraudulent and it is won by a margin of victory of at least 20 percent. The figure in the text excludes vote buying before the day of the election as well as any other pre-electoral tactics of manipulation covered by my data. In this calculation, I do not distinguish by regime type; for a breakdown of the incidence of excessive electoral manipulation by regime type see Table 5.2 in Chapter 5.

[41] My argument is sketched earlier in this chapter, and further elaborated in Chapters 4 and 5.

[42] A supermajority in this literature is understood as electoral support in excess of the victory threshold. I discuss the work on the slightly different concept of supermajorities in legislatures (e.g., Groseclose and Snyder 1996) in the Appendix to Chapter 4.

[43] The logic is that the military cares about levels of popular support, and that it is able to tell a genuine supermajoritarian victory from one manufactured via electoral manipulation.

verify the notable's capacity to mobilize people and resources (14, 27).[44] Enter elections: "modern autocracies have solved [the dictator's] monitoring problem via the institution of elections," because electoral results are "an imperfect but public signal of [a notable's] influence" (5). The logic is similar to that in Cox, Geddes, and Magaloni's analyses, in the sense that elections signal popular support. Consistent with this logic, Boix and Svolik argue that if elections are to be a valuable signal, they cannot be more than "partially fraudulent" (4), as wholly fraudulent results would bear no relationship to that which the notable is supposed to signal – that is, his ability to influence those over whom he rules. Honest electoral results, in contrast, would reflect peoples' true allegiances as well as the degree to which their livelihoods are linked to the notable via state jobs and other long-term patronage (10, 25). In sum, these analyses argue that electoral manipulation undermines the potential for elections to signal popular support and, therefore, to deter challengers.

This book's arguments depart from the literature just reviewed on two counts. First, I propose that *supermajorities, even when obtained via electoral manipulation, can signal power*. For one thing, power does not solely rest on popular support, as the histories of many electoral systems attest. Access to wealth and resources, control over financial, electoral, legal, and judicial institutions, and the allegiance of intelligence and security bureaucracies, among other things, are decisive pillars of power, and supermajorities manufactured via electoral manipulation can certainly signal power resting on such pillars.[45] In other words, even "dishonest" supermajorities can be informative.

Second, I have suggested, for this very reason, that supermajorities manufactured via electoral manipulation can, and do, *influence the behavior of a wide range of political actors to the benefit of the perpetrator*, including those actors considered in the literature just reviewed (regime insiders, the military, and, from the point of view of local politicians, the dictator), as well as others – including bureaucrats, voters, political parties, their financial supporters, labor unions, and other organizations. It is worth noting that the literature's perspective on electoral supermajorities, and the ideas I have proposed here, have at least one sharply divergent observable implication: according to the logic of the works just reviewed, highly popular rulers should not manipulate elections because, without manipulation, they stand to obtain honest supermajoritarian victories – a highly advantageous outcome. For such rulers, manipulating could be counterproductive: it could mask their true supermajoritarian popularity by making it difficult for onlookers to discern, on the basis of the electoral results, where the popularity ends and the manipulation begins. In contrast, this book's notion of indirect effects implies that even rulers who can count on an honest supermajoritarian victory might have much to gain from manipulating the

---

44 The dictator simultaneously cares about the notable's capacity to help to defend him from rival attacks, and about the notable's capacity to challenge the dictator's rule.

45 For a discussion of the sources of political power in Zimbabwe and in Russia, see Chapter 6.

election to expand the size of their victory. In the following chapters, I discuss various examples of rulers who substantially manipulated elections that they could have easily won cleanly, including Robert Mugabe in the 1980s and early 1990s, Vladimir Putin, and Belarus' Lukashenko. Many other examples exist. On the basis of my data, I estimate that *popular rulers were at least as likely to manipulate elections as unpopular ones* in the past two decades or so, and they were more likely to manipulate them excessively.[46] In sum, I argue, in contrast with the literature, that both "honest" and "dishonest" supermajorities can be effectively utilized to enhance power. The key point is that popularity is only one among a variety of facets of the manipulator's strength that supermajoritarian results might signal.

Finally, I briefly discuss a handful of works on dominant-party or fully authoritarian regimes containing ideas about the role of electoral manipulation that are closer to the present book's arguments than the rest of the literature. Greene (2007), in his study of how dominant parties sustain themselves in power, argues that the use of patronage by the dominant party influences party elite recruitment and defections, opposition party coordination, and political donations. In other words, Greene attributes to dominant-party patronage effects akin to what I term here indirect effects, in relation to these outcomes. There are, however, important differences with the arguments presented in this book. First, when it comes to electoral manipulation more generally, our approaches diverge. Greene's treatment of election fraud, for example, is consistent with the prevailing wisdom (i.e., the view that the purpose of election fraud is to win the election at hand), as mentioned earlier. Second, information plays a central role in my arguments, but not in Greene's.[47] Third, the arguments presented here apply to a broader range of actors than those considered in Greene (2007), as well as to regimes that are not dominant-party authoritarian.

An important exception to the literature's view about the role of supermajoritarian victories is Lisa Wedeen's analysis of the 1999 presidential election in Yemen (Wedeen 2008). Wedeen argues that the Yemeni government could easily have won the 1999 presidential election cleanly (73–74), but the government nevertheless engaged in substantial manipulation. Wedeen argues

---

[46] For this calculation, popularity is based on the latest opinion poll prior to an election that I could locate, considering an incumbent party popular if the poll gives it a plurality of electoral support, and unpopular otherwise. The next two chapters provide further details on the data and on the measurement of electoral manipulation; Chapter 5, Section 5.3, discusses the relationship between incumbent popularity and patterns of manipulation.

[47] Consider, for example, our respective accounts of the mechanism linking electoral manipulation (specifically patronage, in Greene's study) to opposition party coordination. Greene's mechanism emphasizes ideological (i.e., programmatic) differences among opposition parties (2007, 63 and 308–309). In contrast, in the theory advanced here, coordination success or failure depends on beliefs about how other parties and actors are likely to behave, an issue on which electoral manipulation can provide information.

that it did so to signal its power: "the 'elections' conveyed to politicians in the opposition and to disaffected ordinary citizens that the regime could actively intervene to foreclose certain democratic possibilities" (75). In contrast with Magaloni, Geddes, and Cox, Wedeen rightly notes that the regime's actions signaled (and generated) power even though it was plain to everyone that the election was a sham and did not accurately reflect the preferences of the people – in other words, even though the large margin of victory was not an "honest supermajority." In fact, Wedeen argues, the very fact that the election was a sham could have helped to convey the authoritarian message: "the excessive bogusness operated both as a signaling device and a mechanism for reproducing the quasi-autocratic political power it signaled" (74). Her account of the Yemeni election is in line with the relevant part of my argument: excessive and blatant electoral manipulation can be used by the regime to communicate its power to the public at large. Because electoral manipulation is not Wedeen's primary focus – the chapter where this analysis is found focuses on the relationship between state power and the experience of citizenship – she does not theorize about the role of electoral manipulation more generally, nor does she investigate how her perspective on electoral manipulation might generalize beyond the Yemeni case. Nevertheless, she does theorize about the power of charade-like spectacles more generally, of which elections can be an instance.[48] Also close in spirit to some of the arguments presented here is Przeworski and Gandhi's suggestion, in their seminal article on the role of democratic institutions in authoritarian regimes, that the reason that dictators hold elections is to intimidate potential opposition (2006, 21). In contrast with the theory advanced here, which focuses on incentives to manipulate, their insight focuses on the decision of dictators about whether or not to hold elections in the first place.[49]

Regime Type and Electoral Manipulation

What is the relationship between the type of regime in place and electoral manipulation? And, in particular, is excessive and blatant manipulation associated with a specific kind of regime? When thinking about regime type, it is helpful to follow the literature on the topic and move beyond the authoritarian-democratic dichotomy. A few years after the number of electoral regimes around the world exploded in the early 1990s, scholars and analysts remarked on the fact that many of these regimes fell short of democratic standards (Carothers 1997; Joseph 1997). Moreover, scholars noted that these regimes

---

[48] Another exception to the literature is Simpser (2003), which argued that "electoral fraud is not only about creating, obtaining or eliminating ballots, but also about transmitting messages to potential voters – messages, for example, that discourage those who favor opposition forces from voting," and that electoral manipulation could have effects that transcend those on the election in which it is perpetrated, for example by reinforcing "beliefs about the invincibility of the incumbent" (3, 24–25; see also Simpser 2005 for further elaboration).

[49] Also, Gandhi and Przeworski devote only a few sentences to this idea.

were neither fully democratic nor fully authoritarian, but they appeared to be stable, and therefore to constitute regime types of their own. Collectively, such regimes have been called hybrid or electoral authoritarian.[50] Within this general category, scholars have identified "competitive" and "hegemonic" subcategories. Levitsky and Way (2002) coined the term "competitive authoritarianism," and identified it as a subcategory of electoral authoritarian regimes, one that displays real electoral competition albeit in a substantially biased playing field. They and Schedler draw a distinction between competitive and hegemonic authoritarian regimes – in the latter, elections are regularly held but are of limited significance in the contestation of power, "little more than a theatrical setting" (Schedler 2002, 47).[51] Howard and Roessler (2006), drawing on this and other work, provide the following classification of regimes, in decreasing order according to the degree of their democratic quality: liberal democracy, electoral democracy, competitive authoritarianism, hegemonic authoritarianism, and closed authoritarianism. All but closed authoritarian regimes hold regular, multiparty elections.[52] There is also a literature on dominant-party regimes. Greene (2007) defines a dominant-party authoritarian regime (DPAR) as a competitive authoritarian regime (in the sense of Levitsky and Way 2002) in which the ruling party has held office for either four consecutive elections or twenty years. For Magaloni (2006), an electoral regime is one-party dominant if the incumbent has been in power for at least twenty years. In her study, a regime is a "hegemonic-party autocracy" – a category roughly equivalent to Greene's DPAR – if it is one-party dominant and authoritarian.[53]

Having mapped out the different regime types, I now return to the questions at the beginning of this subsection. Consider first the general relationship of regime type and electoral manipulation. Empirically, electoral manipulation is found in all regime types, whether democratic or authoritarian; but its excessive or blatant incarnation should be more frequent in authoritarian regimes than in democratic regimes (and even more frequent in the most authoritarian among electoral authoritarian regimes). The reason for this, drawing from the theory advanced in this book, is that the enabling conditions for excessive or blatant manipulation are more common in some regime types than in others – in particular the power and discretion of incumbents are generally greater in authoritarian regimes.

---

[50] Different authors used different terminology. See Carothers 2000; Diamond 2002; Levitsky and Way 2002; Schedler 2002, 2006; and Ottaway 2003, among others.

[51] See also Sartori 1976 for an earlier conceptualization of a hegemonic party system.

[52] It is not entirely clear whether Howard and Roessler consider single-party regimes that hold national elections to be hegemonic authoritarian or closed authoritarian (but it is clear that, in their scheme, many if not all hegemonic authoritarian regimes hold regular, multiparty elections). Hyde and Marinov (2011) provide necessary and sufficient criteria for an election to be "competitive," independent of regime type: opposition must be allowed, multiple parties must be legal, and more than one candidate must be allowed to compete.

[53] For a more precise enumeration of conditions, and for Magaloni's subtle approach to distinguishing between democracy and autocracy, see Magaloni 2006, 36–38.

This leads to the second question – about the relationship between authoritarianism and excessive or blatant manipulation. Both conceptually and empirically, the main point is that excessive or blatant manipulation straddles regime types, and regime types straddle patterns of manipulation. On a conceptual level, the conditions that render excessive/blatant manipulation likely – strong and relatively unconstrained incumbents – can be found in all types of authoritarian regimes. At the same time, nothing in the definition of these regimes requires that manipulation, when present, should necessarily be excessive: rulers in competitive authoritarian and in dominant-party authoritarian regimes, even if strong, may not be strong enough to pull off excessive manipulation. Therefore, while excessive electoral manipulation is more likely to arise where the level of authoritarianism is higher, there is no reason to expect that the type of authoritarian regime will fully predict either the incidence or the pattern of electoral manipulation.

These expectations are borne out in the data: all authoritarian regime types – competitive, hegemonic, closed, or dominant-party – exhibit elections that are manipulated marginally and elections that are manipulated excessively or blatantly. Within competitive authoritarian regimes, as classified by Levitsky and Way (2010), examples of marginally manipulated elections include the presidential elections in Ukraine in 1994 and in Zimbabwe in 2002; an example of an excessively manipulated election is the 2004 Russian contest. The 2006 election in Belarus is an instance of excessive electoral manipulation in a hegemonic authoritarian regime.[54] More generally, among competitive authoritarian regimes, only about half of all elections are excessively or blatantly manipulated. Nevertheless, the majority of authoritarian regimes – whether competitive, hegemonic, or dominant-party – have at some point experienced excessive manipulation. These findings are based on the analysis of my original data presented in Chapter 5.

In a sense, then, excessive or blatant electoral manipulation is a more widespread phenomenon than either competitive authoritarianism or party dominance: the set of countries that have exhibited one or more excessively manipulated election is appreciably larger than the set of competitive authoritarian regimes (Levitsky and Way 2010), or the set of dominant-party authoritarian regimes (Magaloni 2006; Greene 2007). Of the 132 countries for which I have information, 82 (or 62 percent) witnessed at least one excessively manipulated election in the 1990–2007 period.[55] As a point of comparison, Levitsky

---

[54] Regime type classifications taken from Levitsky and Way (2009, chapter 1, 31). They consider Ukraine in the 1992–2004 period, Zimbabwe since 1980, Russia in the 1992–2007 period, and Belarus in the 1992–1996 period to be competitive authoritarian. They find that by 2000, Belarus' regime had become hegemonic authoritarian (Levitsky and Way 2009, chapter 5, 31). For details on the operationalization of excessive manipulation see my Chapter 3.

[55] In this count, an election is considered excessively manipulated if it was substantially manipulated and the margin was at least 20%. Restricting to cases with margins of at least 30% yields a total of seventy-one countries. Restricting the data to the 1990–1995 period (the time period in which Levitsky and Way (2010) count the number of competitive authoritarian regimes)

and Way (2010) count thirty-four countries with competitive authoritarian regimes between 1990 and 1995. Magaloni enumerates twenty hegemonic-party autocracies (2006, 40), and Greene (2010) counts seven dominant-party authoritarian regimes.[56]

Finally, a few additional notes are in order regarding the conceptual relationship between party dominance and excessive/blatant electoral manipulation. First, party dominance need not be related to electoral manipulation, whether marginal or excessive. Sartori (2005, Ch. 5), for example, distinguishes a "predominant system" from a "hegemonic" one – in both cases one party dominates politics, but only in the latter is power obtained through extra-democratic means.[57] Along similar lines, Greene (2007) contrasts dominant-party authoritarian systems with dominant-party democratic systems (e.g., Sweden under the Social Democrats).[58] Second, even when dominance relies on electoral manipulation, existing definitions of dominance do not require that such manipulation be excessive: most authors define dominance as the consistent attainment of absolute majorities, not supermajorities. Sartori, for example, defines dominance as the attainment of an absolute majority of seats across three consecutive elections (2005, 176); Greene (2007, 2010) requires holding executive office and, in parliamentary systems, an absolute majority in the legislature, across four consecutive elections or twenty years.[59] In sum, party dominance is, on the conceptual level, compatible with no electoral manipulation, with marginal manipulation, and with excessive manipulation.

Nevertheless, in light of this book's arguments, there is good reason to expect that the authoritarian variety of party dominance will often be found in association with excessive/blatant manipulation. There are two reasons for this. First, as suggested earlier, authoritarian dominance entails a kind of power imbalance that is an enabling condition for excessive/blatant manipulation. Second, excessive/blatant manipulation enhances the power of the perpetrator, and therefore can help a party to establish, or increase, dominance.[60]

Single-Party Elections and Excessive/Blatant Manipulation

I have contrasted this book's arguments with the view of electoral manipulation that emerges from the study of competitive systems – what I call the prevailing wisdom. But there is another perspective in the literature, associated with

---

yields fifty-three countries. I describe my original data in Chapter 2 and provide further details on this analysis in Chapter 5.

[56] For the list of countries see Table 5.3 in Chapter 5.

[57] Sartori also distinguishes between a dominant party and a dominant-party system (2005, 173).

[58] Thus, party dominance is found in different regime types: a dominant party can exist in a democracy, a competitive authoritarian regime, or a hegemonic authoritarian one.

[59] The dominance threshold for Pempel (1990) is a plurality of votes and seats, for Ware (1996) it is 40–50% of the vote. For critical takes on approaches to dominance see Bogaards 2004; Magaloni 2006; Greene 2007.

[60] I discuss the dynamic aspects of my argument in Chapter 5, Section 5.3.

single-party, or almost-single-party elections, such as those in Syria in the past few decades, Iraq before 2003, the Soviet Union, the former East Germany, or Cambodia between 1946 and 1981. These are distinct from all types of electoral authoritarian or dominant-party regimes previously discussed in that only one party is legally permitted to win elections. In practice, this can mean that only one party can run (as in Soviet local elections) or that multiple parties can run but must be part of a government-run "meta-party" or "front," as in the former East Germany or in Syria.[61] In general, such elections are viewed as shams by scholars and observers, because it is virtually impossible, by construction, for the ruling party to lose office.[62] In the Soviet Union, for example, voting meant either approving or disapproving the single Communist Party candidate on the ballot. Cases such as Suharto's Indonesia are similar, if not as clear-cut: multiple parties were on the ballot and obtained votes, but the ruling party had such formal (not to mention informal) control over the process that it was, again, for structural reasons extremely difficult for it to lose an election.[63]

It would seem, then, that the only thing these exercises have in common with the multiparty elections that constitute the focus of this book is that they are both called – perhaps somewhat misleadingly in the single-party case – elections. Although this is true on one level, on another level I would submit that the dynamics at work in single-party elections bear a family resemblance to the logic of excessive and blatant manipulation that this book puts forth: even though single-party elections are hardly arenas for the contestation of power, their outcomes can be, and have been, informative and discouraging to potential regime opponents – citizens, organizations, bureaucrats, and regime insiders, for example – much like excessive and blatant manipulation can be in a multiparty electoral system. Observing 99 percent of one's fellow citizens cowed into "approving" the single Communist Party candidate on the ballot, as was normal in the Soviet Union, in all likelihood resulted in indirect effects similar to the ones that I enumerated earlier.[64]

Electoral Manipulation and Popular Rebellion

I have argued that excessive and blatant electoral manipulation can influence the behavior of the political class and the public in ways that serve the manipulator's interests. Isn't it equally plausible, however, that electoral manipulation could backfire? The manipulator's popularity or "legitimacy" could

---

[61] Moreover, in Syria and in the Soviet Union, the ruling party was constitutionally enshrined as the "leader" of the state.

[62] See, for instance, Hyden and Leys (1972), Sakwa and Crouch (1978), Lewis (1990), Anderson (1996), and Taylor (1996b).

[63] On Indonesia see Anderson 1983; Slater 2008.

[64] I further discuss electoral manipulation in single-party elections in Chapter 3.

suffer (Taylor 1996; Birch 2012), or the ruling party could face popular unrest (Tucker 2007; Fearon 2011). I have discussed the question of popularity earlier in this chapter and I revisit the issues of popularity and legitimacy in Chapter 4. Here, I focus on the possibility of manipulation-related post-electoral unrest.

My argument suggests that whether or not electoral manipulation sparks a popular rebellion *depends on the information conveyed by the manipulation.* Excessive and blatant manipulation can convey the message that the manipulator is strong, while failure to manipulate excessively/blatantly can make the manipulator be publicly perceived as weak.[65] Accordingly, my argument implies that, all else equal, popular protests are less likely to arise following excessive electoral manipulation than following marginal manipulation. Even when a ruling party manipulates elections blatantly, this need not spark a popular rebellion so long as the public perceives the ruling party to be powerful enough.

The empirical record suggests that large-scale popular rebellion after excessive electoral manipulation is comparatively rare, and for the most part it is marginal electoral manipulation that has sparked such rebellion. All four Colored Revolutions, for example, followed on instances of marginal manipulation. Ukraine's ruling party's efforts at manipulation in 2004 were substantial, but they attained merely a slim margin of victory (less than 3 percent of the vote in the first runoff). In Georgia's 2003 legislative election, electoral manipulations reported by European observers as "widespread," "systematic," and "egregious" only garnered the incumbent party slightly more than 3 percent of the vote in excess of the main challenger Saakashvili's party's (OSCE/ODIHR 2003b, 1). In the 2000 election in Serbia, the incumbent barely managed to reach the vote threshold needed to avert a runoff despite considerable vote rigging. And, while vote totals for Kyrgyzstan's 2005 election were only partly announced before the election was annulled, European election observers writing before the vote perceived the 2005 contest as "more competitive than previous elections" (OSCE/ODIHR 2005, 1).[66] In all four Colored Revolutions, thus, the pattern of electoral manipulation conveyed relative weakness. By way of contrast, Putin's Russia has displayed variation both in terms of the information that electoral manipulation has conveyed, as well as in the public's reactions to such electoral manipulation. All Russian national elections since at least 2003 (including the presidential elections of 2004 and 2008 and the legislative elections of 2003, 2007, and 2011) were highly manipulated (Myagkov et al. 2009; White and Barry 2011). So long as the manipulation was

---

[65] For a fuller discussion of these propositions see Chapter 4.

[66] Mexico's PRI experienced the largest election-related protests after the 1988 election, a fraudulent affair where the PRI's performance was its lowest in decades. In contrast, traditionally widespread electoral manipulation had failed to elicit such protests for decades. And allegations of election fraud in Mexico's 2006 election, also an incredibly close race, gave rise to large post-election protests.

excessive, however, no popular rebellion occurred. It is only in 2011, when the ruling party obtained its worst ever result despite the very substantial electoral manipulation, that the public chose to take to the streets.[67] More generally, my data analysis suggests that marginal electoral manipulation is statistically and substantively associated with post-election protest, while excessive electoral manipulation is not.[68]

Electoral Manipulation and the Choice to Hold Elections

Unlike some of the literature on authoritarian institutions, this book does not seek to explain why authoritarian regimes choose to hold elections. The reasons why such regimes begin to hold elections are many and varied – in some instances, rulers operate under constraints or threats (domestic or external) that virtually force them to hold elections. In other cases, the holding of elections is

---

[67] The sources of the weakening of the incumbent party in 2011 have been argued to include an increasingly prosperous middle class, Putin's very unpopular decision to "castle" yet again – that is, to run for office once more in 2012 (Whitmore, December 8, 2011; January 25, 2012) – and the associated capital flight and elite divisions (Galeotti 2012). Gazetta.ru, for instance, wrote that "... the decline in United Russia's approval rating following the announcement of the shuffle at part one of the congress on September 24 and the drain of capital from the country, which accelerated after this, and the business of the booing at the Olympic Stadium are vivid confirmation of the citizenry's weariness with the new old regime" (cited by Whitmore, November 29, 2011).

[68] On the basis of 115 country-level elections for which I collected information on the incidence and approximate size of post-election protests. Although this statistical finding is consistent with the discussion of cases and the argument offered in the body of the text, I consider the statistical finding tentative because of the relatively small proportion of cases in my dataset for which I have data on this matter. On election-related protests see also Arriola and Johnson 2012; Hafner-Burton, Hyde, and Jablonski 2012. In a related argument, Tucker (2007) has argued that election fraud is especially likely to elicit post-election protests when it is perceived to have changed the identity of the winner (536). Our respective arguments throw similar predictions about the relationship between electoral manipulation and popular protests in many instances. Nevertheless, in contrast with Tucker's, my argument predicts an increased likelihood of post-election protests even in cases where the public believes that the manipulator was the rightful winner, so long as the outcome makes the manipulator look weak. A possible example of such a situation is the 2011–2012 set of Russian elections. Although it was widely acknowledged that Putin would have won the 2012 presidential election cleanly, the fact that both the 2011 legislative and the 2012 presidential elections were perceived to be substantially manipulated and yet failed to yield victories as large as earlier elections presumably contributed to making Putin appear somewhat weakened in the eyes of the public (the legislative election yielded the lowest proportion of the vote for Putin's team in recent history, and the presidential election yielded a margin somewhat smaller than Putin's in 2004 and Medvedev's in 2008, although Putin's 2012 margin of victory was still formidable). My argument implies that post-election protests should have been likelier after those elections than after any other Russian national election since Putin rose to power, while Tucker's argument predicts no protests after the presidential election, because there was no dispute that Putin was the rightful winner. Protests did materialize, but they were relatively modest in size.

a choice that brings with it certain advantages, even for authoritarian rulers.[69] The analysis in this book begins at the moment when elections are held and investigates the causes of their manipulation. It is conceivable that, at least in some instances, the decision to hold elections in the first place – or to abolish elections altogether – could be informed by the ruling party's perceptions about the likelihood that it might be able to subsequently manipulate them. Therefore, the present study speaks to the question of the holding of elections – in other words, of the choice to begin to hold elections – by furthering existing understandings of what it is that parties, politicians, governments, and other political actors might hope to gain or lose down the line in the decision tree that begins with choices about whether to hold elections, to participate in them, and to permit opposition parties to contest them. Still, on a practical level, the institution of elections appears to be quite often a resilient fact, not one subject to constant and short-term reevaluation.[70] This makes it possible to separate, at least in such cases, the study of why elections are held in the first place from the study of strategic choice *given* that elections are held.[71]

The Variety of Tools of Electoral Manipulation

The present analysis does not set out to explain the choice of *means* or *tools* of electoral manipulation – that is, of why a party might choose to stuff ballot boxes versus tamper with the vote count versus buy votes versus intimidate voters, to take a few examples. It also does not seek to explain how specific tools of manipulation ought to be implemented, and in particular whether vote buying or vote suppression target, or ought to target, swing versus core voters. These are interesting questions in their own right and they are the subject

---

[69] Carothers, for example, writes that many governments hold elections because they "crave the attention, approval, and money that they know democracy attracts from the Western international community," and therefore pursue a "balancing act" in which "they impose enough repression to keep their opponents weak... while adhering to enough democratic formalities that they might just pass themselves off as democrats" (1997, 90–91; on why elections are held see also Przeworski 1991, Anderson 1996, Ross 2004, and Levitsky and Way 2010, among many others).

[70] Chacón (2009), for example, argues that democratization is associated with irreversible investments (e.g., in organizational capacity) that help to lock in an electoral system once it is adopted. Another factor behind the resilience of the practice of elections is the fact that international pressures to hold them are much greater than the pressures to uphold high democratic standards (see Karl 1995, Carothers 1997, and Joseph 1997, among many others). The resilience of elections is perhaps most remarkable in the most authoritarian of electoral regimes (which have been termed "hegemonic" by various authors) in which ruling parties are extremely advantaged with respect to their opponents (Levitsky and Way 2002, 2010; Schedler 2002; Howard and Roessler 2006). The timing of elections is often the subject of strategic machinations, especially in parliamentary systems.

[71] This is not to say that there do not exist instances in which both choices ought to be analyzed simultaneously, but merely that in many, and probably most scenarios, such separation is analytically possible.

of excellent recent work.[72] In the present study, I largely abstract from these issues: for purposes of the analysis in this book, different tools or techniques of electoral manipulation function largely as substitutes – as different means to the same end. The focus here is on understanding choices about the extent and the visibility of electoral manipulation, irrespective of the specific choice or mix of tools.

As a first approach to the question of the choice of tactics of manipulation, one can think of a "supply curve" of electoral manipulation, according to which those means of manipulation that yield the greatest benefits at the lowest cost will be chosen first (implying that electoral manipulation is likely to have increasing marginal costs).[73] For instance, for a party with easy access to social networks, vote buying may be a cost-effective means of obtaining votes corruptly, as in Argentina (Calvo and Murillo 2004; Levitsky 2007; Szwarcberg 2009) or in British colonial Africa (Golder and Wantchekon 2004, 9). For a party with control over the electoral bureaucracy, tampering with voter lists may be a readily accessible means of rigging an election – examples include Paraguay 1989 (NDI 1989; Molinas et al. 2006), and Mexico under the PRI, among many others. And a party with connections to specialists in violence may have ample possibilities to engage in voter intimidation, as in Nigerian elections (Adejumobi 2000, 70); or in Ghana, where Rawlings used preexisting militia-like organizations for electoral purposes after he began holding elections, as did Zimbabwe's Mugabe.

To the extent that my theory makes distinctions between different tactics of electoral manipulation, it is mostly along the dimension of *visibility* or blatancy. Choices about visibility may have implications for the choice of tactics of manipulation. To be sure, some tools of electoral manipulation tend, by their nature, to be more visible than others – for example, vote buying and vote intimidation tend to be more visible than tampering with voter registration lists or falsifying vote tallies. The choice about visibility, however, does not fully pin down the choice of tools of electoral manipulation. It is possible to intimidate voters or stuff ballot boxes, for example, with different degrees of blatancy.[74]

---

[72] See for example Scott 1969; Cox and Kousser 1981; Dixit and Londregan 1996; Dahlberg and Johansson 2002; Calvo and Murillo 2004; Stokes 2005; Díaz-Cayeros et al. 2007; Nichter 2008; Rosas and Hawkins 2008; Dekel et al. 2008; Gans-Morse et al. 2009; Szwarcberg 2009; Weitz-Shapiro 2012. Some of these pieces focus exclusively on vote buying, others study redistributive spending more broadly understood. Schaffer (2007) is a book-length treatment of vote buying.

[73] As Schedler put it, electoral transgressions should work "like the tubes of a pipe organ. If some go down, others must go up" (2002, 46). According to my data for the 1990–2007 period, among elections with manipulation, 81% exhibit more than one form of electoral manipulation (the average number of forms of electoral manipulation, given that some manipulation is present, is 3.9). The empirical relationship between the amount and the cost of electoral manipulation remains a question in need of additional research.

[74] I discuss the issue of blatancy further in Chapters 3 and 4. The extent of electoral manipulation may have implications for its visibility.

Ultimately, the question of why some tactics of electoral manipulation are chosen over others in particular circumstances remains an open one.

A growing body of work has recently focused on vote buying. Although vote buying is certainly an important category of electoral manipulation, it is rarely the only one utilized, as I document at various points in this book (through the case studies and through the quantitative analysis in Chapter 2). Moreover, it is almost always utilized in combination with other forms of manipulation. On the basis of my data, I estimate that among elections in which vote buying is used, in 91 percent of the cases it is used in combination with other forms of electoral manipulation. This discovery points to a potential gap in the literature on the targeting of vote buying: if choices about vote buying are inscribed within larger strategic choices about electoral manipulation, then it may be difficult to understand vote buying in isolation from the strategically simultaneous choices about utilizing other forms of electoral manipulation.[75]

Additional Related Literatures

There exist additional important literatures that center on other aspects of electoral manipulation. The literature on *election forensics* utilizes statistical techniques to identify anomalies in electoral figures that might indicate electoral manipulation. Forensic techniques are acquiring increasing prominence, both in scholarship and in broader publics.[76] While forensic techniques focus on detection and this book focuses on strategic choice, it is not possible to separate the two. As the forensics literature points out, election forensics indicators must be informed by a theory about the process that generated the electoral data. I discuss some implications of my arguments for forensics indicators based on turnout patterns in the context of my analysis of Mexican elections in Chapters 7 and 8. I also utilize findings of the forensics literature at various points in the book, especially in my discussion of Russian elections in Chapter 6. A related body of work studies institutional and legal reforms aimed at decreasing possibilities for electoral manipulation.[77] A central question in that literature is whether such reforms have salutary or harmful effects on levels of

---

[75] Could this speak to the debates in the vote-buying literature, e.g., about whether core or swing voters are targeted by vote buying strategies? This remains an open question awaiting additional research. Suppose, for example, that in a particular setting it is easier to buy votes (or turnout) in areas with lots of core supporters, and cheaper to tamper with vote counts in areas with lots of swing voters; then we might observe that vote buying or turnout buying targets areas with core voters for this reason alone.

[76] See Hausmann and Rigobon (2004) and Taylor (2005) on the 2004 referendum in Venezuela; Mebane (2007) on the 2006 presidential election in Mexico; Beber and Scacco (2009) and Ansari (2009) on the 2009 election in Iran. See also Wand et al. 2001; Mebane, Sekhon and Wand 2003; Myagkov and Ordeshook 2005; Mebane 2006, 2008; Mebane and Kalinin 2009; Myagkov et al. 2009; Cantú and Saiegh 2011. For an experimental approach see Hyde (2007).

[77] See Alvarez et al. 2008; Ansolabehere and Persily 2008; Ansolabehere 2009; Erikson and Minnite 2009; *Purcell v. Gonzalez*, 549 US 2006, Per Curiam; Schaffer 2002, 2008.

political participation, and specifically on voter turnout. I touch on this issue in Chapters 7 and 8.[78]

1.3 ORGANIZATION AND CHAPTER-BY-CHAPTER OVERVIEW

The book is structured in three sections. The first section, consisting of the first three chapters, motivates the study and presents some basic empirical facts. Chapter 2 discusses issues of definition and measurement, introduces the cross-national dataset, and uses the dataset to provide a descriptive "snapshot" of manipulation's institutional, socioeconomic, and geographical correlates. One of the findings of the descriptive analysis is that, although electoral manipulation in any given election generally involves a mix of different tactics of manipulation (e.g., vote buying, stuffing ballot boxes, and intimidating voters), some tactics have been more prominently used in some regions than in others in recent decades. On average, there has been more election-day fraud, for example, in the former Soviet region than elsewhere, vote buying has been most common in Asia, and obstacles to candidate entry have been greatest in the Middle East and North Africa.[79] In addition, the descriptive analysis explores the correlation between overall levels of electoral manipulation, on the one hand, and various governance, economic, institutional, demographic, and regional indicators.

---

[78] Bearing a certain resemblance to this book's concept of indirect effects, is the idea, developed in the study of American politics, that incumbent "war chests" – sums of money that candidates can use for electoral campaigning – can deter high-quality challengers and political donors (e.g. Hersch and McDougall 1994; Goodliffe 2001). Some versions of that argument consider signaling mechanisms that are formally similar to those I propose in this book (and to signaling arguments in general), but the literature on incumbent war chests is silent about electoral manipulation (see Box-Steffensmeier 1996; Milyo and Groseclose 1999; Goodliffe 2001; Ansolabehere and Snyder 2002; Goodliffe 2005; Gordon and Landa 2009, among others). An additional difference is that, in that literature, margins of victory are generally seen as a consequence, not a cause, of incumbency advantage. In my account, in contrast, incumbency advantage can be obtained by inflating margins of victory through electoral manipulation. More generally, while this book focuses on electoral manipulation, the logic of the argument advanced here could have further reach. Electoral manipulation is not the only possible means to elicit information-based effects of the kind I have described. Tactics other than electoral manipulation, such as electoral mobilization, campaign fundraising, and media efforts, for example, can potentially convey information and therefore be used for more than winning. The excessive use of such tactics (that is, their use substantially beyond the point at which they can reasonably contribute to victory in the election at hand), or the attainment of needlessly-large electoral victories through these (or through a combination of electoral manipulation and non-manipulative tactics), can function much like excessive and blatant manipulation do in this book's account: by conveying or distorting information about the strength of the different parties, they could potentially influence the behavior of a wide range of actors in ways akin to the indirect effects of electoral manipulation. For the general notion of electoral overinvestment, of which excessive and blatant electoral manipulation is an instance, see Simpser (2011).

[79] These newly-identified patterns call for an explanation (a task that lies beyond the scope and goals of this book).

Chapter 3 further discusses what I have termed the prevailing or conventional wisdom about the incentives that motivate electoral manipulation. It then utilizes the dataset mentioned earlier to document patterns of electoral manipulation that do not conform to the prevailing wisdom. In particular, the chapter documents the prevalence of excessive and of blatant electoral manipulation in country-level elections around the world in the 1990–2007 period.

The second section of the book develops my theory of electoral manipulation. The main goal of Chapter 4 is to explain the role of information in causally linking electoral manipulation, on the one hand, with the behavior of social and political actors, on the other. In other words, the focus of the chapter is primarily on the consequences of electoral manipulation. The chapter develops the concept of the indirect effects of electoral manipulation and provides extended examples of such effects, as mentioned earlier. It then elaborates, with the aid of simple formal models, the two information-based mechanisms underpinning the indirect effects of electoral manipulation discussed earlier: costly signaling and coordination.

The first half of Chapter 5 focuses on the prior step in the causal chain: it discusses the logic of strategic choices about electoral manipulation. A key theoretical result is that the prospect of indirect effects can provide incentives to manipulate excessively and blatantly. Additionally, the chapter considers the relationship between the vigor of electoral competition and patterns of electoral manipulation. Chapter 5 also discusses how variation in the background conditions – specifically those relating to the distribution of power and resources, and the discretion of the government to use its power in arbitrary ways – maps onto variation in equilibrium incentives and possibilities to manipulate and, therefore, onto observed patterns of manipulation (Section 5.3). The last section of Chapter 5 (Section 5.4) considers alternative explanations for excessive electoral manipulation, including the ideas that uncertainty, a low cost of manipulation, a high stakes of office, or the need to keep the manipulation machinery "well oiled," might motivate excessive manipulation. The respective opening sections of Chapters 4 and 5 verbally convey each of the chapter's main ideas and results.

The final section of the book, consisting of Chapters 6 and 7, explores a range of empirical implications of the theory in light of qualitative and quantitative data, as described in detail earlier in this chapter. As mentioned previously, Chapter 6 contains the qualitative evidence, while Chapter 7 presents quantitative analyses based on various kinds of information. The concluding chapter, Chapter 8, briefly discusses some further implications of the book's ideas.

2

Electoral Manipulation

Definition, Measurement, and a Snapshot

This chapter explores some of the theoretical challenges involved in defining and measuring electoral manipulation and a manipulated election. It then presents an original dataset with information on country-level elections for the 1990–2007 period, collected for purposes of the analysis in this book. Next, it implements summary measures of electoral manipulation constructed on the basis of the dataset. Finally, on the basis of the dataset, the chapter presents a brief global picture of electoral manipulation and its association with a range of institutional, economic, demographic, and governance-related variables.

2.1 WHAT IS ELECTORAL MANIPULATION?

Scholars and practitioners use a variety of terms to normatively qualify elections, including free and fair, clean, fraudulent, corrupt, and manipulated, among others. Similarly, actions that render an election unacceptable have been described as election fraud, electoral corruption, electoral manipulation, electoral malfeasance, patronage, and clientelism. In this study, I call an unacceptable election *manipulated* (and an acceptable one *clean*), and I call the actions that contribute to rendering it so instances of *electoral manipulation*.[1]

What is electoral manipulation? As is the case for many concepts in the social sciences, any definition is likely to leave room for disagreement. I believe, however, that it is possible to establish conceptual guidelines that, although not perfect, nevertheless make it possible to productively study the topic. The concept of electoral manipulation hints at a deviation from an ideal type – a "clean," "free and fair," or "fully democratic" election. In practice, no election

---

[1] Later in this chapter, I discuss the relationship between electoral manipulation and related terms and concepts.

attains the ideal type (Dahl 1956; Schedler 2002), but the degree of departure from it varies widely.

One approach to defining electoral manipulation is to utilize a principle to partition the universe of election-related actions into those that constitute instances of electoral manipulation and those that do not. Schedler, for example, speaks of "the introduction of bias into the administration of elections" (2002, 44) and Minnite and Callahan of "corruption of the process of casting and counting votes" (2003, 14). But "bias" and "corruption" are too general – further elaboration of these principles would be necessary to apply them to specific scenarios.[2]

One principle that meets the requirement of specificity is legality: an action is an instance of electoral manipulation if and only if it concerns elections and breaks the law. This is the position taken by Lehoucq (2003) in his review of the literature: "[A]n act [that potentially affects election results] is fraudulent if it breaks the law" (235). This approach is intuitively appealing and has been productively used in empirical studies that measure electoral manipulation on the basis of legal complaints (e.g., Lehoucq and Molina 2002 on Costa Rica in the first half of the twentieth century; Ziblatt 2009 on Germany in the late nineteenth and early twentieth centuries).

Nevertheless, legality has important limitations. First, using legality as the defining principle may work well in countries that have reasonably fair legal and political institutions. But in many situations, the law itself is bent for partisan and electoral purposes. For example, in the 2000 presidential election in Kyrgyzstan, a number of prominent opposition leaders were excluded from the election because of a restrictive candidate registration process that included, among other things, an "onerous language test" that constituted "an unfair obstacle to participation for many candidates," especially candidates belonging to national minorities (OSCE/ODIHR 2000a, 5–6). In his second term as president of Peru, Fujimori used the law to close down a hostile television channel, presumably for electoral motives, and changed the internal voting rules of the Junta Nacional Electoral (the National Board of Elections) to his own benefit (Levitsky 1999, 78–80). In Armenia, as the 1995 parliamentary election approached, the Armenian Revolutionary Federation, an opposition party, was banned for six months. The timing and duration of the ban were criticized by observers as electorally motivated (CSCE 1995). In Zimbabwe, President Mugabe's government has consistently used the law to attack its opponents in what Comaroff and Comaroff have called "lawfare – the resort to legal instruments ... to commit acts of political coercion" (2006, 30). In Mexico, buying votes or even coercing voters is not always illegal – a Mexican survey in 2000 found, for instance, that only 21 percent of the reported vote

---

[2] The use of "corruption" as the defining principle presents the additional problem that it is generally defined as "private gain at public expense" (Friedrich 1972), while "electoral manipulation" can be perpetrated also by parties not holding public office.

buying and election-related coercive acts were illegal (FLACSO-IFE 2000 in Cornelius 2004). Such practices, however, are widely perceived by Mexicans to be "deceptive, manipulative and exploitative" (Schedler 2004, 81–85). In other words, legal actions pertaining to elections may themselves constitute acts of electoral manipulation. As Mark Philp writes, "[T]he law... may not cover cases which are widely perceived as corrupt... [and] the law itself can originate in corrupt practices: that an act is legal does not always mean that it is not corrupt" (1997, 441). In sum, the principle of legality by itself may not suffice to adequately distinguish acts of electoral manipulation from normatively acceptable election-related acts. Where the legal system is considerably biased in favor of one of the parties, one would need to apply a prior criterion of fairness to supplement the criterion of legality.[3]

An alternative approach begins with a principled specification of what constitutes a democratic election, and then defines electoral manipulation as a departure from it. In a memorably-titled article, "The Menu of Manipulation," Schedler lays out a "chain of democratic choice" based on Robert Dahl's classic body of work on democratic theory, such that an election is considered acceptable ("democratic" is the language used by Schedler) if and only if all seven links in the chain remain "whole and unbroken" (2002, 39–43). The links in the chain of democratic choice can be summarized as follows:

1. Empowerment: offices filled via elections ought to wield real power.
2. Free supply: a wide-enough range of candidates to choose from, other than the state-sponsored ones, must be available.
3. Free demand: voters must be free to form their preferences, implying, among other things, that plural public sources of information about the candidates must be available.
4. Inclusion: the franchise must be universal.
5. Insulation: the vote must be free from bribery and coercion.
6. Integrity: votes must be counted honestly and weighted according to the principle of "one person, one vote."
7. Irreversibility: winners must be able to access office, exercise power, and complete their terms in office.

The chain of democratic choice is helpful for organizing ideas about what constitutes electoral manipulation. Electoral fraud – stuffing of ballot boxes, tampering with the vote count, and multiple voting, for example – constitutes a violation of the sixth link in the chain, integrity. Vote buying and voter intimidation violate the fifth link, insulation. Schedler also argues that the fifth link entails ballot secrecy. Arbitrary obstacles to voter registration violate

---

[3] This point is likely to apply even in countries with judicial systems generally regarded as fair. The practice of gerrymandering – the redrawing of electoral boundaries for partisan electoral purposes – for example, is often considered anti-democratic (for one thing, it creates safe districts) and some consider it a form of election fraud (e.g., fraudfactor.com).

the fourth link, inclusion. Media restrictions favoring government-sponsored candidates, as well as some campaign finance violations, contravene the third link, free demand. Bans on opposition parties or candidates, such as are present in contemporary Iran or were present in Mubarak's Egypt, violate the second link, free supply.[4]

A broad understanding of electoral manipulation, such as one based on the chain of democratic choice, works well with my theory. In the context of my argument, different tactics of electoral manipulation (such as violations of different links in the chain of democratic choice) function as different, normatively unacceptable means to a common end – whether electoral victory, some kind of indirect benefit, or both. For empirical purposes, however, there are practical reasons to take a more focused approach. Therefore, in this study I utilize two approaches to "defining" electoral manipulation: a capacious one for conceptual purposes and a more restricted and focused one for empirical tractability (in the latter case, it might be more precise to speak of an operationalization or an operational definition, rather than simply of a definition).

In the sections that follow, I develop the operational definition of electoral manipulation that I utilize for empirical purposes at various points in this study. This operationalization lays no claim to universality, but it has analytical and practical advantages. My operational definition consists simply of a list of common tactics of electoral manipulation.[5] In putting together such a list, I seek to meet three goals. First, there should be relatively little ambiguity as to whether or not the action listed constitutes an instance of electoral manipulation (I say more on this later in the chapter). Second, every listed act should be a commonly utilized tactic of electoral manipulation. Third, the list should cover a reasonably large portion of the incidences of electoral manipulation. The list includes the following main items:

- stuffing ballot boxes (or destroying ballots)
- falsifying results or otherwise tampering with the vote count
- tampering with voter registration lists
- vote buying before the election[6]
- vote buying during the election

---

[4] Note that even a principled approach may not be universally applicable without modification. Consider, for instance, the fact that the acceptability of some electoral practices has varied over time (and varies even today, albeit in relatively minor ways, from place to place). Vote buying in the United States in the nineteenth century, for example, was defended by public figures (Cox and Kousser 1981, 654) and considered an entitlement by possible voters. Today, however, it is regarded as unacceptable even by poor citizens in the post-colonial world (Schaffer and Schedler 2005, 16). To take another example, home visits by party operatives are legal in present-day United States, but they are illegal in Mexico.

[5] In determining what is "common" I draw on prior literature, on my own data collection efforts, and on informal consultations with experts on contemporary electoral practice.

[6] Including paying people to vote or refrain from voting, and/or to change the direction of their vote.

- creating obstacles to voter registration
- creating obstacles to candidate registration
- intimidating voters before the election
- intimidating voters during the election
- intimidating candidates
- voting multiple times
- voting by those who are ineligible, such as minors

In comparison with a prescriptive approach – that is, one based on an abstract principle – this list has advantages and disadvantages. On the plus side, it is concrete and therefore reduces the indeterminacy associated with overly general principles such as bias or corruption. Also, in contrast to the criterion of legality, the list avoids the definitional problems that result when legality is itself unfairly manipulated. The list is also transparent, and therefore both easy to critique and to refine. Additionally, on a practical level, the list is amenable to empirical implementation – a key advantage for the purposes of this study. Furthermore, the items on the list largely satisfy the property that when one of them is observed, it is highly likely that it constitutes an act of electoral manipulation. To see this final point, consider again the question of ambiguity. From the perspective of the analyst, potential acts of electoral manipulation become more difficult to unambiguously identify as manipulation as their temporal distance to the election increases. Whereas ballot box stuffing, when observed, can unambiguously be recognized as an instance of electoral manipulation, a law concerning media ownership, even if it obviously introduces bias in elections, can be more difficult to pin down with certainty as an action intended to influence elections – the law could be justified on alternative, non-electoral grounds (in contrast, the same is not true for ballot box stuffing).[7]

Relatedly, the items on the list are all likely to reflect deliberate choices on the part of the manipulator. To elaborate, electoral unfairness can arise either from deliberately chosen acts or from factors that, although not deliberately chosen for the purpose of influencing elections, nevertheless have such an effect. For example, certain institutional legacies may persistently bias the electoral playing field in ways that may not be attributed to deliberate choice, at least in the short term and the medium term.[8] Because my theory concerns strategic choice,

---

[7] Note, accordingly, that most of the items on my list constitute violations of those links in Schedler's chain of democratic choice that are most closely associated to election day, i.e., links five and six. See Simpser (2008) and Simpser and Donno (2012) for a detailed discussion of the notion of ambiguity in the determination of what constitutes electoral manipulation from the viewpoint of an external observer.

[8] In the long run, of course, most structure can be viewed as endogenous to agency. Birch (2012) provides a typology of electoral manipulation ("malpractice") according to whether it concerns institutions, vote choice, or the voting act. Insofar as institutions are difficult to manipulate and persist over time, electoral bias stemming from these might be closest to "structure," while electoral bias stemming from the manipulation of vote choice and of the voting act might be seen as reflecting "agency." The items on my operational definition of electoral manipulation

it is desirable that my measure of electoral manipulation reflect deliberate choice.

The coverage of the list could be deemed either too broad or too narrow. The former charge is empirically difficult to sustain: all of the items on the list are commonly used, often in combination, as tools to boost electoral results (Lehoucq and Molina 2002; Schedler 2002; Minnite and Callahan 2003; Simpser 2005).[9] Therefore, at least on empirical grounds, there is no clear basis for pruning down the list. On the other hand, the list is likely to exclude at least some instances of electoral manipulation that do not fall under any of the items covered. But this merely strengthens some of the book's central empirical findings: for example, insofar as my operational definition omits part of the manipulation that is actually taking place, this means that there may exist even more cases of excessive electoral manipulation than those I have identified.[10]

It is helpful to clarify the relationship of the above list with the concepts of "clientelism" and "patronage." These terms are used with different meanings in the literature, making it necessary to specify what is meant in order to make it possible to discuss their relationship to my operational definition of electoral manipulation. Clientelism is sometimes understood as a long-standing relationship of diffuse reciprocity in non-electoral realms, which can spill over into the electoral realm via emotional attachment or "moral debt" (Auyero 2000, 22–23; Schaffer and Schedler 2005, 9). Therefore, some argue, it is possible that clients might freely *want* to vote for their patrons, an act which should not be understood as resulting from electoral manipulation. Heise (1982), for example, writes that in nineteenth-century Chile, "the clients voted spontaneously for their patron."[11] Paraphrasing O'Gorman (1989), Posada-Carbó argues that "neither deferential nor clientelistic relationships necessarily imply the distortion of the will of voters; thus they should not themselves be equated with corrupt electoral practices" (2000, 630). According to this view, clientelism is normatively different from electoral manipulation – including what one might call election fraud, electoral corruption, or even vote buying. Along similar lines, Christie (1872) – an opponent of "electoral corruption" in Great Britain in the nineteenth century – considered that there existed "a palpable difference between bribery of voters and distribution of favours" (121). This view of clientelism, therefore, does not overlap with my operational definition of electoral manipulation.

(reflecting the list presented above) correspond mostly to the latter two categories in this typology.

[9] See also the evidence presented further below in this chapter.

[10] More generally, this kind of measurement error should attenuate any differences between the subset of manipulated and non-manipulated elections, rendering any significant differences all the more striking. In any case, to partly address the issue, for coding purposes I add the catch-all "other electoral manipulation" category to those on the list, as discussed later in this chapter.

[11] Author's translation from Spanish. Cited in Posada-Carbó 2000, 630.

Contemporary political science, however, often espouses a somewhat different, and more comprehensive, understanding of clientelism. Stokes (2007), for instance, defines clientelism as the conditional exchange of resources for electoral support.[12] This definition encompasses patronage and vote buying as sub-categories. Patronage is clientelism perpetrated with public resources.[13] Vote buying is the conditional exchange of resources for a vote (clientelism is more general in that it is not only the vote, but "electoral support" more generally – for example, effort to secure others' votes – that the recipient of the resources is supposed to provide). Under these definitions, my operational definition of electoral manipulation overlaps with the notion of clientelism, insofar as vote buying is an instance of it. My operationalization also overlaps with patronage, insofar as my definition captures vote buying funded by public resources.

There are other ways to understand patronage. For example, some scholars add a temporal criterion so that patronage is the exchange of resources for electoral support in the period preceding an election.[14] My list would overlap with this understanding of patronage because both include pre-electoral vote buying (as well as other pre-electoral actions such as voter and candidate intimidation). Finally, patronage is often understood as specifically involving government jobs in exchange for political support (see Folke, Hirano, and Snyder 2011). This view of patronage does not overlap with my operational definition of electoral manipulation.

In sum, my theory is compatible with a broad understanding of electoral manipulation, but for empirical purposes I operationalize electoral manipulation more narrowly. Specifically, I define it as any action covered by the above list. There exist other reasonable ways to conceptually and empirically delimit the meaning of electoral manipulation; different research goals may call for different approaches.

2.2 MANIPULATED ELECTIONS

What is a *manipulated election*? An adequate answer to this question will be informed by the central goal of the present study – to illuminate the logic of choices about electoral manipulation.[15] Accordingly, the sought definition

---

[12] This is close to Kitschelt and Wilkinson's characterization of a clientelistic relationship as a contingent exchange of goods for political support (2007, 10).

[13] Stokes's (2007) definition of patronage is quite similar to Greene's (2007). Others use clientelism and patronage interchangeably in the broad sense reflected in Stokes's definition of clientelism (e.g., Kitschelt and Wilkinson 2007, 7). Horowitz (1999) equates urban clientelism with patronage, understanding patronage as the exchange of government jobs in return for political support.

[14] Greene (2007).

[15] Note that the enterprise of determining whether an election is manipulated differs from that of classifying electoral regimes (although a regime classification might conceivably utilize

should be *procedural*; in other words, it should pay attention to the electoral process but not to its outcome – one would want to call an election manipulated when political actors made the choice to engage in electoral manipulation, regardless of who ends up winning. To illustrate this point, consider two hypothetical elections: "election 1" and "election 2." In both, a political party engages in electoral manipulation to the same extent. In election 1, the manipulating party wins. In election 2, however, the manipulating party loses. For certain purposes (e.g., to determine who was the legitimate winner of the election), one might care about electoral manipulation only in election 1, because it is clear that in election 2, the perpetrator of electoral manipulation did not manage to change who wins. For purposes of understanding the logic of elites' choices to utilize electoral manipulation, however, both scenarios are interesting.

One alternative approach is suggested by Hartlyn and McCoy, who argue that an election can be considered successful whenever the results are acceptable to key political actors, including "all major political parties or electoral movements participating in the election" (2001, 2). A second possible approach is to deem an election manipulated when the manipulation, whatever its scale, changes who wins. Such an approach is routinely used by practitioners: an assessment as to whether an election reflected the "will of the people" often plays an important role in the overall assessment of the election by international election monitors.[16]

These criteria – whether electoral manipulation changes who wins or whether the results are acceptable to key political actors – are intuitively appealing as a means to determine whether an election is acceptable, but they are nevertheless inadequate for purposes of the present study, as they are incompatible with the idea that the acceptability of an election should be determined on procedural grounds. The 2000 Mexican presidential election exemplifies this issue. The results of that election were recognized by all major political actors and were considered to reflect the "will of the people" (Hartlyn and McCoy 2001, 4). And, because, that election unseated the ruling party after seventy years in power, discussions of the election tend not to pay attention to the use of electoral manipulation in it. Nevertheless, there exists considerable evidence that the incumbent party, the PRI, (and other political parties) engaged in extensive vote buying and other practices of electoral manipulation (Cornelius 2002) (this is reflected in my coding of this election in the

information about, say, the incidence of electoral manipulation). See Diamond 2002; Levitsky and Way 2002, 2005 and 2010; and Schedler 2006; among others.

[16] Social choice theory suggests that the "will of the people" may not be a well-defined concept, and may depend, for example, on the electoral rules used to aggregate the preferences of individuals (e.g., Arrow 1951; Sen 1999). Nevertheless, what is usually meant by the "will of the people" in this context is the (counterfactual) outcome of the election had it been conducted without electoral manipulation. I revisit the issue of the relationship between electoral manipulation and the "will of the people" in Chapter 8.

dataset to be described further below). Additionally, there exist elections in which the outcome is not in doubt, but the front-runner nevertheless perpetrates large-scale electoral manipulation. One example is the 2005 presidential election in Kazakhstan in which preelection polls put the incumbent's popularity at around 70 percent, buoyed by high oil prices, yet the incumbent party engaged in large-scale manipulation. Other examples include some elections in pre-1990s Mexico, in Paraguay under Stroessner, and in Russia under Putin and Medvedev, among many others. In fact, elections such as these constitute an important subset of the cases to which this book devotes close attention. On procedural grounds, these examples constitute clear instances of manipulated elections, even though in some cases one could not say that electoral manipulation changed the outcome (or even had the potential to change the outcome, given that the perpetrator was practically assured victory in a clean election), and, in other cases, all key political players accepted their results. Similar issues are raised by a third alternative approach, where the quality of an election is judged by the size of the margin of victory or by the proportion of the vote obtained by the winner – for instance, by assuming that elections in which the winner obtains more than 70 percent of the vote reflect electoral manipulation by the winning party.[17]

For purposes of this study, I call an election manipulated if it is associated with acts of electoral manipulation on a scale that exceeds a predetermined threshold. From a practical viewpoint, this approach has several advantages. First, given the appropriate information, it is possible to conduct robustness tests by varying the threshold. Second, this approach does not require estimating how much manipulation would have been necessary to change the outcome or to assess whether an election reflects the "will of the people" – both elusive tasks. Third, and perhaps most importantly, the focus on procedure is consistent with this study's goal of investigating the logic of choices about electoral manipulation.

This approach raises the question of what the appropriate threshold ought to be – of how much electoral manipulation is "too much." Should a small-scale, isolated instance of electoral manipulation render an election as a whole a manipulated election? The use of a threshold could mean that such an election would not be classified as manipulated, even if the consequences of the manipulation (e.g. for the identity of the winner, or for social conflict) were substantial. In other words, a nonzero threshold could potentially "misclassify" some instances of manipulated elections, in which the scale of manipulation is small, as clean.[18] The threshold-based approach also implies that highly-manipulated

---

[17] The 1991 election in Zambia, for example, was won by the *challenger*, not the incumbent, with more than 75% of the vote.

[18] This type of bias is unlikely to influence the main empirical tasks of the present study, for example the task of establishing the prevalence of excessive electoral manipulation. Nevertheless, where relevant, I conduct sensitivity analyses to address this issue (see, for instance, the

elections in which there is no doubt that the rightful winner actually won (e.g., elections manipulated by a popular ruling party) would be classified as manipulated, even when all actors agreed that the outcome reflected the "will of the people."[19]

2.3 A CROSS-NATIONAL MEASURE OF ELECTORAL MANIPULATION

In the discussion that follows, I describe the empirical implementation of the previously mentioned ideas on the basis of an original dataset. Before proceeding with that task, I briefly review other existing empirical measures of electoral manipulation. One cross-national measure of electoral manipulation that has been publicly available for several years now is the variable "FRAUD" in the Database of Political Institutions (henceforth DPI; Beck et al. 2001). This variable simply codes an election as corrupt when the sources consulted report fraud or corruption "serious enough to alter the outcome of the election" (Beck et al. 2001). As a result, the DPI coding is inaccurate, from a procedural standpoint.[20] For example, the DPI codes as "clean" the presidential elections of Zimbabwe in 2002, Peru in 2000, and Mexico in 2000. For each of these, there is strong evidence of widespread manipulation. My data on electoral manipulation differ from the DPI in about 30 percent of the cases.

Another early effort to assess the "quality" of elections at the national level was undertaken by Pastor (1999). He reviewed the brief reports about upcoming and past elections in the "Election Watch" section published at the end of

---

discussion of the distribution of margins of victory in clean versus manipulated elections in Chapter 3).

[19] The threshold could conceivably be zero – in which case even a minor act of electoral manipulation would suffice to deem an election as manipulated. There are, however, good reasons to set the threshold at a point higher than zero. For one thing, from a *purely procedural* viewpoint, very small amounts of electoral manipulation might be ignored – normatively, the gravity of the offense might be deemed to be proportional to the scale of the violation. But even if one focused on the effect of electoral manipulation *on the outcome* of the election, there is a normative case to be made for setting a threshold greater than zero. The reason for this is that when an election is very close, random imperfections in the voting and counting process could be responsible for yielding victory for one or another candidate, even in the absence of any electoral malfeasance. It could be argued that in such a situation, the precise identity of the rightful winner is not well-defined; one of the front-runners should win, but it may be impossible to determine which one in fact deserves to win. In other words, in a very close election, the outcome is essentially a coin toss (assuming two front-runners), and therefore a very small amount of electoral manipulation may not make a difference – in some cases, electoral manipulation could even have the effect of "correcting" small random errors and therefore yielding the "true" outcome. Moreover, even if a small amount of electoral manipulation did alter the outcome of the election, the unrightful winner would represent roughly the same proportion of the electorate as the party whose victory it usurped, rendering the injustice in some sense a minor one. And, when the race is *not* tight, a very small amount of electoral manipulation will not change the outcome.

[20] Additional inaccuracies are likely to stem from the source used to code this variable (personal communication with one of the investigators heading the DPI).

every issue of the *Journal of Democracy*, and categorized elections as flawed whenever a political party "objected to the process or rejected the results." As Pastor acknowledges, his approach suffers from the problem that "the reports are brief, and do not always provide enough information to determine the cause or even the seriousness of the electoral problem," and therefore his classification should be viewed as "illustrative rather than definitive" (1999, 16). Also, losing parties often stand to gain from crying foul even when it is not warranted, and therefore are not particularly reliable sources of information about electoral manipulation.

Other datasets containing country-level measures of overall election quality include Kelley's Quality of Elections dataset, Hyde and Marinov's National Elections Across Democracy and Autocracy (NELDA; Hyde and Marinov 2012), and Birch's Index of Electoral Malpractice. Kelley's data were compiled on the basis of State Department Country Reports on Human Rights Practices for 172 countries for the 1978–2004 period. These data contain an indicator of overall election quality, and one of election-day fraud, but no coding for specific tactics of cheating. NELDA contains an indicator for whether or not Western election monitors claimed that significant vote fraud was present in an election. These data cover all states in existence from 1945 to 2006 (although election monitoring has only come into existence more recently; see Bjornlund 2004). Finally, Birch (2012) collected original data on electoral manipulation for 161 elections between 1995 and 2007, on the basis of election observers' reports by the European Union, the Organization of American States, and the Organization for Security and Cooperation in Europe. Birch's Index aggregates data on a variety of forms of electoral misconduct. My own data, to be described presently, contain substantially more detail than Kelley's and Hyde and Marinov's in the realm of electoral manipulation. Compared with Birch's, my data have substantially greater coverage, encompassing 874 elections in the 1990–2007 period. Finally, my data contain information of relevance to the present study that is not contained in any of the existing datasets (including data on the preelection public opinion polls).

Scholars have found other ways to proxy for electoral manipulation. For example, various authors have recently utilized records of legal complaints to estimate the extent of electoral manipulation (Molina and Lehoucq 1999, 2002; Ziblatt 2009). Others have utilized newspaper reports (Cox and Kousser 1981, Nyblade and Reed 2008). One common issue with such measures is reporting bias, although the gravity and relevance of this problem will vary from case to case.[21] Hyde (2007) has compared the proportion of the vote obtained by the ruling party in precincts with and without election monitors, while

---

[21] The sources utilized for compiling cross-national datasets, such as those described previously, are also open to different kinds of bias. For example, Birch raises the possibility that State Department human rights reports could suffer from such a bias (2012, 41); and international election monitors may suffer from their own biases (Carothers 1997), although these are presumably milder for the higher-quality monitoring groups.

randomly assigning the monitors to precincts in the 2003 Armenian election. She finds that the ruling party's proportion of the vote is significantly lower in the monitored precincts. Ichino and Schundeln (2012) use a similar approach for the 2008 election in Ghana and obtain a similar result, but they also find that there is displacement of the electoral manipulation to nearby areas that are not monitored. Election forensics – the statistical analysis of official electoral results – has been used to produce circumstantial, yet often persuasive, evidence of electoral malfeasance (Lyubarsky and Sobyanin 1995; Wand et al. 2001; Mebane, Sekhon and Wand 2003; Hausmann and Rigobon 2004; Myagkov and Ordeshook 2005; Taylor 2005; Mebane 2006, 2007; Beber and Scacco 2009; Mebane and Kalinin 2009; Myagkov, Ordershook, and Shakin 2009; Cantú and Saiegh 2011; Kobak et al 2012; Enikopolov et al. forthcoming; among others). All these ways of measuring electoral manipulation have contributed enormously to the stock of knowledge about electoral manipulation, and in subsequent chapters, I refer to the findings of studies that have utilized many of these methods. Nevertheless, in practice, forensics methods do not currently constitute an adequate basis for broad cross-national comparative analysis. The reason for this is that they require special kinds of information that are not readily available for a large cross-section of countries; they are also labor intensive. And forensics approaches, as well as those based on legal complaints, are heavily context-specific. Finally, survey data have been used to measure perceptions about electoral manipulation (more on this in Chapter 7).

Implementing a Cross-National Measure of Electoral Manipulation

In what follows, and on the basis of the approach just outlined, I describe a dataset which contains information about electoral manipulation that includes, for the 1990–2007 period, virtually every country-level election in the world in which more than one party was legally permitted to compete, for countries with a population of at least 1 million.[22] One advantage of focusing on the contemporary period is that more information is available than for previous periods. Moreover, if one could choose any period in history to code, this period would perhaps be the most desirable, as it contains more elections in a wider variety of regions and institutional settings than any other similarly long period in history.

The unit of analysis is the "election round" (subsequently called an "election" for simplicity). For every election, with the aid of a team of research assistants (RAs), I collected information on the incidence of different kinds of electoral manipulation and on related topics from secondary sources that

---

[22] Focusing on the country level is helpful for describing the range of empirical variation. However, the ideas that I develop in this study need not apply only at the country level. For discussion of electoral manipulation at the subnational level see the Appendix to Chapter 4, the case study of Russia in Chapter 6, and the subnational analysis of Mexico in Chapter 7.

included reference works on elections (including the Europa Yearbook and Dieter Nohlen's handbooks of elections), the reports of international election observers (such as NDI, the Carter Center, and OSCE/ODIHR), reports by NGOs (such as International IDEA and IFES) and journalistic sources. The information covers every category of electoral manipulation on the list provided earlier in this chapter. A residual category was included to cover instances of electoral manipulation reported by the sources but not included on the list. Information on vote buying and voter intimidation was collected separately for the preelection period and the election period.

For each category of electoral manipulation reported in the sources, the scope was recorded as "small and insignificant" or "widespread." I also permitted an "intermediate" category, utilized in cases where the manipulation was decidedly greater than "small and insignificant" but not quite "widespread." If sources specifically reported that the kind of manipulation in question did not take place, a o was recorded. The numbers 1 through 3 correspond respectively to "small and insignificant," "intermediate" and "widespread." This coding scheme acknowledges the difficulty of making fine-grained judgments about the scope of electoral manipulation on the basis of the information available for most elections, and it permits sensitivity analyses to address some potential challenges.[23]

In addition, I collected information on other aspects of each election, including the results of the latest available electoral poll before the election, vote and seat percentages, turnout, whether the winner of the election belonged to or was sponsored by the incumbent party, and whether there were indications before the election that manipulation was likely to take place or after the election that electoral manipulation had taken place (I describe these variables in Chapter 3), among other things. In the Appendix to this chapter, I provide a list of all the variables from this dataset that are used in the book and basic descriptive statistics (see Table 2.1A).

In designing the data collection, I followed the principles of transparency and of fidelity to sources. By transparency, I mean that every piece of information in the dataset is referenced to its source, making it possible to audit the data.[24] By fidelity to sources, I mean the minimization of inferences about the data when coding the sources. For example, if the data sources were silent about vote buying, this was explicitly recorded as an NA. Only if the sources specifically

---

[23] For example, to guard against the possibility that it might be difficult to distinguish between "widespread" and "intermediate," the categories can be analyzed either separately or together. Moreover, to homogenize coding criteria, I created a website on which I posted guidelines, as well as responses to research assistant questions as they arose, and I required all research assistants working on the project to read through these.

[24] An example of a major dataset that has recently come under criticism for lacking an evidentiary trail is the widely used Militarized Interstate Disputes (MID) dataset, which does not provide information on how each of the disputes was coded or what the source for each data point was. See Cohen and Weeks (2009) for a critique of the MID dataset.

stated that vote buying did not take place (or that no irregularities took place in the election in question) did I record a 0. In many cases, it would be reasonable to suppose that if a specific form of manipulation was not mentioned, it was not detected or did not take place. Such an inference, however, should be made explicit, so the analyst can reanalyze the data under different assumptions.[25]

All sources are potentially subject to some form of systematic bias. Losing parties, for instance, may have incentives to exaggerate claims that the winner perpetrated electoral manipulation. High quality election monitoring groups, in contrast, are unlikely to be subject to this kind of bias.[26] Monitoring groups have been criticized for bias when emitting overall assessments about elections – for example, they may choose to soften their criticism to avoid fanning social strife, reward a government for relative improvements, or ensure that they are invited to monitor in the future (Carothers 1997; Kelley 2012).[27] This kind of bias, however, is likely to affect the overall assessment of monitors, and not the specific instances of electoral manipulation that they document in their often detailed reports.[28] For example, the OSCE press conference following the Russian presidential election of March 2000 gave the election "a clean bill of health" (Fish 2005, 47) and the written report concluded that the election had been conducted "under a constitutional and legislative framework that is consistent with internationally recognized democratic standards" (OSCE 2000c, 3), the content of the report documented very serious allegations of electoral manipulation, including the stuffing of ballot boxes, the inclusion of dead people in voter lists, and the falsification of vote protocols (the sheets that tally the results at the precinct level) "by reversing or increasing the vote totals recorded for Putin over Zyuganov" (OSCE 2000c, 31). Therefore, in coding the

[25] Unless otherwise stated, when analyzing the data, I make the inference that when sources did not report a specific form of manipulation, it was unlikely to have taken place.

[26] I provided the RAs with a list of high quality election monitoring organizations. This list includes the Organization of American States (OAS), the Carter Center, the National Democratic Institute (NDI), the International Republican Institute (IRI), the United Nations (UN), the European Union Commission (EU), the Council of Europe (COE), the Organization for Security and Cooperation in Europe (OSCE/ODIHR), the CSCE Helsinki Commission, Commonwealth, EISA, the Asian Network for Free Elections (ANFREL), the European Network of Election Monitoring Organizations, and IFES.

[27] More generally, for each data point on electoral manipulation I categorized the source into one of six categories. This permits sensitivity analyses about source reliability by distinguishing, for example, between claims by parties who lose an election and claims by reputable international election monitoring groups. The categories are: (1) the losing political party, (2) a high quality election monitoring organization, (3) a low quality election monitoring organization, (4) independent courts or electoral tribunals, (5) severely partisan courts or tribunals, and (6) a residual category.

[28] The individuals who participate in high quality election monitoring missions are generally committed to democratic values and therefore would be unlikely to countenance the suppression of their findings. The drawing of conclusions on the basis of their collective factual findings, however, is a more ambiguous task and therefore one about which there can be room for disagreement.

scope of electoral manipulation, I ignored overall assessments by monitoring groups, but used the factual information they provided on instances of electoral manipulation. Low quality monitoring groups often function as rubberstamps for elections in friendly countries and are therefore less useful as sources of reliable information.[29] Finally, it is conceivable that the data sources I utilize are better suited to capturing medium- or large-scale manipulation, and that they could therefore miss some instances of small-scale manipulation. I consider this possibility when presenting empirical findings based on these data later in the book. Where relevant (e.g., in Chapter 3) I conduct appropriate sensitivity checks. The book's empirical findings are robust to such checks. The data on electoral manipulation cover 874 election rounds, including 416 in executive elections and 458 in legislative elections, in 133 countries. Coverage for each variable is described in Table 2.1A. Lastly, I supplement my data collection efforts with demographic, economic, institutional, and political information from preexisting data sources, including the Database of Political Institutions (DPI; Beck et al. 2001, data updated in 2010), the Penn World Tables 6.3 (PWT; Heston et al. 2009), the World Bank's World Development Indicators (WDI), Political Risk Services' International Country Risk Guide (ICRG), Freedom House (FH), and the Cingranelli-Richards Human Rights Data Project (CIRI; Cingranelli and Richards 2008).

Summary Measures of Electoral Manipulation

For descriptive and analytical purposes, it is helpful to construct summary measures of electoral manipulation at different levels of aggregation, such as: the election round, the election, the country-year, the country, the region, and the "spell in government" (i.e., the period during which a political party or candidate holds power). Most of these can be derived in a straightforward manner from a summary measure for the election round, simply by averaging. Therefore, the basic issue is how to aggregate information on the extent of manipulation for each of the many forms of manipulation included in the data, into a summary measure for the election round with which they are associated.

For both theoretical and practical reasons, one would like to know whether the different forms of manipulation are capturing different dimensions of choice on the part of the manipulators, or simply function as substitutes and all capture one same dimension of choice – an overall choice about the extent of manipulation. In the previous chapter, and earlier in this one, I espoused the latter perspective. The idea behind that perspective, put somewhat starkly, is that the decision about how much, and how blatantly, to manipulate comes first and reflects strategic considerations, and the decision about how exactly to manipulate comes second and reflects the different assets and resources that the manipulating party has at its disposal, but is not of special strategic consequence.

---

[29] For example, the Commonwealth of Independent States mission to Ukraine certified the 2004 election as "legitimate," while the OSCE documented widespread fraud (Baker 2005).

TABLE 2.1. *Scoring Factors, Principal Components Analysis*

First Principal Component	
Voter intimidation during election	0.37
Ballot stuffing	0.35
Pre-electoral voter intimidation	0.34
Falsification of results	0.32
Other irregularities	0.31
Tampering with voter registration lists	0.30
Multiple voting	0.30
Obstacles to voter registration	0.22
Vote buying during election	0.22
Candidate intimidation	0.21
Pre-electoral vote buying	0.20
Underage voting	0.18
Obstacles to candidate registration	0.17

Source: Author's data.

To investigate whether this perspective is supported empirically, I conduct a principal components analysis (PCA). This statistical technique summarizes the information contained in the set of variables by reducing it into a smaller set of unobserved or latent variables or "principal components." Filmer and Pritchett (2001), for example, utilize PCA to create an index of household expenditures, which are unobserved, on the basis of data on household asset ownership, which is available. As their index of household expenditures, they use the first principal component. Analogously, I utilize data on the extent of thirteen specific tactics of electoral manipulation to construct an overall index of the extent of electoral manipulation. As it turns out, the first principal component has by far the most explanatory power, capturing about a third of the total variation.[30] Therefore, the first principal component can be seen as a reasonable summary measure of the overall extent of manipulation.

Table 2.1 displays the scoring factors (or "loadings") for the first principal component. The loading on each type of manipulation represents the contribution of that type of manipulation. Note that all of the types of manipulation make substantial positive contributions to the first principal component. In other words, the first principal component resembles a simple average over all of the kinds of manipulation. In fact, the correlation between the first principal component and the simple average over the thirteen types of manipulation is greater than 0.99.[31] As a robustness check, I conduct a common-factor analysis (a technique related to PCA). The correlation between the first factor (the

---

[30] As a point of comparison, Filmer and Pritchett's (2001) first principal component only explains about a quarter of the variance in their data. The second principal component in my data captures about one-tenth of the total variation. The first eigenvalue is 4.3, the second is 1.2.

[31] This is the Spearman rank correlation.

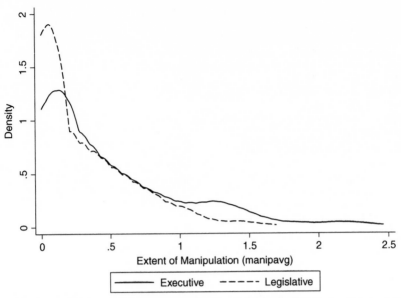

FIGURE 2.1. Distribution of Extent of Electoral Manipulation by Type of Election, 1990–2007
Notes: Based on *manipavg*.
Source: Author's data

analogue of the first principal component) and the first principal component is greater than 0.99, as is the correlation between the first factor and the simple average of manipulation.

These results suggest that a simple summary measure of the overall extent of electoral manipulation in a given election year is the *average of the extent of manipulation across all types of manipulation*. Therefore, as a measure of the overall extent of manipulation in an election round, I construct the variable *manipavg* as the average extent over the thirteen reported forms of electoral manipulation in that election round. Therefore, the theoretical range of the variable is 0 to 3, with 0 meaning that no manipulation was present at all, and 3 that all forms of manipulation were present to a widespread extent. The actual range of *manipavg* is 0 to 2.46, with a median value of 0.23. Figure 2.1 displays the empirical distribution of *manipavg*, distinguishing between executive and legislative election rounds. As the figure suggests, electoral manipulation is more prevalent in executive than in legislative elections (the median values of *manipavg* are 0.31 and 0.15, respectively).[32]

As a second measure for the overall extent of manipulation in an election round, I construct the variable *manipmax*, containing the maximum extent that

[32] Looking at the country-year level (instead of at the election round level), the median values for country-years with executive and legislative elections are 0.27 and 0.19, respectively (in this calculation, country-years with both executive and legislative elections are counted in both categories).

TABLE 2.2. *Incidence of Widespread Electoral Manipulation, 1990–2007*[33]

	Total	Widespread Manipulation	
	(N)	(N)	(%)
Executive	416	107	25.7%
Legislative	458	63	13.8%
All	874	170	19.5%

Notes: Based on *manipmax*.
Source: Author's data.

any one of the thirteen forms of manipulation in Table 2.1 takes in the election round in question. Whereas *manipavg* is a "continuous" variable, *manipmax* is discrete, taking the values 0, 1, 2, or 3.[34] This is the variable I use in the next chapter to construct a measure of *excessive* electoral manipulation (note that electoral manipulation can be widespread without being excessive, as the latter requires that the manipulation be associated with a large margin of victory). Table 2.2 displays the proportion of election rounds for which at least one form of manipulation is coded as widespread (i.e., level 3) in the data.

The table shows that one in four election rounds in executive elections, and about half as many in legislative elections, are highly manipulated.[35] There exist many other possible ways to aggregate the information about electoral manipulation contained in the dataset. It is possible, for example, to weight the different categories of manipulation differently, or to first aggregate them into sub-categories (e.g., election-day manipulation versus preelection manipulation) and then weight the sub-categories.

In sum, the data I have collected are flexible enough to permit different ways of classifying elections in terms of electoral manipulation, and therefore should prove useful in other research projects requiring information on the topic. Finally, as I show further in the next section and in Chapter 3, the data display some patterns that had not been previously documented in a systematic way and that call for explanation.

2.4 A SNAPSHOT OF ELECTORAL MANIPULATION AROUND THE WORLD, 1990–2007

In this subsection, I temporarily step out of the main line of argument of the book, and utilize my data to describe patterns and correlates of electoral

[33] In this table, every election round is counted separately, as are concurrent legislative and executive elections. Elections in the rightmost columns are those for which *manipmax* = 3.

[34] Including or excluding the residual category of manipulation "other" in either *manipavg* or *manipmax* makes very little difference.

[35] The lower incidence of electoral manipulation among legislative elections might be indicative of the fact that, on average, parliamentary systems are found in countries with stronger democratic and rule-of-law institutions than presidential systems. It may also reflect differences in the incentives to manipulate created by different electoral rules. I discuss the role of electoral rules later in the book.

manipulation in the contemporary world (1990–2007). The facts and patterns that I document here are not intended to directly speak to this study's central arguments and findings.[36] I provide them for completeness, because they are interesting in their own right, and because at least some of them have not been noted before. Some of these facts call for explanation and otherwise suggest avenues for further theoretical and empirical research beyond the scope of the present study.

I begin by dividing the countries in my data into seven groups, roughly corresponding to geographical regions, and describing the incidence of different tactics of electoral manipulation within each group. The country groups include a group of wealthy countries (encompassing Western Europe, the United States, Canada, Australia, New Zealand, Japan, and Israel) and six regional groups: sub-Saharan Africa, Middle East and North Africa (MENA), Latin America, former Soviet countries, Eastern Europe, and Asia. For simplicity, I shall henceforth refer to these groups as "regions." Table 2.3 displays the average incidence of each tactic or category of electoral manipulation, on the 0–3 scale, for each region. The first line in the table shows that, overall, the highest incidence of electoral manipulation is in the former Soviet region, followed by MENA, and then by a virtual tie for third place between sub-Saharan Africa and Asia. Latin America and Eastern Europe come in at a distant fourth place, while electoral manipulation in the group of wealthy countries is virtually inexistent.[37]

I next disaggregate this figure into three sets of sub-categories. First, I divide the tactics of electoral manipulation into those that take place before the election, and those that take place during (or closely after) an election (second panel in Table 2.3).[38] Pre-electoral manipulation is greater in magnitude than election-day manipulation in all groups except for the former Soviet region. The difference, however, is quite small in Eastern Europe and among the wealthy countries. The most notorious gaps are in MENA and Asia, where pre-electoral manipulation is almost twice as high as election-day manipulation.

The third panel in Table 2.3 breaks down the tactics of electoral manipulation into four substantive sub-categories: obstacles to candidate entry, obstaclesto voter entry, vote buying, and electoral fraud.[39] This panel shows that

---

[36] For example, in this subsection I do not differentiate between marginal and excessive manipulation empirically (I do that in the next chapter and subsequently).

[37] This is not to say that electoral manipulation is wholly absent from such countries, but merely that those forms of electoral manipulation included in my operational definition, as described earlier, are only rarely observed there. Other categories of actions that could potentially be part of a broader measure of manipulation, such as campaign finance abuses, malapportionment, or gerrymandering, are likely to be present even in the group of wealthy countries (as well as in the rest of the country groups).

[38] Pre-electoral manipulation includes candidate intimidation, pre-electoral voter intimidation, pre-electoral vote buying, obstacles to candidate registration, obstacles to voter registration, and tampering with voter registration lists. Election-day manipulation covers voter intimidation during the election, vote buying during the election, ballot stuffing, multiple voting, underage voting, and falsification of results.

TABLE 2.3. *Average Extent of Electoral Manipulation by Group of Countries and Type of Manipulation*

	Sub-Saharan Africa	Middle East and N. Africa	Latin America	Former Soviet	East Europe	Asia	Wealthy
Tactics included in operational definition (*manipavg*)	0.48	0.55	0.25	0.75	0.24	0.49	0.03
Timing categories							
Pre-electoral manipulation	0.49	0.64	0.28	0.64	0.20	0.63	0.04
Election-day manipulation	0.39	0.35	0.16	0.78	0.19	0.33	0.01
Substantive categories							
Obstacles to candidate entry	0.37	0.95	0.22	0.78	0.19	0.58	0.04
Obstacles to voter entry	0.69	0.62	0.38	0.73	0.30	0.61	0.03
Vote buying	0.24	0.36	0.22	0.37	0.08	0.68	0.02
Election fraud	0.38	0.30	0.11	0.87	0.18	0.26	0.01
Disaggregated categories							
Candidate intimidation	0.40	0.59	0.35	0.70	0.22	0.77	0.05
Pre-electoral voter intimidation	0.82	1.10	0.62	1.04	0.32	0.93	0.01
Voter intimidation during election	0.64	0.62	0.34	0.86	0.36	0.53	0.02
Pre-electoral vote buying	0.35	0.44	0.28	0.40	0.08	0.94	0.03
Vote buying during election	0.14	0.28	0.16	0.34	0.07	0.42	0.01
Obstacles to candidate registration	0.33	1.31	0.09	0.87	0.16	0.39	0.03
Obstacles to voter registration	0.61	0.13	0.18	0.29	0.22	0.37	0.07
Ballot stuffing	0.50	0.23	0.18	0.98	0.21	0.31	0.00
Multiple voting	0.35	0.33	0.13	1.18	0.28	0.20	0.04
Underage voting	0.20	0.18	0.00	0.00	0.00	0.11	0.02
Tampering with voter registration lists	0.42	0.28	0.14	0.57	0.20	0.37	0.02
Falsification of electoral results	0.48	0.46	0.14	1.30	0.24	0.42	0.00
Other irregularities	0.99	1.15	0.66	1.23	0.72	0.60	0.08
Number of observations	218	39	191	92	130	83	121

Notes: Author's data on multiparty elections, 1990–2007. The unit is the country-year-round. Quantities displayed are average values of the extent of electoral manipulation over the relevant set of tactics. See text for details on the composition of the subcategories.

there is considerable variation across the country groups in the choice of tactics of manipulation. Although every region displays a mix of tactics, different tactics predominate in different regions. The main tactic of electoral manipulation in Asia is vote buying, although obstacles to voter and candidate entry make a close second. In contrast, obstacles to candidate entry are the most heavily used tactic in MENA, while obstacles to voter entry predominate in sub-Saharan Africa. Election fraud is the most highly utilized tactic in the former Soviet region, but obstacles to voter and candidate entry are also heavily used there, and the level of vote buying is also relatively high. The reasons for such regional variation remain to be systematically studied.[40]

Finally, the bottom panel of the table breaks down electoral manipulation into the tactics that go into my operational definition as described in the previous subsection. This panel shows that: (1) a mix of several tactics of electoral manipulation is present in each of the regions, and (2) different tactics predominate in different regions. Point (1) is consistent with the fact that, as cited in the previous chapter, the average number of tactics of manipulation per election is 3.9, as well as with the results of the principal components analysis presented earlier (i.e., that all tactics of electoral manipulation in the third panel contribute substantially to the first principal component).[41] This panel also provides further information about the sources of the gap between pre- and post-electoral manipulation (displayed in the second panel of Table 2.3): in MENA, the gap is in large measure attributable to the high levels of obstacles to candidate registration and to pre-electoral voter intimidation. In Asia, the pre-post gap appears to be largely due to relatively high levels of pre-electoral intimidation of voters and candidates, as well as to pre-electoral vote buying.

I next use my data to study the correlates of electoral manipulation. I consider three categories of potential covariates: formal institutions, economic

---

[39] Obstacles to voter entry encompasses pre-electoral voter intimidation and obstacles to voter registration; obstacles to candidate entry encompasses candidate intimidation and obstacles to candidate registration; vote buying includes the two vote-buying categories; election-day fraud covers ballot stuffing, multiple voting, underage voting, and falsification of electoral results.

[40] Collier and Vicente (2011) provide a formal model to account for the choice between violence or intimidation, on the one hand, and bribery and ballot fraud, on the other. They argue that weak parties will use violence to intimidate swing voters, while bribery and vote fraud will be utilized by strong incumbents. Cox and Kousser (1981), Dunning and Stokes (2007), Nichter (2008) and Stokes et al. (2011) investigate the choice between different forms of bribery, including paying citizens to vote or to abstain from doing so. Some studies of dominant parties have argued that election fraud is used as a last resort, once resources for vote buying and other forms of patronage dry up (see Magaloni 2006 and Greene 2007 for the case of Mexico under the PRI), others that voter fraud gives way to vote buying and intimidation as pressures to democratize mount (Schedler 2002, 46, also regarding Mexico under the PRI) (however, see Cosío Villegas (1973, 396) and Marbry (1974, 221–223) for the view that PRI used election fraud even at the apex of its popularity and power).

[41] It is also the case that the Pearson correlation of the extent of manipulation (0–3) for every pair of tactics of electoral manipulation is positive and statistically significant (the data unit for that calculation is the election round).

and demographic variables, and governance broadly construed. Table 2.4 displays the bivariate relationships of each of these variables with electoral manipulation (*manipavg*).[42] For the institutional variables, which are categorical, the table displays the average level of electoral manipulation for each category. For the economic, demographic, and governance variables, the table displays the Pearson correlation coefficient between each variable and electoral manipulation.

In the raw data, presidential systems display significantly higher levels of electoral manipulation on average than parliamentary ones, with semi-presidential coming in somewhere in between. With respect to legislative electoral rules, when most seats in the lower house are filled via plurality rule, electoral manipulation is higher than when most are filled via proportional representation (PR) (the middle category has even more electoral manipulation, but there are very few cases of it in the data). And elections for executive office display higher levels of manipulation than elections for legislative office. These findings are in line with the hypothesis that winner-takes-all contests magnify incentives for electoral manipulation. Following Carey and Shugart (1995), for example, Hicken (2007, 48–51) argues that incentives to cultivate a personal vote are greater when citizens can vote for individual candidates (as in winner-takes-all executive elections, or plurality-rule legislative elections) than when they cannot (as in close-list PR, where citizens vote for a party list). In turn, incentives to cultivate a personal vote, Hicken argues, can increase the likelihood that candidates will resort to voter intimidation and vote buying. Similarly, Birch (2007) argues that legislative elections in single-member districts (SMD) are more likely to be manipulated than those under PR because, in tight races, a few votes can yield a much greater benefit in the former than in the latter (Birch 2007, 1540).[43]

Political decentralization to states is associated with lower levels of electoral manipulation. Specifically, average electoral manipulation is lower in countries that hold state-level elections both for legislative and executive office. The level of manipulation in countries that hold no state-level elections is about the same as in those that hold elections for a state legislature. I am not aware of any literature about the relationship between political decentralization and electoral manipulation in national elections.[44] Finally, elections observed byreputable international election monitoring groups have, on average, higher levels of

---

[42] The data sources are provided in the Table notes.

[43] However, in safe districts (i.e., when the contest is not tight) incentives to manipulate could be greater under PR, for example, if limits to the capacity to manipulate mean that the potential gain from manipulation in an SMD is negligible. For a relevant discussion see Cox's (1999) analysis of incentives for mobilization under different electoral rules. Empirically, Birch (2007) finds in a sample of 46 elections in post-Communist countries that single-member district rules are associated with higher levels of electoral misconduct.

[44] On decentralization and subnational governance see Eaton (2004); Montero and Samuels (2004); Gibson (2005; 2010); Fan, Lin, and Treisman (2009); Giraudy (2009).

TABLE 2.4. *Correlates of Electoral Manipulation*

Institutions and Elections		Average Manipulation	N
Electoral system	Presidential	0.44	465
	Semi-presidential	0.35	61
	Parliamentary	0.21	200
Legislative elec. rules	Mostly PR	0.24	340
	Equally PR and plurality	0.90	15
	Mostly plurality	0.47	296
Decentralization	No state-level elections	0.36	233
	Elections for state legislature	0.35	190
	Elections for state legislature and executive	0.27	149
Election type	Executive	0.45	414
	Legislative	0.27	347
Election monitoring	Unmonitored	0.22	330
	Monitored	0.49	426

Economy, Demographics, and Development	Correlation	P-value	N
GDP per capita (thousands of US dollars)	−0.36	0.00	743
Population (millions)	0.00	0.94	749
GINI coefficient	−0.13	0.11	147
Literacy (% adults above 15 years of age)	−0.31	0.01	70
Poverty (head count ratio, $1.25/day)	0.27	0.00	139
Infant mortality (per 1,000 live births)	0.43	0.00	336

Governance	Correlation	P-value	N
Physical Integrity Rights Index	−0.42	0.00	695
Rule of law index	−0.33	0.00	635
Bureaucratic quality index	−0.38	0.00	635
Corruption index (reverse scale)	−0.40	0.00	635
Civil liberties index (reverse scale)	0.55	0.00	738
Media freedom index	−0.58	0.00	564
Newspapers (daily, per 1,000 people)	−0.31	0.00	174

Notes: The unit of data is the election round.

Sources: Author's data for electoral manipulation (*manipavg*). Electoral system, legislative electoral rules, decentralization, and election type from Database of Political Institutions (Beck et al 2001); GDP/cap from Penn World Tables 6.3; population, GINI, literacy, poverty, infant mortality, and newspapers from World Development Indicators 2009; Physical Integrity Rights Index from CIRI 2008; rule of law, bureaucratic quality, and corruption from International Country Risk Guide; civil liberties index and media freedom index from Freedom House; international election monitoring from Simpser and Donno dataset (see Simpser and Donno 2012).

electoral manipulation than elections that are not observed by such groups.[45] This could reflect a choice by high quality election monitoring groups to observe elections that they expect to be of lower quality.[46]

The correlations between electoral manipulation and each of the economic and geographic correlates considered in Table 2.4 show that, on average, electoral manipulation is greater at lower levels of socioeconomic development. The extent of electoral manipulation is negatively associated with GDP per capita and adult literacy, and positively associated with poverty and infant mortality (all statistically significant).[47] The correlations with population size and inequality are not statistically significant, although inequality is marginally so (greater inequality is associated with less electoral manipulation, although the sample here is greatly restricted by data availability). Electoral manipulation is also associated with normatively worse governance outcomes. More electoral manipulation correlates with lower levels of respect for physical integrity, a weaker rule of law, lower bureaucratic quality, more corruption, lower levels of civil liberties and media freedom, and fewer daily newspapers (all of these correlations are statistically significant at standard levels).

I next use regression analysis to explore the partial correlations of many of the above covariates, once the correlations with other covariates are taken into account. I emphasize that this exercise aims only to bring out some of the patterns in the data, and is not designed to serve as the basis for causal inferences about the effects of institutional or economic covariates on incentives to manipulate (or the reverse). A causal analysis of these issues is beyond the scope of the present study, and it would require additional theoretical and empirical foundations. Model 1 in Table 2.5 controls for GDP per capita, as well as for the five "institutional" correlates in Table 2.4. Model 2 adds in demographic and governance indicators. Due to high levels of multicollinearity among governance indicators, Model 3 utilizes only two of these (rule of law and media freedom). Models 4 and 5 are specified similar to Models 1 and 2, but also include indicator variables for the country group/region. It should be noted, however, that the region indicators are highly collinear with some of the other covariates.

Overall, the picture that emerges is as follows. The electoral system (presidential versus parliamentary) does not seem to be strongly correlated with electoral manipulation once the other institutional variables in the regressionsare

---

[45] The list of reputable monitoring organizations on which the monitoring variable is based is provided earlier in this chapter.

[46] On the question of how expected election quality influences the sorting of monitoring groups across elections see Kelley (2008) (see also Simpser and Donno 2012).

[47] The correlation with growth in GDP/cap is positive but statistically insignificant (P = 0.13).

TABLE 2.5. *Correlates of Electoral Manipulation, Regression Analysis*

Dependent Variable: Incidence of Manipulation (*manipavg*)

	1	2	3	4	5
Electoral system (o=presidential or semi-presidential, 1=parliamentary)	0.02 (0.038)	0.07+ (0.043)	0.05 (0.042)	0.11** (0.047)	−0.02 (0.051)
Legislative electoral rules (o=mostly PR, 1=equal PR/plurality, 2=mostly plurality)	0.09*** (0.016)	0.05*** (0.018)	0.05*** (0.017)	0.04** (0.016)	0.01 (0.018)
Decentralization (o=no state elec., 1=state legislature, 2=state leg. and exec.)	0.04** (0.02)	0.06*** (0.021)	0.06*** (0.021)	0.04** (0.019)	0.02 (0.021)
Election type (o=legislative, 1=executive)	0.08** (0.032)	0.11*** (0.034)	0.10*** (0.034)	0.10*** (0.03)	0.12*** (0.031)
International election monitoring (o=unmonitored election, 1=monitored)	0.13*** (0.035)	0.04 (0.04)	0.03 (0.04)	0.16*** (0.035)	0.06 (0.04)
GDP per capita (thousands of US dollars, log)	−0.11*** (0.02)	−0.03 (0.025)	−0.05* (0.024)	−0.04 (0.026)	0.02 (0.03)
Population (millions)	−0.00+ (0)	−0.00* (0)	−0.00* (0)	−0.00* (0)	−0.00** (0)
Rule of law index		0.01 (0.019)	0 (0.017)		−0.02 (0.02)
Corruption index (reverse scale)		−0.03 (0.019)			−0.02 (0.019)
Civil liberties index (reverse scale)		0.04* (0.025)			0.05* (0.025)
Media freedom index		−0.01*** (0.002)	−0.01*** (0.001)		−0.01*** (0.002)
Country group (omitted category=sub-Saharan Africa)					
Middle East and North Africa				0.15* (0.077)	−0.25*** (0.092)
Latin America				−0.20*** (0.055)	−0.27*** (0.062)
Former Soviet				0.44*** (0.089)	0.38*** (0.113)
Eastern Europe				−0.22*** (0.067)	−0.20** (0.079)
Asia				0.08 (0.065)	0.05 (0.072)
Wealthy				−0.33*** (0.09)	−0.07 (0.103)
Constant	1.08*** (0.182)	0.77*** (0.297)	1.16*** (0.202)	0.56*** (0.212)	0.58* (0.307)
N	601	422	422	601	422
R-squared	0.22	0.39	0.38	0.33	0.49

Notes: Standard errors shown in parentheses.

accounted for (Model 1). If anything, in contrast with the bivariate relationship in Table 2.4, it is now parliamentary systems that exhibit slightly higher levels of electoral manipulation. The coefficient on the electoral system is positive in Models 1 through 4 and negative in Model 5, but it is only statistically significant in Model 4, which includes region indicators.[48]

The correlations of electoral manipulation with plurality rule, decentralization, and executive elections are, as in the bivariate case, positive and statistically significant across models, with the exception of Model 5, where the first two remain positive but lose statistical significance. The correlation with international election monitoring remains positive in Model 1, but is substantially diminished and loses statistical significance once the governance indicators are included (Models 2, 3, and 5). In this case, however, the correlation is robust to the inclusion of regional indicators (when governance indicators are omitted – Model 4).

The level of wealth, as measured by per capita GDP (logged), is negatively associated with electoral manipulation (Models 1 through 4), consistent with the sign of the bivariate correlation in Table 2.4. The correlation loses statistical significance when controlling for the governance indicators (Model 2) or the regional dummies (Model 4), both of which are strongly correlated with per capita GDP.[49] In contrast, population size is now negatively and significantly associated with electoral manipulation, in all models. Finally, the association of electoral manipulation with civil liberties and media freedom remains negative, as in the bivariate case, although correlations with corruption and the rule of law are now negligible.[50]

In sum, some of the bivariate correlations survive the regression analysis: electoral manipulation is positively associated with plurality rule, executive elections, political decentralization, and election monitoring. It is negatively correlated with per capita income, civil liberties, and media freedom. The correlation with presidentialism, the rule of law, and corruption are substantially weakened in comparison with the bivariate case. Finally, a new, negative association emerges in the regression analysis between population size and electoral manipulation. Beyond the hypotheses mentioned previously concerning the effect of institutional variables on incentives to manipulate elections, systematic empirical testing and conceptual understanding of these correlations are tasks that call for additional research.

---

[48] The region indicators are strong predictors of the electoral system, however.

[49] In Model 5, GDP per capita has a positive, but statistically insignificant coefficient.

[50] The coefficient on civil liberties is positive, but that variable is coded in reverse scale. Similar to the finding in Simpser and Donno (2012, 507 and Table A2), the probability of high-quality election monitoring is nonlinearly associated with civil liberties, with monitoring most likely at middling levels of civil liberties (regressions for this result not shown).

APPENDIX

Additional Notes on the Data

Criteria for Inclusion of Cases: The unit of analysis is the election round (subsequently "election" for simplicity). An election is admissible in the dataset if it fulfills all of the following characteristics:[51]

- It is a country-level election (not a referendum)
- It took place between 1990 and 2007
- More than one party is legally permitted to run (the number of parties that *actually* ran is not material to decisions about inclusion)
- The country where it took place had a population greater than 1 million people as of 2007

Missing Data: In constructing the variables that measure the overall level of manipulation (*manipmax*, *manipavg*), it is assumed that if a particular type of electoral manipulation is not mentioned, it did not take place. The reason for this is that sources seldom report the absence of specific kinds of electoral manipulation. In contemporary elections in the Scandinavian countries, for example, there is often no information about electoral manipulation, but such elections are widely regarded as clean (nevertheless, the original data point is retained as missing data).

Information on the vote percentage obtained by the winner is virtually complete for executive elections. In legislative elections, it is missing in about one-quarter of the cases. Information for pre-electoral public opinion polls was available for slightly more than one-half of all executive elections, and for slightly less than one-quarter of legislative elections (226 and 100 cases, respectively). The variables coding for generalized expectations about electoral manipulation before elections were obtained for 170 cases, and those for the equivalent post-electoral item for 237 cases. (See Chapter 3 for further details on these variables.)

---

[51] A small number of elections in parts of the former Yugoslavia are not included due to the complexity of the electoral system (elections in Serbia, Slovenia, and Croatia are in the dataset).

TABLE 2.1A. *Descriptive Statistics*

Variable	N	Mean	Std. Dev.	Minimum	Maximum
Year	874	1998.56	5.16	1990	2007
Executive election dummy	416	1	0	1	1
Legislative election dummy	458	1	0	1	1
Margin of victory (%)	761	24.77	24.36	−5.3	100
Intimidation of candidates (preelection)	874	0.39	0.84	0	3
Intimidation of voters (preelection)	874	0.64	0.97	0	3
Intimidation of voters (during election)	874	0.46	0.82	0	3
Vote buying (preelection)	874	0.32	0.75	0	3
Vote buying (during election)	874	0.17	0.53	0	3
Obstacles to candidate registration	874	0.32	0.77	0	3
Obstacles to voter registration	874	0.30	0.70	0	3
Ballot stuffing	874	0.34	0.75	0	3
Multiple voting	874	0.32	0.71	0	3
Underage voting	874	0.07	0.36	0	3
Tampering with voter lists	874	0.28	0.71	0	3
Falsification of election results	874	0.38	0.84	0	3
Other forms of manipulation	874	0.75	0.98	0	3
Average extent of manipulation (*manipavg*)	874	0.36	0.44	0	2.46
Maximum level of manipulation (*manipmax*)	874	1.38	1.12	0	3
Preelection expectation that election will be manipulated	170	0.53	0.50	0	1
Post-election belief that election was manipulated	237	0.39	0.49	0	1
Incumbent margin in pre-electoral poll (%)	326	7.54	21.37	−47	75
Sub-Saharan Africa dummy	874	0.25	0.43	0	1
Middle East and North Africa dummy	874	0.04	0.21	0	1
Latin America dummy	874	0.22	0.41	0	1
Former Soviet region dummy	874	0.11	0.31	0	1
Eastern Europe dummy	874	0.15	0.36	0	1
Asia dummy	874	0.09	0.29	0	1
Wealthy countries dummy	874	0.14	0.35	0	1
Per capita GDP (log) (PWT)	830	8.56	1.07	5.74	10.73
Law and order (ICRG)	728	3.65	1.40	0	6
Investment profile (ICRG)	727	7.28	2.45	0	12
Corruption (ICRG)	728	3.01	1.25	0	6

(*continued*)

TABLE 2.1A *(continued)*

Variable	N	Mean	Std. Dev.	Minimum	Maximum
Checks (DPI)	801	2.97	1.69	1	18
Party years in office (DPI)	833	6.24	5.64	1	44
Political rights (FH)	848	3.07	1.74	1	7
Civil liberties (FH)	848	3.31	1.44	1	7
Polity2 (Polity)	819	5.15	5.08	−9	10

Sources: Author's data; PWT = Penn World Tables; ICRG = Political Risk Services' International Country Risk Guide; DPI = Database of Political Institutions; FH = Freedom House.

3

The Puzzle of Excessive and Blatant Manipulation

3.1 CONVENTIONAL WISDOMS ON ELECTORAL MANIPULATION

This chapter considers existing approaches to the study of electoral manipulation – specifically, of the incentives that drive it – in light of the data that I have collected and described in Chapter 2. The main conclusion is that existing ideas about electoral manipulation do not adequately account for a large proportion of the observed variation, and in particular for the prevalence of excessive and blatant manipulation. Electoral manipulation as a subject of scholarly study has received increasing attention in recent years. Nevertheless, only a small proportion of the analytical effort has been devoted to studying the incentives that drive political parties and governments to pursue it (Minnite 2009). In the literature (which spans political science, history, economics, and sociology), there are two major approaches to the question of what motivates electoral manipulation. The first approach is predicated on the idea that the main – in fact, the only – goal of electoral manipulation is to contribute to winning the election at hand.[1] This idea, and its implications about when and how electoral manipulation is likely to be pursued, is implicitly or explicitly espoused in most of the literature on the topic, and therefore I shall call it the *first conventional wisdom* about electoral manipulation.[2]

The second approach to electoral manipulation, or *second conventional wisdom*, forms part of the broader study of highly authoritarian regimes and the single-party elections that some such regimes hold. Examples of these regimes include the Soviet Union, Iraq under Hussein, and Syria in recent

---

[1] Nyblade and Reed (2008), for example, argue that "[t]he goal of cheating is to win the current election" (928).

[2] In this first approach I include scholarship on both democratic and authoritarian electoral systems, where the latter category includes the work by Geddes (2006), Magaloni (2006), Greene (2007), and other authors, for the reasons discussed in Chapter 1 and later in this chapter.

decades.[3] Two broad ideas or intuitions emerge from this literature. The first idea stems from the observation that single-party elections offer essentially no choice to citizens, no avenue for access to power, and are routinely "won" by governments that organize them with close to 100 percent of the vote (as in the Soviet Union or Hussein's Iraq, for example).[4] In light of this, scholars of these elections have accorded relatively little importance, and also limited attention, to electoral manipulation per se: given the substantial penetration of society by the government's coercive apparatus, overwhelming electoral results are attainable in such settings even without recourse to electoral manipulation. To illustrate this point, consider Soviet elections. To vote in favor of the single candidate on the ballot, all the voter had to do is deposit the ballot into a box. To vote *against* the candidate, however, the voter had to enter a secluded voting room and cross out the candidate's name on the ballot, an act that necessarily "invites attention."[5] Gilison concludes, therefore, that "the environment of pressures is so effective that the desired result – a rousing affirmative vote of more than 99 percent – could be achieved without recourse to such dirty business as falsifying election results." The first intuition that emerges from this literature, then, is that authoritarian control largely obviates incentives to manipulate elections. This idea cannot be extrapolated beyond the most authoritarian of authoritarian regimes and their very restricted elections. Most authoritarian regimes today hold regular, multiparty elections, and electoral manipulation in these is very prevalent (as noted by the literature on electoral authoritarianism, for instance, and corroborated by my data). Therefore, the first intuition in this literature would appear to be of limited relevance for the study of electoral manipulation, even in a large proportion of authoritarian settings. Of greater interest for present purposes is the second broad intuition that emerges from this literature: the idea that elections (under dictatorship) might have goals other than gaining office. This literature observes that elections have had the effect of subjugating citizens to the yoke of the state.[6] This observation is related in spirit to the central arguments of the present book,

---

[3] Authoritarian regimes where multiple parties participate in elections (including dominant-party, hegemonic authoritarian, and competitive authoritarian regimes) are *not* included in this category.

[4] See, for example, Schapiro (1978) and Goldman (2007; 2011) on Soviet elections; Gross (1986; 2002) on Soviet-organized elections in Eastern Europe; Corner (2011) on "plebiscitary elections" in fascist Italy; Sakwa and Crouch (1978) and Lewis (1990) on communist Poland; Jessen and Richter (2011) for a general overview of the historical literature on elections under dictatorship in twentieth-century Europe; on Asia see Taylor (1996b); and on Kenya and Tanzania see Hyden and Leys (1972).

[5] This and the next quote are from Gilison (1968, 816).

[6] Gross writes, for example, that the function of elections in Eastern Europe organized by the Soviets was to drill people "into obedience" (2002, 86). Puzzling over the purpose of the 1929 "plebiscitary election" in fascist Italy, Corner concludes, similarly, that their goal was to render individual citizens complicit with the regime: "Given the unanimity of the plebiscite, the drive towards conformity became extremely strong and, of course, by conforming, the individual became in effect an accomplice of the regime. All of which was exactly what the plebiscite had

and in particular to the notion of indirect effects. The observation, however, is not systematically developed in the literature, it is articulated with a restricted scope (i.e., in reference to single-party elections in highly authoritarian or totalitarian regimes), and its implications for the practice of electoral manipulation receive little attention.

In the rest of this chapter, I critically reconsider the first conventional wisdom in light of fresh data. After reviewing the relevant ideas in greater detail, I describe cross-national patterns of electoral manipulation using the dataset introduced in the previous chapter. The principal finding of this exercise is that a sizeable part of the empirical record does not fit the conventional wisdom. In particular, there are many cases in which electoral manipulation is utilized by a party that does not need it to win, or in which it is perpetrated to a degree that far exceeds the amount necessary for victory; in many cases, it is also perpetrated blatantly. Cases of this sort contrast with the expectations that electoral manipulation ought to be carried out frugally, only insofar as it contributes to victory, and in secret. In sum, electoral manipulation is a more diverse phenomenon than prevailing wisdom would suggest.

3.2 THE FIRST CONVENTIONAL WISDOM

A substantial part of the literature on electoral manipulation – including many single-country case studies,[7] a handful of comparative studies,[8] the work on vote buying,[9] the literature on multiparty authoritarian elections,[10] and the literature on election monitoring[11] – tends to converge on three ideas regarding when and how electoral manipulation is likely to arise. The first idea is that *manipulated elections are associated with small margins of victory* (the margin of victory refers to the difference in vote percentage between the winner and the first runner-up after the election takes place). The logic is that any amount of electoral manipulation beyond that necessary for victory is unlikely

---

been designed to realize" (2011, 184–185). See also Gross (1986); Goldman (2007; 2011); Jessen and Richter (2011).

[7] These cover Costa Rica in the first half of the twentieth century (Lehoucq and Molina 1999, 2002), Spain during the Restoration (Darde 1996), Germany in the late nineteenth century (Ziblatt 2009), Argentina at the turn of the twentieth century (Alonso 1996), Victorian England (Kam 2008), and the United States at various points in its history (Cox and Kousser 1981; Argersinger 1985; King 2001; Campbell 2003, 2005; among others).

[8] These include a monograph by James Scott (1972), a study of electoral practices in Latin America in the nineteenth century by Eduardo Posada-Carbó (2000), a famous article by Schedler in which he surveys the different tools of electoral manipulation (2002), and two recent edited volumes by Schaffer, one devoted to vote buying and the other to electoral reform (2007, 2008). Lehoucq (2003) is a survey article.

[9] For cites on this topic see Chapter 1.

[10] Discussed in Chapter 1 as well as later in this chapter.

[11] Including Carothers 1997; Bjornlund 2004; Hartlyn and McCoy 2006; Hyde 2006, 2011; Hyde and Marinov 2008; Kelley 2008; Simpser 2008; Beaulieu 2009; Beaulieu and Hyde 2009; and Simpser and Donno 2012.

to bring any further benefit to the perpetrator, and therefore would constitute a costly and potentially risky excess – manipulating elections requires considerable effort, money, and personnel, and can lead to punishment or redress.[12] To illustrate this idea, consider a hypothetical set of clean, winner-takes-all, plurality rule elections, displaying a wide range of margins of victory. Suppose now that in some of these, electoral manipulation is used by the formerly losing party up until the point where it yields victory. At the point of victory, the margin is close to zero, because the formerly losing party has used electoral manipulation to bring its vote total to barely exceed that of the formerly winning party (recall the Joe Kennedy quote from the introduction).[13] Examples of this logic include the United States presidential elections of 1892 and 1960, as well as the 2004 Ukrainian presidential election: in all these cases, electoral manipulation was utilized only up to the point where it granted victory, resulting in a very small margin of victory (OSCE/ODIHR 2005, Hersh 1997, Holt 2008). The phenomenon of "fraud on election night," discussed in the next chapter, is another example of the association of electoral manipulation with small margins of victory (Christensen and Colvin 2005).

The second idea is that *electoral manipulation is associated with tight (or "close") races* – that is, with those races in which the front-runner and the first runner-up enjoy similar levels of support before the balloting takes place. The logic is that it is in such races that electoral manipulation has the greatest probability of changing who wins. James Scott, for instance, writes that "when the race is close, the marginal utility of the additional dollar of . . . patronage promises . . . is all the greater" (1972). In his 2003 literature review, Lehoucq concludes that "political competition fuels ballot rigging" (253). In their study of elections in Costa Rica in the first half of the twentieth century, Lehoucq and Molina write that "as competition becomes more intense, parties will resort to more . . . acts of electoral fraud" (2002). Nyblade and Reed (2008), analyzing data from Japan, argue that "cheating is more likely by marginal candidates, those on the cusp between victory and defeat" (927). In a study of electoral manipulation in the United States, Argersinger sums up the logic behind this idea:

only in those areas where relatively minor changes in the recorded popular vote would result in a different electoral outcome was there any incentive for fraudulent activity (1985)

It is important to emphasize the distinction between the *closeness* or *tightness* of an electoral race and the *margin of victory*. Closeness (or tightness) refers to the difference in the popularity of the front-running parties or candidates

---

[12] The costs of manipulation are discussed further in Chapters 4 and 5.

[13] This example assumes the rival party does not have the capacity or the willingness to counter the efforts by the manipulating party (or, alternatively, that it is not a strategic actor). I devote Chapter 5 to the strategic aspects of manipulation.

before the election.[14] The margin of victory, in contrast, refers to the difference in the vote totals obtained by the winner and by the first runner-up. The margin of victory can only be calculated *after* the election. The distinction is important because empirical studies of elections often use the margin of victory to proxy for the tightness of a race (e.g., Cox 1988; Cox and Munger 1989; Nyblade and Reed 2008; Ziblatt 2009). There is nothing wrong in principle with this procedure, so long as the election outcome can reasonably be thought to reflect voter sentiment. When vote totals are distorted by electoral manipulation, however, this need not be the case. To be clear, the presence of electoral manipulation does not necessarily mean that the margin of victory is not a good proxy for the tightness of a race. For example, if the efforts at electoral manipulation of the various contending parties neutralize each other, it is possible that the margin of victory might roughly reflect the tightness of the race. In many cases, however, electoral manipulation efforts do not neutralize each other. In such cases, the margin of victory is not a good proxy for tightness.

The third idea is that *electoral manipulation will be kept secret* – that perpetrators as a rule seek to hide their activities of electoral manipulation from public view, presumably to avoid punishment. This assumption runs deep in the literature; it is virtually unquestioned.[15] Jensen writes, for example, that "successful dirty politics, by definition is never discovered" (1971, 35), and Lehoucq makes secrecy part of the definition of election fraud – "clandestine and illegal efforts to shape election results" (2003, 233).

The first conventional wisdom has made its way to scholarship on both democratic and authoritarian regimes. As noted in the first chapter of this book, the recent literature on multiparty elections in dominant-party authoritarian regimes (also called "hegemonic-party autocracies") takes the view that ruling parties utilize election fraud only insofar as it contributes to electoral victory, in line with the first conventional wisdom (e.g., Magaloni 2006, Greene 2007).[16] I note, as discussed in Chapter 1, that this literature draws a distinction between election fraud – by which it means electoral manipulation on the day of the election – and other forms of government abuse that could affect elections, such as pre-electoral vote buying, or the manipulation of the economy at large. To engage this literature, in what follows, alongside my preferred operationalization of electoral manipulation – which encompasses some forms of pre-electoral manipulation such as vote buying before the election and intimidating voters or candidates in temporal proximity to the election, as described in the previous chapter – I utilize a more restrictive operationalization designed

---

[14] Pre-electoral forms of electoral manipulation can potentially alter the measured tightness of a race (I discuss this issue further later in this chapter).

[15] In fact, it is sometimes cited as a reason why electoral manipulation is difficult to study.

[16] While this claim is made specifically regarding dominant-party authoritarian regimes, it could conceivably apply also to the broader category of electoral authoritarian regimes. Dominant-party authoritarian regimes are a subset of electoral authoritarian regimes. For further details see Chapter 5.

to capture the notion of election-day fraud, (encompassing, therefore, only tactics of manipulation implemented on the day of the election). The chapter's central finding is robust – under either operationalization, the analysis that follows establishes that excessive and blatant electoral manipulation (or fraud) is quite common.

3.3 THE EMPIRICAL RECORD

Do the observable implications of the first conventional wisdom square with the empirical record? In this section I answer this question on the basis of the original cross-national dataset of country-level elections around the world in the 1990–2007 period, described in Chapter 2. I find, first, that excessive electoral manipulation is quite common, and that it constitutes a substantial proportion of the universe of manipulated elections (in other words, excessive manipulation is prevalent in both an absolute and a relative sense). Second, I do not find that manipulated elections on average have smaller margins of victory than clean elections. Third, tight elections are not more likely to be manipulated than elections that are not tight. And finally, electoral manipulation appears to be quite often perpetrated blatantly. I do not interpret these findings as indicating that the conventional wisdom is false, but instead as evidence that, while it may hold in a subset of cases, other important dynamics are often at play.

Electoral Manipulation and the Margin of Victory

Do manipulated elections yield small margins of victory? Perhaps the simplest way to answer this question is to look for counterexamples – for manipulated elections with *large* margins of victory.[17] Various examples of manipulated elections that resulted in large margins of victory were provided in Chapter 1 (e.g., Russia 2004). To investigate how prevalent such instances are, I count the number of elections in my data for the 1990–2007 period that (1) are manipulated and (2) are won by large margins of victory.[18] The total number of elections with information for both the margin of victory and electoral manipulation is 761.[19] I count an election manipulated if at least one kind of electoral manipulation is coded as either *medium* or *widespread*.[20] There are 199 such elections in the data that resulted in margins of victory of 20 percent

---

[17] Note that the first conventional wisdom on electoral manipulation is silent regarding the size of the margin of victory in elections that are not manipulated; therefore, clean elections with large margins would not constitute a relevant counterexample.

[18] Unless specified otherwise, by "election" I refer to an election round.

[19] While information on the margin of victory was collected for the vast majority of elections in the data (87%), for a surprisingly large number of legislative election rounds, my research team was unable to locate the margin of votes. This could mean that my estimate of the number of cases with excessive/blatant manipulation could be an undercount.

[20] This is equivalent to a value of 2 or 3 in *manipmax*. The variables are described in Chapter 2.

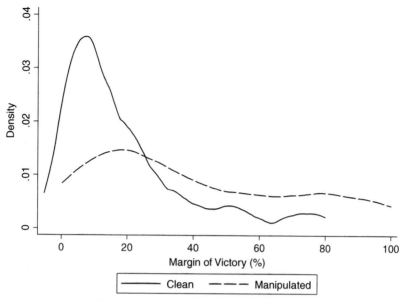

FIGURE 3.1. Distribution of Margin of Victory in Clean versus Manipulated Executive Elections
Source: Author's data

or greater.[21] Restricting the definition of a manipulated election to one that exhibits a *widespread* manipulation of at least one kind, then the number of manipulated elections with a margin of at least 20 percent is 99. As these figures suggest, excessive electoral manipulation is quite common.

Having established the prevalence of excessive electoral manipulation in absolute terms, I now investigate its relative incidence. To this end, I present density plots of the full distribution of margins of victory for the sets of clean and of manipulated elections. Figure 3.1 displays such distributions for executive elections.[22] In the figure, manipulated elections are those in which at least one category of manipulation was coded as widespread in extent; clean elections are those for which every category of manipulation was recorded as 0.[23] The median margin of victory in the set of clean elections represented by the solid line is 12 percent, and a large proportion of the cases are clustered around the median. In contrast, the median margin of victory for the group of manipulated elections depicted in the graph is 30 percent, and the distribution

---

[21] Restricting to election-day manipulation, the equivalent figure is 120.

[22] There is a small number of elections where the winner actually obtained fewer votes than the first runner-up, and therefore the margin of victory is slightly negative.

[23] That is, manipulated elections are those with a value of 3 in *manipmax*. Elections for which manipulation was neither 0 nor 3 are excluded from the figure. The figure represents a total of 97 clean elections and 107 manipulated elections, all for executive office.

is quite spread-out. The figure conveys two important points. First, focusing only on the distribution of manipulated elections, a large proportion of those is won by large margins of victory. Second, comparing the two distributions, there is no evidence that manipulated elections are likely to yield smaller margins of victory than those that are not manipulated – if anything, the opposite seems to be the case.

These data are likely to identify moderate to high levels of manipulation more reliably than small-scale manipulation, and therefore it is possible that some instances of marginal manipulation are simply missed, perhaps because they are kept secret, and mistakenly coded as "clean."[24] If so, it could be that within the set of clean elections in the graph lurk some manipulated elections. Although this possibility cannot be ruled out, it is possible to conduct robustness checks to see if the general pattern changes if one assumes that many of the elections that the dataset codes as clean are actually miscoded and should be recoded as manipulated. As an extreme scenario, which stacks the deck against finding the pattern shown in Figure 3.1, I make the assumption that every clean election outside of the wealthy, established democracies (Western Europe, USA, Canada, Australia, and New Zealand) should instead be in the set of manipulated elections. All such elections are transferred from the solid line to the dashed line, so to speak. The result is shown in Figure 3.2.

The pattern in the figure still conveys the two central messages derived from Figure 3.1: a substantial proportion of manipulated elections yield very large margins of victory, and there is no evidence that manipulated elections yield smaller margins of victory than clean elections. In other words, the reclassification does not manage to "dilute" these messages. The bumps in the distribution of clean elections at high margins of victory are entirely due to four elections: Austria 1998, Portugal 1991, France 2002 (a runoff), and Iceland 2004.These are the only elections in the clean set with margins of victory larger than 40 percent (the total number of cases represented by the solid line in Figure 3.2 is 30, because of the reclassification). The finding in Figure 3.1 is also robust to restricting the measure of manipulation to the election day (Figure 3.1A shown in the Appendix of this chapter). In any event, the data show that there exist many instances of manipulated elections won by very large margins of victory, a fact that does not sit easily with the perspective of the conventional wisdom.

The excessive use of electoral manipulation is also a feature of many manipulated legislative elections. To assess excess in such elections, I focus on seats instead of votes, because it is generally seats and not votes that matter most in those elections, and because the precise way that votes translate into seats varies from country to country. Moreover, I focus on the percentage of seats obtained by the winner, instead of on the margin of seats. The reason for this

---

[24] Elections where the scale of manipulation is smaller than the threshold utilized to classify an election as manipulated would also be categorized as "clean" (see Chapter 2).

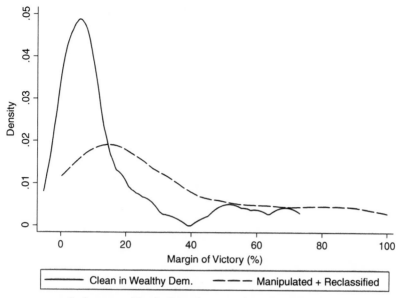

FIGURE 3.2. Robustness Check: Distribution of Margin of Victory in Executive Elections, Clean Elections in Wealthy Democracies versus Manipulated Elections + Reclassified Clean Elections
Source: Author's data

is that, for the purposes of a legislature (e.g., for passing laws or reforming the constitution), the actual percentage of seats can matter greatly while the "margin of seats" (the difference in the percentage of seats obtained by the winner minus that obtained by the first runner-up) is less important.[25]

Figure 3.3 displays the distribution of the percentage of contested seats obtained by the winner in clean and manipulated elections for legislative elections.[26] The graph shows that a sizeable proportion of manipulated legislative elections are won by remarkably large seat percentages, suggesting excessive use of electoral manipulation. In fact, in one-third of the manipulated legislative elections represented in the graph, the winner obtained more than 65 percent of the contested seats (this is true for only 8 percent of clean elections), and in more than one-quarter of the cases the winner obtained more than 80 percent of the contested seats.

---

[25] In addition, data on seats are more widely available for legislative elections than data on votes. For countries with more than one legislative chamber, only one chamber is represented in the data.

[26] There are 121 elections in the clean group and 30 in the manipulated group. The manipulated group includes all elections where at least one type of electoral manipulation is coded as widespread (*manipmax* = 3). In some legislative elections, not all seats in the legislature are contested; for purposes of this graph I do not remove elections for which this is the case.

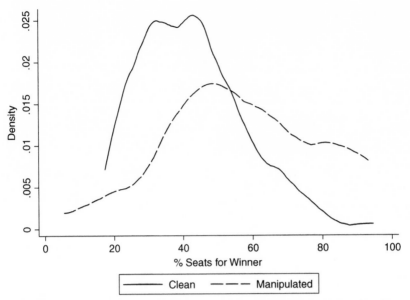

FIGURE 3.3. Distribution of Margin of Seats in Clean versus Manipulated Legislative Elections
Source: Author's data

Overall, the evidence I have presented is inconsistent with the view that, on average, electoral manipulation and small margins go together. This may be true for a subset of cases, but, as I have shown, it is certainly not true for another, quite substantial subset. In other words, it would seem that the prevailing wisdom is incorrect or at any rate incomplete: the latter subset of cases constitutes unexplained empirical variation.

Tight Races and Electoral Manipulation

The data also offer no support for the claim that electoral manipulation is more likely in tight races. Information about the tightness of races was obtained from the latest public opinion poll before the election that could be located. This information was available for 226 executive elections, which is equivalent to 54 percent of the executive elections in the dataset.[27] If the conventional wisdom held broadly, then those elections that are ex ante more competitive should be more likely to be manipulated.

Figure 3.4 is a scatterplot of the extent of electoral manipulation versus the tightness of the race according to the electoral poll, in executive elections.

[27] Data for legislative elections are available for 100 cases, constituting about 22% of the legislative election rounds in the data. I focus on executive elections because the finding is most striking in the context of winner-takes-all contests.

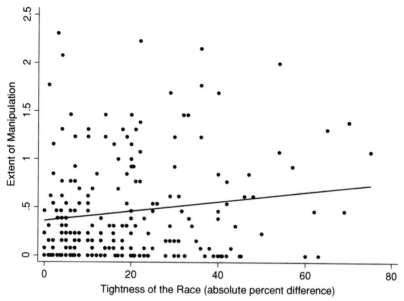

FIGURE 3.4. Tight Races and Electoral Manipulation in Executive Elections
Note: Measure of extent of electoral manipulation is *manipavg*.
Source: Author's data

Tightness is measured as the absolute difference between the percentage of poll respondents who supported the incumbent and the percentage of respondents who supported the strongest non-incumbent contender.[28] The pattern in the figure shows no strong association between the tightness of a race and the extent of electoral manipulation. If anything, the association is *positive*, that is, in the direction opposite to that predicted by the conventional wisdom. The fitted line is a regression of the extent of manipulation on the tightness of the race (the coefficient on tightness is 0.005 and statistically significant at conventional levels).[29]

Could the finding in Figure 3.4 be due to bias in the polls? It is conceivable that strong incumbents might distort polls to indicate a commanding lead in their favor. If those same incumbents are also more likely to manipulate

---

[28] This is not a perfect measure of tightness, but because the incumbent (or incumbent-supported candidate) is often one of the front-runners, it is likely to be the appropriate measure in most cases. In the few instances when the incumbent is not one of the front-runners, this measure will display some measurement error. Such error could potentially attenuate the relationship between the variables in the data, but because it is likely to be rare, it is unlikely to drive the finding. Moreover, the direction and size of the error are unlikely to follow a systematic pattern. I discuss potentially more important sources of error in the closeness variable later in this chapter.

[29] The proportion of manipulated elections is also not positively correlated with the tightness of the race (analysis not shown).

elections, then a spurious correlation could be created between elections that do not appear to be close in the data and electoral manipulation. In turn, that spurious correlation could dilute or reverse any real (and ostensibly positive) association between tightness and electoral manipulation. To check whether this kind of bias might be at work, I divided the sample according to an index of freedom of the press (Freedom House).[30] One would expect that this type of bias would be smaller, or absent, in countries with a sufficiently high level of press freedom, and therefore that any real correlation between tightness and electoral manipulation should be apparent. This is not the case: regressing the extent of electoral manipulation on tightness for the subset of cases in the 75th percentile of freedom of the press yields a coefficient that is statistically indistinguishable from zero.[31] The same result obtains if one repeats the regression for the subset of cases in the 50th percentile of press freedom. Restricting the sample to either the top category or the top two categories of political rights (Freedom House Political Rights Index), the coefficient also yields a statistically-insignificant coefficient.[32] These results indicate that it is unlikely that bias in the polls is driving the observed pattern.

In conclusion, the cross-national evidence does not support the idea that electoral manipulation is on average more likely to arise in tight races. This does not mean that the tightness of a race does not influence incentives to manipulate (in many instances it likely does); rather, it suggests that the incentives driving electoral manipulation differ from those suggested by the first conventional wisdom in a significant proportion of the cases.

Blatant Electoral Manipulation

I suggested in the first chapter that electoral manipulation is often perpetrated blatantly, in full view of the public. Manipulation efforts may be visible to the public at different stages of the election process. Before the election, for example, publicly visible practices can include tampering with the voter registration process in general, vote buying, or intimidation of potential voters and candidates. On the day of the election, ballot box stuffing, intimidation of voters at the polls, and similar tactics of electoral manipulation can be, and have been, practiced openly. Before or after an election, the media and word of mouth can transmit information about practices of this sort.

---

[30] The Freedom of the Press Index takes integer values between 1 and 100. I inverted the original index so higher values indicate greater levels of press freedom.

[31] The coefficient turns slightly negative in this case, but it is statistically indistinguishable from zero (P=0.33, fifty-one observations).

[32] The index of political rights takes integer values between 1 and 7, with 1 indicating the highest level of political rights. There are fifty-four cases with an index value of 1, and fifty-five with an index value of 2. In addition, even if the kind of bias suggested in the text was present in the data, its role would be limited by the pattern of missing data: polls are substantially less likely to be available where the regime is less democratic, disproportionately censoring cases where that kind of bias is most likely.

To obtain a sense for how commonly electoral manipulation is perpetrated in the public view, I collected information on whether there were any public indications of electoral manipulation before the election, according to scholarly sources, election monitors, or the media. Examples of such indications include interference with the registration process, public knowledge that voter lists are inflated and biased, and preelection pronouncements by government or military leaders threatening to win at all costs. I also collected information on whether after the election the population believed that the election had been manipulated. If pre-electoral indications of manipulation, or post-electoral beliefs about it, correlate with actual manipulation, that would suggest that such indications are capturing actual knowledge about electoral manipulation – and therefore that manipulation is carried out in a publicly visible manner. It is possible, of course, that manipulators attempt to keep electoral manipulation secret and do not always succeed. But the higher the proportion of cases for which there is evidence of visibility, the lower the likelihood that such instances are failures of secrecy, and the higher the likelihood that they are instances of blatancy – of manipulation perpetrated without regard for the possibility of detection, or in a purposefully visible fashion.

To assess the degree to which electoral manipulation is perpetrated in the public eye, as opposed to secretly, I first construct a baseline level of visibility by calculating the proportion of *clean* elections where public indications of electoral manipulation were present. I then calculate the same proportion for *manipulated* elections. I do this separately for the pre- and post-election periods. The data contain information on pre-electoral expectations about whether an election would be manipulated for 170 election rounds, and on whether after the election there existed a generalized belief that the election had been manipulated for 243 election rounds.[33]

Table 3.1 displays the results. The table shows that the proportion of clean elections for which there were pre-electoral indications that the election would be manipulated is relatively low. In contrast, such indications were much more common in elections that in fact were manipulated.[34] The difference is striking – once the baseline is subtracted, the likelihood that pre-electoral indications about manipulation were accurate is almost 60 percent.[35] The results are similar for post-electoral beliefs about whether an election had been manipulated: such beliefs appear to be accurate in 45 percent of the cases, once the baseline is subtracted. The finding is robust, and in fact stronger, if one restricts electoral manipulation to election-day tactics: baseline-adjusted pre-electoral

---

[33] Of these, in ninety cases before the election, and ninety-three after, the expectation was that the election would be (or had been) manipulated.

[34] An election is considered clean if *manipavg* has a value of 0, and manipulated if it has a value greater than 0. The table excludes any cases for which it was not possible to determine whether pre-electoral indications or post-electoral beliefs about manipulation existed; only cases where sources explicitly contained such information are included.

[35] This and all other differences on the table are statistically significant at conventional levels in t-tests for equality of means.

TABLE 3.1. *Generalized Beliefs about Electoral Manipulation versus Actual Manipulation*

	Generalized Belief Election Would Be/Was Manipulated					
	Before the Election			After the Election		
Actual Electoral Manipulation		Std.Dev.	N		Std.Dev.	N
None (baseline)	6%	(24%)	34	6%	(25%)	62
Electoral Manipulation	65%	(48%)	136	51%	(50%)	175
Difference	59%			45%		
Election-Day Manipulation	77%	(42%)	96	62%	(49%)	122
Difference	71%			56%		
Excessive Electoral Manipulation	92%	(28%)	36	85%	(36%)	34
Difference	86%			79%		

Notes: All differences calculated with respect to the baseline category.
Source: Author's data.

indications of election-day manipulation were accurate in 71 percent of the cases, and post-electoral beliefs about it were accurate in 56 percent. Finally, pre- and post-electoral indications were accurate for excessive manipulation in the vast majority of cases (86 percent before and 79 percent after the election, baseline-adjusted), indicating that excessive manipulation is quite frequently also blatant.[36] In sum, the data suggest that electoral manipulation is quite often blatantly perpetrated.

3.4 CONCLUSION: PATTERNS OF ELECTORAL MANIPULATION

As the previous analysis shows, not all instances of electoral manipulation fit the pattern described by the prevailing wisdom. For the sake of clarity, I briefly discuss four distinct axes of variation in patterns of manipulation. The first

---

[36] However, the number of cases on which this last finding is based is relatively small, as the table indicates. Excessive manipulation is operationalized as *manipmax*=3 and a margin of votes of at least 20% (for both executive and legislative elections). To further probe the robustness of the findings reported in this paragraph, I compared the subset of cases for which I have data on visibility indicators with the subset of cases with missing data to check for sample balance on per capita income, political rights, civil liberties, and corruption (data from PWT, FH, and ICRG). Differences are substantively small. For example, the log of per capita GDP is 8.52 for cases with data on pre-electoral expectations, and 8.57 for those with missing data on this variable; the FH index of political rights is 3.56 and 2.94, respectively; civil liberties 3.63 and 3.22, respectively; and corruption 2.94 and 3.02, respectively. Further, I ran a linear probability model regressing the presence or absence of indications about manipulation on actual manipulation (*manipavg*), with and without controlling for these four covariates. The coefficient on *manipavg* is positive and highly statistically significant (P<.01) with and without the controls for both the pre- and post-electoral indicators of the visibility of manipulation.

axis of variation is spanned by the distinction between marginal and excessive manipulation. On an intuitive level, marginal manipulation is that which fits the image of the first conventional wisdom of two evenly matched parties manipulating a tight race to win. More precisely, for purposes of this book, an election is said to be *marginally manipulated* if (1) it is manipulated by at least one party and (2) the margin of victory is small. An election is *excessively manipulated* if (1) it is manipulated by at least one party and (2) the margin of victory is large. As an approximate rule of thumb, I shall use, as I have done so previously, a margin of victory of 20 percent as the threshold. Such a margin would be considered in most electoral systems to be a landslide.[37]

It is important to distinguish this dimension of variation – marginal versus excessive – from the scale of the manipulation. The *scale* of electoral manipulation refers to the total amount of manipulation perpetrated by all the parties involved in the election. Examples of elections that were manipulated on a decidedly large scale include those in the Philippines in the 1950s, described by Wurfel (1963) as massive; the first round of the presidential election in Ukraine in 2004, where an estimated 10 percent of the vote was stolen; and the Russian presidential election of 2004, where Myagkov et al. estimate that 10 million votes were suspicious or stolen (2009, 136). In comparison, allegations of electoral malfeasance in the United States elections of 2000 and 2004, if true, would constitute small-scale manipulation. Crucially, the scale of electoral manipulation is independent of its effect on who wins: in the United States, small-scale manipulation could potentially have determined the winner, while in the 2004 Russian presidential election, massive manipulation in all likelihood simply increased the votes and seats margins (Myagkov et al. 2009).

Note that marginal electoral manipulation can vary in scale. Despite the fact that the scale of electoral manipulation in the Ukraine 2004 election, for example, was large, the margin of victory was small, and therefore manipulation was marginal. In contrast, electoral manipulation in the United States in 2000 was at most small-scale. Unlike marginal manipulation, excessive manipulation is generally large-scale.[38] But the converse is not true: large-scale manipulation can be marginal (when it yields a small margin of victory) or excessive (when it yields a large margin). Manipulation in the 2004 Russian election, for example, was large-scale and excessive.

Importantly, whether manipulation is marginal or excessive depends on the outcome of the election, but not on the scale of the effort, nor on the intentions of the manipulators. Consider the 2008 election in Zimbabwe. Although President Mugabe and his party engaged in large-scale electoral manipulation, they only managed to obtain a small (and negative) margin of victory in the

---

[37] In the United States, for example, the largest margin of victory in a presidential election (referring to the popular vote) since 1908 was 26.17%, obtained by Harding in 1920. The average in the postwar period is 8.6%.

[38] Although this is true in practice, on a purely conceptual level this need not be the case (see Chapter 5, Result 3 in the footnotes).

first round of voting. This example highlights the divergence between the colloquial use of the word "excessive" and its use in this book: in ordinary speech,
one could say that Mugabe's approach to the 2008 election was "excessive"
in the sense that it was large-scale and that it overstepped the boundaries of
decency. According to the definition provided here, however, the election *was
not* excessively manipulated – it was marginally manipulated.[39]

A third axis of variation concerns the distribution of manipulation efforts
among competing parties. On one end of this axis is *one-sided* electoral manipulation – that is, the situation where only one party manipulates. On the other
end is what I shall call *two-sided* or *competitive* manipulation, in which two or
more parties pursue manipulation to the same extent. Two-sided manipulation
can resemble a price war or an arms race, where no contender wishes to fall
behind its rivals. This pattern describes some instances of electoral manipulation in the United States in the nineteenth century. In 1880, the Democratic
National Chairman, William Barnum, expecting Republicans to engage in electoral manipulation, asked party workers "to organize some plan to keep even
with them [i.e., with the Republicans]."[40] Similarly, when Democrats contested
the 1878 Minnesota congressional election by providing evidence of voter
intimidation and other illegal forms of electoral manipulation, the Republican
defense was "that such practices were followed by all parties."[41] Scholars of
Latin America have documented similar dynamics. A Colombian leaflet from
1836, for instance, reports that all parties used "every possible trick to gain victory; the opposition and the government, all resorted to condemned weapons:
they all seduced, flattered, attracted, intimidated, and put into practice whatever means they had at hand" (Posada-Carbó 2000, 636). Another example
of two-sided manipulation is furnished by elections in the Philippines in the
1950s, where partisan electoral competition resulted in remarkably expensive
elections (Wurfel 1963). In contrast, in one-sided manipulation, only one of

---

[39] A second feature of the definition of excessive manipulation given here is that it does not depend
on the relative level of manipulation of competing parties. In particular, if the two front-runners
manipulate to the same extent, so that their manipulation efforts neutralize mutually, but one of
them wins by a large margin (e.g., because he is more popular), then the election would be said to
be excessively manipulated. This scenario is unlikely to arise in practice (as discussed in Chapter
5); I point it out to clarify the definition of excessive manipulation. A more common scenario
of excessive manipulation is one where the ruling party is the only perpetrator of manipulation
(as in the case of Putin's Russia). For completeness, consider also a scenario where only one
party manipulates, but that party *loses* by a large margin. According to the definition given in
the text, that is an instance of excessive manipulation. Note that such manipulation could be
aimed at preventing the front-runner from attaining indirect effects (more on indirect effects
and electoral competition in the next two chapters).

[40] William H. Barnum to William H. English, 10 and 18 August 1880, quoted in Argersinger
(1985, 678).

[41] "...and, therefore, not of particular relevance," ends the quote from Martin Ridge, 1962,
Ignatius Donnelly: The Portrait of a Politician, quoted in Argersinger (1985, 682).

the parties engages in a substantial amount of electoral manipulation. Examples include the previously mentioned 2004 presidential election in Ukraine, or elections in Mexico in the 1980s, where the ruling party was primarily responsible for electoral manipulation, among many others. Note that both one-sided and two-sided manipulation can come in different scales, and can be either marginal or excessive. I discuss the strategic logic of choices about electoral manipulation under party competition in Chapter 5.

The fourth axis of variation is the visibility of the manipulation, discussed earlier in this chapter. On either end of this dimension of variation are secret and blatant electoral manipulations. Electoral manipulation is *blatant* when it is perpetrated in such a way that indications about the manipulation are available to the public. The source of the information about electoral manipulation need not be firsthand: it is possible that the mass media could disseminate the information regarding electoral manipulation.

The four dimensions of variation that I have highlighted here – marginal versus excessive, visible versus blatant, one-sided versus two-sided (or competitive), and small-scale versus large-scale – can, and in practice do, vary separately, yielding different patterns of manipulation. A large portion of the literature has occupied itself with *two-sided, marginal* manipulation (with the scale ranging from small to massive). More recently, the literature on electoral authoritarianism has examined *one-sided, marginal* manipulation, either as I have operationalized manipulation or in the more restricted sense of election-day fraud. This chapter has established that a sizeable proportion of the empirical variation does not fit either of these patterns. In particular, it has shown that *excessive* and *blatant* manipulation – as in Zimbabwe in the 1980s, or in Kazakhstan under Nazarbaev – constitutes a sizeable proportion of the universe of manipulated elections.

Excessive and blatant manipulation is not easily accounted for by the conventional wisdom: from the viewpoint of what I have termed the first conventional wisdom, this kind of electoral manipulation is either wasteful (if one supposes that the manipulator needed electoral manipulation to win, but engaged in so much of it that it won overwhelmingly) or unnecessary (if one supposes that the manipulating party stood to win, but decided to engage in electoral manipulation anyway). And purposefully blatant manipulation would seem to incur unnecessary risks, by rendering it more likely that the manipulation effort might be detected, documented, and redressed or punished. In the next two chapters, I develop a theory to explain why different patterns of electoral manipulation might be pursued – marginal versus excessive, secret versus blatant.

By way of transition to the next section, I briefly revisit the ideas in the first conventional wisdom. Underlying it there are two (often implicit) assumptions. The first such assumption is that the goal of pursuing electoral manipulation in a given election is to change who wins that election. The second assumption is that electoral manipulation is costly to those who directly benefit from it, both in terms of resources (like any other policy) and in terms of the risk of punishment (like any other illegal or illegitimate activity; in this case the cost is an expected cost). In constructing my theory, I retain the second assumption, but question the first one – that is, I question the notion that the sole goal of electoral manipulation is to win the election at hand. Instead, I suggest that electoral manipulation often seeks more than winning. As I will show, this simple idea goes a long way toward accounting for the observed variety in patterns of electoral manipulation, including its seemingly unnecessary, excessive, and blatant use in diverse locations and time periods.

APPENDIX

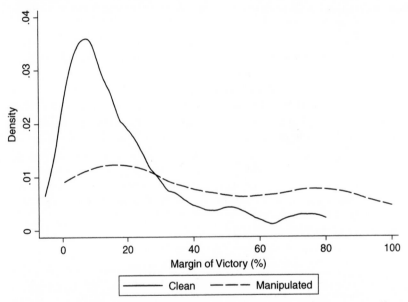

FIGURE 3.1A. Robustness Check: Distribution of Margin of Victory in Clean versus Manipulated Executive Elections, Restriction to Election-Day Electoral Manipulation
Source: Author's data.

4

More than Winning

Information and the Consequences of Electoral Manipulation

How might one account for excessive, unnecessary, and/or blatant electoral manipulation? More generally, what are the causes of variation along the "marginal versus excessive" and the "secret versus blatant" dimensions of manipulation? In this chapter and the next, I present a theory of electoral manipulation that provides an answer to these questions. The theory explains how patterns of electoral manipulation vary as a result of the strategic choices of those who perpetrate it and of the social and political actors who react to it. The core of the argument is that electoral manipulation plays an informational role. By influencing expectations about the strength of the manipulating party, and about the likely reaction of political and social actors, electoral manipulation shapes the behavior of such actors in ways that potentially benefit the manipulator.

I propose two general mechanisms linking electoral manipulation to the behavior of a wide range of social and political actors, via information. These mechanisms are best illustrated by considering the decision process of an individual actor, such as an ambitious politician, a voter, a bureaucrat, a businessman, or a union leader. Consider one such actor – a bureaucrat, for example – and suppose that there are two political parties contesting power via an election. The actor prefers one of the parties over the other, and he or she must choose whether to act on this preference. Suppose that, in considering how to proceed, he or she assesses the potential consequences of different courses of action. Ideally, the actor would like to support its preferred party. However, if that party's prospects of attaining power are dim, the actor's effort is likely to be futile. If, in addition, the institutional framework is "weak" in the sense that it does not effectively restrain the arbitrary use of political power – as is the case in many of the countries that rule themselves via elections today – the actor's support for his or her preferred party could be counterproductive, leading to material or physical reprisals, or to the loss of benefits and privileges.

Therefore, the central task confronting the actor, in choosing how to proceed, is to assess the likely consequences of the available alternatives (to support one of the parties, to do nothing, to actively oppose one of the parties, etc.). Such consequences depend on what I shall term the *strength* of each of the political parties. A party's strength reflects its likelihood of subsequently holding office (which in turn depends in part on the party's popularity, but also on other factors such as resources and dispositions), the kinds and amounts of power it is likely to enjoy, and the level of discretion with which it is likely to be able to act. Hence, the actor's assessment of likely consequences will depend crucially on the information available to him or her concerning the parties' strength. The central claim of my theory is that electoral manipulation can be harnessed to shape such information.

I argue that there are two major categories of information that electoral manipulation can influence. The first one consists of *expectations about the likely collective reaction of other social and political actors*. If I sympathize with the opposition party, for example, the expectation that fellow actors will actively oppose the ruling party could motivate me to take action myself. Conversely, the expectation that fellow actors are unlikely to act on their political preferences could discourage me from actively opposing (because doing so would likely be futile or potentially elicit reprisals). In general, there are various material and expressive reasons to care about how the rest of the public is likely to behave, including the likelihood of success of one's preferred party, and the probability of reprisals. If everyone reasons in a similar manner, expectations about how others are likely to behave become a key driver of social coordination.

The important point is that electoral manipulation can influence such expectations, with consequences for collective social behavior. To continue with the example, if I believe that the sight of excessive electoral manipulation will discourage fellow opposition supporters from actively challenging the ruling party, I myself may be reluctant to challenge; and if others think like me, then excessive electoral manipulation will lead to collective opposition passivity. The example illustrates how electoral manipulation can function as a *focal, equilibrium selection, or coordination device*.

The second category of information that electoral manipulation can influence concerns *attributes (capacities, resources, dispositions) of the manipulating party* that are not readily or fully observable by the public, but are nevertheless relevant to the actor's choice. For example, a bureaucrat who sympathizes with an opposition party may nevertheless work on behalf of the incumbent party (e.g., by diverting resources to it) if she believes that the incumbent party is able and willing to fire her should she fail to do so. Should the bureaucrat come to perceive the incumbent party as unable to fire her, however, she might instead choose to stop working on that party's behalf or even to actively oppose it (e.g., by diverting the resources to a rival). A key idea is that electoral manipulation can convey information about the capacity and the willingness of a party to take actions such as firing disloyal bureaucrats. For example, by pursuing excessive and blatant manipulation, a party can convey the impression that it is able to overstep ethical or legal constraints without facing serious consequences. Conversely, by failing to manipulate excessively or blatantly, a party could convey the impression that it is unable or unwilling to overstep such constraints, potentially eliciting challenges from bureaucrats and others. This example illustrates the role of electoral manipulation as a *costly signal* about the manipulator's strength.

In sum, electoral manipulation has, under conditions to be discussed later in this chapter and in the next, important informational properties. Specifically, it can convey information that shapes the subsequent behavior of a wide range of political and social actors. In particular, electoral manipulation can influence behavior in two capacities: as a coordination device, and as a source of information about the manipulator's attributes. In both capacities, electoral manipulation provides information about party strength. The informational properties of electoral manipulation imply that choices about electoral manipulation will have consequences that transcend any potential effects of manipulation on a party's immediate winning chances. When electoral manipulation signals strength, it can align actors' behavior with the manipulating party's interests. When it signals weakness, incentives can instead become misaligned, to the detriment of the manipulating party.

The coordination and the signaling mechanisms are not mutually exclusive; they may operate simultaneously or even reinforce each other. For one thing, the ability of a ruling party to arbitrarily mete out rewards and punishments depends not only on the party's attributes and resources, but also on the activity of supporters and opponents – in other words, it depends on coordination dynamics. It is easier to reward and punish the odd dissenter than to do the same when opposition is massive and well-coordinated. At the same time, perceptions of a party's attributes can influence coordination dynamics. For example, the greater the perceived capacity of the ruling party to reward and punish arbitrarily, the less likely it is that its opponents will venture to challenge it, and therefore the less likely that a coordinated opposition will arise. In sum, in practice there would appear to be positive feedbacks between the coordination and the costly signaling mechanisms: when electoral manipulation disrupts opposition coordination, it increases the effective capacities of the manipulating party; and when it signals that the manipulator is strong, it renders opposition coordination less likely (which in turn increases the manipulator's effective capacities, and so on).[1]

Electoral manipulation's potential to shape the behavior of a wide range of actors is a major driving force shaping a party's incentives to manipulate. The potential stakes for the manipulating party fall in two categories (as discussed

---

[1] In what follows, I discuss the coordination and costly signaling mechanisms separately. For a model that incorporates both costly signaling and coordination see Simpser (2005).

in Chapter 1 and later in this chapter). First, electoral manipulation can expand or reduce the party's scope for action while in office. Second, electoral manipulation can influence the party's prospects for holding office in future contests. In other words, in the theory presented here, there exist powerful reasons to choose electoral manipulation, other than winning the election at hand.

But could excessive or blatant electoral manipulation also erode the manipulator's popularity or "legitimacy"? This is certainly possible, but two notes are in order. First, the greater the cost in popularity and legitimacy associated with manipulating, the more difficult it becomes to account for the fact, documented in this book, that parties often manipulate elections when doing so cannot reasonably contribute to victory, and that they frequently manipulate blatantly. In other words, considering these potential costs of electoral manipulation (i.e., to the manipulator's popularity and legitimacy) only renders the existence and prevalence of excessive and blatant manipulation more puzzling, highlighting the need to understand the incentives driving such manipulation. Second, and relatedly, the fact that excessive and blatant electoral manipulation is prevalent suggests that any potential loss in popularity and legitimacy associated with electoral manipulation is frequently overwhelmed by some kind of potential benefit deriving from the manipulation. From the viewpoint of a political party, fostering the impression that it is willing and able to punish those who are disloyal, or that fellow opponents are unlikely to coordinate their efforts, may be more important, for the reasons described by my theory, than maximizing legitimacy or popularity.[2]

In this chapter and the next I develop the ideas I have just sketched in greater detail. I present two simple formal models – one focusing on coordination and the other on costly signaling – and describe equilibria with the property that electoral manipulation, through its informational properties, yields indirect effects. In such equilibria, parties that manipulate excessively appear strong to the public, incentivizing behavior that benefits the manipulating party. In contrast, parties that fail to manipulate elections excessively, or to manipulate at all, appear weak in such equilibria, eliciting opposition.[3]

The presentation of the theory over this chapter and the next is organized as follows. This chapter focuses mostly on the consequences of electoral manipulation for the behavior of social and political actors, emphasizing informational dynamics through the mechanisms of costly signaling and coordination. The next chapter focuses on the prior step in the chain of events: it studies how political parties make strategic choices about electoral manipulation. In that chapter, I consider incentives to manipulate in both competitive and

---

[2] I discuss the relationship between electoral manipulation and popularity at greater length later in this chapter.

[3] In the separating equilibrium discussed below, failure to manipulate excessively occurs on the path of play, while in the pooling equilibrium discussed below, failure to manipulate excessively occurs off the path of play.

uncompetitive elections, when indirect effects are absent and when they are present.

The rest of this chapter is organized as follows. Section 4.1 develops the idea of indirect effects and provides several examples. Section 4.2 elaborates in detail the steps in the causal mechanisms that give rise to indirect effects. That section contains two simple formal models, corresponding respectively to the coordination and the costly signaling mechanisms. The end of the section elaborates on various aspects of the argument: timing, blatancy, and electoral manipulation at subnational levels of government. I provide brief concluding comments in Section 4.3. The chapter Appendix discusses the concept of indirect effects in the context of legislative elections.

4.1 THE DIRECT AND INDIRECT EFFECTS OF ELECTORAL MANIPULATION

At the core of my theory is the idea that, under conditions that are common in many electoral systems today, there is often more to be gained from electoral manipulation than winning. To be sure, practices such as stuffing ballot boxes, voting multiple times, and tampering with the voter lists may contribute to winning by directly changing vote totals. In addition, however, I argue that electoral manipulation can influence the subsequent behavior of a wide variety of political actors – such as bureaucrats, voters, and party leaders, among others to be detailed later – potentially yielding benefits to the perpetrator that could encompass not only the election, but also the post-electoral period, subsequent elections, and realms beyond the electoral. For example, blatant displays of electoral manipulation before an election, such as vote buying by the incumbent, can discourage opposition supporters from turning out to vote. To take another example, a large margin could also bolster the winner's bargaining stance after the election with respect to labor unions, business organizations, and other actors by showing that no one actor is indispensable in a winning coalition.

I collectively denote effects such as these as the *indirect effects* of electoral manipulation. The indirect effects of electoral manipulation refer to its impact on the *subsequent voluntary behavior of political actors*, as in the examples just given. Of course, electoral manipulation can also have *direct effects*, which refer to its *contribution to winning the election being disputed*. Direct effects correspond to the standard way of thinking about electoral manipulation. The theory proposed here augments the conventional understanding of electoral manipulation by introducing the notion of indirect effects. Indirect effects have significant implications for incentives to pursue electoral manipulation. Most importantly, the prospect of inducing indirect effects that advance its own interests can motivate a party to resort to electoral manipulation beyond the point needed to win the election in question, when manipulation is unnecessary to win, and/or in a publicly blatant manner – in other words, to manipulate elections excessively and/or blatantly. In contrast, if electoral manipulation only had direct effects, virtually the only reasonable motivation to pursue it would be to reach the victory threshold.[4]

The following is a list of the main kinds of indirect effects that can ensue from the informational properties of electoral manipulation. This list covers what I view as the most important categories of indirect effects, but it is not exhaustive – additional indirect effects may exist that I have not listed. The list is organized according to the political or social actor whose behavior is affected. Electoral manipulation, beyond possibly contributing to victory, can potentially:

1. Affect *subsequent voting behavior*. In terms of timing, there are various possibilities: electoral manipulation preceding an election could affect voting behavior in that election; or electoral manipulation in one election could affect voting behavior in a subsequent election, or a series of subsequent elections. (I say more about timing later in the chapter.)

2. Influence the *electoral strategies of out-of-power political parties*; for example, an opposition party's leadership could react to such manipulation by calling for an electoral boycott, or by abandoning ship and joining the ruling party.

3. Affect *the behavior of political elites inside the ruling party* – for instance, by shaping the choice of intra-party factions or politicians about whether to leave the party and compete independently.

4. Influence *other kinds of electoral behavior by elites*; for instance, the choices of *donors* regarding funding or supporting political contenders in a future electoral contest, or about funding mass-mobilization efforts, or the choices of *activists* as to when to fight and when to compromise on policy.[5]

5. Influence the support of citizens and elites for *mass mobilizations and protests* that may not be related to elections.[6]

6. Allow regional or local *power brokers* with resources of their own (e.g., state governors) to display their loyalty or their capacity as political operators, and to thereby curry favor with their superiors.[7]

7. Affect the *choices of bureaucrats* whose actions are of consequence to the different parties' abilities to govern, to appropriate rents, and to get elected.

8. Impact the post-electoral *support for, or opposition to, policy initiatives* by the winner. In particular, electoral manipulation can influence the

---

[4] Some additional nuances arise in legislative elections. I discuss these in the chapter Appendix.

[5] Activists are sometimes counted as political elites.

[6] See Chapter 1 for further discussion of this issue.

[7] I discuss this issue further later in this chapter as well as in the case study of Russia in Chapter 6.

post-electoral bargaining power of the winner vis-à-vis other social and political actors, such as labor unions or organizations of businesses (for example, by making such actors seem more, or less, powerful in relation to the ruling party – e.g., less pivotal in a current or future winning or policy coalition).

9. For the same reason – that is, because of its effect on actual or perceived bargaining power – electoral manipulation could mitigate (or increase) pressures on the ruling party to redistribute or *share rents* with other groups.

While I have defined indirect effects as effects on the *behavior* of diverse actors, it is also possible to speak of the "indirect benefits" that could potentially accrue, or fail to accrue, to the perpetrator as a result of the effects of electoral manipulation on actors' behaviors. With respect to their consequences for the manipulating party, indirect effects can be grouped into two broad categories: first, those that relate to the *value of holding office*; second, those that pertain to the ruling party's subsequent grip on power and, more generally, the *chances that one or another party will hold power*. As shorthand, I refer to those indirect effects of electoral manipulation that pertain to the value of holding office as *non-electoral*, and those that relate to the likelihood that one or another party will hold power as *electoral*.

Consider non-electoral indirect effects first – those that pertain to the value of holding office. The value of holding office depends in large measure on the degree to which the party in office is able to pursue its preferred goals – to implement a policy program or capture rents, for example. Bureaucrats, labor unions, business organizations, and outside politicians can often place some limits on the freedom of the party in government to pursue its own objectives. Bureaucrats can help or hinder policy implementation, unions can push for policy concessions, and politicians may seek a portion of the licit or illicit rents captured by the government. These actors can not only constrain the ruling party, they can also help it to implement and attain its goals. But the degree to which a bureaucrat, union, politician, or other actor might press or challenge the government for concessions, policies, or rents will depend on bargaining power. Electoral manipulation can influence actors' perceptions about their bargaining power. Similarly, the willingness of a bureaucrat, politician, or businessman to do the ruling party's bidding will depend on its perceptions of that party's power and prospects. For example, a large margin of votes obtained via electoral manipulation can persuade the bureaucrat – or voter, politician, or others – that the ruling party's capacities to resist pressures for policy concessions or rents are relatively large, and that therefore the bureaucrat stands to gain from working with or for the party in government (as opposed, for instance, to supporting another politician's interests).

A similar logic underlies indirect effects of the electoral kind. The actions of potential voters, party activists, donors, opposition party leaders, regional governors and notables, wealthy individuals and businessmen, labor unions, business organizations, and other organized groups (including ethnic and religious groups) can importantly influence not only the ability to govern, as in the case of non-electoral indirect effects just discussed, but they can also shape electoral outcomes. Electoral manipulation, by influencing the perceived ability of each of these kinds of actors to make a difference in subsequent elections, can affect their election-related behavior. For example, a politician choosing between leaving the ruling party and challenging it, or staying within it in a lesser position, may be less likely to defect and challenge if he or she perceives that the probability of a successful challenge is small. Similarly, the motivation of an opposition sympathizer to turn out to vote may suffer if he or she perceives that the party in office is likely to remain in power. It is also possible for a single act of electoral manipulation to result in both categories of indirect effects – electoral and non-electoral.

Excess and blatancy are distinct concepts. Nevertheless, both play a similar role in the present theory: either of them (or both together) can convey similar information. With this in mind, I will often speak of "excessive and/or blatant" electoral manipulation, to emphasize the similar function that excess and blatancy play in the context of my theory. Of course, for some purposes it will be appropriate to discuss excess and blatancy separately and to indicate their differences (more on this later). Before continuing with the theoretical discussion, I present two brief examples to further illustrate the idea of the indirect effects of electoral manipulation.

Example: Electoral Manipulation and Union Acquiescence

As an example of the non-electoral indirect effects of excessive and blatant electoral manipulation, consider the case of labor unions in Mexico under the PRI (the ruling party from 1929 to 2000).[8] For present purposes, I focus on one aspect of the relationship between the PRI government and the labor unions, namely the effects of the PRI's electoral predominance – attained with the aid of fraudulent electoral practices – on the behavior of labor unions with respect to the PRI's policy priorities. Labor in Mexico constituted a very important political coalition partner for the PRI (Collier and Collier 1979, 977–978). Collectively, therefore, labor in all likelihood had the potential to effectively constrain the PRI's freedom to set policy, for instance, to protect labor's interests. In practice, however, even the largest confederations of labor unions in Mexico acquiesced and, in some instances, actively supported the PRI's policy goals while gaining minimal concessions, even when such policies directly threatened the interests and welfare of unions and their rank-and-file.

The interaction between the most important confederation of unions, the CTM, and the PRI-government in the 1980s and early 1990s, starkly

[8] The party was called PNR during 1929–1938, PRM until 1946, and PRI thereafter.

illustrates this point. In response to the severe economic crisis in 1982, the De la Madrid administration (1982–1988) pursued structural adjustment and inflation-control policies. These policies involved a series of tripartite pacts between labor, business, and government that required wage restraint among other measures that stood to appreciably reduce workers' income as well as the privileges of labor elites. In fact, both the minimum wage and the industrial wage dropped by more than 30 percent in real terms between 1982 and 1987, and as late as 1993 still remained below their pre-crisis levels (Pastor and Wise 1997, 43). Strikingly, the CTM nevertheless signed on to these pacts, first under De la Madrid, and then under the Salinas administration (1988–1994). Additionally, when the PRI presented a law initiative in Congress in 1992 to reform the institutions of social security and low-income housing – the IMSS and INFONAVIT, respectively – in ways that importantly reduced union privileges, the CTM representation in Congress voted in favor of it (Bensusán 1994, 63). And when president Salinas pushed to integrate Mexico into the North American Free Trade Agreement, the CTM not only acquiesced, but at some points provided active support to Salinas's initiative without gaining any significant concessions from the government in return, despite the dangers that free trade posed to important sectors of labor (Murillo 2000, 139).[9]

A key factor behind union subservience to PRI goals was the PRI's electoral predominance, attained with the aid of regularly excessive and blatant electoral manipulation.[10] Such predominance shaped the behavior of labor unions and confederations in at least two ways. First, it meant that the balance of power favored the PRI with respect to any one union or confederation of unions. From the early days of the PRI, labor was fragmented into a number of confederations of unions – including the CROC, CROM, and CTM, among others. And while labor, collectively, might have had the potential to effectively constrain the PRI's freedom to set policy, no one union or confederation of unions had enough power to do this on its own. The threat by a confederation of labor unions to abandon the PRI and become affiliated with a rival party was essentially empty, as opposition parties had no prospects of access to the state and its resources, either at the national or subnational level, and therefore had little to offer. And the threat by an individual union to defect to a rival confederation – for example, in reaction to its own confederation's subservience to the PRI-government – was similarly empty, as the available alternatives were also affiliated with the PRI. In other words, individual labor unions and confederations had no credible "exit" option. Second, the PRI

---

[9] Labor acquiescence to PRI goals was certainly also present before the 1980s. For example, highlighting the role of the PRI's fraudulent electoral practices, Murillo suggests that the PRI's electoral predominance facilitated the implementation of the PRI's economic policy of *desarrollo estabilizador* (stabilizing development) and import substitution in the 1950s and 1960s in a climate of labor peace (2001b, 38).

[10] On electoral manipulation by the PRI in its early decades see Padgett (1976); McDonald (1972); Marbry (1974, 223), Durand Ponte (1995, 67), among others.

leveraged its control of the state to make it difficult for labor to overcome its initial fragmentation. By rewarding or punishing confederations according to their willingness to go along with PRI priorities, the PRI undermined incentives for unions to coalesce against it.[11] Tellingly, the subservience of labor to the PRI waned as the PRI's "monopoly" over the state eroded over the course of the 1990s, when deep electoral reforms dramatically curtailed the PRI's ability to manipulate elections.[12]

This example hints at the two general mechanisms for excessive/blatant electoral manipulation that I develop in the rest of this chapter. First, excessive/blatant manipulation has the power to *undermine coordination* among opponents. Second, independent of coordination issues, excessive/blatant electoral manipulation can provide *information about the manipulator's power, resources, and prospects* and as a result deter challenges that might curtail its freedom of action and its grip on office.

Example: Electoral Manipulation and Bureaucratic Support

As a second example of the indirect effects of excessive and blatant electoral manipulation, consider the role of manipulation of this sort by the ruling party in securing the support of bureaucrats – broadly understood to encompass a wide variety of government employees. Bureaucratic compliance is of the essence for a ruling party to be able to implement its agenda and to hold on to power.[13] The following quote from a discussion of electoral authoritarian regimes by Way (2006) illustrates the point:

> ... subordinates in the military, regional governments, and state-run media have generally been less likely to follow orders to favor the incumbent if they thought that he or she faces serious challenges. In such a context, it has often been perceived as much safer for subordinates to ignore autocratic demands in an effort to avoid anything that might offend an opponent who might subsequently gain power. Orders to the media to provide biased coverage, to the military to fire on opponents, or to local governments to steal votes have been more likely to be ignored (Way 2006, 173).

As a specific example of the importance of bureaucratic compliance for the ability of an incumbent to hold on to power, consider Ukraine president Kravchuk's

---

[11] For a sophisticated treatment of union choices about militancy and acquiescence in Mexico and other Latin American countries see Murillo (2000; 2001a).

[12] I discuss such reforms in Chapter 7.

[13] For an illuminating discussion of the issue of bureaucratic compliance, see Brehm and Gates 1993; 1997. Brehm and Gates argue that, due to the agency problem inherent in delegating and supervising, bureaucratic compliance depends greatly on whether bureaucrats themselves wish to comply. The approach I take here is similar in that it emphasizes the bureaucrat's preferences and discretion (Brehm and Gates do not discuss, however, the role of electoral manipulation as a means to inducing bureaucratic compliance). For a general discussion and a formal model of electoral manipulation as a tool for controlling bureaucratic behavior, see Gehlbach and Simpser (2011).

experience in the 1994 presidential election: "local officials and even his own appointees often directly undermined the president during the election. Election commission workers in eastern and southern regions openly supported Kuchma and influenced the voting process in his favor" (Way 2006, 178).

The recent history of Belarus highlights both the importance of bureaucratic compliance and the role of excessive/blatant manipulation in securing it. In a story that echoes Ukraine's Kravchuk's, Belarus' Prime Minister Kebich's failure to control the security and intelligence bureaucracies played a central role in his electoral defeat in 1994 by Lukashenko. In contrast, once in office, Lukashenko consolidated his power and utilized excessive electoral manipulation to signal his control, thereby securing the allegiance of potentially hesitant government officials.[14]

By all accounts – including the opposition's – Lukashenko could have been reelected handily in the 2001 and 2006 presidential elections without recourse to electoral manipulation. Nevertheless, Lukashenko's government pursued substantial electoral manipulation in both instances.[15] In reference to the former election, for example, Hill observes that "it was clear that Lukashenko had decided he would win: the question was 'by what margin'?" (2002, 136). Lukashenko obtained 76.5 percent of the vote against his closest opponent's 15.6 percent, making for a margin of victory of more than 60 percent. Regarding the latter election, Marples writes that there is "little doubt that the incumbent president would have led by a considerable margin with an accurate vote count" because "the degree of popular support for Lukashenko is quite impressive" (2006, 363). And the opposition, even as it denounced electoral manipulation, acknowledged that Lukashenko had won (Ioffe 2008, 217).

The effect of excessive electoral manipulation on government bureaucrats is discussed by Belarussian newspaper editor Alexander Tomkovich (cited in Uzelac 2001). Lukashenko, he observes, "is surrounded by people who could switch sides at the first occasion if given a guarantee that they would keep their posts." Therefore, "a landslide first-round victory is a must – one can never know if the bureaucracy would change its mind in between the two rounds." Therefore, although there existed practically no doubt that Lukashenko would have won the election, albeit with a smaller margin of victory, "politically, he could not afford such a victory," because "only with the certainty of a big first-round victory could he be sure of keeping his hold over state officials." In other words, Lukashenko's use of excessive and blatant electoral manipulation was motivated not by its contribution to winning – because victory was already assured – but instead by its potential to influence bureaucratic behavior. The role of excessive electoral manipulation in securing bureaucratic compliance

---

[14] See Way (2006, 175). On the consolidation of power by Lukashenko see Hill 2002; Way 2005b; Burger 2006.

[15] On the manipulation, see OSCE/ODIHR (2001, 19–24) and Kazakievic (2006, 129).

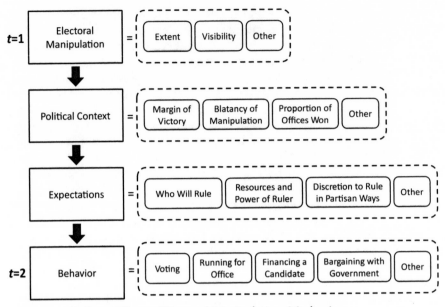

FIGURE 4.1. Indirect Effects of Electoral Manipulation: Mechanism

exemplifies the broader effects of such manipulation on political and social actors in Belarus. As Silitski put it, Lukashenko has worked to "maintain the popular perception that he is invincible at the polls" in the service of a political strategy of "preemption" that seeks to "eliminate threats before they arise" (2005, 84–96).

4.2 CAUSAL MECHANISMS DRIVING INDIRECT EFFECTS

I now provide a more detailed and general description of the causal links between electoral manipulation, on the one hand, and its potential consequences – specifically, its indirect effects – on the other. The mediating link is information: electoral manipulation, as mentioned previously, can convey or distort information concerning (1) the likely behavior of other actors, and (2) the attributes, capacities, resources, and dispositions of the manipulating party. Such information, in turn, shapes the choices of political and social actors. On a general level, the causal chain can be described in three steps. First, *electoral manipulation* shapes the *political context* (to be defined presently). Second, the political context shapes the *expectations* of social and political actors. Third, such expectations influence the actors' *politically relevant behavior*. Figure 4.1 depicts the flow of information through these three steps. In the sections that follow, I elaborate these links, beginning with the last one and proceeding in reverse order.

From Expectations to Political Behavior

At the core of the concept of indirect effects is the idea that expectations are a major influence on the behavior of a variety of social and political actors. As suggested in Figure 4.1, the expectations that matter concern:

(1) Which party will be in government
(2) How much power it will have while in government
(3) What it will be able to do with such power (i.e., its discretion to use power for its own ends)

Consider, for example, the choices of Russian "oligarchs" (i.e., tycoons) in Putin's Russia. Oligarchs faced a predicament: challenging Putin and his associates politically – for instance, by funding opposition parties, or by supporting free media outlets that might criticize the president – could pay off handsomely should the challenge succeed, but if it failed, the consequences to the challenger were likely to be dire. Persuaded that (1) Putin's grip on power was solid and (2) that Putin was able to exercise such power to punish challengers, many oligarchs decided to play along with Putin's agenda – for instance, by selling their assets to the government and moving abroad. The implication is that, had the oligarchs perceived Putin's hold on power to have been weaker, or that his discretion to exercise such power was constrained, some of the oligarchs might have chosen to resist or even to challenge Putin – for instance, by refusing to sell their companies or to leave the country.[16] In fact, the counterfactual scenario (i.e., a ruler with less power) is approximated by the situation under Putin's predecessor, Boris Yeltsin. During the Yeltsin presidency, it was clear that political challenges to Yeltsin stood a considerable chance of success, and this was reflected in the behavior of oligarchs, many of whom backed Yeltsin's opponents at various points in time. Other political actors too – including regime insiders and regional bosses – pressed the Yeltsin government and challenged Yeltsin electorally (I discuss the Russian case in Chapter 6).

To put this in slightly more general terms, it is helpful to reflect on the payoffs for a social or political actor – a bureaucrat, a voter, a party leader, a labor union chief, among others – associated with different courses of action. When the government is both sufficiently powerful and relatively unconstrained to use its power in partisan ways, then opposing the party in government is risky. Therefore, even actors who would prefer to oppose the ruling party, or to pursue their own interests at the expense of the ruling party, might be inclined to forego their wishes and instead cooperate with the government (e.g., by actively supporting it or by refraining from challenging it). In contrast, where the government is either sufficiently constrained – for instance, by the rule of

---

[16] Whether or not such challenges would have succeeded is a separate question – the point is that oligarchs' perceptions of Putin's strength were a major driver of the oligarchs' behavior.

law – or not especially powerful (e.g., because of a lack of resources), then actors might find it worthwhile to pursue their own goals and interests even if they conflict with those of the party in government. One reason for this is that the constraints and relative weakness of the government make it less likely that the ruling party will continue to hold power in the future. A second reason is that, even if the government retains power in the future, its relative weakness and the constraints under which it operates make it less likely that it will be able to utilize its power to reward supporters or punish opponents. In sum, *the returns to political behavior depend on which party holds power, and on its scope to use such power for partisan goals.*

To formalize these ideas in a simple way, consider a sample actor (e.g., a voter, bureaucrat, union leader, or political party chief) who can choose to support or to oppose the ruling party. If the actor chooses to oppose the ruling party and the ruling party retains power, the actor faces an expected "cost" (or set of negative consequences) of magnitude $r > 0$.[17] If the ruling party loses power, the actor does not face such negative consequences.

Let g denote the likelihood that an actor who opposes the ruling party will face cost r down the line. The expected utility for the actor who chooses to oppose the ruling party is decreasing in both g and r. Therefore, when choosing how to behave, expectations about these two variables, g and r, play a crucial role.[18] (Later in this chapter, I present a complete model of actor choice.)

In general, g depends on the chances that the ruling party might retain power for an additional term or time period, and on the ruling party's discretion to utilize government resources and power in partisan ways (for example, to monitor challenges and enforce negative consequences), among other

---

[17] If the actor instead chose to support the ruling party and the party wins, then it faces no such punishment (one could additionally, or alternatively, specify that a *benefit* should accrue to the actor in such a scenario, but this would not yield additional insight). The value r can be understood as an actual "bad" – e.g., a punishment – or as benefit foregone. As one of many possible examples of payoffs of this sort, consider the distribution of "coupons" by Cambodia's CPP, before the 2003 election, to be redeemed for provisions after the election in the event that the CPP won. CPP officials were reported to tell citizens: "If you keep this coupon and our party proves successful, you will receive a great deal three days after the poll" (ANFREL 2003, 43). Of course, the issue of the observability of the vote is important, but as the literature has discussed elsewhere, there exist a variety of ways to circumvent it. For example, when a citizen's partisan preferences are known, it suffices to observe whether she turns out to vote (see for instance Cox and Kousser 1981 on 19th century United States; Hsieh et al 2009 on contemporary Venezuela). Many other examples could be furnished of payoffs with a similar structure – that is, payoffs that *depend jointly on the actor's behavior and on the election outcome* – for voters and for other political and social actors.

[18] The analysis here assumes that a party in office can and will condition payoffs on the actor's behavior, as in fact many ruling parties have been observed to do. Nevertheless, it is necessary to ask why a ruling party may wish to reward or punish an actor ex post (i.e., once the actor has made his/her choice), in view of the fact that meting out rewards and punishments is likely to require resources and effort. A possible answer is based on the idea that interactions between the party and the actors are repeated over time.

factors.[19] When the rule of law, international pressures, or a lack of resources constrain the arbitrary exercise of power by the ruling party, g and r will be smaller, and therefore challenging the incumbent will be less unpalatable. In contrast, where governments have ample discretion, as is the case in many developing countries, then g and r will be larger and the potential negative consequences of challenging the ruling party will weigh more heavily on actors' choices.[20] A concrete example of such payoffs can be glimpsed in Venezuela under Chávez, who has attained considerable discretion over the use of state power and resources. Hsieh et al. (2009) estimate that voting for the opposition in recent years resulted, on average, in a lowering of one's salary and an increased probability of unemployment. The stakes associated with actively opposing Chávez are well-known to the Venezuelan public, and in all likelihood have shaped the political behavior of a wide range of political and social actors.[21]

The argument does not necessitate that the consequences of one's behavior be *material* in nature, as in the study of Venezuela just cited. *Psychological* or *expressive* rewards or frustrations associated with political participation can also be substantial, and depend both on one's behavior and on the overall political outcome. For instance, promoting the vote against an incumbent who nevertheless manages to hold on to power can be greatly frustrating; conversely, working hard against an incumbent that is successfully removed from power can be very rewarding – more rewarding than simply watching from the sidelines as the incumbent is removed through the efforts of others.[22]

From Political Context to Expectations

Having discussed the link between expectations and political behavior, I now focus on the prior step in the causal chain, that is, on the link between political context and expectations (the second arrow in Figure 4.1). The *political context* is the set of circumstances under which social and political actors make political decisions, such as those that concern whether to vote, run for office, or support one or another party. The political context encompasses a potentially wide range of dimensions, including past election results and margins of victory, the proportion of seats or offices won by different parties in a legislative body in the past, the actions and pronouncements of candidates and parties in the

---

[19] The term r could also depend on such discretion.

[20] It is possible, of course, that certain actors' behavior is not only influenced by, but also influences, both g and r. More on this later in this chapter.

[21] The idea here is that the beliefs that (1) Chávez has a solid grip on power and (2) he is willing and able to punish dissent, together have influenced the behavior of political and social actors in ways that reduce active opposition to Chávez's rule and have presumably weakened the (substantial but relatively unsuccessful) opposition.

[22] To use a sports analogy, no fan would want to miss the game where his or her favorite team finally wins a tournament.

run-up to an election, and visible indications that electoral manipulation took place (or did not take place) in the past or is likely (or unlikely) to take place in the future, among other things.

Political context matters for present purposes because it provides information that can shape the categories of expectations mentioned previously – expectations about the likelihood that one or another party might be in power in the future, about the magnitude of the power and resources it commands, and about its discretion to utilize these for its own partisan goals. For example, an overwhelming electoral victory in today's election can persuade a potential challenger that the winner will be able to retain power in a subsequent election a few months or years down the line, and/or that the winner commands considerable power and resources. Similarly, the sight of blatant vote buying can lead a citizen to conclude that his or her friends and neighbors have been bribed or intimidated into inaction and that, therefore, the ruling party will have an easy time capturing office. It can also convey the message that the perpetrator is above the law (and therefore does not need to hide its vote-buying activities).

The link between political context and the categories of expectations highlighted in the preceding paragraphs – about which party will win and what it will be able to do in office – can be elaborated in greater detail, as illustrated in Figure 4.2. The first idea, mentioned earlier, is that a party's chances to obtain or retain office, as well as its discretion to act once in government, depend importantly on (a) the *behavior of other political and social actors*, and (b) the party's own *attributes, capacities, and dispositions*.

The key point is that *the political context provides information on the basis of which actors can draw inferences about (a) and (b)*. In other words, the political context helps an actor (a citizen, bureaucrat, opposition party leader, or donor, for example) to answer the following questions. First, how can I expect the electorate, the bureaucracies, opposition parties, their financial backers, labor unions, business leaders, and other political and social actors to behave in the future (either in relation to an election or in between elections)? Second, what can I infer from the political context about the capacities, resources, dispositions (e.g., willingness to condition benefits or punishment on political behavior) of the ruling party (and possibly of other parties)?

Why does the political context provide information on (a) and (b)? I explore two major avenues through which political actors might draw inferences about the aforementioned categories of expectations on the basis of the political context, indicated in Figure 4.2: coordination and costly signaling. The first avenue is based on the idea that the potential influence of any one actor by itself on politics or policy is often relatively small, but can become quite large through the accumulation of efforts of multiple political and social actors pressing in a similar direction. In other words, *coordination* is frequently the foundation of political strength: coordination among sets of citizens to vote for one or another candidate; or among politicians, opposition party leaders, and potential financial backers to form a coalition that has political or electoral weight,

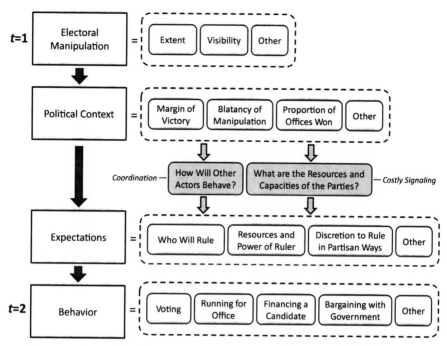

FIGURE 4.2. Indirect Effects of Electoral Manipulation: Detail of Link between Political Context and Expectations

for example. Because of the centrality of coordination as a basis for political strength, expectations about how other political actors – other bureaucrats, voters, union leaders, and political party chiefs, for example – are likely to behave play a crucial role in actors' estimates about the likelihood that one or another party will hold power, and about its likely capacity for partisan action while in power. The first role of the political context, then, is that it can provide information about how other actors are likely to behave.[23]

The second way in which political context provides a basis for inference is a *costly signaling* mechanism. The idea is that excessive and blatant manipulation can be utilized to indicate the broader capacities of the manipulator to the public at large (capacities that cannot be easily or fully observed directly due, for example, to incentives to misrepresent). Excessive manipulation can indicate that the manipulator has access to substantial material and human resources, logistic capacities, and the willingness to go to considerable lengths

[23] In a related argument, Hale (2005) claims that moments of elite succession – for example, the moment at which a president's term limit is about to expire – furnish focal points that can spur elite coordination against an incumbent leader, and that pre-electoral surveys can contribute to such coordination by providing an indication of the vulnerability of the incumbent. His argument does not, however, take the further analytical step of positing that electoral manipulation can constitute such a coordination (or signaling) device, as I argue here.

to hold power. Blatant manipulation can suggest that the manipulating party is above the law, and therefore not only does it not need to hide its efforts at manipulation, but it can purposefully showcase them. These traits – access to resources, ruthlessness, and independence from the rule of law, among others – correlate with a party's ability to attain or retain power, to bargain successfully with other actors, and to inflict costs on those who challenge its hold on power or its freedom of action.

In fact, electoral manipulation can simultaneously drive expectations about the relative strength of parties through both mechanisms – coordination and costly signaling. The coordination mechanism will play a role in a wide range of situations, because many kinds of political actors cannot, on their own, exert much influence. The costly signaling mechanism is important for all categories of actors. It is of special relevance, however, for the small subset of actors who on their own wield considerable influence (such actors are often powerful individuals or small, cohesive groups). This is because such actors are less susceptible to coordination failure (or are likely to have solved their coordination problems). An example of such an actor is a powerful politician with an independent basis of resources and support, large enough that it could influence the ruling party's hold on office and bargaining power. As mentioned previously, the two mechanisms can also reinforce each other.

These ideas point to two ways of formally modeling the relationship between electoral manipulation and the behavior of political and social actors: as a coordination game (Schelling 1960) and as a costly signaling game (Spence 1973). In the coordination game, electoral manipulation plays a focal role. For example, actors that observe excessive/blatant manipulation or the consequences of such manipulation might expect fellow actors to be discouraged and therefore passive, undermining the potential for collective action to challenge the ruling party.[24] In the signaling game, a strong ruling party can utilize excessive/blatant electoral manipulation to differentiate itself, in the eyes of the public, from a presumably weaker ruling party which would not be able to pull off the same kind of feat.[25] In terms of the simple formalization presented here, both coordination and costly signaling can underpin the public perception that g and r are large.[26]

An interesting feature of this framework is that excessive electoral manipulation can shape public expectations *even if it is known that the manipulation took place* and that the excessive electoral result is due to manipulation. To

---

[24] The question of why this kind of expectation, and not a different one (e.g., that actors will be angry and become politically active or rebellious in the face of excessive or blatant electoral manipulation), might become focal is an interesting one. I say more on this later (see also the discussion of popular rebellion in Chapter 1).

[25] This is the logic of a separating equilibrium; I also discuss a pooling equilibrium where manipulation plays a slightly different information-related role.

[26] Such perceptions could result either from updating the values of g and r upwards, or from failure to update these downwards.

revisit a point from the first chapter, some prominent works in the contemporary political science literature on elections and authoritarianism have argued that large margins of victory obtained through electoral manipulation cannot effectively deter or discourage potential challengers – they can only do so if they are obtained "honestly" (see Geddes 2006). The theory I have described implies, in contrast with this view, that even if it is publicly known that an excessive result – such as a large margin of victory – was obtained through cheating, such a result can still shape the behavior of the politically relevant public. I have described two mechanisms yielding such an outcome: first, a large margin (or blatant manipulation) can disrupt the coordination of political and social actors. The issue is not whether or not the manipulation is known to have taken place, but how an actor expects fellow actors to react to it. Second, an excessive electoral result (or blatant manipulation) can provide an indication of the manipulator's capacities – its access to resources, the scope of its networks and its logistical possibilities, its independence from the strictures of the law. For this reason, an excessive result can deter potential challengers even if it is known (or *precisely because* it is known) that it was produced through manipulation.

A Model of Political Action under Electoral Manipulation

I now make these ideas a bit more precise with the aid of a simple formal model. The purpose of the model is to explore whether and under what circumstances indirect effects, such as those described earlier, might arise in equilibrium. Consider a set of generic political and societal actors (subsequently "actors" for simplicity), potentially representing bureaucrats, politicians, their financial backers, citizens, and organizations such as labor unions, among others. As an initial approximation, the formalization does not differentiate among categories of actors, and it is assumed that the number of actors is large and that any one individual actor has, on his or her own, negligible influence on electoral or policy outcomes (but groups of actors have substantial influence).[27] Actors are indexed by i and the set of all actors is I. In the description of the game, I also refer to a ruling party (or, equivalently, an incumbent) and an opposition party, although these are exogenous to the analysis of the coordination model presented in this chapter.[28]

Coordination. Consider a one-shot game in which every actor $i \in I$ (the set of all actors) chooses an action $a_i \in \{0, 1\}$. The choice $a_i = 1$ represents an action that potentially harms the ruling party's interests and power (or that fails to advance them), while 0 stands for one that does not harm (or benefits) the ruling

---

[27] Later I discuss the possibility that individual actors might have substantial influence.

[28] In the next chapter, the parties are allowed to choose how much and how blatantly to manipulate elections.

party. For example, in the case of a bureaucrat j, action $a_j = 1$ might stand for channeling resources to help opposition, and $a_j = 0$ for channeling the resources to the ruling party's coffers.[29] For a citizen k, $a_k = 1$ might represent the action of casting a vote on behalf of an opposition candidate or party, while $a_k = 0$ could denote abstention. For a union chief l, $a_l = 1$ could mean fighting the ruling party and $a_l = 0$ could represent leaving the union to take a position in the government (i.e., allowing oneself to be co-opted).

Payoffs to an actor $i \in I$ are constructed as follows. Actor i receives utility $d_i \in \mathbb{R}$ if he or she takes action $a_i = 1$. This is a payoff intrinsic to challenging the ruler (or failing to support him). In addition, if he or she takes action $a_i = 1$, with probability $g(\alpha)$ he or she incurs cost $r > 0$, where $\alpha \in [0, 1]$ is defined as the proportion of actors $j \in I$ who choose action $a_j = 1$. As mentioned previously, in substantive terms the cost r represents a material, expressive, or psychological disutility that depends jointly on the actor's behavior and on the system-level political outcome. For example, r could represent some sort of material retaliation on the part of the ruling party – the withholding of a government benefit or job, or physical intimidation – toward an actor who chooses $a_i = 1$. But the capacity of the ruling party to mete out such retaliation depends, in turn, on the proportion of actors who choose action 1, that is, on α. If only a handful of actors choose action 1, the ruling party's power remains largely unaffected, and the probability g that those who took action 1 will suffer for it will be relatively high. In contrast, if a large proportion of actors choose action 1, the ruling party's power is weakened and the probability g is lowered. For example, when α is large, the ruling party could be thrown out of office and in consequence lose most or all of its capacity to mete out payoffs r. In other words, g represents the likelihood, from the viewpoint of i, that taking an action that does not accord with the incumbent's best interest (i.e., choosing $a_i = 1$) will result in negative consequences for i of magnitude r. The likelihood of negative consequences is assumed to be smaller the greater the proportion of actors that take action $a_i = 1$; that is, g is decreasing in α. Payoffs to action $a_i = 0$ are normalized to zero.[30] The quantities d_i and r are treated as exogenous parameters, while α is endogenous because it depends on the players' choices.[31] Thus, for any given actor $i \in I$, expected utility is given by:

$$(d_i - g(\alpha)r)\,a_i, \tag{4.1}$$

---

[29] As the number of actors increases, the effect of an individual actor's actions on the incumbent's power will diminish. Nevertheless, groups of actors would still be able to have a measureable effect.

[30] Alternatively, it is possible to posit that taking action $a = 0$ might result in a "prize" that accrues with probability g. The approach in the text is simpler and suffices to produce the key insights.

[31] Of course, as suggested previously, r could also be considered endogenous to α. To simplify the exposition and the analysis, I take r as exogenous and I assume the function g is exogenous.

which immediately implies that i will choose action 1 if and only if:

$$g(\alpha) < \frac{d_i}{r}; \quad r \neq 0. \tag{4.2}$$

that is, if the likelihood of receiving negative payoff r is less than a threshold d_i/r. The threshold depends directly on the net payoff associated with action $a_i = 1$ (represented by d_i) and inversely on the magnitude of the possible negative consequences of taking that action (represented by r). Letting d_i vary from actor to actor, it follows that those actors for whom $d_i < 0$ will always choose action 0; and those for whom $d_i > r$ will always choose action 1. The analysis is interesting, therefore, for the subset of actors whose choice of action depends on g; that is, those for whom $d_i \in (0, r)$. In what follows, the analysis focuses on this subset of actors (let I be the set of such actors); for simplicity these are called "actors" or "the public," with the implicit understanding that there may exist other actors whose choices are exogenous to the model. The specific way in which I have set up the payoffs means substantively that these actors are those who naturally prefer to act in ways that harm (or fail to benefit) the incumbent, either out of partisan preference (e.g., they prefer the opposition party), material self-interest (e.g., when supporting the incumbent requires effort), or some other reason. Examples of such actors include citizens who sympathize with the opposition, ambitious politicians within the ruling party who might wish to skip over party hierarchy and run independently, opposition candidates and party elites, bureaucrats who would prefer to avoid the arduous work of supporting the ruling party's political goals, and organizations whose policy interests could reduce the scope of action or the rents available to the ruling party.[32]

All actors make their choices simultaneously. Thus, a strategy for actor i is a choice of action $a_i \in \{0, 1\}$. The game potentially has multiple Nash equilibria in pure strategies. For example, there can exist a "low" and a "high" equilibrium. In the low equilibrium, a small fraction ($\underline{\alpha}$) of actors I choose $a_j = 1$, which is incentive-compatible when $d_j - g(\underline{\alpha})r > 0$ for those actors $j \in I$ who chose action 1, and $d_k - g(\underline{\alpha})r < 0$ for $k \in I$ who chose action 0.[33] In the "high" equilibrium, a larger fraction $\bar{\alpha} > \underline{\alpha}$ choose $a = 1$, with analogous incentive-compatibility conditions. To keep the analysis interesting, I assume

[32] For some substantive interpretations about the identity of the actors, it may be possible to enrich the action set. For instance, if the actors are voters, one might suppose that there are two candidates, incumbent and opposition, and model supporters of the incumbent differently from supporters of the opposition. For instance, while opposition supporters face cost r with probability g when they vote, incumbent supporters could be modeled as not facing such a cost, or even as facing a benefit of magnitude r (or some other magnitude) with probability g when they vote. Such a model would slightly complicate the analysis without adding much by way of substantive insight. Thus, when considering actors with partisan preferences, the analysis in the text can be understood as focusing on *opposition supporters*, because it is they who face potentially negative consequences from taking action against the incumbent.

[33] For simplicity, I ignore the case in which utility is exactly 0.

that parameters and functional forms are such that these two equilibria exist unless otherwise specified.

Substantively, the low equilibrium can be interpreted as a situation where a large proportion of actors are "cowed," discouraged, or apathetic, and therefore do the incumbent's bidding. This is a self-enforcing state of affairs, as most individual actors would not like to be one of the few to shirk or to actively act against the interest of the incumbent, because the expected consequences of doing so are too undesirable. The high equilibrium, in contrast, corresponds to a situation in which a sufficiently high proportion of actors fails to act on behalf of the incumbent (or actively opposes the incumbent), with the consequence that the incumbent's hold on power is weakened. This is also a self-enforcing state of affairs: because the prospect of negative consequences is relatively lower (e.g., because the incumbent is unlikely to retain power, or to have the capacity to utilize its power to inflict costs to those who challenged him), many individual actors prefer to pursue their own interests, even if they conflict with the incumbent's (for instance, by shirking, voting against the incumbent, or supporting an opposition candidate).

Suppose now that before actors choose how to proceed, they observe a public signal μ that depends on electoral manipulation by the ruling party (for the moment, suppose that the opposition party is not able to manipulate – this assumption is fully relaxed in the next chapter). For example, μ can represent a binary signal that takes the value of 0 if a recent election was clean, and 1 if it was manipulated excessively or blatantly (for present purposes, electoral manipulation is exogenous; the next chapter renders choices about manipulation endogenous). The signal μ thus, corresponds to the notion of "political context" discussed previously.[34]

Now, actors can condition their actions on the signal. The key idea is that the signal can convey information to actors about the likely consequences of their actions, a. I have described two ways in which the signal can do this. The first way is that the signal can shape the actor's expectations about *how others might act* – that is, about α (see Figure 4.2).[35] Suppose that $\mu = 0$ is taken by the actor to indicate that other actors are likely to actively oppose the incumbent – that is, that α will be large and therefore $g(\alpha)$ will be low, while $\mu = 1$ is taken to mean, in contrast, that other actors will be passive, α low, and $g(\alpha)$ high. In this example, an actor who observes the signal $\mu = 0$, expects that the high equilibrium will ensue, and if he/she observes $\mu = 1$, he/she will expect the low equilibrium to be realized. Accordingly, on observing $\mu = 0$, his/her best response is to "participate" – to choose $a = 1$ (because in the high equilibrium, α is large, $g(\alpha)$ is therefore low, and the participation condition (4.2) is met). By the same logic, on observing $\mu = 1$, his/her best response is

---

[34] In a multi-period model, the signal could be viewed as a state variable.

[35] The second possibility is that the signal could convey information about an attribute of the manipulator. I discuss this possibility in the next subsection.

not to participate. If all actors interpret the signal in a similar manner, each value of the signal will give rise to a different equilibrium: $\mu = 0$ to the high equilibrium and $\mu = 1$ to the low one.

The indirect effect of excessive electoral manipulation in this model is the difference in the fraction of actors who take the anti-ruling-party action, α, in a scenario with excessive electoral manipulation, compared to one with no excessive manipulation:

$$\alpha\,(\mu = 1) - \alpha\,(\mu = 0),$$

where I have written α as a function of μ and I have not made explicit the dependence of μ on electoral manipulation. Rendering the dependence of the signal on electoral manipulation explicit and letting x represent the chosen amount of electoral manipulation, the indirect effect of an amount of electoral manipulation $x = X$ can be written as:

$$\Delta\alpha(X) = \alpha\,(\mu[x = X]) - \alpha\,(\mu[x = 0]). \tag{4.3}$$

In the current example – where $\mu = 0$ is associated with the high equilibrium and $\mu = 1$ with the low one – the indirect effect of excessive electoral manipulation (which yields the signal $\mu = 1$) consists of a decrease in the proportion of actors who actively oppose the ruling party.

Equilibrium Selection and Learning. In the example in the previous section, excessive/blatant manipulation is associated with low levels of opposition to the manipulating incumbent. In general, however, the relationship between the signal and actors' expectations could be of different sorts. To see this, consider that a pure strategy for an actor in the one-shot game with a binary signal consists of a map $\{0, 1\} \to \{0, 1\}$ from the signal to an action. Actors can choose to condition their action on the signal, or to ignore the signal altogether. Restricting attention to pure strategies, four possibilities exist. In two of these, the signal is ignored. In the other two, a different action corresponds to each of the two signal values. There is a symmetrical equilibrium in pure strategies (i.e., an equilibrium where all actors choose the same pure strategy) corresponding to each of these four possibilities. In two of these equilibria, actors ignore the signal and there are no indirect effects.[36] In the other two, an actor's action depends on whether or not electoral manipulation is used excessively/blatantly, giving rise to indirect effects. The equilibrium just discussed, where actors choose action 1 when the signal is 0, and action 0 when the signal is 1, belongs to the latter category. This establishes that there exists an equilibrium where electoral manipulation (specifically, excessive manipulation) has indirect effects.

In this setup, the reason that electoral manipulation has indirect effects is because it plays a role in equilibrium selection – excessive manipulation leads to the low equilibrium, while the absence of excessive manipulation leads to

[36] When actors' strategies do not depend on the signal, we have $\alpha(\mu = 1) = \alpha(\mu = 0)$.

the high equilibrium. In other words, electoral manipulation has a *focal effect* (Schelling 1960). The existence of multiple equilibria to the game with a signal raises the question of when and why one might expect this precise equilibrium – where manipulation deters challenges to the perpetrator – to be played, instead of another equilibrium (for instance, one where excessive manipulation is ignored or one where excessive manipulation is associated with the high, instead of the low equilibrium). For one thing, as an empirical matter, a relationship between more manipulation and less participation, especially by rivals of the manipulator, is commonly observed. I document various instances of such a relationship in Chapters 6 and 7.[37] Additionally, there exist powerful reasons why one might expect excessive electoral manipulation to deter challenges. Conceptually, the issue of equilibrium selection might be approached by postulating an over-time, off-equilibrium learning process. Loosely stated, the idea is that actors who challenge a ruling party that manipulates excessively/blatantly are likely to receive a low payoff (for example, due to punishment or reprisals by the ruling party) and therefore to become more likely to refrain from challenging when next encountering excessive/blatant manipulation. Over time, the proportion of actors who are deterred from challenging by excessive/blatant manipulation grows, and the system approaches a steady state where the distribution of actors' strategies resembles the Nash equilibrium to the coordination game described previously. In other words, the idea is that strategies different to the equilibrium strategy described previously are weeded out over time as individual actors learn from their experience.[38]

---

[37] Although Christie's account of "electoral corruption" in nineteenth century English elections corresponds to a somewhat different setting, it can be read as a vivid description of the "low" equilibrium described here: "[T]his evil of electoral corruption has taken hold of the nation like a nightmare; the victims desire to get rid of it, but they are bound down and cannot move" (1872, 119).

[38] These ideas are predicated on the notion that a party's capacity to condition payoffs to actors on their behavior – for example, by withdrawing benefits from or inflicting costs on those who challenge them – is likely to be positively correlated with the party's capacity to manipulate excessively and blatantly, and inversely correlated with the proportion of actors who challenge the party. Therefore, the distribution of strategies used by actors in the steady state will depend on the initial proportion of actors choosing to challenge. When the initial proportion of actors who challenge is "low enough," the Nash equilibrium in the text – i.e., do not challenge if manipulation is excessive/blatant, challenge otherwise – is likely to be reached. Now, precisely what initial proportion is "low enough" will depend on the parameters of the model: the weaker the rule of law, the greater the ability of the ruling party to punish actors who challenge, and therefore the larger the set of initial conditions (i.e., initial proportions of actors who challenge) under which the Nash equilibrium in the text is eventually reached. Therefore, this learning model suggests that the equilibrium in the text, and therefore the potential for indirect effects, is more likely to arise in developing countries, where the rule of law and constraints on the government are often mild or weak (and where, in many instances, the initial conditions under which multiparty elections were held include a powerful party – often a holdover from authoritarian times – that few might have been willing to challenge). In the next chapter, I document a strong empirical association between excessive electoral manipulation

Party "Strength" and Indirect Effects.[39] To lay the groundwork for a later discussion of the background conditions under which excessive and blatant manipulation is likely to arise (in the next chapter), I briefly discuss the conditions under which electoral manipulation has the potential to yield indirect effects. The potential for indirect effects exists only when the information conveyed by electoral manipulation has the capacity to influence the behavior of social and political actors. This is not always the case. A solid and effective rule of law, for example, can limit the discretion of a ruling party to arbitrarily condition benefits and punishments on actors' behavior. In such a situation, any information potentially conveyed by electoral manipulation would likely be of limited relevance to the choices of actors.[40] Similarly, on the other end of the strength spectrum – when it is evident to the public that the ruling party is too strong and unconstrained – any information provided by electoral manipulation may also be superfluous to actors' choices. In other words, when party strength is known to be either too low or too high, the information contained in electoral manipulation about how other actors are likely to behave may matter little for the choices of individual actors, mitigating the potential for electoral manipulation to yield indirect effects via the coordination mechanism.[41]

To incorporate this intuition into the formalization presented above, I introduce an additional parameter to the model, γ, representing the party's "strength." As mentioned earlier, g (the likelihood that negative consequences r will accrue to an actor who chooses $a = 1$) depends on the probability that the ruling party will retain office, as well as on the power of the government and its discretion to utilize such power in partisan ways. Therefore, shifts in these factors can shift g for given α – that is, they can shift the likelihood that negative consequences will result for an actor who challenges the ruling party

and the weakness of institutions. The learning model I have sketched here is based on a simple evolutionary game with replicator dynamics. For alternative approaches to equilibrium selection in coordination games see Carlsson and van Damme (1993); Morris and Shin (2001); Medina (2007). One advantage of explicitly describing or modeling an over-time process of equilibrium selection (e.g., via a learning model) is that the description is intuitively appealing and it can potentially have observable features.

[39] Note that I am not using the phrase "party strength" in the sense that it is often used in the literature on political parties. In that literature, it often refers to the "rootedness" of a party in society (for a discussion of the various meanings of party strength in that literature see, for instance, Mainwaring and Scully 1995, 170).

[40] Information about certain attributes of the party, or about how others are likely to behave, might be relevant to actor behavior in an institutionally strong democracy, but in a much more limited sense (since the stakes of actors' choices are more limited than in a situation in which the ruling party has greater discretion to arbitrarily reward and punish). For example, the literature on bandwagon effects studies the influence of perceptions about whether and how others are likely to vote on individual vote choices (e.g., Bartels 1988; Schuessler 2000).

[41] Similarly, the costly signaling mechanism (to be discussed below) can underpin indirect effects only when differences in unobserved party attributes could be potentially relevant to actors' utilities. A strong rule of law, for instance, might reduce the relevance of party attributes in actors' utilities.

(the same factors could also influence the magnitude of the consequences r; but for simplicity I take r to be constant). Let the probability that the ruling party will retain office be given by p, which is a weakly decreasing function of α. In addition, let the government's power and resources, and its discretion to use these in partisan ways, be parametrized by $\gamma \geq 0$, with greater values of γ denoting greater power and discretion for the ruling party. Specifically:

$$g\,(.) = \gamma p(.).\tag{4.4}$$

Then, for low values of γ, the prospect of negative consequences becomes unlikely, and therefore will fail to deter any actor from challenging the ruling party, irrespective of his or her beliefs about how other actors are likely to behave. When γ is known to be small enough, there is no longer a connection between electoral manipulation and the actor's behavior. Formally, $d_i > \gamma p\,(\alpha)r$ for any α and all $i \in I$ so that $a_i = 1$ becomes dominant for all $i \in I$ (by condition 4.2). This renders the "low" equilibrium infeasible, and therefore precludes the possibility of indirect effects. That is, $\Delta\alpha\,(X) = \alpha\,(\mu\,[X]) - \alpha\,(\mu\,[0]) = 0$, even if $X > 0$. And, if γ is thought to be large enough, it becomes dominant for all actors to comply (so long as $p(\alpha)r$ is not too small), ruling out the "high" equilibrium. In this situation, too, electoral manipulation cannot yield indirect effects via the coordination mechanism.[42]

Costly Signaling. As mentioned earlier, there is a second way in which the signal μ can convey information to the actors about the potential consequences of their choices (i.e., choices of action a) independent of the coordination issues just discussed. Suppose that the ruling party's "strength" can vary, where strength reflects the resources and capacities likely to be available to the party to utilize in a discretionary manner for partisan purposes, and its willingness to utilize them thus. Insofar as the strength of a party is not directly or fully observable by the public, electoral manipulation can function as a costly signal of the party's strength. The key idea is that the party's ability and willingness to manipulate elections are correlated with the party's ability and willingness to overstep the law with impunity, provide rewards and punishments conditional on partisan loyalty, or bargain with other social and political actors. Therefore, in the signaling mechanism, the central issue for an individual actor deciding how to behave is not how others are likely to act (as in the coordination mechanism described earlier); instead, *the challenge for the actor is to assess the capacities and resources (i.e., the "strength") of the ruling party.*[43] Individual

---

[42] Additionally, as discussed in the next chapter, when competing parties are evenly matched in terms of strength, it may be difficult for any party to effectively utilize electoral manipulation to convey information in the first place.

[43] As mentioned earlier, an actor could care about both issues: party attributes, and how other actors are likely to behave.

actors who perceive the ruling party to be strong may be reluctant to oppose it. In the context of the participation model provided previously, thus, by signaling strength a ruling party could elicit the "low" equilibrium.

To elaborate the costly signaling mechanism, consider a game with a ruling party and a single actor, where the ruling party's strength, or "type" (to use the terminology of costly signaling games), is unknown to the public (i.e., to the actor). To emphasize the point that costly signaling can drive excessive electoral manipulation, suppose in what follows that ruling party is sure to retain power (formally, let $p = 1$). Under this assumption, any equilibrium electoral manipulation is by definition aimed at more than winning, and it is excessive, because it cannot contribute to victory in the election at hand. For simplicity, let the ruler be characterized by one of two types: "strong" or "weak." Let the parameter γ denote party strength, with $\gamma = \gamma'$ denoting a weak party, $\gamma = \gamma''$ a strong one, and $0 < \gamma' < \gamma''$. Assume $d < \gamma'' r$ so that when the ruling party is strong, the dominant choice for the actor is $a = 0$ (this follows from (4.2) using the parametrization $g(.) = \gamma p(.)$ suggested previously, and the assumption that $p = 1$). Analogously, let $d > \gamma' r$ so that $a = 1$ is dominant for the actor who knows the ruler is a weak type.[44]

Let parameter $\pi \in [0, 1]$ denote the actor's prior – that is, his/her initial belief about the probability that the ruling party is strong, before any electoral manipulation takes place. The game proceeds as follows. First, the ruling party learns its type (which is chosen by "nature," and remains unknown to the actor) and chooses the extent of electoral manipulation $x \geq 0$. Next, the actor observes signal μ, the value of which depends on the ruler's choice of the extent of electoral manipulation, x. After observing the signal, the actor chooses an action $a \in \{0, 1\}$ such that action $a = 0$ favors the ruling party and action $a = 1$ challenges or undermines the party. Finally, payoffs are distributed. For simplicity, suppose that $\mu(x) = x$. Under this assumption, and to simplify notation, I use x to stand in for the publicly observable signal μ.[45]

Note that the actor is better off having supported the ruling party in the event that the party is a strong type, but he/she is better off having challenged it when the party is weak. Specifically, the actor's payoff to choosing $a = 1$ is $d - \gamma'' r < 0$ when the party is strong, and $d - \gamma' r > 0$ when it is weak. Let the ruler's payoff be given by $(1 - a) - x/\gamma$ with $\gamma \in \{\gamma', \gamma\}$, reflecting the idea that a strong party can more easily manipulate (it has a lower cost of doing so). The payoff function also reflects the fact that the ruling party prefers that the actor comply (i.e., choose $a = 0$) rather than challenge ($a = 1$).

---

[44] Therefore, we have $0 < \gamma' < \frac{d}{r} < \gamma''$.

[45] Other assumptions are possible here. For example, one might suppose that the public cannot observe the precise extent of electoral manipulation, but can observe whether the extent of manipulation was either low or high. In that case, $\mu(x)$ might be modeled as an indicator variable, with $\mu(x) = 1$ when $x > \hat{x}$, for some threshold $\hat{x}$, and $\mu(x) = 0$ otherwise. The analysis that follows is compatible with this approach.

The costly signaling game has pooling and separating equilibria in which electoral manipulation yields indirect effects. In such equilibria, manipulating excessively elicits compliance from the actor (i.e., $a = 0$) while failing to manipulate excessively leads the actor to believe that the party is weak, therefore inviting the actor to challenge ($a = 1$). This dynamic can be seen in a separating equilibrium in which a strong ruling party chooses $x = \gamma' > 0$, a weak party chooses $x = 0$, and the actor chooses to comply ($a = 0$), if and only if $x \geq \gamma'$.[46] In this equilibrium, the strong type manipulates, not to win the election at hand (by assumption victory is assured), but to elicit compliance from the actor. In other words, the strong type manipulates excessively in equilibrium, motivated by manipulation's indirect effects. The actor challenges when the party does not manipulate excessively, but complies under excessive manipulation. From the viewpoint of the strong party type, actor compliance more than justifies the cost of excessive manipulation (the weak party type does not manipulate excessively only because doing so is prohibitively costly).[47]

A similar logic of manipulation holds in a pooling equilibrium in which both a weak and a strong ruling party engage in excessive electoral manipulation, and the actor complies if and only if manipulation is excessive.[48] Such an equilibrium is possible when the actor initially believes that the ruling party is likely to be strong (i.e., when π is high enough). Because of pooling, the actor obtains no new information about the party's type, and therefore chooses to comply. In this equilibrium, as in the one just described, excessive manipulation is utilized to influence the behavior of the actor; that is, for its indirect effects: should the ruling party manipulate less than the equilibrium amount, it would convey weakness and elicit opposition from the actor (in this case, however, no party manipulates less than the equilibrium excessive amount on the path of play).[49]

---

[46] Incentive compatibility for the actor follows from the above payoff structure and the fact that, due to separation, the actor learns the ruler's type from the signal. For a weak ruling party, any amount of electoral manipulation $x > \gamma'$ is strictly dominated, and deviating to any positive but smaller amount of manipulation is undesirable since it is costly and cannot elicit favorable behavior from the actor (for simplicity I ignore the generic case where $x = \gamma'$). For a strong ruling party, using further excess in manipulation $x > \gamma'$ is costly and provides no additional benefit in terms of the actor's behavior, while a lesser amount $0 < x < \gamma'$ fails to elicit compliance from the actor but is nevertheless costly. Moreover, $x = 0$ yields a payoff of zero while the equilibrium choice yields a positive payoff.

[47] Letting $\mu(x) = 0$ for $x < x^* = \gamma'$ and $\mu(x) = 1$ otherwise, and noting that in this equilibrium $\alpha(\mu = 1) = 0$ and $\alpha(\mu=0)=1$, the indirect effect of excessive electoral manipulation is given by equation 4.3.

[48] Off the path of play, the actor believes that only a weak type would not manipulate excessively.

[49] Formally, the equilibrium level of electoral manipulation for either type in this equilibrium is $x = x^*$, where $0 < x^* < \gamma'$. Any $x^* > \gamma'$ would be unaffordable (i.e., strictly dominated) for the low type, and therefore could not be part of a pooling equilibrium. Off the path of play, the actor believes that a ruler who manipulates less than x^* is a low type. Deviations to $x > x^*$ are costly for either type and do not yield any additional benefit, as the actor is already complying.

Both the separating and the pooling equilibria have an information-based logic, but the specifics of the logic differ in the following sense. In the former, electoral manipulation reveals new information about type; in the latter, it potentially distorts or obscures such information: specifically, it preserves pre-existing beliefs about type even when they do not correspond to actual type. In both cases, electoral manipulation yields indirect effects, that is, it influences the actor's behavior.

To further illustrate the information dynamics at play, consider the following example. Suppose that the ruling party can be one of three types: weak, strong, or bluffing. The weak and strong types are as previously defined, and the bluffing type is closer to the weak type in strength, but has a greater capacity to manipulate. Specifically, suppose that a weak type cannot manipulate enough to produce the signal value $\mu = 1$, but that the bluffing and the strong type can do so. Let p_W, p_S, and p_B respectively denote the prior probabilities that the ruler is weak, strong, or bluffing, and let all be nonzero. For simplicity, suppose that the actors have solved any coordination problems and are therefore adequately modeled as a unitary actor. Such an actor would like to know the ruler's type, because he/she would choose $a = 0$ if the ruler was strong, but would challenge (i.e., choose $a = 1$) if the ruler was either weak or bluffing. Now, if the actor observes the spectacle of excessive or blatant manipulation, represented by signal $\mu = 1$, he/she cannot tell whether the ruling party is actually strong or merely pretending to be so – namely, bluffing. However, he/she can rule out the possibility that the ruler is outright weak, and update his/her assessment about the probability that the ruler is strong (or bluffing) accordingly. Let $\tilde{p}_s$ denote the posterior probability that the ruler is strong. Then, on observing the signal $\mu = 1$, the actor concludes that:

$$\tilde{p}_s = \frac{p_S}{p_S + p_B} > p_S.$$

This means that excessive electoral manipulation increases the actor's probability assessment that he/she is facing a strong ruler, and therefore decreases the chances that he/she will challenge him. To exemplify these three types and the corresponding logic, consider the following (imperfect but illustrative) set of examples. As an example of a weak ruler, consider Ukraine's Yanukovich. His party was able to manipulate the first realization of the 2004 election enough to win, but only by a narrow margin of victory. In the model, the signal conveyed by such an electoral result is $\mu = 0$, which reveals that the ruling party is a weak type. In consequence, a large number of actors decided to challenge the incumbent party (both through protests and in the repeat of

---

Deviations to $x < x^*$ are all strictly dominated by $x = 0$ (because the actor does not comply and manipulation is costly), which in turn is less desirable for either actor than the equilibrium choice, because $x = 0$ yields a zero payoff to both types and the equilibrium choice yields a strictly positive payoff to either type.

the runoff, after courts invalidated the first runoff vote). Belarus' Lukashenko, in contrast, exemplifies a strong type. Going into the presidential election of 2001 as the incumbent, even opponents acknowledged that he could have won without manipulation, but Lukashenko utilized excessive and blatant manipulation and obtained a large margin of victory (in the model, $\mu = 1$). Having indicated that he was not a weak type, a variety of actors (such as bureaucrats and voters) were discouraged from challenging him. Finally, Egypt's Mubarak in 2010–2011 potentially exemplifies a bluffing type. His successful manipulation of the 2010 legislative election, in which he obtained an impressive margin of seats, signaled that he was not a weak type (again, $\mu = 1$) and for some time this sufficed to keep rivals at bay. It is only after the fact, on the basis of subsequent events largely unrelated to the election (e.g., the protests and fall of the government in Tunisia), that we are able to conclude that Mubarak was a bluffing type and not a strong one: he was not able to resist an all-out opposition challenge.[50]

Note that costly signaling can also function to elicit compliance or deter opposition in a setting with a large number of actors, each of whom has little influence on his/her own. Whether or not such actors have overcome their coordination problems, the belief that the incumbent is a strong type can lead such actors to avoid choosing to challenge. As mentioned previously, however, coordination and costly signaling mechanisms are not mutually exclusive – electoral manipulation can simultaneously drive expectations about the relative strength of parties through both mechanisms (e.g., for different kinds of actors, or for the same actors in different situations), and the two mechanisms can potentially reinforce each other.

In sum, the simple model presented here shows that electoral manipulation, by shaping the political context (modeled here as μ) can influence the actor behavior, potentially in ways that favor the perpetrator – that is, electoral manipulation can yield indirect effects. I have shown two information-based mechanisms through which electoral manipulation can do this. The first mechanism involves influencing actor coordination. The second mechanism consists of shaping public perceptions about the strength of the manipulating party.

From Electoral Manipulation to the Political Context

I now briefly consider the relationship between electoral manipulation and signal μ, the topmost link in the mechanism depicted in Figure 4.2. As mentioned previously, μ is a simple way to formalize the notion of "political context." The question of interest in this subsection is: under what conditions will

---

[50] This brief example, of course, does not delve into the sources of Mubarak's "strength" or "weakness," which presumably had much to do with his control over the military. In terms of the formalization, both Lukashenko and Mubarak's use of manipulation produced the signal $\mu = 1$, even though the former was truly strong and the latter was likely a bluffing type.

electoral manipulation shape the signal μ. There exist a variety of possibilities for the substantive referent for μ. It could represent the margin of victory, the margin of seats, or the blatancy of manipulation, among other things. The point is that, to yield indirect effects, electoral manipulation must influence the political context. However, while electoral manipulation may affect any or all dimensions of the political context, it need not always do so. Suppose, for example, that the political context μ consists solely of the margin of victory in the most recent election. If two competing parties manipulate to the same extent, so that their respective manipulation efforts neutralize each other, then the margin of victory will remain unaffected. In contrast, if one of the parties manipulates to an appreciably greater extent than the other, the margin of victory will certainly change as a result of the manipulation.

As this example suggests (and the following chapter demonstrates), for electoral manipulation to affect the political context, a certain measure of initial inequality in the capacities and resources of the competing parties is needed. Consider once again the relationship between electoral manipulation and the margin of victory. In the Philippines in the 1950s, in Colombia and Costa Rica in the nineteenth and early twentieth centuries (respectively), and in the United States at various points in its history, the two major competing parties were relatively evenly matched in terms of their resources and capacities, and therefore electoral manipulation had only small effects on margins of victory. Instead, electoral manipulation took the form of an arms race where one contender's efforts mostly cancelled the other's. In contrast, in Putin's Russia, Mugabe's Zimbabwe through most of the 1990s, or Mexico in the 1970s and 1980s, ruling parties enjoyed advantages that allowed them to manipulate to a substantially greater extent than other parties. In these cases, electoral manipulation had dramatic effects on margins of victory, and therefore held the potential to yield strong indirect effects (I discuss these three cases in detail in Chapters 6 and 7).

While the example of the margin of victory focuses on the balance or imbalance in the *extent* of electoral manipulation, a similar logic applies to the *visibility* of manipulation, changing a few nuances. Consider an election among two parties that are evenly matched and choose to manipulate equally blatantly. Of course, the blatancy of one party's manipulation will not, strictly speaking, neutralize the blatancy of the other party's. Instead, the idea is that, because the blatancy of each party's manipulation is similar, their efforts at manipulation are unlikely to cause a partisan bias in the behavior of actors. Suppose, for example, that blatant manipulation turns actors (voters, donors, or potential candidates, for instance) off from politics. The point is that, insofar as each party's efforts are equally blatant, the set of actors who is turned off will not disproportionally consist of one of the party's sympathizers. Therefore, blatant manipulation will have had an indirect effect (because it will have changed the behavior of political actors), but one that does not favor any of the parties. In contrast, when one of the parties manipulates more blatantly than the other, the ensuing indirect effect will have a clear partisan bias.[51] These ideas describe the notion of *directional visibility*: the degree to which the blatancy of one party's manipulation exceeds the blatancy of the other's. Once again, this suggests that initial disparity in the capacities of competing parties is needed to yield indirect effects that favor one of the parties.[52] This idea stems from the strategic logic of party competition, a logic that the next chapter examines.

Blatant Manipulation and Popularity

The models presented in this chapter focus primarily on the extent, not the visibility or blatancy, of electoral manipulation. However, the basic logic of the argument applies to secret as well as to blatant electoral manipulation. In this subsection, I discuss some of the nuances that arise from this distinction in relation to each of the two mechanisms I have proposed, coordination and costly signaling. When electoral manipulation is secret, it can shape the political context through its effect on electoral margins of victory (or margins of seats, or proportion of subnational offices captured). When manipulation is visible to the public, it can still influence such margins; in addition, its very visibility is a constitutive element of the political context.[53] For purposes of my argument, both secret and visible electoral manipulation have the capacity to influence the political context (formalized as μ) and therefore to potentially unleash indirect effects on the basis of coordination or signaling dynamics such as I have described previously.

Nevertheless, it stands to reason that the public might have different reactions to the specific manner in which electoral manipulation shapes the political context, and in particular to the blatancy of manipulation. Blatant manipulation could potentially anger the public, reduce the manipulator's popularity, and erode the manipulating party's "legitimacy."[54] Several notes are in order regarding this possibility.

---

[51] It is possible that supporters of different parties have different sensitivities to the blatancy of manipulation. The general idea of directional visibility will still hold, although the precise levels of blatancy at which parties efforts cause or fail to cause a partisan bias will differ according to the sensitivity of rival actors to blatancy.

[52] Of course, the issue is what choices parties make in equilibrium. The next chapter shows that disparity in equilibrium choices is proportional to initial disparity in the capacities and resources of the competing parties.

[53] Note that, even when electoral manipulation is secret, Nash equilibrium implies that the actor(s) may know the extent of it (because in equilibrium, players know the other players' strategies). Even when that is the case (i.e., when manipulation is secret and actors know its extent in equilibrium), it is possible that blatant manipulation could have behavioral effects that differ from those of secret manipulation – cheating that is flaunted may discourage, or anger, more than the same cheating when it is not flaunted. (See also the discussion of the relationship between electoral manipulation and public protests / rebellions in Chapter 1.)

[54] If there exists the possibility that secret manipulation could come to be publicly revealed, then these dangers would apply, albeit to a lesser degree, to secret manipulation as well.

First, whether or not, and to what extent, blatant electoral manipulation influences popularity or legitimacy is likely to depend on context. For example, even if blatant manipulation is universally disliked by the public, a party that has in the past manipulated blatantly may not experience any additional loss in popularity or in legitimacy as a consequence of manipulating blatantly once again. It is also possible that the manipulating party's supporters and opponents could react quite differently to the allegation or the knowledge that such a party manipulated blatantly, with opponents being more sensitive. The overall effect on popularity and legitimacy would depend on the proportion of supporters and opponents (in which case the impact of blatant manipulation on popularity would vary with the party's initial popularity). Moreover, actors' preferences over parties are likely to depend on a multiplicity of dimensions – such as the economy, security, social issues, and ethnicity, among others – in addition to the issue of electoral conduct.[55] If so, even if blatant manipulation erodes the manipulating party's legitimacy, the impact of the manipulation on the party's level of popular support remains an open question (and one possibility is that such impact could be small or negligible).

Second, even when blatant manipulation carries with it a cost in terms of popularity and legitimacy, such a cost – or the prospect of it – is one among various considerations influencing choices about manipulation. A party might be willing to incur a cost in popularity, in exchange for the benefits of appearing strong to the public, for example. As mentioned earlier, the indirect benefits of electoral manipulation could include a greater freedom to act while in office as well as a greater likelihood of retaining office in the future, even after considering the loss in popularity and legitimacy.[56]

Third, and relatedly, when electoral manipulation is visible, it cannot effectively signal popularity: the public would know that the electoral result resulted from the manipulation.[57] Nevertheless, the strength of a party depends on a number of attributes, of which popularity is only one, and manipulating blatantly can shape public perceptions about other such attributes. Attributes relevant to strength other than popularity include: the capacities of the manipulator (e.g., control over legal processes and institutions), resources available to the manipulator (e.g., ability to somehow muster financial or logistical resources for partisan ends), and dispositional traits (e.g., inclination to engage in normatively unacceptable practices such as manipulating elections, repressing or

---

[55] Rose and Mishler (2009), for example, find on the basis of survey data collected in Russia in 2007 that endorsement of the current regime is much more strongly influenced by approval of the current economic system than by electoral unfairness (129–131).

[56] For example, in their study of post-Communist Slovakia and Serbia, Bunce and Wolchick (2010) find that "[v]ulnerable regimes can endure, however, if both civil society and the opposition are demobilized" (150).

[57] However, when manipulation is blatant but its extent cannot be precisely assessed by the public, it could still be possible to utilize such manipulation to shape perceptions about the manipulator's popularity.

otherwise punishing opponents, and rewarding supporters). Blatant manipulation can also shape perceptions about how other social and political actors are likely to behave: even when it is known that a ruler is unpopular, it does not necessarily follow that those who dislike it will venture to challenge it.

It would certainly be possible to explicitly incorporate popularity or legitimacy costs into the analysis. So long as those costs are not prohibitive, blatant manipulation could continue to be desirable in equilibrium. The fact that, in practice, electoral manipulation is often blatant (as discussed in Chapter 3) suggests that when it comes to choices about electoral manipulation, popularity and legitimacy costs can be trumped by other factors – for example, by the prospect of eliciting indirect effects that benefit the manipulator.

The Time Dimension in the Mechanisms

The previous discussion and Figures 4.1 and 4.2 make explicit the dynamic nature of the argument: electoral manipulation in time-period one influences political behavior in time-period two. The two time periods have more than one relevant substantive interpretation. For example, time-period one could refer to the months or weeks immediately preceding an election, and time-period two to the election itself. In this interpretation, blatant indications of electoral manipulation in the preelection period could potentially influence political behavior in the election itself. A second possibility is that time-period one refers to the time period surrounding an election (and including the election), and time-period two to the post-election period. In this scenario, electoral manipulation associated with the election could potentially influence policy, bargaining between government and other actors, distribution of rents, and acquiescence of political and social actors with the manipulator's agenda (assuming that the manipulator wins the election). A third possibility is that the first and second periods span a longer period of time. For example, time-period one can refer to a country's (or a region's) electoral history, and time-period two to an electoral or interelectoral period following that history. In this case, a history of manipulated elections might shape the behavior of political and social actors in the period following it. A fourth possibility, similar to the last one, is that the two periods refer to consecutive elections – for example, a presidential election in May and a legislative election in October. In this instance, electoral manipulation in the May election could influence political behavior in the subsequent October election. All of these scenarios are compatible with the basic argument, that electoral manipulation today can importantly influence the behavior of a wide range of political and social actors tomorrow, with potential indirect effects in both the electoral and the non-electoral realms.

Indirect Effects and the Level of Government

The potential for indirect effects, and therefore the incentive to manipulate excessively and blatantly, can exist at different levels of government. For one thing, the mechanisms I have discussed can be applied wholesale to elections for subnational office: the "ruler" in question could be a governor, for example.[58] In addition, however, subnational actors can have incentives to manipulate excessively, from the viewpoint of their locality, in elections for *national* office. As noted earlier, one category of indirect effects consists of positive career externalities for subnational politicians, who in some contexts stand to curry favor with their superiors by demonstrating that their ability to deliver the vote is substantial, or that it exceeds that of other subnational politicians (Ames 1970, Ichino 2006, Boix and Svolik 2007). In practice, the incentives and possibilities for excessive/blatant manipulation by subnational politicians in national elections need not coincide with those of national politicians. Subnational politicians may wish to maximize manipulation in their locality in order to enhance their own career prospects, while a national government may, in contrast, wish to allocate resources and effort differently, keeping national and not local outcomes in mind. Excessive manipulation at the national level, therefore, could reflect either the aggregate consequences of the incentives of subnational politicians, or a deliberate national-level choice to manipulate excessively.

The balance of power between national and subnational politicians, as well as the level of government from which resources for manipulation flow, will play an important role in determining whose incentives are reflected in actual patterns of manipulation. It is also necessary to distinguish, of course, between the *locus of decision-making* about the extent or visibility of electoral manipulation, on the one hand, and the level of government or administration at which such decisions are *implemented*, on the other (noting that agency problems could drive a wedge between central directives and actual implementation).

In the case of Mexico, for example, there is evidence that electoral manipulation under the PRI – the party in government – was, to an important degree, centrally planned, both as recently as 1988 (when massive manipulation was planned and implemented at the highest levels of government) and as far back as in the times of the Mexican president and dictator Porfirio Díaz (who would himself decide the list of candidates that would stand for election and win).[59] In Carbonell's (2002) account of the chain of command for electoral frauds in Mexico under the PRI in the twentieth century, decisions were made centrally. Molinar and Weldon (1994) and Magaloni (2006) find evidence that considerable resources were centrally allocated for electoral purposes in Mexico under the PRI. A similarly centralized organization of vote buying is described by Wang and Kurzman (2003) for the case of Taiwan (discussed further in the next chapter). In the case of Ukraine, evidence from the Melnychenko tapes (discussed in Chapter 1) suggests that directives about the extent of electoral

---

[58] I discuss excessive/blatant manipulation in the states of Mexico under the PRI in Chapter 7. For electoral manipulation in Russia's regions see Hale (2003).

[59] Posada-Carbó 2000, for instance, refers to a letter that Mr. Díaz wrote to the Governor of Puebla detailing a list of "candidates" (615).

manipulation originated at the highest level of government. Similarly, suggestive evidence is available for the case of Zimbabwe, and there is evidence that in Putin and Medvedev's Russia, subnational governments follow manipulation targets set by the national government (more on these cases in Chapter 6).[60] I discuss the issue of the centralization of decision-making about electoral manipulation in Russian elections in Chapter 6.

4.3 CONCLUSION

To sum up, this chapter has explored the mechanisms through which electoral manipulation might influence the behavior of a wide range of political and social actors – that is, the mechanisms behind indirect effects. These mechanisms are based on the idea that electoral manipulation can play an informational role. The causal chain runs from electoral manipulation to expectations (via the political context) to behavior, as summarized in Figures 4.1 and 4.2. I have elaborated the logic of the argument with the use of simple formal models where the political choices of actors depend, in equilibrium, on a signal that in turn reflects electoral manipulation. How exactly such a signal is generated in the context of electoral competition is the subject of the next chapter.

The preceding discussion also began to explore the background conditions under which electoral manipulation is capable of yielding indirect effects. Institutional settings where the rule of law is relatively well-established help to insulate social and political actors from the discretion of politicians, also reducing or eliminating the potential for electoral manipulation to yield indirect effects: bureaucrats may be able to resist entreaties by the ruling party to behave in particular ways, without suffering for it; voters may be able to support opposition parties without the fear of losing state benefits; and ambitious politicians may face limited consequences if they challenge the incumbent and lose, as well as better prospects of winning in the first place. This point was made in

---

[60] It is possible for both national and subnational incentives to manipulate excessively to operate simultaneously. Ames (1970), for example, suggests that local PRI politicians independently sought to manipulate excessively with the purpose of currying favor with superiors. In such cases, it is conceivable that the national government is the marginal manipulator (understanding the term "marginal" in the economic sense – that is, to denote the actor that makes the decision as to whether or not to pursue additional manipulation). If so, then the coexistence of independent decisions to manipulate excessively at the national and subnational levels might be understood, from a strategic point of view, as implying that subnational-level decisions to manipulate are *not* yielding enough manipulation from the perspective of the national decision-maker (i.e., the ruling party) – otherwise, there would be no need for the national actor to undertake additional electoral manipulation on his/her own, or to abet the manipulation efforts of subnational actors. (In the model presented in the next chapter, the parameter δ could be seen to incorporate not only the incumbent party's popularity, but also any expected effect on the vote stemming from the independent choices of subnational-level actors, either on behalf of that incumbent party or of an opposition party. Taking that as a given, the ruling party would then choose how much (and/or how visibly) to manipulate).

the context of the coordination mechanism, but it holds also for the costly signaling mechanism. Under institutional conditions that limit the difference between "weak" and the "strong" ruler types in terms of resources and discretion, information about type will have little or no effect on the behavior of political actors.

Additionally, at various points in the chapter, I suggested that vigorous partisan competition can make it difficult for electoral manipulation to influence the political context (e.g., when one party's manipulation is neutralized by another party's manipulation). Therefore, loosely speaking, a measure of inequality in the capacities of competing parties is necessary for electoral manipulation to have the potential to yield indirect effects. This intuition is developed with greater rigor in the next chapter. These two results suggest the "comparative statics" hypothesis that, as conditions change in a given country or region (where by conditions I refer to the power, resources, and discretion of the ruling party, and to the balance of resources and power among competing parties), so should the potential for indirect effects. I elaborate these ideas further in the next chapter (especially in Section 5.3); and in Chapter 6, I show how these comparative statics are borne out in the recent electoral histories of Russia and Zimbabwe.

The way I have modeled actors is parsimonious and is designed to capture the essential features of the different sets of choices that different kinds of actors face – voters, activists, donors, bureaucrats, and others. There is no implication, however, that all actors are the same, interchangeable, or analytically equivalent: voters, donors, and union leaders are different in many ways; even the label "bureaucrat" encompasses a wide variety of actors. One could surely construct a slightly different theory and write an accompanying formal model, for each kind of actor. Instead, I have provided here a general model and exemplified some of the ways in which it can apply to different categories of actors. This procedure has the distinct advantage of laying bare and emphasizing the essential elements of the argument in a way that abstracts from actor-specific nuances. Such nuances, however, may be interesting in their own right and deserving of analytical attention, and there is certainly room for studies focused on specific kinds of actors.[61]

For these reasons, in the theoretical section of this study I have abstracted from many of the particularities of specific kinds of actors. Nevertheless, I have theorized an important dimension of variation among different kinds of actors: the distinction between small, atomized actors that have little influence on political and policy outcomes, on the one hand, and powerful, influential actors, on the other. The actions of a citizen in isolation casting a vote, or a

---

[61] For a study of the indirect effects of electoral manipulation on the behavior of bureaucrats see Gehlbach and Simpser (2011); for a discussion of the indirect effects of manipulation on voter turnout see Simpser (2012), as well as Chapters 6 and 7 of this book; for the role of excessive electoral manipulation on the behavior of political parties see Donno and Roussias (2009).

low-level bureaucrat who chooses not to divert the resources at his or her disposal to the incumbent's coffers, have a small (and perhaps negligible) amount of influence; in contrast, the choices of a labor union head, or of a popular governor, may importantly affect the ruling party's scope for action while in office, as well as its ability to win subsequent elections, and its grip on power. The argument I have developed in this chapter – that electoral manipulation can yield indirect effects – may, but need not, rely on the same mechanisms for these two broad categories of actors. The choices of very influential actors are likely to depend on their perceptions of the manipulating party's relative power, perhaps more than on expectations about how less-influential actors are likely to behave. Through a costly signaling mechanism, electoral manipulation can constitute a source of information precisely on the manipulator's strength. Smaller, atomized actors, in contrast, care not only about the relative power of the different parties, but also about the likely behavior of fellow actors. Therefore, electoral manipulation can influence the behavior of such actors by affecting their perceptions of the manipulator's relative power, as well as their expectations about the likely collective behavior of fellow actors. Of course, atomized and unitary actors are extreme types – there also exist actors with middling levels of influence, such as medium-sized businesses or smaller labor unions, whose individual choices have consequences that on their own are not negligible yet not sufficiently weighty to make a big difference, taken on their own, on political outcomes. Such actors, like atomized ones, care both about the ruling party's power as well as about how fellow actors are likely to behave.

The goal of this chapter was to define indirect effects of electoral manipulation and to describe the mechanisms that give rise to them. In doing this, the prior process of choice giving rise to electoral manipulation itself was mostly set aside. Such a process constitutes the focus of the next chapter, where choices about electoral manipulation are made endogenously as the equilibrium behavior of competing political parties.

APPENDIX

Generalizing the Concept of Indirect Effects

Legislative Elections. To state the central ideas of the book with a bit more generality, consider the concepts of an electoral *prize* and an electoral *threshold*. An electoral prize is the good that is at play in the election, that which parties or candidates are contesting. An electoral threshold is the proportion of the vote needed to attain the prize. Consider a winner-takes-all election. In the traditional view of electoral manipulation, the prize is the office being contested, and the threshold is a plurality (or a majority). In this view, any votes beyond the threshold are superfluous, because they do not contribute toward the attainment of the prize. Therefore, this view does not adequately explain the excessive or blatant use of manipulation. In fact, the traditional view provides good reasons why electoral manipulation ought *not* to be pursued excessively or blatantly: doing so would increase the chances that the perpetrator might be punished or the election annulled, for example, without contributing to obtaining the prize.[62]

To define excessive manipulation for the case of legislative elections, it will be helpful to generalize the traditional view by noting that different governmental and electoral institutions give rise to different prizes and thresholds. For example, in legislative elections, the prize could consist of a plurality of the seats, where a plurality of seats grants the privilege to form the government. The prize could also consist of an absolute majority, or a two-thirds supermajority of the seats, if this would permit a party to unilaterally approve laws or amend the constitution.[63] But the basic logic would be the same as in the winner-takes-all case: there is an electoral threshold associated with a prize, and once the threshold is reached, further electoral manipulation does not contribute to the attainment of the prize. The definition of excess, of course, depends on the threshold in question. Therefore, it is possible that in some legislative elections, margins of victory of, say, 30 percent of the seats could be justified by an extended version of the conventional wisdom, if that size margin is what is needed to reach the relevant threshold of seats – e.g., that associated with the ability to unilaterally pass a law.

There is an additional subtlety to consider in the case of legislative elections. Because of the way that legislatures function, legislative coalitions can shift in the course of their normal functioning – in fact, they can shift on any occasion where the legislature votes. This means that parties must not only win enough seats, they must also maintain their coalitions in an environment in which opponents may attempt to lure legislators away. Groseclose and Snyder (1996) have shown that, in such an environment, it is often optimal to invest in a supermajoritarian coalition to forefend possible attacks.[64] For example, for a party that wishes to maintain a two-thirds majority coalition in the legislature, it could conceivably be optimal to have, say, 70 percent of the seats to prevent potential attacks on the coalition. For theoretical reasons, if a party manipulated and attained 70 percent of the vote in that scenario, I would not call such manipulation "excessive," even though it exceeds the

---

[62] The same basic logic applies in a probabilistic setting: after a certain point, the contribution of additional electoral manipulation to the prize is less than its cost. See Chapter 5 for more on the role of uncertainty.

[63] Blaydes (2010), for example, argues that Mubarak's government in Egypt sought to retain a two-thirds majority to be able to unilaterally pass constitutional amendments and presidential initiatives without the consent of rivals, but with the cover of formal institutions (39).

[64] Of course, the possibilities for attacks on one's coalition will depend on a variety of factors, including party discipline (which in turn will depend in part on the electoral rules) and the resources available to the different parties.

relevant institutional threshold (two-thirds of the seats, in this case). In other words, in legislative elections, I will say that the relevant threshold is the institutional threshold (e.g., two-thirds of the seats) adjusted for the optimality considerations introduced by Groseclose and Snyder.[65]

Empirically, however, allowing for this adjustment of the threshold introduces some complications: to determine what constitutes an instance of excessive manipulation in a legislative election, it is necessary to first determine the relevant adjusted threshold. But the adjustment is difficult to estimate empirically without additional case-specific information.[66] Strictly speaking, therefore, the evidence I presented in Chapter 3 on legislative elections should be seen as suggestive that excessive manipulation is taking place in such elections – perhaps strongly suggestive, but not as incontrovertible. Note that Groseclose and Snyder's insight does not apply to elections for executive office, where, technically speaking, winning by one vote is the same as winning by millions.[67] Therefore, large margins of victory are very strong evidence of excessive manipulation in executive elections.[68]

To account for excessive and/or blatant electoral manipulation, what I am proposing is a broadening of existing understandings of what it is that parties, governments, and rulers can potentially obtain through the use of electoral manipulation. In the language of prizes and thresholds, I am suggesting the following:

(1) There exist prizes stemming from electoral manipulation other than those defined by the electoral and institutional rules – for example, the wholesale discouragement of opposition in an upcoming election can be of great value, above and beyond the obtaining of a plurality, a majority, or a filibuster-proof supermajority.

(2) Prizes stemming from electoral manipulation need not be confined, in terms of timing, to the electoral period; they may also accrue later in

---

[65] The reason for this is that the threshold thus adjusted is still motivated by the goal of attaining (and maintaining) the associated institutionally determined threshold – and not by the possibility of deterring opponents (or of eliciting other indirect effects), for example.

[66] Such a task is beyond the scope of what I attempt here.

[67] Note that the possibilities for the impeachment of an executive office-holder depend on *legislative* coalitions, and not on the margin of victory with which the executive obtained office.

[68] Concurrent elections for executive and legislative offices introduce an additional twist: it is possible that manipulation aimed at reaching a given threshold of seats in the legislature could "drive" the manipulation of the executive result. This could be one source of excessive manipulation in executive elections. Nevertheless, it is unlikely to be an important source for various reasons. First, many executive elections are nonconcurrent with legislative ones. Second, even in those that are concurrent, it is likely that the executive election would be at the center of any efforts at manipulation, because, in systems with a directly elected president, the presidency is often a very powerful office (this is true for Latin America and for many formerly Communist countries, for example).

time. For example, a landslide victory in a federal election could enhance the government's bargaining power vis-à-vis business interests or unions.

(3) Prizes stemming from electoral manipulation need not be of a discrete nature. Winning an office or a cabinet position is a discrete prize, in the sense that it is either attained or not attained, and therefore votes beyond the victory threshold are wasteful. But discouraging opponents could, in many instances, be a matter of degree: for example, the degree to which opposition morale is wrecked by a large or a blatant victory could be proportional to the size of the margin of victory or to the blatancy of the victory.

(4) Prizes stemming from electoral manipulation need not be confined to the electoral and institutional realms: the margin of victory could, for example, influence the winner's post-electoral bargaining power in a variety of policy areas (e.g., by conveying the message to business interests, labor unions, and other political and social actors that no actor is indispensable in the winning coalition).

It is possible to restate the definition of direct and indirect effects using the previous language. The *direct effects* of electoral manipulation consist of the contribution of electoral manipulation to the attainment of discrete prizes being contested in the election in question, as specified by the constitutional rules.[69] The *indirect effects* of electoral manipulation consist of the contribution of electoral manipulation to the attainment of additional sorts of prizes – prizes that may concern arenas other than the electoral, may accrue outside the time frame of the election in question, may not be formally defined by the constitutional rules, and may not be discrete.

Electoral Manipulation Tactics and Voter Contact. Finally, a small nuance arises in cases where the specific form of electoral manipulation involves voters or potential voters in the very act of manipulation. To see this, it is helpful to distinguish between tools of electoral manipulation that are purely mechanical (e.g., ballot box stuffing or tampering with the vote count), and tools that involve voters or potential voters (for example, the bribing or pressuring of citizens to control the direction of their vote and/or whether they vote at all).[70] Both kinds of tools of manipulation – those that operate mechanically and those that are "voter mediated" – can have both direct and indirect effects. Consider, for example, the case of vote buying. Suppose that, in the context of an election in period t, party X successfully buys the vote of citizen A, unsuccessfully tries to buy the vote of citizen B (who refuses the bribe), and all of this is witnessed by citizen C and by politician D. The direct effect of the

---

[69] Of course, the actual allocation of the prizes could take place a few months after the election is completed.

[70] Vote buying is often illegal, and even when it is not it is often widely regarded as illegitimate. I discuss this issue further in Simpser (2012).

vote-buying effort, then, is to increase the vote tally for party X by one vote.[71] In addition, the vote-buying effort could have an indirect effect on the subsequent behavior of all actors A through D. For example, it could discourage B and C from actively supporting an opponent of party X in the election at t and in subsequent elections, and diminish D's perceived bargaining power vis-à-vis the manipulator (it could also discourage citizen A from supporting X's opponents on elections subsequent to t). In other words, to be slightly more precise, the direct effect of electoral manipulation refers to its impact on vote totals either via mechanical means (as in the case of ballot box stuffing) or via the response of members of the electorate *directly and successfully targeted* by the manipulation efforts (such as A in period t). In contrast, the indirect effect of electoral manipulation refers to its impact on the choices of all political actors, including those not directly targeted and those directly but unsuccessfully targeted, by the process of manipulation (such as B, C, and D in periods t and thereafter), as well as those directly and successfully targeted, subsequent to the instance on which they were targeted (such as A in periods after t).

---

[71] A minor precision: if citizen A planned to vote for a party other than X, then the direct effect of X buying A's vote is to both increase the vote tally for X by one vote and to decrease the vote tally for that other party by one vote.

5

The Strategic Logic of Electoral Manipulation

The previous chapter examined the consequences of electoral manipulation by developing the idea that electoral manipulation can yield both direct and indirect effects, and by describing the causal mechanisms underpinning the latter. This chapter extends the theoretical discussion by focusing on the prior step in the causal chain, that is, on how choices about electoral manipulation are made in the first place.[1] Specifically, I examine the strategic logic of electoral manipulation in a setting where political parties compete in elections. The goal of the analysis is to elucidate the patterns of electoral manipulation that are likely to arise in equilibrium in a competitive setting, and how such patterns are influenced by the possibility of indirect effects. In addition, the chapter has two additional goals: to examine the relationship between background conditions and patterns of manipulation (Section 5.3); and to consider potential alternative explanations for excessive and blatant manipulation (Section 5.4).

The analysis in the first part of this chapter proceeds on the basis of a model of party competition where two rival political parties can choose the extent of electoral manipulation.[2] Electoral manipulation can benefit its perpetrator by contributing to the probability of victory (its direct effect) and potentially yielding indirect effects. Manipulating, however, is costly: it requires resources, manpower, and organization, and can lead to punishment both domestically and internationally. This simple model helps to study the basic logic of choices about electoral manipulation, the role of indirect effects in such choices, and alternative explanations for excessive manipulation.

---

[1] That step corresponds to time period $t = 1$ in the schematic depiction of the argument in Figures 4.1 and 4.2.

[2] The parties' choices can be reinterpreted as choices about the visibility of manipulation, as discussed later.

The central result is that equilibrium electoral manipulation is excessive and blatant when the following two conditions hold. First, there is a *motive* – that is, manipulation has the potential to yield more than victory. In other words, the potential for indirect effects provides the motivation to manipulate excessively and/or blatantly. Second, excess/blatancy is *feasible* – that is, one of the parties has a large enough capacity to manipulate that it can do so excessively (and/or blatantly), despite possible competition from a rival.[3] The results can be loosely summarized as follows:

Result 1:   When the potential for indirect effects does not exist, any equilibrium electoral manipulation is marginal and secret.

Result 2:   When electoral manipulation has the potential to yield indirect effects, equilibrium electoral manipulation is excessive and/or blatant, provided the following feasibility condition holds:

Condition A: The capacity for manipulation of one of the parties is large, and greater than that of other parties.[4]

The intuition behind these results can be stated in simple terms. Consider the extent of manipulation (I return to the visibility of manipulation later). When the potential for indirect effects does not exist, there is little to gain from manipulating beyond the victory threshold, and therefore the equilibrium margin of victory in a manipulated election will be small. This is true even when a party is capable of manipulating excessively, because the motive to manipulate in such a manner is lacking. This is the intuition behind Result 1.

In contrast, when the potential for indirect effects is substantial, there is much to gain from manipulating beyond the point of victory (i.e., to elicit indirect effects). For such a gain to be realized, however, it is necessary that one of the parties be capable of manipulating excessively. A subtle but important point that emerges from the analysis that follows is that party competition can render excessive manipulation difficult or infeasible. The reason for this is that the potential for indirect effects will simultaneously motivate competing parties to manipulate (either to realize the benefits of indirect effects or to prevent a rival from doing so). Therefore, their respective efforts at manipulation will partly or wholly neutralize each other. Therefore, in general, excessive

---

[3] Feasibility, of course, also requires that the expected cost of manipulation, in relation with its expected benefit, not be prohibitive. When the cost is high enough, elections will be clean. In what follows, I assume that budget constraints are not binding. I discuss the substantive sources of the cost of manipulation later in this chapter.

[4] There exists an additional theoretical scenario where excessive or blatant electoral manipulation arises in equilibrium even when Condition A does not hold. Denote such a scenario as Result 3. Result 3 requires, similar to Result 2 in the text, that the potential for indirect effects exists. Result 3 also requires an alternative feasibility condition: Condition B. Condition B is that one of the contenders be exceptionally popular among the electorate. For reasons discussed later, in practice, Result 3 is unlikely to arise.

manipulation will only be feasible when one of the parties has a sufficiently-large relative advantage in the capacity to manipulate. In contrast, when the competing parties have similar capacities to manipulate, electoral manipulation is unlikely to be excessive (even though its overall scale could be large).[5]

A similar logic governs the visibility of manipulation: when the blatancy of the two parties' manipulation is comparable, the indirect effects of blatancy will not unduly favor either of the parties. But a disparity in blatancy opens the door to indirect effects favoring the party that manipulated most blatantly.[6] Where relevant, I indicate how the intuitions and results about the extent of manipulation apply also to the visibility of manipulation.

Results 1 and 2 are derived in Sections 5.1 and 5.2. After deriving these results, the chapter discusses in greater detail the empirical background conditions that are likely to give rise to different patterns of electoral manipulation (Section 5.3). The two main points in that discussion are as follows. First, the set of empirical conditions under which there exists a *motive* to manipulate excessively or blatantly – namely, the conditions under which electoral manipulation has the potential to yield indirect effects – overlaps considerably with the set of conditions under which excessive/blatant manipulation is *feasible*. Such conditions are present, to simplify somewhat, in situations where the rule of law is weak and the distribution of power and resources among parties is skewed (generally in favor of the ruling party). A weak rule of law and an unequal distribution of resources and power exist in many electoral regimes in less developed countries, but in few established democracies. Therefore, excessive and blatant manipulation is likely to arise in the former set of countries, but not in the latter (in contrast, marginal electoral manipulation can arise in both groups of countries). The second point, which follows from the first, is that excessive or blatant manipulation has self-reinforcing properties: excessive or blatant manipulation requires that one of the parties be relatively powerful in the first place, and in turn such manipulation serves to further enhance or preserve its power. The self-reinforcing nature of excessive/blatant manipulation raises the possibility of "excessive-electoral-manipulation traps." Section 5.3 discusses over-time dynamics, traps, and how countries might get into and out of them.

Can excessive electoral manipulation be explained by other factors, such as uncertainty, a low cost of manipulation, a high stakes of holding office, or the need to keep the electoral manipulation machinery "well oiled"? I consider these questions in the last part of the chapter (Section 5.4). My analysis suggests that these factors cannot by themselves account for excessive manipulation except in unique and rare circumstances.

---

[5] Recall that excessive electoral manipulation is manipulation yielding a large margin of victory. When competing parties with similar levels of electoral support manipulate to a similar extent, the ensuing margin of victory will be small. Therefore, as mentioned in earlier chapters, it is possible for manipulation to be large-scale but not excessive in the sense I have defined the term.

[6] See the previous chapter for further discussion of this point and the idea of the "directional visibility" of electoral manipulation.

A Model of Party Competition with Electoral Manipulation

The basic model depicts two parties, a ruling party (or incumbent) and an opposition party, against each other in a winner-takes-all election.[7] Both parties can engage in electoral manipulation to increase their chances of winning, but electoral manipulation is costly. I begin by modeling a situation where there are no benefits to be had from electoral manipulation beyond victory – that is, I do not allow electoral manipulation to have indirect effects. In this model, any equilibrium electoral manipulation is of the *marginal* kind (Result 1). In the next subsection, I add indirect effects to the model, and show that *excessive* electoral manipulation can arise in equilibrium (Result 2), but it will generally require a significant disparity in the capacities of the parties to manipulate (which generally stems from an unequal, or concentrated, distribution of power and resources among the parties).

5.1 EQUILIBRIUM ELECTORAL MANIPULATION WHEN ONLY WINNING MATTERS

Suppose first that there are no benefits to be had from electoral manipulation beyond victory – that is, no indirect effects.[8] The central goal of the analysis in this section is to characterize the extent of electoral manipulation chosen by the parties in equilibrium under this scenario, with attention to the distinction between marginal and excessive manipulation. Let $j = 1, 2$ respectively denote the incumbent and the opposition parties. The party that obtains the most votes wins the election. A party obtains utility $w > 0$ if it wins, 0 if it loses. Each party chooses an amount of electoral manipulation, $x_j \geq 0$, $j = 1, 2$. When party j obtains x_j votes via manipulation, the fraction of the vote in its favor increases by x_j and the fraction of the other party's vote decreases by the same amount.[9] Electoral manipulation is costly. Costs are intended to represent both resource costs as well as the possibility of punishment, for example by domestic courts or via the action of foreign powers.[10] The total expected cost of amount x_j of

---

[7] I focus on the winner-takes-all (plurality) rule for simplicity and because it is often used in scholarly discussions of electoral manipulation. As mentioned in previous chapters, however, the basic logic travels to other electoral rules such as two-round majoritarian systems and proportional representation.

[8] For a discussion of the factors that determine the potential for indirect effects see Chapter 4.

[9] This form of electoral manipulation has been called "vote-switching," as it entails substituting a vote for one's opponent with a vote for oneself. An example of a vote-switching technology is the "renting" of voter IDs of likely opposition voters by party operatives, who then use them to cast a vote themselves (Schaffer 2008, 119). This form of manipulation is convenient to work with algebraically, but the model's results do not require it – other forms of manipulation (e.g., exclusively adding ballots for oneself, or exclusively destroying opponents' ballots) could be used instead.

[10] For a discussion of the reasons why electoral manipulation is costly see the section on alternative explanations later in this chapter.

electoral manipulation is given by $c_j(x_j)$ with $c_j(0) = 0$ and the marginal cost $c'_j(x_j)$ is assumed to be strictly positive for $x_j \geq 0$. In this setup, the *capacity of a party to engage in electoral manipulation* is captured by the cost function c_j; the high costs of manipulation reflect a low capacity to manipulate and vice versa (therefore, whether Condition A holds will depend on the shape of the cost functions).[11]

Let p denote the probability of an incumbent victory. The probability of victory p is a function of the parties' popularity, represented by δ (to be defined presently), and of their use of electoral manipulation (indicated by x_1 and x_2). Let the incumbent party's "natural advantage," $\delta \in [-0.5, 0.5]$ be defined as the fraction of the electorate intending to vote for the incumbent party minus the victory threshold (which for present purposes is 0.5). Positive values of δ indicate that the incumbent is more popular than the opposition (and therefore would win in an election where neither of the parties utilized electoral manipulation) and negative values indicate that it is less popular than the opposition. For example, if 43 percent of those who intend to vote favor the incumbent, then $\delta = -0.07$. We can write p as follows:

$$p(x_1, x_2 | \delta) = \Pr\{\delta + x_1 - x_2 + \varepsilon \geq 0\} = 1 - F(-\delta - x_1 + x_2). \qquad (5.1)$$

In this expression, ε is a stochastic term with cumulative distribution F and mean 0; and it represents factors that affect the parties' assessment of p but are not explicitly modeled – for example, any factors that create uncertainty about the parties' popularity, δ.[12] Let the incumbent party's "net advantage" be defined as its natural advantage adjusted for the parties' choices of electoral manipulation, namely $\delta + x_1 - x_2$, and note that p is a function of this quantity. Denote the negative of the incumbent's net advantage as the "opposition's net advantage." Utility for the parties, written as a function of the parties' choices and the popularity parameter, is given by:

$$u_1(x_1, x_2) = wp(x_1, x_2 | \delta) - c_1(x_1)$$
$$u_2(x_1, x_2) = w(1 - p(x_1, x_2 | \delta)) - c_2(x_2),$$

where I have not made explicit the dependence of u on δ. The incumbent party's margin of victory is given by m and it is defined as the fraction of the vote

---

[11] The notion of a "supply curve" for tactics of electoral manipulation introduced in Chapter 1 suggests increasing marginal costs.

[12] I follow Roemer's "error-distribution model of uncertainty" and assume that parties experience uncertainty (e.g. about their vote share, or about the effectiveness of manipulation), but voter preferences and the process of manipulation are not stochastic (Roemer 2001, 45–46). Hence, the uncertainty term ε plays a role when modeling decision-making by the parties, but not when describing realized outcomes such as the margin of victory (e.g., from the viewpoint of the analyst, expression (5.2) is the actual margin of victory, not an expected value that averages over the values of ε). I discuss various possible sources of uncertainty in the later section on alternative explanations.

obtained by party 1 minus that obtained by party 2, all things considered:[13]

$$m = \frac{1}{2} + \delta + x_1 - x_2 - \left(1 - \left[\frac{1}{2} + \delta + x_1 - x_2\right]\right).$$
$$= 2\left(\delta + x_1 - x_2\right). \tag{5.2}$$

Expression (5.2) is written from the viewpoint of the analyst and reflects the assumption that, while parties face uncertainty (as reflected in the term ε) voter preferences and the manipulation technology are not stochastic. For simplicity, in the rest of the model analysis, by "margin of victory" I refer to the "incumbent's margin of victory" as defined in (5.2), unless otherwise specified. Note that the margin of victory, similar to the probability of victory, is a function of the incumbent's net advantage (specifically, it is equal to twice the incumbent's net advantage). This is intuitive: both the margin of victory and the chances of an incumbent victory are directly proportional to the fraction of the vote secured by the incumbent. This connection (between the margin of victory and the probability of incumbent victory) will be helpful to show why equilibrium electoral manipulation in this setup is generally not excessive.

The parties make their choices simultaneously. An equilibrium is a pair of choices $\left(x_1^*, x_2^*\right)$ such that no party, after learning the other's choice, wishes to deviate. The equilibrium margin of victory, therefore, is:

$$m^* = 2\left(\delta + x_1^* - x_2^*\right). \tag{5.3}$$

That is, the equilibrium margin of victory reflects the combined effects of the popularity of the parties and the difference in their equilibrium choices of electoral manipulation. Note that it would be possible to make the model more complex by allowing parties to also choose platforms, as in a Downs-like model (Downs 1957, Roemer 2001). Supposing that platforms are chosen before electoral manipulation, both parties would choose the platform preferred by the median voter, and therefore no party would have a natural advantage – that is, $\delta = 0$. Therefore, $m^* = 2\left(x_1^* - x_2^*\right)$, that is, the equilibrium margin of victory would depend only on the difference in choices of electoral manipulation. This would be a special case of the analysis that follows, which is more general because it applies for values of δ in the range $[-0.5, 0.5]$.

Normatively speaking, from a procedural point of view, the most desirable outcome is one where (1) the margin of victory reflects the preferences of the electorate – that is, $m^* = 2\delta$ – and (2) there is no electoral manipulation – that is, $x_1^* = x_2^* = 0$. Note that the same margin of victory, $m^* = 2\delta$, can be attained even in the presence of electoral manipulation (e.g., when one party's efforts neutralize the other's – that is, when $x_1^* = x_2^* > 0$), although in that case

---

[13] Therefore, if the ruling party loses the election, the margin of victory is negative. Note that this differs from the definition of the margin of victory that I utilized for empirical purposes in Chapter 3, which was computed as the winner's percent of the vote minus the first runner-up's. Note also that uncertainty term ε does not enter into the actual outcome, but only into the probability calculations by the parties (see previous footnote on this point).

condition (2) would not be satisfied (and therefore the most normatively best outcome would not be achieved).

Following the discussion in Chapter 3, I say that electoral manipulation is *excessive* whenever (1) the margin of victory is large and (2) one or both parties manipulate. Electoral manipulation is *marginal* when (1) the margin of victory is small and (2) one or both parties manipulate. The first result from the basic setup of the model is that, when there is no potential for electoral manipulation to yield indirect effects, *excessive electoral manipulation is unlikely to arise in equilibrium*. To show this, I proceed as follows. I first demonstrate that the equilibrium margin of victory is bounded, and then I show that the bounds on the margin of victory are likely to be reasonably tight. Specifically, the size of the bounds on the margin of victory will depend on the degree of uncertainty, and at plausible levels of uncertainty the bounds are fairly restrictive (and, by definition, when the margin of victory is small, electoral manipulation is not excessive).[14]

The logic behind the result is as follows. Consider a party's maximization problem, given the model's parameters and the other party's choice about manipulation, and suppose that the problem is concave.[15] If the party chooses a nonzero amount of electoral manipulation in equilibrium, then at that level of manipulation the marginal benefit – the value of office times the probability of winning – must equal the marginal cost of manipulation (this is simply the first-order condition that must hold at an interior maximum). The crux of the matter is that the marginal benefit of manipulation will decrease rapidly once manipulation has closed the vote gap with the other party. Therefore, the party will optimally manipulate precisely up to a point that makes the margin of victory small.

To see this formally, consider the first-order conditions that must respectively hold for each of the parties at an equilibrium with nonzero amounts of manipulation:

$$wf(-\delta - x_1^* + x_2^*) = c_1'(x_1^*). \tag{5.4}$$

$$wf(-\delta - x_1^* + x_2^*) = c_2'(x_2^*). \tag{5.5}$$

In these expressions, f is the density function associated with F. When only one of the parties manipulates in equilibrium, only the corresponding first-order condition will hold, and the arguments that follow will apply to that party. The first-order conditions suggest that the margin of victory is unlikely to be large (in favor of either of the parties). Intuitively, the reason for this is that, as the net advantage of one of the parties (i.e., the magnitude of $\delta + x_1^* - x_2^*$) grows, the marginal benefit derived from additional electoral

---

[14] I provide empirical evidence on uncertainty later on in the chapter (see especially Section 5.4).

[15] In other words, that the party's utility function is concave. One set of sufficient conditions for this to be the case is: $p' > 0, p'' < 0, c' > 0, c'' \geq 0$. I assume throughout that all the functions are differentiable and "well-behaved," and that maximizers exist and are unique.

manipulation decreases rapidly, while the cost of electoral manipulation for that party remains positive.[16] Because of this, there is a limit to the degree to which a party wishes to invest in continuing to grow its net advantage. Because the margin of victory is simply twice the net advantage, the magnitude of the margin of victory will also be limited.[17]

To fix ideas, suppose that F is the uniform distribution with support on the interval $[-\varphi/2, \varphi/2]$. A reasonable value for φ will reflect the fact that, in general, parties know more or less how they will do in an election after all is said and done. They may not know this exactly, but they are likely to be able to give something like a confidence interval – for example, a candidate might say that with 90 percent certainty he will obtain somewhere between 45 percent and 55 percent of the vote. Note that what is being assumed here is *not* that parties know whether they will win or lose, but rather that they know more or less what proportion of the vote they are likely to receive, once their popularity, efforts at manipulation, and other potentially relevant factors are taken into account.[18] In other words, the parameter φ can be taken to represent, roughly speaking, the width of a "confidence interval" for the fraction of the vote that a party will obtain. In practice, it should be rare for φ to exceed 0.1 or 0.2.

In an equilibrium with nonzero levels of manipulation, the marginal benefit of electoral manipulation must be positive. This means that f must be positive, and therefore its argument, $-\delta - x_1^* + x_2^*$ must lie in $[-\varphi/2, \varphi/2]$. Because the argument of f is (minus) the incumbent's net advantage, this means that the incumbent's net advantage cannot be too large in absolute value – that is, neither the incumbent nor the opposition can be too far ahead of the other. As mentioned previously, the margin of victory is simply twice the incumbent's net advantage. Therefore, the margin of victory also cannot be too large in absolute value. In fact, the first-order conditions place an upper bound on the absolute value of the margin of victory:

$$-\delta - x_1^* + x_2^* \in [-\varphi/2, \varphi/2]$$
$$-\frac{m^*}{2} \in [-\varphi/2, \varphi/2]$$
$$|m^*| < \varphi$$

[16] This statement assumes a density function where the mass is concentrated near the mean, as in a Normal distribution where the variance is not too large (more on the size of the variance later). It is also possible to approximate such a scenario using a Uniform distribution with narrow support, as I do later.

[17] Using expression (5.3), it is possible to rewrite the argument in the left-hand side of the first-order conditions explicitly as a function of the margin of victory.

[18] A party could be 99% certain that it will receive between 49% and 51% of the vote – quite a narrow confidence interval – and still be very uncertain as to whether it will win. Conversely, a party could have a 99% confidence interval that is much wider (e.g., 65 to 85%), and yet be virtually certain that it will win.

Here I have used (5.3) to rewrite the left-hand side of the expression. This shows formally that the margin of victory is unlikely to be excessively large. This is because the returns to manipulating beyond the point necessary for victory are small. Therefore, electoral manipulation will only be pursued to the extent that it contributes to winning, with some adjustment for uncertainty.[19] I used the uniform distribution for simplicity, but the logic can be applied to distributions other than the uniform.[20]

Moreover, this reasoning merely establishes bounds for the equilibrium margin of victory with manipulation. The actual margin need not reach those bounds. In fact, the equilibrium margin of victory will differ from o only insofar as one of the parties has an advantage in terms of capacity to manipulate. In the model, the capacity to manipulate is captured by the cost function: loosely speaking, a lower cost of electoral manipulation is equivalent to a higher capacity to manipulate (e.g., in terms of votes per dollar). For example, if the incumbent's marginal cost of manipulation is lower than the opposition's at any given level of manipulation, then the incumbent can be said to have a greater capacity to manipulate.[21] The first-order conditions (5.4) and (5.5) imply that, in equilibrium, the marginal cost of an additional vote obtained through electoral manipulation will be equal for both candidates. In other words, $c_1'\left(x_1^*\right) = c_2'\left(x_2^*\right)$. This equality implies that, loosely speaking, the party with the greatest capacity to manipulate will manipulate to a greater extent, and the disparity in equilibrium choices of manipulation will be proportional to the disparity in cost structures (within the bounds derived previously).[22]

When the candidates have the same cost structure, they will manipulate to the same extent – that is, $x_1^* = x_2^*$ – and the incumbent party's net advantage will equal its natural advantage, δ. In this case, the margin of victory m^* will equal 2δ (the normatively ideal margin of victory). In other words, in equilibrium, the parties' efforts at electoral manipulation will fully neutralize each other if the parties have identical capacities to manipulate. As in Chapter 3, I refer to an equilibrium outcome where parties manipulate to roughly the same extent

---

[19] Therefore, electoral manipulation leading to very large margins of victory would be difficult to explain on the basis of uncertainty alone (more on this in Section 5.4).

[20] For example, if F was a Normal distribution with small enough variance, the marginal benefit of electoral manipulation would be overwhelmed by its marginal cost as $|-\delta - x_1^* + x_2^*|$ diverged from zero, giving rise to similar bounds on the margin of victory.

[21] There are other ways to model parties' capacities to manipulate – for example, by incorporating budget constraints in the model.

[22] Suppose, for example, that the marginal cost of manipulation is strictly increasing (as suggested by the idea of a "supply curve" of electoral manipulation tactics introduced in Chapter 1), and say, for simplicity, that party 1 has a "greater capacity to manipulate" than party 2 if the marginal cost of electoral manipulation for party 1 is smaller than the marginal cost for party 2 for any given extent of manipulation. Then the equality of marginal costs in equilibrium implies that the party with the greatest capacity to manipulate will manipulate to a greater extent (weaker assumptions about the cost curves can yield the same result).

as "competitive" or "two-sided" manipulation. In practice, instances of two-sided manipulation seem to arise, as the model predicts, in situations where the parties' capacities to manipulate are not-too-dissimilar – as in the Philippines in the 1950s and 1960s (Wurfel 1963), in Costa Rica in the first half of the twentieth century (Lehoucq and Molina 2002), and in some United States elections (such as the one of 1876).

The overall level of manipulation – namely, the sum total of electoral manipulation by all parties, $x_1^* + x_2^*$, or the "scale" of manipulation – will be determined by the balance between the costs and the benefits of manipulating (this can readily be seen in the first-order conditions (5.4) and (5.5)). If costs are relatively low in comparison with the possible benefits (i.e., the probability-adjusted stakes of winning), the total amount of electoral manipulation could be large. System-level factors that raise the expected costs of manipulation will reduce the equilibrium level of manipulation for both parties. Such factors might include a strong rule of law, independent electoral management bodies, and certain kinds of international pressures, potentially exerted in connection with election monitoring. A clean election will ensue when the cost of manipulating is prohibitive for both parties, in relation to its potential benefit.

In sum, the analysis in this section shows that in a simple setup that mimics the assumptions of the conventional wisdom – what matters is winning the election (i.e., there is no possibility for indirect effects), and electoral manipulation is costly – excessive electoral manipulation is unlikely to arise. Note that if the model is augmented to allow the parties to make choices about the visibility of electoral manipulation, insofar as increasing the visibility of manipulation increases its expected costs (e.g., by making punishment to the perpetrator more likely), then parties will always choose the least visible form of manipulation. Therefore, there would be no rationale for purposefully blatant electoral manipulation. In other words, the drive to win can yield marginal electoral manipulation, but it does not suffice to produce excessive or blatant electoral manipulation.[23]

Aside: Election-Night Fraud

Election-night fraud arises when one of the parties obtains information about the electoral returns on the night of the election, after most of the votes have been counted but before the results are announced, and can use such information to decide whether and to what extent to pursue electoral manipulation with the purpose of closing the gap between its proportion of the vote and the

---

[23] To be precise, it is possible to produce incentives for excessive manipulation in the basic model as presented in the previous section, by picking extreme values of the parameters (in particular, a very high stakes of victory w and/or a very high level of uncertainty φ). This possibility is discussed at length later in the chapter (Section 5.4). For now it suffices to say that, in practice, such values of the parameters would appear to arise in relatively uncommon circumstances.

winning threshold (this is probably most feasible with small electorates; e.g., in local elections). In terms of the model, election-night fraud corresponds to the special case in which uncertainty is very small (i.e., $\varphi \cong 0$) and only one of the parties is able to manipulate.[24] Students of elections in the United States have argued that election-night fraud results in razor-thin margins of victory (Christensen and Colvin 2005). This is consistent with the theoretical prediction of the model, namely that the margin of victory is bounded by uncertainty and, because uncertainty is small, so is the margin.

5.2 EQUILIBRIUM ELECTORAL MANIPULATION WHEN MORE THAN WINNING MATTERS

The previous section showed that, when winning is the focus, equilibrium electoral manipulation is marginal and discreet, not excessive, nor blatant. In this section, I show that when electoral manipulation has the potential to result in indirect effects – when it can potentially deter challenges from different social and political actors and keep their demands in check, for example – excessive and blatant manipulation can arise in equilibrium. I augment the model by allowing electoral manipulation to have indirect effects in addition to direct effects. In the previous chapter, I derived indirect effects from first principles as equilibrium behavior by actors responding to electoral manipulation – I do not repeat that derivation here. Instead, I utilize a reduced form representation of indirect effects: let $q(x)$ represent the utility to the incumbent party associated with the indirect effects of amount x of electoral manipulation, with $q(0) = 0$ and $q'(x) > 0$ for all $x \geq 0$.[25] Substantively, $q(x)$ represents the effect of electoral manipulation on both the value of holding office (therefore, the variable w now represents the "baseline" value of holding office, when no indirect effects are present) and on the future likelihood of retaining power (i.e., on p at a future time period), in accordance with the discussion of indirect effects in earlier chapters.

When the potential for indirect effects exists, excessive electoral manipulation arises in equilibrium under two sets of circumstances. First, when one of the parties – generally the incumbent party – has a substantial advantage

---

[24] It is interesting to ask whether the party that did not have access to the electoral returns on election night knows, going into the election, that the other party might have access to such information. The answer would have implications for equilibrium choices of electoral manipulation.

[25] This "reduced form" representation skips over the different steps in the mechanism linking electoral manipulation with indirect effects detailed in the previous chapter. Rendering those steps explicit (using equation 4.3), one would write: $q(x) \equiv q(\Delta\alpha(x)) \equiv q(\alpha[\mu(x)] - \alpha[\mu(0)])$. The expanded expression indicates the different steps in the causal chain underpinning indirect effects (Figure 4.1): electoral manipulation x influences the political context μ, which in turn affects the behavior of actors, summarized by α. Finally, the behavior change induced by electoral manipulation impacts the party's utility.

in capacity to manipulate (the capacity to manipulate is modeled as the cost structure c). This is Condition A. This condition renders electoral manipulation feasible on a scale large enough to increase the size of the margin of victory for the advantaged party. The second set of circumstances under which excessive electoral manipulation arises in equilibrium is mostly a theoretical possibility; I defer discussion of this to the end of this section.

The role of indirect effects on incentives for electoral manipulation can perhaps be seen most clearly by assuming first that only one party can engage in electoral manipulation (let that party be the incumbent). This corresponds to a scenario of extreme inequality in the capacity to manipulate – because one party cannot manipulate at all. Utility for the incumbent party is now given by:

$$u(x) = wp(x) + \beta q(x) - c(x). \tag{5.6}$$

As mentioned previously, q represents the indirect effect of electoral manipulation as a utility term that depends on the level of electoral manipulation x, and $\beta \in [0, 1]$ is a parameter. Parameter β could be seen as a time-discount factor: indirect effects are, in general, temporally posterior to the implementation of electoral manipulation.[26] I have omitted subscripts denoting the party because only the incumbent can make choices in this scenario, and I have also omitted a variable denoting the level of manipulation by the opposition party, because it is 0 by assumption. Note that when $\beta = 0$, the model simplifies to the case without indirect effects presented in the previous section (for the case in which only one party can manipulate).

The distinguishing feature of the augmented model can be seen in (5.6). Now, the incumbent's choice of electoral manipulation, x, can have an impact not only on the probability of victory p, as in the base model, but it can potentially bring additional benefits to the incumbent (i.e., indirect effects). Such additional benefits are captured by the second term in (5.6), $\beta q(x)$. For example, such benefits could consist of lower subsequent levels of political opposition, or of greater bargaining power for the incumbent. If such benefits are attractive enough, they can motivate excessive electoral manipulation (by a similar logic, they could also motivate blatant manipulation).

To gauge the impact of indirect effects on equilibrium electoral manipulation, I compare two scenarios. In the first scenario, electoral manipulation, as in the base model, has no indirect effects. To represent that scenario I simply set $\beta = 0$. I call the situation where $\beta = 0$ the "base case." In the second scenario, electoral manipulation can potentially yield indirect effects. I represent this scenario by setting $\beta > 0$. The question is whether equilibrium electoral manipulation x^* is greater in the second scenario than in the first. I assume

---

[26] The substantive meaning of the temporal dimension of the argument is discussed in the previous chapter (see also Figures 4.1 and 4.2).

throughout that the utility function is strictly concave to guarantee the existence and uniqueness of a maximizer.[27]

The following result shows that, whenever electoral manipulation can yield more than winning, equilibrium electoral manipulation will indeed be greater than in the base case. Technically, the result shows that equilibrium manipulation x^* is increasing in β whenever the indirect effect q is strictly increasing in electoral manipulation. In other words, Proposition 1 shows that the presence of indirect effects gives rise to excessive electoral manipulation as an equilibrium outcome.[28]

Proposition 1 (Excessive Manipulation): *Consider the model where only the incumbent can pursue electoral manipulation, and let q be strictly increasing. Let $x^*(\beta)$ maximize incumbent utility for given β and suppose that $x^*(0) > 0$. Then equilibrium manipulation when $\beta > 0$ is greater than in the base case (i.e., when $\beta = 0$).*

Proof: By strict monotone comparative statics (Edlin and Shannon 1998), a sufficient condition for the maximizer x^* to be strictly increasing in β is for incumbent utility (5.6) to be supermodular in (x, β). Supermodularity follows when the cross-partial derivative of incumbent utility with respect to (x, β) is positive. Because only the second term in the right-hand side of (5.6) depends on β, it is sufficient for supermodularity that q be strictly increasing. □

Note that a similar result can be obtained for the case of blatant manipulation. To see this, hold the extent of manipulation fixed and suppose that x is a choice about the blatancy, not the extent, of electoral manipulation.[29] Suppose that rendering manipulation more blatant increases the cost (as before) and the magnitude of the indirect effect of manipulating, q (it is possible to assume that the probability of victory p is constant with respect to x, because the visibility of electoral manipulation is unlikely to change the probability of victory). Clearly, in the absence of indirect effects, there would be no incentive to increase the visibility of electoral manipulation – doing so would simply increase the costs and yield no benefits. However, when the visibility of manipulation has the potential to elicit indirect effects, Proposition 1 goes through: the incumbent will purposefully increase the blatancy of manipulation.

I now consider the more general case where both parties can manipulate. Let utility for the parties, as a function of their choices, be:

$$u_1(x_1, x_2|\delta) = wp(x_1, x_2|\delta) + \beta q(x_1, x_2|\delta) - c_1(x_1)$$
$$u_2(x_1, x_2|\delta) = w(1 - p(x_1, x_2|\delta)) - \beta q(x_1, x_2|\delta) - c_2(x_2).$$

---

[27] I provide an example with explicit functional-form assumptions on the different elements of the utility function later in this chapter.

[28] The result could hold also for q weakly increasing, depending on the functional forms.

[29] One might wish to model both decisions – about extent and about visibility. To make the point in the text, however, it suffices to simply reinterpret the meaning of variable x. One could suppose, for example, that the choice about extent was made prior to the choice about blatancy, and is not made explicit in the model.

Here q represents the indirect effect of electoral manipulation as a benefit to party 1 (and as a loss to party 2). The indirect effect of electoral manipulation affects the parties in opposite directions in accordance to the intuition that indirect effects, insofar as they benefit one of the parties, harm the other one (for example, discouraging opposition voters, donors, and politicians from actively supporting the opposition clearly benefits the incumbent at the expense of the opposition). In line with the discussion in the previous chapter, I suppose that indirect effect q is a function of the incumbent's net advantage, $\delta + x_1^* - x_2^*$. The indirect effect q is increasing in the incumbent's net advantage and decreasing in the opposition's net advantage, implying that $q(x_1, x_2)$ is increasing in x_1 and decreasing in x_2.[30]

In an interior equilibrium (implying nonzero levels of manipulation), the marginal benefit must equal the marginal cost for each of the parties:

$$wf\left(-\delta - x_1^* + x_2^*\right) + \beta q'\left(\delta + x_1^* - x_2^*\right) = c_1'\left(x_1^*\right). \tag{5.7}$$

$$wf\left(-\delta - x_1^* + x_2^*\right) + \beta q'\left(\delta + x_1^* - x_2^*\right) = c_2'\left(x_2^*\right). \tag{5.8}$$

As in the base case without indirect effects, the first-order conditions require that the equilibrium marginal costs be equal – namely, $c_1'\left(x_1^*\right) = c_2'\left(x_2^*\right)$. This implies, as in the case without indirect effects, that the party with a cost advantage manipulates more in equilibrium.[31] But there is now a key difference stemming from the potential for indirect effects: now *the bounds on the margin of victory are much less constraining*. To see this, use (5.3) to rewrite the first-order conditions as a function of the equilibrium margin of victory. Assuming that f is symmetric about 0, we obtain:

$$wf\left(-m^*/2\right) + \beta q'(m^*/2) = c_1'\left(x_1^*\right)$$

$$wf\left(-m^*/2\right) + \beta q'(m^*/2) = c_2'\left(x_2^*\right)$$

From this expression, it is apparent that, as the margin grows, even if its contribution to the probability of victory in the election at hand, $f\left(-m^*/2\right)$, declines steeply or becomes 0, a marginal benefit could still accrue from the indirect effect, as denoted by $q'\left(m^*/2\right)$ (because indirect effects "kick in" precisely at higher margins of victory, as discussed in the previous chapter).[32]

This difference opens the door to excessive electoral manipulation. Specifically, it has the following implications for equilibrium electoral manipulation. First, if the disparity in cost structures is sufficiently large, the advantaged party's equilibrium margin of victory will also be large – that is, equilibrium electoral manipulation will be excessive. Because of the indirect effect, the

---

[30] In general, the indirect effect of electoral manipulation q depends also on δ (this does not change the analysis that follows). Note also that, as before, setting $\beta = 0$ yields the base model presented in Section 5.1.

[31] This is true, for example, under increasing marginal costs as mentioned earlier.

[32] Because f is symmetric about 0, what matters is the absolute value of its argument.

first-order conditions will now potentially support equilibria at a greater disparity in cost structures than in the case without indirect effects.[33] This is the logic behind Result 2, described at the beginning of this chapter.[34]

Second, even if the parties' capacities to manipulate are equal, it is possible in theory for excessive manipulation to arise in equilibrium. In this case, the margin of victory would not be the result of excessive manipulation, but rather of the difference in popularity. The point is that, because of the presence of indirect effects, the parties could engage in electoral manipulation even when the difference in popularity is large.[35] Because parties' capacities are roughly equal, the equilibrium margin of victory will be close to that which would have ensued in a clean election – that is, $m^* \cong 2\delta$. Although this scenario describes an alternative way in which excessive manipulation could arise, in practice it is unlikely to arise. The reason for this is that the assumption that parties' capacities are equal will generally reflect the existence of more than one center of power and resources in society. When multiple centers of power of comparable strength exist, they can check each other and neutralize each others' efforts, reducing the scope for the arbitrary use of power and resources that underpins indirect effects. In that case, the relevant scenario is one *without* indirect effects. In the absence of indirect effects, a large disparity in party popularity can certainly give rise to a large margin of victory, but there would be no motive to manipulate (and therefore no excessive electoral manipulation).

An Example with Specific Functional Forms

To provide additional intuition, I present a version of the model with specific functional forms. In so doing, because the purpose is to illustrate the logic, I privilege simplicity over realism. Let the probability of incumbent victory be given by $p(x_1, x_2) = ln(2 + x_1 - x_2 + \delta)$; and the cost of manipulation by $c_j(x_j) = \kappa_j x_j^2 / 2$, $j = 1, 2$, where $\kappa_j > 0$ is a party-specific parameter (with lower values representing a greater capacity to manipulate).[36] Without losing generality, assume that the incumbent has a greater capacity to manipulate – namely, $k_1 < k_2$. Denote the indirect effects of manipulation by $q(x_1, x_2) = ln(2 + x_1 - x_2 + \delta - \mu)$, where $\mu \in [0, 1]$ is a parameter that,

---

[33] Recall that, in contrast, in the case without indirect effects, even a large disparity in cost structures will not yield a large margin of victory in equilibrium, as shown in Section 5.1.

[34] Of course, the lower the popularity of the party with the advantage in capacity to manipulate, the larger such an advantage needs to be to produce excessive manipulation in equilibrium.

[35] This was not possible in the case without indirect effects, when the marginal benefit of manipulation in a scenario with a large disparity in popularity would have been too small to motivate electoral manipulation (here the marginal benefit is bigger because of the indirect effects of manipulation). Note that the scenario described in this paragraph corresponds to "Result 3" in Footnote 3 near the beginning of the chapter.

[36] To retain the interpretation of p as a probability, it is necessary to restrict the parameter space so that p ranges in [0,1]. I utilize the logarithm for algebraic simplicity. One drawback of this functional form is that it does not reflect the intuitive notion that the probability mass is highly concentrated around the point at which the incumbent's net advantage is close to o.

loosely speaking, captures the notion that indirect effects "kick in" when the incumbent's net advantage is at least μ. Note that $p' > 0$, $p'' < 0$, $c' > 0$, and $c'' > 0$. Therefore, utility for each of the parties, given as before by $u_1 = wp + \beta q - c_1$ and $u_2 = w(1 - p) - \beta q - c_2$, is strictly concave in the respective party's choice of electoral manipulation. The first-order conditions at an equilibrium with nonzero levels of manipulation are summarized as follows:

$$\frac{w}{2 + x_1^* - x_2^* + \delta} + \frac{\beta}{2 + x_1^* - x_2^* + \delta - \mu} = \kappa_1 x_1^* = \kappa_2 x_2^*.$$

Note that x_1^* and x_2^* are unique.[37] For κ_2 large enough (I revisit this presently), the second-order conditions confirm that x_1^* and x_2^* are maximizers:

$$-\frac{w}{\left(2 + x_1^* - x_2^* + \delta\right)^2} + \frac{\beta}{(2 + x_1^* - x_2^* + \delta - \mu)^2} - \kappa_1 < 0$$

$$\frac{w}{\left(2 + x_1^* - x_2^* + \delta\right)^2} + \frac{\beta}{(2 + x_1^* - x_2^* + \delta - \mu)^2} - \kappa_2 < 0$$

The SOC for the incumbent (the first expression above) holds immediately, because all the terms on the left-hand side are negative. The SOC for the opposition party holds for κ_2 large enough – for instance, $\kappa_2 = w + \beta$.[38]

Equilibrium electoral manipulation for the incumbent is strictly increasing in the strength of indirect effects, represented by β. This can be seen by applying the implicit function theorem to the first-order condition for the incumbent party:

$$\frac{\partial x_1^*}{\partial \beta} = -\frac{\dfrac{1}{(2 + x_1^* - x_2^* + \delta - \mu)^2}}{-\dfrac{w}{(2 + x_1^* - x_2^* + \delta)^2} - \dfrac{\beta}{(2 + x_1^* - x_2^* + \delta - \mu)^2} - \kappa_1} > 0.$$

Finally, I illustrate the logic of this result with a numerical example.[39] Figure 5.1 displays the marginal cost and benefit curves as a function of incumbent electoral manipulation, for the following parameter values: $\delta = 0.05$, $w = 1$, $\mu = 0.1$, $\kappa_1 = 1.5$, and $\kappa_2 = 2$. The solid, downward-sloping curve represents the marginal benefit of electoral manipulation for the incumbent when $\beta = 0$ – that is, in the absence of indirect effects. The upward-sloping curve represents

---

[37] The marginal benefit (i.e., the left-hand-side of the expression) is greater than the marginal cost (the middle expression) at $x_1 = 0$ and it is strictly decreasing in x_1^*, while the marginal cost is strictly increasing. Uniqueness of x_2^* follows from the second equality.

[38] Due to the assumption that the incumbent has an edge at manipulating, in equilibrium $x_1^* > x_2^*$, hence a lower bound for the denominator of each of the first two terms of the SOC is 1.5 (since $\delta \geq -0.5$ and $\mu \geq 0$). Therefore, $k_2 \geq w + \beta$ is sufficient (although more stringent than necessary).

[39] The numbers in this example are not intended to be taken literally as estimates of the corresponding real-world quantities; the example has been constructed with clarity, not realism, in mind.

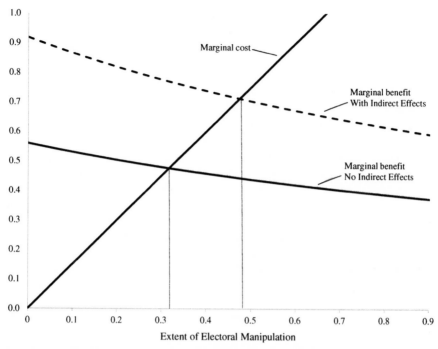

FIGURE 5.1. Equilibrium Electoral Manipulation for the Incumbent Party, Numerical Example

the marginal cost of electoral manipulation for the incumbent. The intersection of the solid lines determines the equilibrium level of electoral manipulation.[40] Allowing for indirect effects – specifically, setting $\beta = 0.5$ – shifts the marginal benefit curve of the incumbent party outward. The new intersection with the marginal cost curve gives the equilibrium level of electoral manipulation for the incumbent – greater than in the case that does not consider its indirect effects. The opposition party's equilibrium level of manipulation also increases, but less than the incumbent's and therefore the margin of victory is larger in the scenario with indirect effects.

5.3 BACKGROUND CONDITIONS, OVER-TIME FEEDBACKS, AND PATTERNS OF ELECTORAL MANIPULATION

Institutional Setting and Excessive/Blatant Manipulation

It is possible now to revisit the question of the conditions under which excessive/blatant electoral manipulation is likely to arise. I focus on two sets of conditions: those that underpin the potential for indirect effects and therefore

---

[40] This takes into account, of course, the opposition party's best response function.

provide the motive to pursue excessive/blatant manipulation (discussed in the previous chapter), and those that render excessive/blatant electoral manipulation *practicable* or *feasible* – discussed earlier in this chapter. The empirical scenarios under which these conditions hold turn out to overlap considerably, and loosely correspond to the "level of development," which is often associated with the concentration of resources and power in the hands of government and with constraints on government discretion.

The discussion in the previous chapter suggested that the potential for indirect effects – which is necessary to motivate excessive or blatant electoral manipulation – rests in large measure on the degree to which the ruling party has the discretion to utilize the resources and power of the government in arbitrary ways.[41] *Constraints on government*, as might stem from a strong rule of law, determine the scope for the party in office to utilize government resources and power in arbitrary or partisan ways, and therefore the potential for electoral manipulation to have indirect effects. More generally, the discretion of government depends on a number of factors including the effectiveness and neutrality of law and its enforcement, the constitutional configuration of government (checks and balances), the degree to which the government controls the bureaucracy and the economy (e.g., state-owned companies and the independence of central banks could be relevant), the presence of NGOs concerned with human rights and corruption, the strategic and economic importance of the country in the international arena, and international constraints on government behavior. The distribution of power and resources can also matter: when multiple centers of power and resources coexist, they can mitigate or neutralize each other's efforts at arbitrarily rewarding and punishing social and political actors.[42]

The second set of conditions underpinning excessive or blatant manipulation is that one of the parties have the requisite *capacity to manipulate* in this manner. When various parties have similar capacities for electoral manipulation, no one party may be able to manipulate excessively (or more blatantly than rival parties). Even if constraints on government are lax, vigorous electoral competition may place excessive manipulation out of reach, as argued earlier in this chapter.[43] For excess or blatancy to be practicable, it is necessary that one of the parties have a *substantially greater capacity to manipulate*, in terms of

---

[41] Otherwise, the behavior of social and political actors becomes relatively insensitive to the kinds of information that underpin indirect effects (e.g., information about the likely behavior of other actors, or about attributes of the manipulating party), as explained in Chapter 4.

[42] Note, however, that competition among elites need not suffice to constrain these from wielding disproportionate political influence in comparison with non-elites. McCormick (2006; 2011), for example, argues that the institutions of modern democracy translate wealth inequalities into political ones, and he has proposed a variety of extra-electoral institutional arrangements through which elite accountability might be enhanced.

[43] For an exception, albeit one with limited empirical relevance, see the discussion of "Result 3" in Footnote 3 in this chapter.

extent and/or blatancy, than any other party. In other words, excessive/blatant manipulation requires a certain inequality among the manipulating parties' capacities to manipulate.[44] The capacities of different parties to manipulate will depend on a range of factors. Some such factors are party-specific, others derive from the position in the system occupied by each party: when the government is powerful, the party that controls it is likely to be able to benefit from that power.[45] It is frequently the case that ruling parties have a considerably greater capacity to manipulate than their rivals. This, however, is not always the case: as mentioned previously, there are numerous instances in the history of elections, recent and past, where the government party does not hold an especially large advantage over opposition parties in its capacity to manipulate (e.g., Costa Rica in the first half of the twentieth century, to name an example studied by Lehoucq and Molina (2002)). Additional factors impinging on the capacities of parties to manipulate include the presence of independent electoral management bodies with enforcement power, independent courts with jurisdiction over electoral matters, international election monitoring coupled with the credible threat of sanctions (here, the economic and strategic importance of the country will matter), and resource limitations (e.g., stemming from economic crisis) or bonanzas (e.g., from rising oil and gas prices).

What is the role of the parties' relative popularity among voters? An unpopular incumbent party that wishes to manipulate excessively faces a greater challenge than a popular one – that is, it must manipulate to a greater extent, all else equal. Therefore, popularity has consequences for the *feasibility* of excessive electoral manipulation. For example, in the 2004 presidential election in Ukraine, the incumbent president Yanukovich and his team engaged in large-scale manipulation yet barely managed to win, obtaining a margin of only 0.6 percent in the first round.[46] Russia's Yeltsin, too, faced an uphill battle in the 1996 election, where he won the first round of a seriously manipulated election with scarcely a 3.3 percent margin. Another illustration of the role of popularity is the near-loss of the 1988 Mexican presidential election by the ruling PRI which, despite its usual pre-electoral manipulation efforts, found itself compelled to engage in last-minute "cooking" of the vote tally.[47]

---

[44] Absolute levels matter too, of course: the party with the advantage at manipulation must also have a large-enough capacity to manipulate in absolute terms to be able to manipulate excessively or blatantly.

[45] The degree to which it can do so, of course, depends on government constraints, as argued previously. Therefore, government *constraints* and *capacity* to manipulate are connected.

[46] There is evidence that background conditions in Ukraine were such that manipulating excessively had the potential to pay off (as suggested by the episode related in Chapter 1). For a discussion of the capacities of the Ukrainian government under President Kuchma, see Way 2005a.

[47] The jury is still out on whether the PRI lost the 1988 election, or won it but manipulated it in order to increase its proportion of the vote. For an illuminating account of the indirect benefits for the PRI associated with exceeding the 50% vote threshold (vs. merely obtaining a plurality of the vote) see Castañeda (1999).

Popularity may also matter in a limited way for the *motivation* to manipulate excessively and blatantly: the scope for deterring opposition is presumably
greater when opponents are more numerous – although, as just mentioned, the
difficulty of doing so may be greater as well. The evidence suggests that many
popular rulers (e.g., Putin and Medvedev, Kazakhstan's Nazarbaev in 2005,
and possibly Mexico's PRI in the 1970s) are greatly motivated to manipulate
excessively and blatantly. In my data, in fact, excessive electoral manipulation
is more common among popular incumbents than among unpopular ones.[48]

As an empirical matter, the two sets of conditions I have just discussed –
those relating to constraints on government, and those pertaining to the distribution of capacities to manipulate – are associated with the broader and
somewhat more fundamental issue of "institutional strength," by which I refer
to the rule of law and checks and balances. Generally speaking, a weak rule of
law frequently goes together with a powerful government and with an unequal
distribution of capacities to manipulate. Therefore, the strength of institutions
provides a rough indication of where to expect, empirically, that different patterns of electoral manipulation might arise. Powerful, relatively unconstrained
incumbents are most common in developing countries. This is in part because
many electoral systems of recent vintage inherited weak rule of law and a highly
unequal distribution of resources and power among political and economic
actors.[49] Powerful incumbents are rarer in wealthier democracies. Incumbents
appear to have an electoral advantage even in the most competitive of today's
electoral systems (see Ansolabehere and Snyder 2002); but viewed in comparative perspective, the incumbency advantage in such competitive systems would
appear to be relatively small, and to be available to whichever party happens to
be in power. Consistent with these ideas, excessive and blatant manipulation
are seldom observed in established democracies, which tend to exhibit stronger
institutions.[50]

---

[48] The difference may be partly because of the feasibility issue just discussed. Considering the
subset of the data for which I have information on preelection polls, among elections where the
preelection poll indicated that the incumbent was ahead, 28% were excessively manipulated,
while only 10% of elections where the incumbent was behind were excessively manipulated (a
t-test for difference of means is significant at the 1% level). The result holds up in the subset
of cases where I have information that the main manipulator was the incumbent. It also holds
up when considering only excessive election-day fraud (i.e., excluding preelection vote buying,
candidate intimidation, etc.).

[49] As Linz writes, many regimes "have been established as successors of monarchical traditional
despotisms or traditional political systems, where authority was limited by customs rather than
by law and in which no other groups including religious organizations and authorities could
challenge or limit political authority" (2000, 267–268). Although Linz was writing in the 1970s,
his observations apply to many of the electoral regimes that emerged in the wake of the Cold
War.

[50] Note that the analysis could be applied to elections at different levels of government, and it
is possible for subnational variation to exist (see Gibson 2005, Gervasoni 2010). Therefore, it

I emphasize, however, that among cases with a weak rule of law there nevertheless exists considerable variation in terms of the degree to which power and resources are concentrated in the hand of the government. In fact, there are many developing countries where ruling parties face substantial competition from rivals. I discuss this kind of variation in detail in the next chapter for the cases of Zimbabwe and post-Soviet Russia.

With the purpose of connecting these ideas to the models presented in this and the previous chapter, let the parameter γ represent the ruling party's discretion and power (as in the preceding chapter). According to the previous discussion, γ drives both the strength of potential indirect effects and the degree to which one of the parties has the capacity to manipulate excessively/blatantly. The relationship between incumbent power and discretion, γ, on the one hand, and the strength of indirect effects was formalized in expression (4.4) in the previous chapter. The connection between γ and the capacity to manipulate can be formalized by rewriting the cost function for the ruling party as $c_1(.) = \gamma \kappa(.)$ and the cost function for the opposition party as $c_2(.) = \kappa(.)$.[51] Then at an equilibrium with nonzero levels of electoral manipulation, the first-order conditions in the model of party competition discussed earlier in this chapter require that $c_1'\left(x_1^*\right) = c_2'\left(x_2^*\right)$ or $\gamma \kappa'\left(x_1^*\right) = \kappa'\left(x_1^*\right)$, from which it is clear that values of γ further from 1, in either direction, increase the disparity between equilibrium choices of manipulation x_1^* and x_2^*, and therefore increase the feasibility of excessive/blatant manipulation.[52]

The empirical record is consistent with these expectations. Table 5.1 compares various proxies for the rule of law and government discretion in countries where excessively manipulated elections took place at any point between 1990 and 2007, with those in countries where no election was excessively manipulated in that period. The figures in the table are averages of the 1990 and 1991 values for each group of countries, with the idea of capturing the background conditions at the beginning of the period. An election is counted as excessively manipulated if it displayed an excessive margin of victory (greater than 20 percent) and it was manipulated to an intermediate or widespread extent, as coded in my data. The first three lines on the table are measures of the rule of law, contract enforcement, and government corruption, respectively. These variables are taken from Political Risk Services' International Country

---

is conceivable that excessive/blatant manipulation in elections for subnational office could be present in some subnational units of a country and not in others. I explore subnational variance in electoral manipulation empirically in the analysis of Mexico in Chapter 7.

[51] Note that, in contrast to the numerical example of the model presented earlier in the chapter, where the symbol κ was a parameter in the cost function, here κ represents a function.

[52] In particular, supposing for example that the marginal cost κ is positive and increasing, when $\gamma > 1$ the incumbent party has the greatest capacity to manipulate and manipulates more in equilibrium.

TABLE 5.1. *Initial Institutional Setting and Subsequent Excessive Manipulation*

	Ever Displayed Excessive Manipulation?	
	Yes	No
Rule of Law	2.2	4.1
Contract Enforcement	5.2	6.2
Government Corruption	2.8	4.2
Civil Liberties (reverse scale)	4.4	2.3
Checks and Balances	1.9	3.3
GDP per capita (USD)	3,499	13,114

Notes: The time period covered by the manipulation data is 1990-2007. The variable values displayed are 1990-1991 averages. The number of countries covered by each of the items ranges between 101 and 127, depending on data availability.
Sources: Author's data, ICRG, FH, DPI 2010, and PWT 6.3.

Risk Guide (ICRG).[53] The next line corresponds to the Freedom House (FH) civil liberties variable, which measures "the freedoms of expression and belief, associational and organizational rights, rule of law, and personal autonomy without interference from the state" (Freedom House 2012). Next is a measure of checks and balances from the 2010 version of the Database of Political Institutions (DPI; Beck et al. 2001; Keefer and Stasavage 2003). This variable reflects the formal setup of government (i.e., electoral rules) as well as electoral outcomes (e.g., whether the president's party has a majority in the legislature). It is therefore potentially correlated by construction with the presence or absence of excessive manipulation; nevertheless it is included in the table for completeness. The idea is that these five measures proxy for different aspects of the underlying theoretical dimensions – the level and concentration of power and resources in the hands of the government, and government discretion. Finally, the table displays real per capita income (in real 1996 U.S. dollars) as a proxy for the "level of development," from the Penn World Tables 6.3, also for completeness.

Consistent with the preceding discussion, the table indicates that, on average, those countries where excessive electoral manipulation ever took place in the period covered by the data had initially worse values in all of these measures. Mean values for all variables in the table are statistically different between the two sets of countries (P < .01).[54] A second way to assess the relationship between the strength of institutions and the pattern of electoral

[53] The ICRG variable names are, respectively: "law and order," "investment profile," and "corruption." Investment profile considers contract viability/expropriation, among other things. Law and order refers to the "strength and impartiality of the legal system," as well as to the "popular observance of the law." Corruption covers bribery, import/export restrictions, secret party funding, and capture of politics by business, among other things (Political Risk Services). See Knack and Keefer 1995 for a more detailed description of the ICRG variables.
[54] Based on t-tests for equality of means.

manipulation is to divide the sample of countries into those with initial (1990–1991) above-median and below-median values of the rule of law, contract enforcement, and so on; and then measure the proportion of countries in each group that exhibited excessive manipulation in the period covered by the data. Excessive manipulation is substantially more likely to arise in the group with below-average values: the proportion of countries that ever exhibited excessive manipulation is greater by 55 percent, 28 percent, 47 percent, 308 percent, and 143 percent, respectively, for each of the first five variables in Table 5.1.[55] Both analyses are consistent with the claim that the likelihood of excessive electoral manipulation is associated with the "weakness" of institutions.[56]

Regime Type and Excessive/Blatant Electoral Manipulation

The background conditions I have highlighted as propitious for excessive/blatant manipulation – government discretion and a relatively high level of government power and resources – often characterize less-than-democratic electoral regimes, such as competitive authoritarian regimes (Schedler 2002; Levitsky and Way 2002). This raises the question: is excessive/blatant electoral manipulation exclusive to a specific regime type – perhaps even a defining feature of a particular regime type? In the first chapter, I reviewed the existing literature and discussed this issue on a conceptual level. Here I supplement that discussion with a more systematic assessment of the relationship between regime type and electoral manipulation based on my country-level dataset.

To operationalize competitive authoritarianism, I follow the procedure outlined in Howard and Roessler's (2006) influential article on the topic. Although the article focuses on competitive authoritarian regimes, it provides operational definitions of four regime types: democratic, competitive authoritarian, hegemonic authoritarian, and closed authoritarian.[57] One advantage of Howard and Roessler's procedure is that it is based on publicly available data, and is therefore readily reproducible.[58] Their classification is based on Polity and Freedom House (FH) data (which respectively measure democracy and political and civil freedoms), which are available yearly at the country level for a large number of countries. Any regime with a FH score smaller than 3, or

---

[55] The differences are significant for these five measures at $P < 0.1$ (based on t-tests for equal means).

[56] I use quotation marks because the theoretical concepts of relevance – the distribution of power and resources, and the discretion of the government – only partially stem from institutions; and because the proxies I have used for these dimensions at least in part reflect outcomes – e.g., of government choices – as well as institutions (the measure of checks and balances being the closest to a measure of institutions).

[57] The article also distinguishes between electoral and liberal democracy; I collapse that distinction here.

[58] One downside is that the data on which it is based do not perfectly capture the underlying theoretical dimensions.

TABLE 5.2. *Incidence of Excessive Electoral Manipulation by Regime Type, 1990–2007*

Democratic	11%
Competitive or Hegemonic Authoritarian	57%
Competitive Authoritarian 43%	
Hegemonic Authoritarian 85%	
Closed Authoritarian	55%

Notes: Proportion of country-years in each regime category that displayed at least one excessively-manipulated election, 1990–2007. Excessive manipulation operationalized as a margin of victory of 20% or greater and manipulation of level 2 or 3. Author's data.

with a Polity score greater than 5, is classified as a democracy.[59] A regime with a FH score of 7 or a Polity score lower than −7 is a closed authoritarian regime. All other regimes are either competitive or hegemonic authoritarian. The distinction between these two categories depends on the proportion of the vote obtained by the ruling party. The regime is hegemonic authoritarian if the ruling party obtained at least 70 percent of the vote, otherwise it is competitive authoritarian.[60] The regime classification for a given country-year is based on the Polity and FH scores for the preceding year.[61]

For each of these four regime types, I calculate the proportion of elections that were excessively manipulated within each regime type (Table 5.2).[62] For completeness, the table displays hegemonic and competitive authoritarian regimes together (these two categories together have been called "electoral authoritarian") and as separate categories. The table shows that not all elections in competitive or hegemonic authoritarian regimes are excessively manipulated – only 57 percent are.[63] Moreover, excessive electoral manipulation is not exclusive to any one regime type – a small number occur in regimes that

[59] FH scores range between 1 (most free) and 7 (least free). Polity scores range between −10 (most authoritarian) and 10 (most democratic).

[60] By Howard and Roessler's own account (2006), the criterion they utilize to distinguish between competitive and hegemonic authoritarianism is ad hoc. This criterion is not universally embraced in the literature. For example, Levitsky and Way (2010) include in their set of competitive authoritarian regimes many countries where elections were won by more than 70% of the vote (including Russia, Belarus, and Zimbabwe, among others). One problem with utilizing electoral outcomes to distinguish regime types is that it predetermines, to an extent, the relationship between regime type and the pattern of manipulation (when one party obtains 70% of the vote, the margin of victory is at least 40%) – precisely the relationship that this subsection seeks to elucidate.

[61] Howard and Roessler exclude founding elections. I do not, but the empirical patterns I describe later are unlikely to change if these are excluded.

[62] More precisely, the table displays the proportion of country-years in each regime category that displayed at least one excessively manipulated election.

[63] The proportion of "hegemonic authoritarian" regimes that exhibit excessive manipulation is especially high because Howard and Roessler's classificatory procedure to differentiate between competitive and hegemonic authoritarian selects on the margin of victory.

TABLE 5.3. *Countries with At Least One Excessively Manipulated Election in the 1990–2007 Period*

Albania [c]	East Timor	Kyrgyzstan	Russia [c]
Algeria	Egypt	Liberia [h]	Rwanda
Argentina	El Salvador	Macedonia [c]	Senegal [chd]
Armenia [c]	Ethiopia	Madagascar [c]	Serbia [c]
Azerbaijan	Gabon [ch]	Malawi [c]	Sierra Leone
Bangladesh	Gambia [hd]	Malaysia [chd]	Singapore [hd]
Belarus [c]	Georgia [c]	Mali [c]	South Africa [h]
Benin [c]	Ghana [c]	Mauritania	Sri Lanka
Bolivia	Guatemala	Mexico [chd]	Taiwan [chd]
Burkina Faso	Guinea	Montenegro	Tajikistan
Cambodia [c]	Guinea-Bissau [h]	Mozambique [ch]	Tanzania [chd]
Cameroon [ch]	Guyana [ch]	Myanmar	Thailand
Central African Republic	Haiti [c]	Nicaragua [c]	Togo
Chad	Indonesia	Niger	Tunisia
Colombia	Iran	Nigeria	Uganda
Congo (DRC)	Jamaica	Pakistan	Ukraine [c]
Croatia [c]	Jordan	Paraguay [h]	Uzbekistan
Côte d'Ivoire [h]	Kazakhstan	Peru [c]	Venezuela
Djibouti [h]	Kenya [ch]	Philippines	Yemen
Dominican Republic [c]	South Korea	Congo (Brazzaville)	Zambia [c]
		Romania [c]	Zimbabwe [ch]

Notes: Excessive manipulation operationalized as a margin of victory of 20% or greater and manipulation of level 2 or 3. Data for 1990-2007. Codes: c = competitive authoritarian in 1990-1995 (Levitsky and Way 2010), h = hegemonic party autocracy at some point in 20th century (Magaloni 2006), d = dominant-party authoritarian (Greene 2007). Author's data.

Howard and Roessler classify as democratic; and (less surprisingly) a large proportion of elections in regimes that Howard and Roessler classify as closed authoritarian are also excessively manipulated.[64]

Another way to examine the relationship between regime type and excessive manipulation is to look at the country level. Table 5.3 lists those countries that displayed at least one excessively manipulated election in the 1990–2007 period, according to my data. The table indicates whether the country was classified by Levitsky and Way (2010) as a competitive authoritarian regime, or by Magaloni (2006) as a hegemonic party autocracy, respectively with a "c" and/or an "h" in brackets after the country name.[65] A "d" indicates that the country is classified by Greene (2007) as a dominant-party authoritarian

---

[64] Note that Howard and Roessler's theoretical and empirical classifications diverge: while they define closed authoritarian regimes as those that do not hold elections, according to their empirical classification, a good number of closed authoritarian regimes do hold elections.

[65] Note that Magaloni's "hegemonic party autocracy" is distinct from the category of "hegemonic authoritarian" regime. See Chapter 1 for a discussion of these concepts.

regime.[66] Two conclusions emerge from the table. First, most countries listed by Levitsky and Way as competitive authoritarian or by Magaloni as hegemonic-party autocracies have exhibited at least one excessively manipulated election in the 1990–2007 period.[67]

Nevertheless, the set of countries that have exhibited excessive electoral manipulation is substantially larger than the sets of competitive authoritarian regimes or of dominant-party authoritarian regimes. Of the 132 countries in my data with the requisite information, 82 (equivalent to 62 percent) had at least one excessively manipulated election in the 1990–2007 period. Levitsky and Way (2010) count thirty-four countries as competitive authoritarian (they focus on the 1990–1995 period), Magaloni (2006) lists twenty hegemonic-party autocracies (2006, 40), and Greene (2010) mentions seven dominant-party authoritarian regimes (it is not clear that Greene's enumeration is intended to be exhaustive). Restricting my data to the 1990–1995 period, for comparability with Levitsky and Way's count, yields fifty-three countries. If the operationalization of excessive electoral manipulation is restricted to require a margin of votes of at least 30 percent, the total is seventy-one countries. Finally, restricting the definition of excessive manipulation to exclude pre–election day electoral manipulation – following Greene's (and possibly Magaloni's) usage of the term election fraud – yields sixty-three countries. In sum, excessive electoral manipulation appears to be a substantially more widespread phenomenon than competitive authoritarianism, or party dominance or hegemony.

Feedbacks, Over-Time Dynamics, and the Excessive/Blatant Electoral Manipulation Trap

The factors I have described as causally underpinning the extent and visibility of electoral manipulation – the distribution of power and resources among political parties, the discretion of government, and the strength of institutions – are "proximate" in the sense that they determine the incentives and possibilities for different patterns of electoral manipulation in the short and the medium terms. These factors may be considered as exogenous in the short and medium

---

[66] Levitsky and Way classify countries from 1990 to 1995; Magaloni appears to have looked as far back as the early twentieth century. I was not able to locate a full list of dominant-party authoritarian regimes in Greene (2007), therefore the set of countries marked as "d" is presumably a subset of such regimes.

[67] Botswana is considered to be a dominant-party authoritarian system by both Magaloni (2006) and Greene (2007), but its elections have not been excessively manipulated. This is the only country in Magaloni's list that is not present in Table 5.3. Also not on the table are Moldova and Slovakia, whose elections have not been excessively manipulated, although both countries are considered by Levitsky and Way (2010) as competitive authoritarian in the 1990–1995 period (the controversial 2001 legislative election in Moldova, for instance, was praised by OSCE international observers as having met democratic standards; on Slovakia see Bunce and Wolchik 2007). This highlights the point that authoritarianism neither requires nor entails excessive/blatant electoral manipulation (although it renders it more likely).

terms: when deciding whether, how much, and how to manipulate elections, parties and governments must take the existing distribution of resources and power, and of the prevailing strength of institutions, as facts.

It is also helpful, however, to consider long-run dynamics – to reflect on how such factors might themselves be influenced, over time, by the patterns of electoral manipulation to which they give rise. Consider excessive manipulation first; it is likely to arise under a situation where resources for manipulation are concentrated and government discretion is relatively high. In turn, excessive manipulation is likely to further weaken opponents of the perpetrator, potentially making it possible for the manipulator to progressively increase its sphere of discretion by capturing additional levers of power and/or weakening institutions that could check its behavior. Therefore, it seems plausible that, over the long run, excessive manipulation could reinforce or deepen the background conditions that gave rise to it in the first place. In other words, excessive manipulation and the conditions that are likely to give rise to it are self-reinforcing. One can in effect speak of an *excessive/blatant electoral manipulation trap*, where an initially powerful incumbent party routinely manipulates excessively/blatantly, in turn reinforcing its hold on power.

The claim that power conditions and excessive/blatant manipulation mutually reinforce each other over time does not imply that they exist in a relationship of unresolvable endogeneity. Instead, the lines and the direction of causation that link them can be clearly traced at every point in time. This is, in part, the consequence of the discrete, episodic nature of elections and of electoral manipulation. To put this somewhat differently, consider the following dynamic model. Let t index a series of discrete time periods, and let γ_t describe the power conditions (i.e., distribution of resources and power among parties, strength of institutions, discretion of the incumbent) in period t. Incentives and possibilities to manipulate at time t are shaped by γ_t. In turn, manipulation at t denoted by x_t shapes power conditions in the subsequent period, $t + 1$ – that is, x_t shapes γ_{t+1}. Similarly, in period $t + 1$, it is the power conditions γ_{t+1} that shape incentives and possibilities to manipulate and, therefore, actual manipulation choices in that period, x_{t+1}, and so on. In other words, the sequence of causation is: $\gamma_t \rightarrow x_t \rightarrow \gamma_{t+1} \rightarrow x_{t+1} \rightarrow \ldots$ Power conditions γ, therefore, are a state variable, and manipulation x is a choice variable. At any given point in time, the state variable shapes the possible choices and the associated payoffs, but the choice variable does not shape the state variable at that point in time – it shapes the state variable in the subsequent period.

This structure of feedbacks suggests two dynamic paths, each potentially approaching a different steady state: first, an initially concentrated distribution of power renders excessive manipulation more likely, which in turn reinforces the subsequent concentration of power, which again provides incentives for excessive manipulation, and so on. Conversely, an initially dispersed distribution of power limits possibilities for excessive manipulation (and possibly reduces incentives for such manipulation too), rendering any manipulation at most marginal, which in turn is unlikely to lead to significant changes in the subsequent distribution of power, and so on. Eventually, each of these two processes is likely to converge to a different steady state – namely, at some point, power conditions are likely to level off, either at a "low" or a "high" equilibrium, depending on the path. The former path approaches a "low" equilibrium (referring back to the previous chapter) or an "authoritarian" state of affairs, and the latter path approaches a "high" equilibrium or a "democratic" state of affairs. In other words, initial conditions or exogenous events that shape the state variable – the power conditions – can set the polity on one of two self-reinforcing paths: one "democratic," the other "authoritarian." Zimbabwe's government, for example, at independence in 1980 inherited a disproportionately powerful state apparatus from the colonial government, which set it on a path of excessive manipulation and increasing concentration of power.

How might a system move from one of these dynamic paths (or their equilibrium endpoints) to the other – for example, from a vicious cycle of excessive and blatant manipulation and increasing authoritarianism to one of limited (or no) manipulation and greater political competition, or vice versa? The previous chapter discussed two mechanisms underpinning the indirect effects of electoral manipulation – coordination and costly signaling. Each of these two mechanisms points to a way in which movement between different equilibria could take place. Consider first a scenario in which an authoritarian path or equilibrium is sustained by a *coordination failure*: the ruling party is disliked and could be removed if its opponents acted together against it, but this does not happen because every individual actor – bureaucrat, politician, citizen, and businessman, among others – thinks it unlikely that fellow rivals of the ruling party will take action, and therefore is not inclined to take such action him-/herself. In such a situation, authoritarianism is sustained by a *belief*. A change in beliefs, therefore, can lead to a change in behavior and, potentially, to a change in the political outcome.[68]

One way in which the prevailing set of beliefs can change is suggested by Kuran (1989), who famously argued that mass action can result from an informational "bandwagon." For example, an initial "spark" motivates a group of opponents to publicly take action against the ruler. In turn, this alters public perceptions about how likely fellow incumbent rivals are to take action, motivating an additional group of actors – citizens, bureaucrats, and others – to follow suit. Eventually, this process emboldens a large-enough number of opponents of the ruler, and the political state of affairs changes.[69] The

---

[68] For a discussion of various cases that fit this stylized description in the post-Soviet region, see Bunce and Wolchik 2010.

[69] In his 1989 article, Kuran emphasizes the rapid nature of shifts from one equilibrium to another and when such shifts occur, rather than the off-equilibrium adjustment process that might describe how such shifts take place (see also Simpser 2008).

question, then, is what the initial spark might be and where it might originate. Suppose that the main stumbling block for opposition is a high level of apathy or cynicism (among politicians, donors, and voters, among others) surrounding elections. A publicity campaign designed to motivate citizens to vote, politicians to run, and donors to support them, if successful, could provide the needed spark. An example of such an effort is furnished by an advertising campaign that ran before the 2006 election in Haiti. Haiti's history created mistrust among the electorate about the usefulness of elections, and the run-up to the 2006 election was rife with problems that likely exacerbated such mistrust – for example, a candidate with ties to the exiled former president Aristide (Gerard Jean-Juste), was jailed and then barred from registering for the election, and his party threatened to boycott the poll. A Haitian interviewee, for instance, expressed that "who Haitians vote for doesn't matter, many Haitians believe that US decides who governs"[70] and a 58-year-old mason out of work explained why he did not register to vote: "I was discouraged, I didn't want to vote because I've been voting for a long time and have never gotten anything from it" (Flintoff 2006b). In this context, the commonly heard get-out-the-vote slogan "vote now, so you won't regret it later" (Flintoff 2006a), and the following radio skit, which was broadcast across Haiti during the last week before the election, can be understood as government efforts to shift the electorate from a "low equilibrium" – one characterized by voter apathy – to a "high equilibrium," one with high levels of electoral participation:

The woman, Jeanine, calls through the window of her friend, Elifat to wake him up on voting day.

Unidentified Man: (As Elifat) (Through Translator) Jeanine, I don't think I'll vote today. It won't make any difference whether I vote or not.

FLINTOFF: But Jeanine insists. She points out that Elifat's vote, combined with hers, combined with the neighbors, could help their candidate win the election. Elifat is convinced. (Flintoff 2006b)

The radio skit points both to the existence of a generalized tendency toward abstention (which, in the case of Haiti, had clear historical roots), and to the social-coordination or "focal" aspects of voting patterns: Elifat is persuaded to vote by rendering salient the "high-equilibrium" – the imagined situation in which both she, her friend Jeanine, and her neighbors all turn out to vote.[71]

The spark that unleashes opposition coordination could also stem directly from the actions of the government. Weingast (1997) suggests, for example, that a social compact about what constitutes acceptable government behavior,

---

[70] National Public Radio, *All Things Considered*, February 5, 2006.

[71] Why the Haitian government might have wanted to do this is an interesting question, which I do not address here.

when transgressed, can spark mass action against the government. Constitutions, he argues, can play precisely this role when there is a general expectation that a constitutional transgression will spark mass action from fellow citizens. When this is the case, Weingast argues, the threat of mass action underpins the rule of law – namely, the respect of constitutional restraints by government. Fearon (2011) provides a model where a government's failure to hold elections can spark mass action against it. In practice, the factors capable of triggering opposition coordination might include international pressures (e.g., the support of opposition groups by foreign powers), domestic political events, exogenous shocks (e.g., an economic crisis), and gradual structural changes, among other things. Moreover, I submit that such triggers can consist of the *interaction* of various factors. For example, individual opponents of the regime could believe that their fellow opposition supporters are likely to be passive in the face of excessive or blatant manipulation, but that they are likely to actively oppose the ruling party (e.g., by taking to the streets in the case of citizens or by supporting opposition politicians in the case of bureaucrats or businessmen) if excessive or blatant manipulation is *combined* with clear support from the West (which would reduce the likelihood that actively opposing the ruling party might result in repression). It is interesting to think about the post-electoral popular mobilization in Ukraine in 2004 (and possibly also those in Iran in 2009) in this light – as having ensued from a combination of a public violation by the regime of the social compact, coupled with the perception of strong Western support for regime opponents.[72] Importantly, while Kuran's, Weingast's, and Fearon's articles focus on the possibility of citizens rebelling, the relevant coordination (or failure of coordination) might involve actors other than citizens, such as high-level bureaucrats, officials in charge of security forces, leaders of organizations, and elite politicians. Even though such categories of actors are clearly less numerous than citizens, they are also prone to facing coordination problems.[73]

A failure of opposition coordination is not the only possible source of an excessive/blatant manipulation trap. Even a perfectly well-coordinated opposition could be discouraged and deterred by the knowledge (or the belief) that its efforts are likely to be insufficient to overcome a powerful ruling party – one

---

[72] Bunce and Wolchik, for example, emphasize the importance of international factors on the willingness and ability of the opposition to actively oppose a ruling party (2010, 51).

[73] Bunce and Wolchik (2010) suggest that agency – e.g., in the form of tactical electoral savvy on the part of opposition parties – plays a central role in the possibilities for opposition parties to unseat authoritarian incumbents through elections. In the context of the discussion here, such agency could be understood as providing the needed spark. Note, however, that their account of opposition success differs in some ways from that offered here: while they acknowledge the importance of opposition coordination, they argue that such coordination is not sufficient for electoral success – tactics matter too, as do "structural" factors (which could render even a tactically savvy and enthusiastic opposition effort unsuccessful; see my discussion of costly signaling below).

able to comfortably cheat its way into office despite the opposition's best efforts. Such a ruling party could utilize excessive/blatant manipulation to signal "invincibility," discouraging opponents and entrenching itself in power.[74] This is the second mechanism behind the indirect effects of electoral manipulation discussed in the previous chapter. One way out of a "low equilibrium" sustained by this mechanism would begin with a *shift in power* – in the level of power of the ruling party, as well as in the balance of power between the ruling party and other political forces. Shifts in power can have multiple causes, including a change in the price of a commodity such as oil or gas, an economic crisis sparked by world events or by mismanagement, and international pressures for policies and reforms (such as privatization) that reduce the government's relative power.[75] Such shifts in power can potentially limit the ruling party's capacity for excessive manipulation and reduce the potential for indirect effects, leading the political system away from a situation of ruling party entrenchment.[76] In Zimbabwe, for example, the economic crisis that brewed in the 1990s erased some of the ruling party's formerly overwhelming advantages, opening the door for a powerful opposition movement to consolidate and leading to much more competitive elections in which excessive electoral manipulation was no longer feasible.[77] But just as certain economic shocks can lead out of an excessive/blatant electoral manipulation trap, other such shocks can enable a leader to push a country or region onto the path toward a low equilibrium. Such a shift is illustrated by the case of post-Soviet Russia, where a relatively free and competitive party system under Yeltsin gave way to one in which power has been re-centralized in the hands of Putin and his associates.[78]

---

[74] I draw the term "invincibility" from Simpser (2003); "strength" or "power" might be substituted here.

[75] It is also possible for a "low" equilibrium driven by the costly signaling mechanism to be sustained by beliefs. The logic of the pooling equilibrium discussed in Chapter 4, for example, requires that the actor initially believe that the incumbent party is likely to be strong. If the actor did not initially believe this, it would challenge instead of complying. In some instances (i.e., when the incumbent is actually weak), such a challenge could potentially bring the incumbent down (note that the costly signaling model in Chapter 4 considered only a situation in which all incumbent types are assured to remain in power).

[76] Greene (2007) utilizes a similar idea to explain the survival of dominant parties (the argument here applies to electoral systems more generally). Greene argues that dominance wanes when parties lose their resource advantages for exogenous reasons. Levitsky and Way 2010, chapter 2, contains an excellent discussion of the factors that influence the balance of power between incumbent and opposition. See also Simpser 2005.

[77] This is not to say that Zimbabwe ceased to be an authoritarian system, nor that the government stopped manipulating elections – it has done so, and in brutal ways. Nevertheless, since 2000 the ruling party has barely managed to obtain victory despite such manipulation, and vote margins have been slim in comparison with the pre-2000 period.

[78] The next chapter discusses Zimbabwe's and Russia's movement into or out of a situation of excessive electoral manipulation and incumbent entrenchment.

Note that not all patterns of electoral manipulation are associated with the same dynamic downward spiral just described for excessive/blatant manipulation. In Sections 5.1 and 5.2, I showed that two-sided (or "competitive") manipulation – a pattern of manipulation where two or more parties manipulate to a roughly similar extent – has the property that parties' manipulation efforts largely neutralize each other. Two-sided manipulation is generally less worrisome than one-sided excessive/blatant manipulation on at least two counts. First, two-sided competitive manipulation, even when it alters the election outcome, is unlikely to contribute substantially to entrenchment by one of the parties against the will of its citizenry: neither the coordination nor the costly signaling mechanisms that give rise to indirect effects are likely to operate, as discussed earlier in the chapter. Second, from the point of view of the parties, competitive electoral manipulation dissipates rents. Therefore, in a situation of large-scale competitive manipulation, parties could potentially gain from working jointly to put in place safeguards to reduce the systemic level of manipulation.[79] That is, at least in theory, competitive manipulation would not appear to have the same kind of dynamic stability that one-sided excessive/blatant electoral manipulation seems to have.[80]

Somewhat paradoxically, in light of the preceding discussion, excessive electoral manipulation is often treated as less worrisome than marginal manipulation because it does not change who wins an election. International election monitors, for example, are often concerned about whether an election outcome reflects the "will of the people." An election is said to reflect the will of the people when the citizenry's preferred candidate wins. Excessive or blatant manipulation quite frequently does not subvert the will of the people *thus understood*, and therefore its potentially serious consequences – its indirect effects – fail to garner the attention that they deserve.[81]

5.4 ALTERNATIVE EXPLANATIONS FOR EXCESSIVE ELECTORAL MANIPULATION

In this section, I consider four intuitive alternative explanations for excessive electoral manipulation. They are: uncertainty about the outcome, a low

---

[79] In practice, implementing safeguards against manipulation is a tricky business, and internal party relations, as well as relations between different regions and levels of government, might render the creation of such barriers a difficult task. Whether in practice such incentives have led parties to jointly curb the scale of manipulation is a question open to future research.

[80] Note that, theoretically, there exist conditions under which *competitive manipulation*, as I have defined it, can also be *excessive* – namely when one of the parties is exceptionally popular (see the discussion of Result 3 in Footnote 3 in this chapter).

[81] On normative grounds too, it is not clear that marginal manipulation in a tight race that changes who wins is worse than excessive manipulation that does not change who wins. In the former case, the tightness of the race implies that the (unrightful) winner is only slightly less popular than the loser. In contrast, the contribution of excessive manipulation to incumbent power and entrenchment can lead to much-less-representative electoral outcomes over time.

marginal cost of electoral manipulation, a high stakes of holding power, and the need to keep the manipulation machine "well oiled." I consider each in turn and assess their plausibility in light of the available evidence and some simple analyses. I find that only under unique or extreme circumstances that are unlikely to hold in the generality of cases could these explanations account for excessive electoral manipulation of the size observed in the data.[82]

Uncertainty

Elections where multiple parties are permitted to run generally entail some degree of subjective uncertainty about the outcome.[83] Seemingly excessive electoral manipulation could be understood simply as an effort to increase the probability of victory under conditions of subjective uncertainty: attaining a given chance of victory requires more electoral manipulation when the manipulator's uncertainty is higher.[84] Therefore, high uncertainty could motivate levels of manipulation far exceeding those actually necessary to win.

On a general level, the basic logic of this idea is sound: uncertainty most likely influences choices about electoral manipulation to some extent. It is unlikely, however, that uncertainty by itself could explain observed outcomes. Manipulating when it is unnecessary to do so, or to an extent far exceeding that needed for victory, entails substantial costs and risks (more on these in the next subsection). Therefore, the degree of uncertainty that would be required to yield margins of victory of the observed sizes, say 20 percent, 30 percent, or 40 percent, would be, in general, implausibly high. For one thing, parties and governments often have at the very least a rough sense for where they stand in terms of popularity, as argued earlier in this chapter. Moreover, conducting a public opinion poll is not very difficult. One worry, of course, is whether such a poll would elicit the desired information – under repressive rule, citizens may not respond truthfully (Kuran 1989; Wedeen 1998, 1999). To obtain a sense for whether this worry is justified, I investigate how well pre-electoral public opinion polls are able to predict margins of victory. Figure 5.2 is a scatterplot of

---

[82] While my theory accounts for both excess and blatancy in manipulation with the same basic logic, alternative explanations need not have the feature that they apply equally to excess and blatancy. For example, an obvious alternative explanation for blatant electoral manipulation might be the difficulty of hiding manipulation efforts; however, both my data (presented in Chapter 3) and case-specific evidence (e.g., for Mexico under the PRI, and for contemporary Nigeria and Zimbabwe, among other examples) suggest that manipulation is often purposefully blatant. In the rest of this section, I focus on alternative explanations for excessive manipulation.

[83] What matters is uncertainty from the perspective of the manipulating party – hence the term "subjective."

[84] The object of uncertainty could correspond to a variety of factors that impact the probability that different contenders will end up in power, such as the contenders' level of support among the electorate, the capacity of parties to engage in electoral manipulation, and the connection between a given effort of electoral manipulation and its yield in terms of votes or seats.

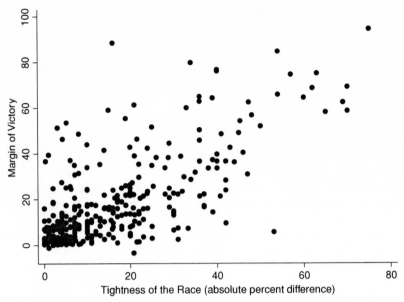

FIGURE 5.2. Margin of Victory and Pre-Electoral Polls, Executive Elections
Source: Author's data

the margin of victory versus the absolute closeness of the election as measured by public opinion polls (the same variable used in Chapter 3).

The figure suggests that polls, while not perfect, are quite informative regarding the likely outcome of executive elections.[85] A regression of the margin on closeness has an R^2 of 0.61, meaning that a large proportion of the variance in the margin of victory is explained by preelection polls. Still, this is an average estimate of the level of information contained in polls, and it is possible that polls are less informative in more authoritarian settings. To check for this possibility, I divided the sample according to an index of political freedoms (Freedom House Political Rights). Even for those cases with low levels of political freedom, polls are reasonably good predictors of actual outcomes $R^2 = 0.52$ (or a similar regression on the subsample with the lowest three levels of political freedom, $N = 52$).[86] Moreover, it is quite possible that those who conduct the polls may often have better quality information than they share with the public (in authoritarian settings, pollsters often work for, or depend on a license from, the government). Finally, while the proportion of missing

---

[85] Note that this is true even if the polls reflect the effects of pre-electoral manipulation – the point here is that polls are informative about outcomes (whether or not they also reflect the underlying true popularity of the parties).

[86] As might be expected, polls are better predictors of outcomes in the subsample with the highest level of political freedoms ($R^2 = 0.82$).

data on preelection polls is greater for countries with lower levels of political rights, there is missing data at all levels of political rights, and the observations for which there is data on pre-electoral public opinion polls include a good number of cases of excessive electoral manipulation.[87]

An additional piece of evidence on the issue of uncertainty comes from Wang and Kurzman's (2003) unusually detailed account of the logistics of electoral manipulation in the 1993 election in Taiwan. They relate that local Kuomintang campaign headquarters set targets for the percentage of eligible votes that each township should buy (townships are subunits of the electoral district), and that, in the township they studied, vote-buying efforts yielded results close to the targets. The campaign headquarters set a target of 70 to 80 percent of the eligible vote, the township campaign officials set a target of 75 percent, and 67 percent of the eligible vote was actually attained (2003, 9–10). This suggests that party operatives had relatively good information about voter preferences and about the effectiveness of their methods for obtaining votes via manipulation.

Another way to assess whether uncertainty might be an adequate explanation for excessive electoral manipulation is to use the formal model to conduct a simple back-of-the-envelope estimate of the amount of uncertainty that would be needed to yield an excessive margin of victory. To do this, recall the expression from Section 5.1 describing the relationship between the size of the equilibrium margin of victory and the level of uncertainty, $|m^*| < \varphi$, and consider a scenario where the candidates have equal levels of electoral support ($\delta = 0$). For simplicity, suppose that only one of the parties can manipulate. In such a scenario, for the manipulating party to have the motivation to manipulate to an extent that would yield a margin of victory of, say, 40 percent, it would have to face an extremely high level of uncertainty. Specifically, the manipulating party would have to be unsure about where its level of support among the electorate lies within a "confidence interval" that is as large as the margin of victory – for example, the interval [30 percent, 70 percent]. Such a high level of uncertainty does not seem generally plausible, in light of the evidence just discussed.[88] In sum, uncertainty does not by itself appear to be a convincing general explanation for excessive electoral manipulation.

---

[87] Of all elections for which there is information on preelection polls, about 14% (30 cases) were both substantially manipulated and won by margins greater than 20%.

[88] The expression for bounds on the margin is based on the uniform distribution. If a distribution with broader support (e.g., the Normal) was used instead, then the bounds on the margin of victory would depend not only on the level of uncertainty (i.e., on the variance of the distribution), but also on the stakes of victory. Therefore, for extremely high stakes of winning (for example, when the life of the ruler would be in danger if he lost power) it would be conceivable that smaller (and more plausible) levels of uncertainty could be associated with excessive manipulation. I discuss the role of the stakes of victory in a later subsection. The combination of extremely high stakes, and high-enough uncertainty, is unlikely to arise often.

Cost

Another possible explanation for the excessive use of electoral manipulation in the absence of indirect effects is that the marginal cost of manipulation is very low. If electoral manipulation is cheap or free, even a small amount of uncertainty about the likelihood of victory could conceivably lead to its excessive use. The problem with this idea is that electoral manipulation is generally neither free nor cheap.[89] Much like any other government policy, implementing electoral manipulation in general entails substantial material costs, associated with logistics, personnel, materials, transportation, and communications, for example. In addition, electoral manipulation can increase the risk of punishment, jail, or a reaction from the public.[90] Overall, electoral manipulation is likely to entail substantial expected costs.

On the material cost and effort required to manipulate elections, Cox and Kousser (1981), in a study of electoral fraud in New York State in the late nineteenth century, list specific electoral practices, including "free transportation to the polls, the use of repeaters, the illegal naturalization of foreigners, the election-day importation of voters from other states, the padding of registration rolls, fraudulent counting, and, most interestingly, payments to citizens not to vote." Wang and Kurzman emphasize the significant effort that goes into recruiting the appropriate campaign managers and building a network of vote brokers to implement vote-buying targets (2003, 6–10). Even under a powerful ruling party, Greene argues that "committing successful fraud requires . . . large amounts of resources to fund the machinery of fraud, including pay for ballot-box stuffers and thugs" (2007, 43).

Precise costs are understandably difficult to estimate for many of these activities, but there exists some information for a specific form of manipulation, vote buying. Cox and Kousser (1981) cite newspaper quotes of the cost per vote in the late 1800s ranging between $10 and $27 (equivalent to roughly $100 to $300 in 2000). By one newspaper account, at least one-third of each party's voters had to be bribed, either to change the way they voted or to stay at home and abstain. Wurfel (1963) estimates the cost per vote in the Philippines in the 1960s at P1 to P25 (equivalent to USD $2 to $58 in 2000). In the Philippines, vote buying was explicitly prohibited by law, and it was also considered illegitimate by the public ("selling one's vote is considered a reprehensible act by a respectable citizen," writes Wurfel). Wurfel estimates that 10 to 20 percent of

---

[89] Moreover, increasing marginal costs (discussed in Chapter 1) would mean that even if some amount of electoral manipulation could be pursued on the cheap, at some point additional manipulation would become expensive.

[90] I have argued that excessive electoral manipulation by a ruling party can actually reduce the possibility of collective action on the part of the ruling party's opponents. However, the possibility remains open that *marginal* electoral manipulation could increase the risk of a rebellion (as discussed in Chapter 1).

the electorate sold their vote. Cost estimates of total spending on vote buying in a single election range from the millions to the billions of U.S. dollars (Tasker and Crispin 2001; Wang and Kurzman 2003, 9; Hicken 2007; Schaffer 2007, 188–190).

As mentioned earlier in this book, the logic of excessive manipulation may be operative at the subnational level – for instance, when a state governor seeks to maximize the margin of victory in a national election, not because such a margin is needed for victory, but because of its indirect effects (on the governor's career prospects, for example). For the governor, such excessive manipulation surely entails considerable costs.[91]

In the limit, one can conceive of circumstances where the marginal cost of electoral manipulation to the party pursuing it is virtually zero. For example, in highly authoritarian states such as Syria, Iraq under Hussein, or the former Soviet Union, the repressive apparatus, already in place for reasons unrelated to elections, could guarantee near-perfect compliance from voters, or even allow the ruler to arbitrarily announce a result of his choosing. In the majority of electoral regimes historically and today, however, the expected cost of electoral manipulation to the party deciding to what extent to pursue it is likely to be substantial.

The Stakes of Office

When the stakes of holding office are sufficiently high, they could conceivably dwarf the costs and risks associated with excessive electoral manipulation. To assess the plausibility of this explanation, I conduct a back-of-the-envelope estimate based on the formal model. The main insight from this exercise is that the stakes would have to be unusually high to justify observed levels of excess in electoral manipulation.

The analysis here indicates that the optimal level of manipulation, and therefore the margin of victory, depends on the relationship between the cost of electoral manipulation and the stakes of office: holding everything else equal, higher stakes imply more manipulation, and a higher cost implies less manipulation. For any given margin of victory, it is possible to back out what the ratio of the cost parameter to the stakes of victory, κ/w, would need to be to motivate enough manipulation to yield such a margin. Let the cost be given by $c(x) = \kappa x^2$. The cost parameter κ can be interpreted as the expected cost of obtaining an amount of votes equivalent to the full size of the electorate

---

[91] From the viewpoint of the national government, in this example the excessive outcome is paid for at the subnational level (however, insofar as subnational governments rely on resources from the center, the cost of manipulation may be partly or fully borne by the center). See Chapter 4, and the case study of Russia in the next chapter for a discussion of subnational incentives to manipulate.

via electoral manipulation. Suppose that the candidates are equally popular ($\delta = 0$). Under simple assumptions,[92] it follows that a margin of victory of 10 percent implies a ratio $\kappa/w \cong 1/20$, which means that the hypothetical value of holding office would have to be 20 times greater than the cost of stealing an amount of votes equivalent to the full electorate, for a margin of 10 percent of the vote to result. In contrast, a margin of victory of 50 percent implies a ratio $\kappa/w \cong 0$, meaning that either the cost of stealing a full electorate's worth of votes is insignificant, or the value of holding office is extremely large in comparison with the cost of stealing a full electorate's worth of votes. As discussed previously, the cost of electoral manipulation is likely to be considerable. If so, a large margin of victory – say of 50 percent, to continue with the example – would require that the stakes of holding office be extremely high. One way to obtain a sense for the plausibility that the stakes of office-holding might be large enough to support excessive manipulation is to consider the monetary stakes that might be associated with office. Consider the most extreme case, that of Indonesia's Suharto. According to Transparency International, having pocketed about USD $35 billion, Suharto tops the list of ruler embezzlement in modern times (2004, 13). If this were the value of holding office, would it suffice to provide incentives to manipulate strong enough to yield a margin of victory of 50 percent? The estimate I have constructed suggests that, for this to be the case, the cost of obtaining *any amount* of votes via electoral manipulation (even as many as the size of the electorate) would have to be virtually zero. As discussed previously, this is generally unrealistic. Therefore, there would not seem to be any plausible monetary amount associated with office that could explain excessive manipulation in the scenario under consideration. It is still theoretically possible, however, for the non-monetary stakes of office to be high enough to account for excessive manipulation, but such stakes would have to be extremely high – for example, the possibility of lifetime jail or death on failing to win the election. Because losing an election seldom promises to yield such an outcome, this analysis suggests that the stakes of office could account for excessive manipulation only in exceptional circumstances.

Keeping the Machine Well Oiled

Could the explanation for excessive electoral manipulation be that ruling parties need to keep their machinery of electoral manipulation "well-oiled" – in other words, that they cheat even when they do not need it to win, with a view

---

[92] I assume that the uncertainty parameter ε follows a Normal distribution, to make it possible for the stakes of victory to matter enough (under the Uniform distribution, the stakes cannot matter in the region of zero probability mass). For the numerical exercise, I assume a standard deviation of 0.025, implying a plausible level of uncertainty (a 90% confidence interval for the level of support of the incumbent is about 8% wide). The first-order condition, expressed in terms of the optimal margin of victory, is $\kappa/w = f(-m^*/2)/m^*$.

to making sure that their manipulation machinery will exist in the future if and when they happen to need it? Perhaps the setting where this hypothesis (henceforth the "machine oiling" hypothesis) is most likely to have bite is in relation to urban political machines in the United States. American political machines are often perceived to have dominated politics in the cities where they operated. However, even successful machines generally faced stiff political competition and operated under severe resource constraints that made it impossible for them to obtain anything more than "city-wide electoral pluralities" and a "minimal winning coalition" (Erie 1998, 7–8 and 69). Menes (2006) finds, similarly, that "elections remained competitive, even in cities like Chicago, Boston, and New York with large and influential machines" and "[p]olitical bosses were regularly defeated" (85–86). Even Boss Tweed, in James Scott's estimation, had a "tenuous" hold on power (1969, 1149). In the 1886 New York mayoral election, for example, Tammany Hall "barely beat back the challenge of Henry George and the United Labor Party," even as "uncounted ballots ... were seen floating down the Hudson for days after the election" (Erie 1988, 11–12).[93] In sum, U.S. urban bosses may have indeed kept their machines well oiled, but, at least during the Progressive Era, they generally did so to meet the short-term threat of losing elections, not as a long-term precaution (as the machine oiling hypothesis would suggest).[94]

The machine oiling hypothesis is also unlikely to furnish an adequate explanation for excessive electoral manipulation more generally. For one thing, this hypothesis is predicated on the existence of some kind of "machinery" – a structure or asset with the specific function of manipulating elections, such as a network of vote brokers. But not all tactics of electoral manipulation necessitate a specialized, manipulation-specific, structure. The personnel and labor needed to stuff ballot boxes or to cast multiple votes, for example, could potentially be found elsewhere – among government employees, or temporary workers. Moreover, some tactics of electoral manipulation require the participation of only a relatively small number of individuals. Examples include tampering with voter registration lists and obstructing possibilities for candidates to register on the ballot.[95]

---

[93] Election fraud in the 1886 election mentioned in the text was mostly perpetrated by Tammany Hall, and therefore constitutes an example of marginal, one-sided manipulation – a pattern of manipulation also mentioned in Chapter 3 and in the discussion of Russia under Yeltsin in the next chapter.

[94] Machines during the Progressive Era generally conformed to this pattern. The rule appears to have been competitive elections, and electoral manipulation aimed at winning. However, after World War I some "truly dominant machines ... that ruled for decades without significant opposition" developed, such as the Chicago machine under Daley (Menes 2006, 86).

[95] Even in cases where there is a specialized, manipulation-specific apparatus, such as a network of vote brokers, it is not clear why these could not be paid off without activating the machine. If they could be thus paid off, then oiling the machine would not be synonymous with manipulating elections.

Additionally, in the absence of indirect effects, only a party that could potentially lose clean elections in the foreseeable future would have the need to invest
in keeping a manipulation machine well oiled. Many examples can be cited,
however, of popular ruling parties safely entrenched in office, which nevertheless manipulate elections excessively. As documented in the next chapter, for
example, Russia's Vladimir Putin has manipulated elections excessively from
the moment of his ascent to power, despite remarkably high levels of popularity
that would have assured him and his team electoral victory without manipulating. Mexico's PRI, also, manipulated elections excessively in the 1950s, 60s,
and 70s, a period during which the notion of its losing an election, even a clean
one, was unimaginable.[96] In sum, while it is possible that the need to keep a
manipulation machine well oiled could give rise to excessive manipulation in
specific cases, the machine oiling hypothesis would not appear to constitute
a convincing general explanation for the phenomenon of excessive electoral
manipulation.

[96] The case of Mexico is discussed in Chapters 4 and 7.

6

The Theory at Work

Evidence from Case Studies

This chapter and the next are devoted to assessing some of my theory's main empirical implications in light of quantitative and qualitative evidence from a variety of sources. This chapter contains two in-depth case studies of the experiences of post-Soviet Russia in the 1991–2008 period and of Zimbabwe in the 1980–2008 period. These case studies accomplish the following tasks. First, they document the fact that electoral manipulation in Putin's Russia and in Mugabe's Zimbabwe (before 2000) was utilized far beyond the point to which it might reasonably have contributed to electoral victory, and it was perpetrated quite publicly. Second, the cases show that such excessive and blatant electoral manipulation was perpetrated in pursuit of its indirect effects, that is, with the aim of influencing the behavior of voters, regional bosses, organizations, party leaders and other political elites, and their financial backers, in ways that enhanced the manipulating party's power and discretion while in office, as well as its ability to subsequently retain office. In the case of Zimbabwe, this rationale for manipulating excessively and blatantly was explicitly articulated by Mugabe. Third, the cases show how largely-exogenous variation in background conditions – specifically, in the power and discretion of ruling parties – gave rise to variation in patterns of manipulation as predicted by my theory, and that this relationship between background conditions and patterns of manipulation unfolded in similar ways in countries as different as Russia and Zimbabwe. Fourth, the cases illustrate the link between the pattern of manipulation and the behavior of a variety of social and political actors. Consistent with theory presented earlier in the book, marginal manipulation under Yeltsin reinforced the perception that Yeltsin's hold on power was tenuous, contributing to elicit substantial political challenges, while excessive manipulation under Putin conveyed strength and, in consequence, helped to align actors' behavior in ways that benefited Putin's team.[1] Finally, the case studies make it possible to assess some alternative explanations for excessive manipulation, supplementing discussions of alternative explanations provided earlier in the book (e.g., in Section 5.4).

In the next chapter, I present quantitative empirical evidence bearing on my theory. The first two analyses focus on voters. Using survey data for elections in fifty-six countries, I study the relationship between perceptions about the quality of elections and the propensity of individual citizens to cast votes. The analysis supports two empirical implications of the theory. First, a citizen who believes that elections are manipulated is less likely to cast a vote. Second, this effect is stronger for opposition supporters. In the second quantitative analysis in the next chapter, I study the same issue – the indirect effects of electoral manipulation on voter participation – on the basis of aggregate data from Mexico. I exploit the fact that Mexico undertook major electoral reforms in the 1990s to estimate such effects. Before the reforms, Mexican states varied in the extent of electoral manipulation; after the reforms, national elections became uniformly clean in all states. I find that voter participation rates in pre-reform Mexico were depressed by the practice of excessive and blatant electoral manipulation, consistent with the survey findings and with the proposition that such manipulation was pursued by the PRI for its indirect effects. The last piece of empirical analysis in the next chapter takes up one of the most general empirical implications of my theory, namely the effect of excessive electoral manipulation on duration in office. I have argued that excessive electoral manipulation potentially yields two categories of benefits: it increases the freedom to act while in office, and it enhances possibilities for subsequently retaining office. I test the "reduced-form" prediction that excessive electoral manipulation increases duration in office through a statistical analysis based on my original dataset. I find strong support for that prediction.

6.2 ELECTORAL MANIPULATION IN RUSSIA AND ZIMBABWE: CASE STUDY EVIDENCE

In what follows, I present detailed case studies of post-Soviet Russia (1990–2008) and Zimbabwe (1980–2008), with attention to those aspects of the cases that can speak to the theory advanced in this book. At the core of the analysis is the question of what drives variation in patterns of electoral manipulation, with a focus on the underpinnings of its excessive and blatant incarnation.

---

[1] Recall, for example, that in the separating equilibrium to the costly signaling model discussed in Chapter 4, excessive electoral manipulation by the ruler elicits actor compliance, while the failure to manipulate excessively elicits a challenge. Similarly, in the pooling equilibrium, manipulation on the path of play is always excessive, while off the path of play the failure to manipulate excessively would elicit a challenge.

There are three general ways in which the case studies advance this goal. On the most basic level, they provide "proof of concept" – that is, they document specific instances of excessive electoral manipulation and the associated indirect effects. Second, they furnish evidence for the causal mechanisms described in the theory. For one thing, excessive/blatant manipulation is found to be associated with indirect effects, while marginal manipulation is not. In addition, the cases demonstrate that the background conditions that I have described as proximate drivers of incentives to manipulate – the power, resources, and discretion of the ruling party, loosely speaking – correlate with patterns of electoral manipulation, as hypothesized. To give these associations – that is, between background conditions and patterns of manipulation, and between patterns of manipulation and indirect effects – a causal interpretation, I utilize longitudinal variation in background conditions within each of the cases to approximate counterfactual scenarios. Such variation is present in both Russia and Zimbabwe, and it provides some causal leverage. Third, I use the case study evidence – in particular the Russian case – to assess alternative explanations for excessive/blatant manipulation, as a nuts-and-bolts empirical addendum to the general discussion of alternative explanations in the preceding chapter.

Like any empirical analysis, qualitative or quantitative, the case study approach has strengths and weaknesses. Without revisiting ongoing methodological discussions, I emphasize that an important strength of qualitative analysis is that it permits a richness of detail and specificity that, in practice, quantitative work is generally unable to match. It is in part for this reason, that the use of case studies to assess causal theories has a long pedigree in comparative politics, political economy, and other social science disciplines.[2]

The cases are chosen to represent some variation in the relevant background conditions – those conditions that I have described as proximate determinants of incentives to manipulate: both Russia and Zimbabwe exhibit longitudinal variation in the degree to which the ruling party concentrates resources and power, both relative to other actors and in absolute terms.[3] In Zimbabwe, a period of high concentration of power and resources comes first, and later gives way to a period where a strong rival to the ruling party emerges. In post-Soviet Russia, resources and power are initially more dispersed, but subsequently – under Putin – they come under the control of the ruling party (the transition point in both cases is at the end of the 1990s). In both cases, the

---

[2] On the use of qualitative evidence in political science see King et al. (1994), Brady and Collier (2004), George and Bennett (2004), Lieberman (2005), Beck (2006), Mahoney and Goertz (2006), and Slater and Simmons (2010), among many others. Of course, any kind of evidence – including that produced via randomized experiments – has limitations. In my view, what ultimately matters is whether the evidence changes one's understanding about how the world works. As Rodrik put it: "the real test of any piece of research is the Bayesian one: does the finding change our priors on the issue of interest?" (2009, 27); see also Weil (2009, 123–124).

[3] On the selection of cases, see King, Keohane and Verba (1994, especially 137–138) and George and Bennett (2004).

relevant variation is observed in recent decades, which greatly increases the availability of information.[4] In terms of classical research design approaches, the within-country comparison can be understood as a "most similar case" design. In comparing Yeltsin's Russia with Putin's Russia, for example, a range of country-specific variables are held roughly constant, while theoretically relevant causal variables (e.g., the distribution of power and resources) change.[5] The cases represent some geographic and institutional variation, which has the advantage of showing that the central ideas of the book are not specific to any particular time, place, "culture," or set of formal institutions – for example, Zimbabwe was a parliamentary system for a few years of the period studied here, and presidential thereafter. Neither case played a role in the generation of the theory. I construct the case studies on the basis of scholarly sources, supplemented with various original interviews with country experts and with some quantitative data.

I note that, while the cases exhibit some variation in terms of the proximate determinants of incentives to manipulate, they do not represent the full range of empirical or theoretical variation: for example, they do not cover the scenario where a strong rule of law constrains government action, or one where two parties are evenly matched in their capacities to manipulate.[6] Instead, the case studies emphasize the range of the variance in background conditions that has received less attention in the study of electoral manipulation.[7]

6.3 POST-SOVIET RUSSIA

After the fall of the Soviet Union, Russia adopted a multiparty presidential electoral system.[8] It held its first presidential election in 1991. Subsequently, presidential elections were held in 1996, 2000, 2004, and 2008; and legislative elections were held in 1993, 1995, 1999, 2003, and 2007. The lower house

---

[4] In Latin America, for example, conditions favorable for excessive/blatant manipulation have become rare in recent decades. Two Latin American cases that exhibited such conditions in the second half of the twentieth century include Stroessner's Paraguay and Mexico under the PRI.

[5] The "most similar case" design is closely related to Mill's "method of difference." Of course, as the sole basis for inference, the strict application of this method has well-known limitations; therefore, the cases that follow pay heed not only to the presence or absence of conditions (as Mill's method would require) but also to the causal mechanisms at work (see George and Bennett 2004, chapter 8).

[6] In both Yeltsin's Russia and Zimbabwe after 2000, the ruling party faced important electoral challenges, but in both cases the ruling party retained considerable advantages exceeding the "incumbency advantage" observed in today's liberal democracies.

[7] For a discussion of the literature on electoral authoritarian and competitive authoritarian regimes, see Chapters 1 and 5.

[8] Some authors called Russia's electoral system prior to 1993 a "semi-presidential" one, but after the 1993 referendum, the constitution strengthened the powers of the president. Some scholars trace the beginning of political openness to 1988, when both independent candidates and regime-sponsored candidates were allowed to run for office.

of parliament, or State Duma, consists of 450 legislators. The upper house, or Federation Council, consists of two representatives from each of Russia's eighty-three administrative regions (the methods of selection for both houses have changed over time).[9] Unless specified otherwise, by "the legislature" I refer to the State Duma.

Most post-Soviet Russian elections have exhibited substantial levels of electoral manipulation, as I document in the discussion that follows. Although it is lamentable, it is perhaps not surprising that this was the case in the 1990s, because the incumbent Boris Yeltsin was – with the exception of an early "honeymoon" period in 1991–1992 – quite unpopular, and therefore in need of all the electoral manipulation that he could muster to merely hold on to office.[10] Yeltsin resigned in 1999, after which Vladimir Putin became acting president, and was subsequently elected president in 2000. In contrast with Yeltsin, Putin has maintained consistently very high approval ratings since he took office. However, all elections under Putin, and under his associate and successor to the presidency Dmitry Medvedev, have been very heavily manipulated – even more heavily, in all likelihood, than under Yeltsin. This observation is certainly at odds with conventional intuitions about the motivations underpinning electoral manipulation, according to which Putin's popularity should have obviated the need for manipulation – and most certainly for manipulation on a scale larger even than in the Yeltsin period.[11] The electoral history of post-Soviet Russia, thus, presents the puzzle of excessive and blatant manipulation – of what drives its use – quite starkly.

In what follows, I provide evidence that Putin's Kremlin has manipulated excessively and blatantly because it has stood to gain from doing so, even knowing that victory was secure. The payoff from such manipulation has been a variety of *indirect benefits* (i.e., "indirect effects" that benefit the Kremlin) along the lines described in previous chapters. By showing that they can win any election handily, Putin and his associates have established themselves as "the only game in town." This, in turn, has shaped the political behavior of political parties, their financial backers, politicians in the ruling party and in the opposition, regional executives, bureaucrats, and voters, in ways that have strengthened the Kremlin's hold on power even further, by increasing their

---

[9] The Russian Federation as of 2008 encompasses eighty-three federal subjects (before 2005, there were eighty-nine federal subjects), of which fifty-five are Oblasts or Krais (i.e., "provinces" or "territories"), twenty-one are Republics, and the remaining seven fall in other special categories. Republics have nominal autonomy and have presidents; Oblasts and Krais have governors; and both have local legislatures. Some Republics, such as Bashkortostan, Dagestan, and Tatarstan, have relatively large populations. The next smallest administrative unit is the rayon, or district. As of 2004, there were 2,756 rayons (Myagkov et al. 2005, 92, fn.2).

[10] For presidential approval data see Treisman 2009.

[11] For a description of the "prevailing wisdom" see Chapters 1 and 3; for a discussion of the relationship between single-party elections, such as Soviet elections, and this book's theory see Chapter 1.

subsequent discretion, bargaining power with respect to other political and social actors, and ability to win and to manipulate future elections.[12]

The case of post-Soviet Russia is of special interest for a number of reasons. First, the period since Vladimir Putin became president in 2000 exemplifies the excessive and blatant use of electoral manipulation. Second, the contrast between the Yeltsin years (1991–1999) and the "Putin years" (1999-present) provides a source of theoretically relevant within-case variation: the degree of concentration of power and resources in the hands of the government was quite different in these two periods. Third, a wealth of information is available. Fourth, the Russian case played no role in the generation of the theory, and therefore it is valuable as evidence either supportive or inconsistent with the theoretical ideas I have presented earlier in this book. Finally, because of Russia's geo-political importance, Russian elections and their manipulation are of interest in their own right.

The case study is organized as follows. First, I describe the relevant *background conditions*, contrasting the Yeltsin period, when power was relatively dispersed, with the Putin period, during which power was re-concentrated in the hands of the government. I then explore the *patterns of electoral manipulation* under each of these sets of background conditions, showing that, while Yeltsin needed electoral manipulation to stay in power and Putin (and his associates) did not, nevertheless electoral manipulation in the Putin years was greater in extent than in the Yeltsin years. To explain this paradox, I explore some of the *indirect effects* of excessive electoral manipulation under Putin – on the behavior of politicians, that of their financial backers, the fate of political parties, and voter participation – and draw a contrast with the behavior of comparable actors under Yeltsin. Finally, I consider a variety of alternative explanations for excessive manipulation under Putin. Overall, the electoral experience of post-Soviet Russia strongly supports the theoretical account of electoral manipulation developed in previous chapters.

The Distribution of Power and Resources in Post-Soviet Russia

Under Yeltsin, the resources that could be brought to bear to win elections were relatively dispersed among competing groups. There existed various independent bases of power and resources among elites, including businessmen, politicians, and regional governors. For one thing, the center was unable to discipline the regions. Because of the perceived threat of secession, the center did not believe itself to be in a strong bargaining position. As Stoner-Weiss documents, there was widespread non-compliance by *regional executives* with federal law – for example, tax receipts were often not passed on to the central government (2006, 60–63). Second, a small number of *business elites* – the

---

[12] For a conceptual discussion of the dynamic relationship between the distribution of power and electoral manipulation see Chapter 5 (especially Section 5.3).

so-called oligarchs – had become extremely influential. According to one account, by the mid-1990s a mere seven oligarchs controlled half of the Russian economy and 80 percent of national TV (Freeland et al. 1997, 17; Sakwa 2009, 54). Many oligarchs had political ambitions of their own and were able to leverage their wealth into political power – some of them became legislators (which granted them immunity from prosecution), others ran as presidential candidates in 1991 and 1996. Many utilized the media for political purposes (Kryshtanovskaya and White 2005, 298–299).

This is not to say that Yeltsin's government did not enjoy any incumbency-related advantages when it came to elections – for example, Yeltsin was able to divert state money for partisan purposes. The "rule of law," both in general and specifically in the realm of elections, has been quite weak in Russia since the Yeltsin years and through today. An activist for the opposition in the 2000 election said, for example, that "for [the Republic of] Tatarstan, the definition of a court is: Something that takes a lot of energy but provides a very equivocal result," to explain why complaining about electoral fraud is futile (Borisova 2000a). Moreover, post-Soviet Russia consistently enjoyed a large degree of insulation from international pressures for clean elections. Foreign powers have been reluctant to lean against Russia on electoral matters because of Russia's oil and gas – as Myagkov et al. (2009) put it, "Gazprom's vote counts more heavily in international affairs than does that of the Russian electorate" (135).[13] Nevertheless, it is beyond question that politically relevant resources, power, and support were relatively dispersed in the Yeltsin period, both in comparison to Soviet times and in comparison to what was to come under Putin, in the sense that – in the Yeltsin period – there existed more than one center of real power and wealth.

A key difference between the Yeltsin and the Putin/Medvedev periods is the dramatic re-concentration of power and resources in the hands of the Kremlin that took place in the latter period. The important rise in the prices of oil and gas provided Putin and his government with very substantial resources just as he first acceded to the presidency. Oil prices more than doubled between 1998 ($12/barrel) and 2000 ($27/barrel), and eventually reached $90 in 2007.[14] As the second-largest oil producer and largest producer of natural gas in the world, Russia benefitted handsomely from this price increase. Between 1999 and 2007, GDP growth averaged 7 percent per year, and total GDP increased from $200 billion in 1999 to $1.26 trillion in 2007 (constant USD).[15] Riding on such favorable conditions, Putin moved quickly to enhance his control

---

[13] Levitsky and Way argue that "larger countries with substantial military and/or economic power (e.g., China and Russia)...have the bargaining power to prevent pressure from being applied...by Western powers" (2010, chapter 2, loc. 1750).

[14] All figures in this paragraph refer to USD and are from Rutland (2008) and Merlevede, Schoors, and Van Aarle (2009).

[15] On the Kremlin's participation in oil production see Aslund (2004) and McFaul and Stoner-Weiss (2008).

and rein in political competition. Scarcely two months after the 2000 election, which elected him as president, Putin's team implemented reforms to curtail the independence of the regional governors, culminating in the elimination of their direct election in 2004 (Kryshtanovskaya and White 2009, 286–287). Second, with respect to the oligarchs, beginning in 2000 the Kremlin established an informal principle of "non interference," meaning the oligarchs who refrained from getting involved in opposition politics would be left alone, but those who strayed from this principle would face serious consequences.[16] The activities of nongovernmental organizations were also severely curtailed. Moreover, Putin set out to create a comprehensive political organization under the name of United Russia, a mass party that would encompass broad sectors of the elite and the public (Gel'man 2008). Finally, the Kremlin took steps to assert control over the mass media (McFaul and Stoner-Weiss 2008).[17]

In sum, the oil and gas windfall, together with Putin's connections with the security bureaucracy, gave Putin an initial edge, which he swiftly leveraged to consolidate the Kremlin's power. The concentration of power and resources in the hands of the state quickly became – and until today has remained – considerably greater under Putin than under Yeltsin. In what follows, I describe how this initial edge increased the possibilities and the incentives for Putin and his team to manipulate elections excessively and blatantly. In turn, such manipulation threw the Kremlin's opponents into disarray, further enhancing the Kremlin's power, and enabled further legal and institutional changes that subsequently cemented the Kremlin's dominance, as well as the possibilities and the incentives to continue to manipulate elections excessively and blatantly.

"From Russia with Fraud"[18]

This subsection discusses electoral manipulation in Russian elections. I focus on the Putin period first, and return to the Yeltsin years later in the case study. At

---

[16] For example, Vladimir Gusinsky, owner of the relatively independent television station NTV, was jailed after his channel criticized the government. He subsequently was freed, fled the country, and sold his media empire to the state-controlled energy company Gazprom. Another oligarch, Boris Berezovsky, moved to England and gave up his seat in the Duma, and was subsequently charged with fraud by the state. He also lost control of an important television channel which aired criticism of Putin's government. Mikhail Khodorkovsky, who controlled the energy giant Yukos, was overtly seeking political influence and, after various warnings, he was arrested in 2003 on charges of fraud and tax evasion and sentenced to jail in 2005, where he has remained since. Various other oligarchs were harassed and pressured to divest from their businesses, and left Russia (see Kryshtanovskaya and White 2009, 288–289; Sakwa 2009).

[17] On freedom of the media in Russia see also Gehlbach and Sonin (2009) and Gehlbach (2010). On the relationship between oil wealth and media freedom, see Egorov, Guriev, and Sonin (2009).

[18] Taken from the headline of the April 20, 2008 article by Luke Harding in *The Guardian*. An alternative title for this subsection is: "Electoral Manipulation in Russian Elections."

least since 2004, there has been scarcely a doubt as to who would win Russian presidential and legislative elections. Nevertheless, all national elections since Putin won the presidency have been very substantially manipulated. According to the available evidence, and to virtually all scholars and pundits, Putin, his associates, and his party – United Russia – have been clear favorites in every national election. Rose writes, for example, that "the personal popularity of Vladimir Putin has been doubly outstanding; not only is it high on average but it also has been consistently high" (2007, 102). Treisman, citing figures from what is perhaps the most reputable Russian polling agency reports that "in his eight years as president, his [Vladimir Putin's presidential approval] rating rose as high as 87 percent and never fell below 60 percent" (2009, 2).[19] Both with respect to average level and to range of variation, Putin's popularity compares favorably not only to Yeltsin's but to that of many leaders of established democracies such as the United States and England.

Putin's popularity has naturally translated into considerable electoral advantage. Regarding the 2004 presidential election, for example, Myagkov, Ordeshook, and Shakin write that "Putin surely would have easily won the 2004 vote without fraud" (2009, 178). Similarly, Brzezinski's view regarding the 2007 legislative election is that "Putin could have in all probability prevailed even in a truly contested electoral process" (2008, 104).[20] The consensus regarding the 2008 presidential election, which brought Putin's candidate Dmitry Medvedev to the presidency, and the 2009 regional election, also seems to be that Putin's team would have easily won both without resorting to electoral manipulation. Before the 2008 election, for example, Medvedev was polling at "up to 82% of the vote" (BBC 2008), and Putin's approval was close to an all-time high.[21] Even in the 2000 presidential election, when Putin was first elected president, according to Steven Fish "Putin did not need fraud to win," and "he probably would have beaten Zyuganov in the second round had the event taken place – even had it been a squeaky clean affair" (Fish 2005, 53). Public opinion polls from January and February of 2000 (i.e., before the election) estimated Putin's level of support at 60 percent, and that of Zyuganov at 15 percent.[22] Even Communist Party members who denounced the first (and only) round of the 2000 election as fraudulent "freely conceded that Putin would have easily won in a second round anyway" (Borisova 2000a).

---

[19] Because of the high degree of control of the media by the state, it is natural to question the reliability of the polling data. Treisman's data come from a reputable polling organization, the Russian Center for Public Opinion Research or VCIOM. In 2003, the head of VCIOM, Yuri Levada, was dismissed, presumably because of his lack of subservience to the regime, and set up the private Levada Center to continue its polling work.

[20] He calls the fact that the Kremlin engaged in extensive electoral manipulation "the ultimate irony."

[21] Based on Treisman 2009, Figure 1.

[22] ROMIR, VCIOM Surveys, and New Russia Barometer VIII, cited in Hesli and Reisinger 2003, 5.

Despite Putin's, Medvedev's, and United Russia's remarkable popularity, there exists considerable evidence that every presidential and legislative election under their tenure was massively manipulated, and that the manipulation has increased over time. How do we know that such manipulation took place? Multiple sources of information point to it. First, there is anecdotal evidence produced by international election monitors, local NGOs, and from individuals who witnessed it themselves and reported it to the media, to political parties, or to the courts. There is some investigative reporting on the matter, published in Russian newspapers and blogs. In September 2000, Yevgenia Borisova published a remarkable three-part article in the English-language daily *The Moscow Times*, based on a six-month-long investigation, documenting electoral manipulation in the March 2000 presidential election. Borisova and her associates report a large number of serious anomalies and outright manipulations of the vote. For example, a police officer guarding the entrance to a government building in Dagestan saw government officers stealing bags full of votes for the opposition candidate Zyuganov and destroying them. Other interviewees reported witnessing various modalities of ballot box stuffing, as well as extensive bullying of citizens to vote for Putin. And, inexplicably, between December 1999 and March 2000, the voter registry increased by 1.3 million people. Demographers and government officials were unable to come up with a compelling explanation for the increase. Because Russian citizens are automatically registered by the government upon turning 18, therefore the sudden increase in the registry could not be explained by rates of registration. The then-head of the Central Electoral Commission (CEC), Alexander Veshnyakov, said that around 550,000 Russians turned 18 between December 1999 and March 2000, a claim that flies in the face of demographic data, which show that the Russian population actually shrank in 1999 by more than 800,000 people. One specialist in Russian demography said he was "very confused by these data"; a second specialist suggested that "perhaps this boom [of 1.3 million people] is just made up" (Borisova 2000d). The most likely explanation is that the 1.3 million new voters are fictional, or "dead souls."

In some instances, the perpetrators themselves, or their associates, plainly admit to their role in the manipulation (knowing they can do so with impunity). For example, after the 1999 legislative election, Irek Murtazin, the spokesman to the President of Tatarstan, confirmed when interviewed "that he had been given 50 rubles for stuffing a ballot" (although he added that he cheated the cheaters by stuffing a ballot for a parallel regional election instead of one for the national election) (Borisova 2000b). Vladimir Shevchuk, who headed the Press Center during Tatarstan's 2000 election, not only admitted that a special system of ballot box stuffing called "the caterpillar" had been used – he also explained how it works:

"There are people standing near the elections precincts and when they see a voter coming up, they offer him or her 50 rubles or a 100 rubles so that he or she takes a pre-filled-in ballot to drop in the box, and then returns with a blank ballot," Shevchuk said. "Then [the fraudsters] fill in the new clean ballot and offer it to the next voter."

(Borisova 2000b)

International electoral observers have also reported widespread manipulation of the 2000 election (despite the fact that they were reluctant to condemn the election as a whole).[23] They were more overtly critical of the 2004 election, of which they said that "the process overall did not adequately reflect principles necessary for a healthy democratic election" (OSCE/ODIHR 2004, 1). In 2007, OSCE international monitors were not issued visas and therefore were not able to observe the election.[24] The elections, however, were observed by a delegation from the Parliamentary Assembly of the Council of Europe. The head of that delegation, Luc van den Brande, said that "we can't say these were fair elections" (Fox News, December 3, 2007).

A second kind of evidence about electoral manipulation comes from the quantitative analysis of official election results. A variety of graphical and statistical methods have been used to identify anomalies. Collectively, such procedures have come to be known as "election forensics." It is important to note, as most practitioners of such analyses do, that while the anomalies uncovered via election forensics can suggest the possibility that electoral manipulation took place, such analyses do not by themselves suffice to *prove* such manipulation. Coupled with evidence from reporters and observers, however, forensic analysis can contribute importantly to the formation of a compelling picture about electoral manipulation.

Myagkov, Ordeshook, and Shakin (2009) conduct a thorough forensic analysis of post-Soviet Russian elections. They utilize a variety of graphical and statistical indicators, as well as case-specific knowledge, to uncover evidence of electoral malfeasance in Russia, focusing on national elections between 1995 and 2007. Independently, Sergey Shpilkin, a Russian physicist, analyzes the official electoral returns of the Russian elections of 2008 and thereafter.[25] Mebane and Kalinin (2009) utilize precinct-level data and nonparametric methods to conduct a variety of forensic analyses on the elections of 2003, 2004, 2007, and 2008. Fish (2005, Ch.3) reproduces interesting data-based evidence on electoral manipulation from a number of sources in elections up until 2004. Broadly speaking, these analyses shed light on three features of the data. First, they point to anomalies in the distribution of turnout. An unusually high level of turnout in a region known for its tradition of dirty elections could indicate

---

[23] For a critique of the OSCE's evaluation of the 2000 election see Borisova (2000a, 2000b, and 2000c) and Fish (2005).

[24] This was denied by the head of the Central Electoral Commission Vladimir Churov (Spiegel November 16, 2007).

[25] Author's interview; see also Abdullaev, April 14, 2008, *The Moscow Times*, reproduced in Levitt, April 16, 2008, *The New York Times*; and Harding, April 20, 2008, *The Guardian*, "From Russia with Fraud."

tampering of various forms – ballot box stuffing, the padding of voter lists with "dead souls," vote buying or intimidation, and outright falsification of the results. Second, they can find suspicious patterns in the relationship between turnout, on the one hand, and the proportion of the vote received by the various candidates or parties, on the other. Suppose that some precincts record above average turnout. If it can be shown that in those precincts, the "extra" votes mostly favor a specific party or candidate, that suggests that the vote was artificially manipulated in favor of that party or candidate (again, through a potentially wide array of methods).[26] Third, Myagkov et al. (2009) study something that they call the "flow of votes." This kind of analysis tries to ascertain the origin of votes for each party or candidate, by comparing how the electorate voted in a prior election with the way they voted in the election being analyzed. The finding, for example, that roughly 7 million votes for Putin in 2004 originated from people who did not vote in the 2003 election (after adjusting for the differences in turnout between parliamentary and presidential elections), points to large-scale electoral manipulation.[27]

To provide a flavor for the kind of data that form the basis for forensic analyses, consider the official electoral data for the 2004 presidential election for a single district in Tatarstan, the Nurlatinskii district, reproduced in Myagkov et al. (2009, 81, table 3.3). In every one of the forty-four polling stations in the district, both turnout and the proportion of the vote for Putin were greater than 95 percent. In fully one-half of all polling stations, turnout was 100 percent and Putin's vote was 100 percent. Perhaps even more striking are the numbers for Chechnya. Despite the high level of violent confrontation with, and contempt for, Putin's government in that region, in the 2007 legislative election, 99.4 percent of the vote in Chechnya went to Putin's party United Russia, and average turnout was 99.2 percent.[28] Electoral outcomes of this sort are very difficult to explain other than as instances of manipulation.

More systematically, forensic analysis of the distribution of turnout across electoral districts (*rayons*) in Russia shows "bumps" that indicate anomalously high turnout. The idea behind this analysis is that, in a clean election, districts with exceptionally high or low turnout should be less common than districts with middling turnout levels, and therefore the distribution of turnout across districts should be bell-shaped. Deviations from this pattern could indicate electoral manipulation. For example, if there is a subset of districts where

[26] See Shpilkin (2009). For forensic analyses of recent Russian elections see Kobak, Shpilkin, and Pshenichnikov (2012); Enikopolov et al (forthcoming).

[27] Mebane and Kalinin (2009) conduct a fourth kind of analysis, based on the "second-digit Benford's Law." That analysis looks for discrepancies between the theoretically predicted distribution of second digits in precinct vote totals, and their empirical distribution.

[28] As Myagkov et al. write, "of the 580,000 registered voters in Chechnya, only 3,000 are reported to have failed to find their way down winding mountain paths and bomb craters to their polling stations – fewer than the number of people reported 'missing' under the brutal regime of the republic's autocratic president, Ramzan Kadyrov" (2009, 125).

ballot stuffing takes place, this would create a "bump" in the right tail of the distribution.[29] In all post-Soviet elections since 1995, such bumps are large, and they are observed precisely in the regions of Russia where one would expect manipulation to be most likely – Russian Republics (often ruled by powerful bosses). Anomalously high turnout bumps are clearly identifiable in the data since the Yeltsin period, indicating substantial manipulation as early as 1995 and 1996, but the bumps have become increasingly pronounced in later elections, since Putin took power, suggesting that the extent of manipulation has increased considerably (Myagkov et al. 2009, 82–89; see also Mebane and Kalinin 2009, figures 1 and 2).

Bumps in the distribution of turnout across districts suggest malfeasance, but they do not say which party might have benefitted. One way to get at this question is to explore the relationship across districts between turnout, on the one hand, and the proportion of the vote going to the different parties, on the other. The idea behind this analysis is that, in the absence of manipulation, one would expect that the proportion of the vote going to each of the parties should not vary much with turnout: if Party X overall received, say, 35 percent of the vote, Party X's percentage in each district should hover around 35 percent, and there is no obvious reason why Party X's percentage of the vote should vary systematically with the level of turnout in a district. Therefore, if we observe that in districts that record especially high turnout it is also the case that Party X obtains, say, 90 percent of the vote, that provides grounds for suspicion: it suggests that "extra" votes were added on behalf of Party X in those districts, increasing both the proportion of the vote going to Party X and the level of turnout, as in the case of the Nurlatinskii district described earlier.

Using this kind of analysis – plotting the proportion of the vote obtained by each candidate versus the level of turnout, with the precinct or the district as the unit of data, or regressing the former on the latter – Myagkov et al. find that, in many Russian regions, there is evidence that one or another of the candidates on the ballot was *disproportionately advantaged by high levels of turnout*, suggesting that the "extra" votes that yielded the higher recorded turnout were obtained via manipulation. In 1996, either the incumbent or the Communist Party candidate was disproportionately advantaged in sixty out of the eighty-nine regions of Russia; in 2000 that was true in sixty-four regions; and in 2004 in sixty-two regions. This analysis is able to distinguish, of course, *which* of the candidates or parties were advantaged. In 1996 (first round of voting), Yeltsin, the incumbent, was advantaged in this manner in nineteen regions, while his Communist Party opponent Zyuganov was advantaged in forty-one (that is,

---

[29] Bumps could be created by any form of electoral manipulation that increases the total number of votes – e.g., stuffing ballot boxes, bribing or pressuring citizens who would have abstained otherwise to cast a vote (what in Russia is often called "applying administrative resources"), adding "dead souls" to voter lists, and outright falsification of the vote tally by adding votes for one of the candidates.

they were advantaged in the sense that "extra" votes were primarily "cast" in their favor). This pattern suggests that Yeltsin and Zyuganov were engaged in vigorous electoral competition, with both sides engaging in substantial electoral manipulation. This pattern changed quickly under Putin. In 2000, Putin was disproportionately advantaged in fifty regions, and his Communist opponent in only fourteen; and in 2004, Putin was advantaged in fifty-one and his main challenger Haritonov in eleven. Moreover, restricting the analysis to regions where this kind of advantage was especially strong,[30] the results are even more striking: in 2004, Putin was thus advantaged in thirty-nine regions, Haritonov in *none* (Myagkov et al. 2009, 99, table 3.5). Similar analyses by Myagkov et al. (2009), Mebane and Kalinin (2009), and Shpilkin (2008, 2010) support these conclusions also for the 2007 and 2008 elections, as well as for the 2010 Moscow regional elections.

Using the third kind of technique, the analysis of the "flow of votes," Myagkov et al. (2009) find additional support for the finding that manipulation under Putin increased. They are also able to generate additional evidence that is strongly suggestive of electoral manipulation, and to estimate the number of votes obtained via manipulation. For the 2004 presidential election, they estimate that the amount of votes obtained via electoral manipulation was 9.4 million, equivalent to about 20 percent of the total vote obtained by Putin. This figure contains about 6 million votes that the "flow of votes" analysis attributes to people who had not voted in previous elections, over and above the expected increase in turnout in 2004 (with respect to 2003) due to the fact that it was a presidential election (Myagkov et al. 2009, 114–115). Their findings for the 2007 election are similarly impressive: they estimate that 20 to 25 percent of the vote obtained by Putin's party, United Russia, in the 2007 legislative election was the product of manipulation. Shpilkin estimates that about 35 percent of the votes for United Russia in the 2007 election, or about 14 million votes, may have been "added."[31] Concerning the 2008 presidential election, won by Putin's candidate Dmitry Medvedev, Myagkov et al. cite an assessment that about 10 million votes were obtained via manipulation (2009, 136–137). Using an entirely different approach – comparing the original count of the votes at the precinct level with the official count – the *Moscow Times* estimated the number of votes obtained through electoral manipulation in the 2000 election, in the republic of Dagestan only, could have exceeded 500,000 (Borisova 2000a).[32]

There is also some evidence that electoral manipulation is quite *blatant* – Wilson writes, for example, that "voters themselves are aware of the manipulation and of how it is achieved. . . . After the 1999 elections, . . . 29 percent

---

[30] Specifically, to regions where a 1% increase in turnout was associated with an increase in the vote beyond the normal share for one of the candidates of 0.25% or more.

[31] Personal interview, May 7, 2010, Moscow.

[32] Citing this figure, Myakgov et al. speculate that their estimates for the amount of manipulation in the 2004 election might be "too low" (2009, 115).

thought the administration and/or counting of votes was unfair" (Wilson 2005, 44). More generally, he observes that since Yeltsin's time, "the crude use of administrative resources (i.e., the more traditional abuses of the electoral process) has become much more obvious" (39). Fish reports that in a major 2002 survey, "two thirds of respondents said that they regarded elections as window dressing." Fish concludes that "an overwhelming majority of Russians consistently say that their country's elections are not honest or even determinative of who rules" (Fish 2005, 54). In sum, while it is not clear whether individual citizens knew the specific logistical details about how the vote was manipulated, these findings suggest that many citizens had information about the fact that elections *had* been manipulated.

Exactly by what method were elections manipulated? The available evidence indicates that there is no one dominant method of manipulation; a wide variety of methods are routinely used. These include the stuffing of ballot boxes with votes for a specific candidate (generally the incumbent), the physical destruction of ballots cast for opponents, the padding of voter registration lists with inexistent people, the alteration of protocols (the sheets indicating the vote totals at the precinct level, filled out at the end of election day), the falsification of results at higher levels of aggregation, the bribing and intimidation of voters and candidates, organized multiple voting by the same individuals (the so-called carousel), organizational pressure to vote in a particular way (e.g., in hospitals or military units), and the abuse of absentee voting, among others. Borisova reports, for example, that in the village of Permiyevo "the head of the collective farm told villagers that if they vote for Zyuganov, he would find out – and they would not get tractors for sowing, or wood, or food," scaring the villagers into voting for Putin, reported an interviewee. In Tatarsky Saplik, another village, an interviewee who wanted to vote for Zhirinovsky reported that the head of the village "took away my ballot and signed it for Putin." In Tatarstan, the "caterpillar," described previously, was widely used. Following up on an eyewitness account that votes for Zyuganov had been burned, the *Moscow Times* confirmed the presence of burned ballots at the reported site. There is also evidence of outright falsification of the vote totals in protocols. Borisova and her associates, for example, hunted down 245 of Dagestan's 1,550 precinct protocols for the 2000 election. They then compared these protocols with the totals reported by the territorial commissions (one level higher up the chain of vote tallying), and found that the vote total for Putin had been inflated by more than 87,000 votes. If the rate of falsification was the same in those precincts for which the original protocols were not available, then about 550,000 out of the roughly 880,000 votes for Putin in Dagestan could have been "manufactured" (Borisova 2000a, 2000b, 2000c; Fish 2005). This diversity of methods of manipulation of the vote is consistent with the view, expressed in Chapter 2, that the different techniques of electoral manipulation function as substitutes; that is, as different tools utilized for one same goal – to alter the vote totals. The precise choice of method will depend on the resources and capacities available to the perpetrator.

Motives for Electoral Manipulation in Russia

How might one understand the use of massive electoral manipulation in Russia in the Putin years, when victory would have been attained without it? Given the discrepancy between the "need" for electoral manipulation (according to the popularity of Putin and his associates) and the fact that copious amounts of votes were nevertheless obtained via manipulation, it would be difficult to attribute electoral manipulation to a concern about victory, which has been assured since Putin's election in 2000.[33] I have argued, instead, that excessive electoral manipulation is motivated by its indirect effects: such manipulation shapes expectations about who is likely to be in power tomorrow, and such expectations, in turn, influence the behavior of a wide range of political actors, including opposition parties, political elites, their financial backers, regional governors, and voters – especially those who sympathize with opposition. In Putin's Russia, the indirect effects of excessive electoral manipulation have included discouraging opposition supporters from turning up at the polls, deterring politicians inside and outside the ruling party from opposing the Kremlin, and persuading wealthy individuals to avoid supporting Putin's political opponents (or becoming political opponents themselves), among other things. Excessive and blatant manipulation has also contributed to re-shaping the party system, by providing strong incentives for politicians and political parties to work with, or join, United Russia, and strong disincentives to belong to or support opposition parties. An additional category of indirect effects accrues directly to regional governors: by manipulating excessively in their territory, they can seek to curry favor with their political superiors.[34] In what follows, I elaborate on these indirect effects.

The sector of the electorate who would support the opposition has been dispirited by the persistent use of excessive and blatant electoral manipulation. Clifford Levy (2009) writes that "the thinking seems to be that Mr. Putin is in charge and the opposition is feeble, so there is no point in trying to get your voice heard, no matter that the country faces serious problems." According to Andrei Gerasimov, a Moscow statistician whose analysis finds evidence of manipulation in the 2009 regional election, "people are passive because they feel that there is absolutely no opportunity to change the system" (cited in Levy 2009). In a discussion of Russia, Ukraine, and Belarus, Wilson argues that "disillusioned voters sell their support lightly and cheaply, without too much thought" (2005, 42–43). Elites, Wilson writes, "want the masses to remain

---

[33] This puzzle is perhaps most evident in presidential elections, where it is very clear that all that is needed to win is a majority of the votes. For a discussion of the nuances involved in establishing the equivalent threshold in legislative elections, see the Appendix to Chapter 4.

[34] Of course, insofar as their political superiors provide instructions about how and how much to manipulate, and resources with which to do so, this may not always be possible – it could simply not be feasible to do more than the central government has asked. I revisit this topic later in the case study.

demobilized" (2005, 48). In other words, excessive and blatant manipulation has had an effect on the *attitudes* of potential opposition *voters*, and thereby on their behavior. The underlying cause for such an effect is the perception that Putin and his associates are unassailable – a perception which in turn stems from the government's spectacular and relentless electoral victories, and from their widespread and blatant use of electoral manipulation to crush opposition.[35]

The issue, however, is not just one of psychology or attitude: often, there are tangible material goods at stake for potential voters. As Victor Sheinis, a respected social scientist and one of Yabloko's leaders, put it: "if some babushka comes to vote, and she is completely dependent on the administration chief for getting wood and fodder for her animals, she will of course vote the way he tells her to" (Borisova 2000b). Rinat Gabidullin, secretary of the Communist Party in Bashkortostan, claims that such pressure is widespread so that villagers as a class have been cut out of the electoral process (Borisova 2000b). In sum, for either material or psychological reasons, in post-Soviet Russia, the returns to voting or to voting in a particular way often depend jointly on the individual's choice (to abstain or to vote, and for which party or candidate) and on which party or candidate ends up in power. This corresponds to the logic behind the model of voter choice presented in Chapter 4.[36] Under Putin, citizens' expectations about who will be in power are quite clear, and they strongly influence voting behavior in ways that favor Putin and his government.

Clarity regarding the fact that Putin and his associates will be in power has influenced not only the behavior of voters, but also that of *political elites*. As Olga Shvetsova argues: "divided as they may be in their preferences over possible presidential candidates, elites first and foremost want to support the future winner, whoever he turns out to be" (2003, 217). Similarly, Myagkov et al. write that "elites have an incentive to back the winner" – and it is clear in Putin's Russia who the winner is (2009). Under the assumption that a sufficiently large number of elites, if coordinated, could defeat Putin's team, the decision problem of an individual member of the political elite resembles a coordination problem where focal signals play a key role, as in the voting model of Chapter 4. Putin's excessive and blatant use of electoral manipulation has provided such a focal signal across Russian society.

Myagkov (2003) argues that this kind of payoff structure (i.e., whereby elites will support the candidate they believe is likely to win) shapes the political choices of *regional governors*. He suggests that the Kremlin's endorsement

---

[35] Focusing on the regional level, Myagkov observes, along these lines, that "the governor's control over how other people vote might well be a *psychological* phenomenon" (2003, 137; emphasis added).

[36] The babushka's payoff structure, or "babushka's dilemma" (unrelated to the prisoner's dilemma) could be depicted as follows: vote for Zyuganov + Putin wins = no wood; vote for Putin + Putin wins = wood (other alternatives – i.e., those when Zyuganov wins – are assigned essentially zero probability).

of Unity, a political party, in the context of the 1999 legislative election moti-vated "almost all governors [to] work hard for Vladimir Putin" by utilizing the resources at their disposal to influence the popular vote in their regions on behalf of Unity (Myagkov 2003, 154–157). In support of this view, he finds that Unity's performance in the election was especially good in regions whose governors were *unaffiliated* with any political party (and, of course, in regions with Unity-affiliated governors). The political choices of other elites were sim-ilarly influenced by expectations about the likelihood that Putin would win. Grigory Yavlinsky, a liberal politician who had run for president in 1996 and 2000, decided not to do so in 2004 because he perceived that the result was preordained (von Salzen 2004).[37]

Excessive and blatant manipulation has also contributed to the weaken-ing of *opposition political parties*. In comparison with their counterparts in most established democracies, Russian political parties since the 1990s were weak – that is, they had limited influence both on electoral outcomes and on policy (McFaul 2001, 1160). Nevertheless, excessive and blatant manip-ulation led to progressively more resounding victories by the ruling clique, and, concomitantly, to a dwindling of opposition parties' hopes for winning elections or influencing policy. In turn, this reduced the incentives of opposi-tion politicians to stand firm as principled opposition, and instead encouraged exit or co-optation (Gel'man 2005). By reducing the likelihood, perceived and real, that opposition parties would become a "party in government," exces-sive and blatant manipulation contributed to dashing the prospects of Russian opposition parties and their members or would-be members. Primakov and Luzhkov, for example, once deemed to be the favorites to capture power after Yeltsin, withdrew from the presidential race after Fatherland–All-Russia's lack-luster performance in the considerably manipulated 1999 legislative elections (McFaul 2001, 1167).[38] Similarly, after their dismal result in the 2003 election (they failed to attain the 5 percent threshold needed for representation in the legislature) the Union of Right Forces (URF) – whose leadership was critical of Putin's policies – fell in internal disarray, and some of its talent fled the party. For example, Irina Khakamada, formerly a co-chair of the URF, launched an independent candidacy, and later sought to create her own party (Gel'man 2005, 40).

The story of Yabloko is similarly revealing. After its less than impressive electoral performance in the 2003 legislative elections, to which massive elec-toral manipulation by the Kremlin contributed, the party fell into disarray.

---

[37] Shvetsova provides a fascinating account of the coordination problem faced by governors as they sought to figure out which candidate other governors were likely to back in 1999–2000 (2003, 217–226). Her account is consistent with the coordination mechanism discussed in Chapter 4.

[38] The forensic analysis of Myagkov et al. (2009), the analysis of Fish (2005), and the findings of Borisova (2000a, 2000b, and 2000c) suggest that the 1999 election was heavily manipulated.

Yabloko boycotted the 2004 presidential election, and some of its prominent members were incorporated into the government – Vladimir Lukin, one of Yabloko's co-founders, became the ombudsman for human rights; and Igor Artemev became the head of the Federal Antitrust Services (Gel'man 2005, 43), regional activists and Duma deputies also left the party (Gel'man 2008, 926). Moreover, Yabloko lost major *financial sponsors*, discouraged by Putin's dominance (Gel'man 2008, 926).[39] The Communist Party has been remarkably resilient in spite of major electoral setbacks in the 2000s, retaining its leadership and policy positions. However, students of the Russian political system point to the danger that the marginalization of the Communist Party might provoke an "exit" strategy, leading to further marginalization (Gel'man 2008, 925).

Overall, the confidence, strength, and strategies of opposition parties seem to have suffered as a result of their diminished electoral prospects. Tanya Lokshina, deputy director of Human Rights Watch in Moscow, observes that, in response to Putin's dominance, opposition parties "have adopted an underground mentality, criticizing the government nonstop and not offering anything positive" (Knight 2010, 27), and this has had real consequences on their choices, leadership, and performance. The effect of Putin's dominance on the ruling party, in contrast, has been the opposite: since 2002, diverse political parties, including Fatherland, All-Russia, and Unity – have given up their individual identities to join the Kremlin's party, United Russia (Hesli 2003, 8–9).[40] Tellingly, the effective number of parties in the State Duma declined from 8.5 in 1994–1995 to 1.92 in 2007–2008 (Gel'man 2008, 914, table 1).[41]

Thus far, I have focused on indirect effects of excessive and blatant electoral manipulation from the viewpoint of the *central government*. I now consider a category of indirect effects that accrues to *regional governors*: by manipulating excessively, the presidents and governors of Russia's regions can secure "nice" electoral results for the Kremlin and thereby *curry favor with their political superiors* (or, equivalently, avoid "looking bad" by failing to obtain a good-enough result). This presumably creates incentives for regional executives to manipulate excessively of their own initiative, and not only when ordered

---

[39] Of course, not all of Yabloko's troubles can be ascribed to electoral manipulation by the Kremlin – Yabloko made tactical mistakes of its own, and the Kremlin acted in ways that weakened it, other than electoral manipulation (for example, the arrest of Khodoskovsky was a major blow to Yabloko) (Gel'man 2005, 239–240 and 2008, 926–927). However, voluntary defections from the party, and the party's choice to boycott elections were in all likelihood responses to perceptions that the Kremlin was invulnerable.

[40] To be sure, electoral manipulation was not the only tool that the Kremlin wielded to weaken opposition parties – institutional reforms, the creation of satellite parties, and the encouragement of opposition dissident factions were also utilized (Wilson 2005; Gel'man 2008). But electoral manipulation played a central role in manufacturing electoral results that would conform to the Kremlin's interests, and that would send the correct message of powerlessness and futility to the political community at large.

[41] This decline reflects the indirect effects of excessive and blatant electoral manipulation under Putin, alongside other factors.

from the center to do so. To be sure, regional executives play a key role in *implementing* excessive electoral manipulation. This has been pointed out by Borisova (2000a, 2000b, and 2000c), and Myagkov et al. (2009). However, it is an open question to what degree, when pursuing electoral manipulation, regional executives are following orders from the center or, alternatively, their own initiative. Borisova nicely captures the two sides of this still unresolved issue:

It is possible that all of this immense pressure to skew the vote was brought to bear on secret orders that could be traced back to the Kremlin itself. Certainly the artificial enthusiasm with which so many governors fawningly embraced Moscow Mayor Yury Luzhkov's Fatherland-All Russia vehicle – and then, when Luzhkov's star was fading, leapt to join Putin's Unity – suggests a willingness to curry favor with the new boss, whomever he may be.... There is, however, no way to prove direct Kremlin involvement. And some of those who have looked into the fraud came away convinced it was organized by individual governors or lower-tier regional officials on their own initiative.
(Borisova 2000b)

It is interesting to consider the potential effects of the rise of the Kremlin's power under Putin on this issue. Two effects, running in opposite directions, could be at work. On the one hand, as the Kremlin comes to control a greater "piece of the pie" (e.g., oil revenues, political power), incentives to curry its favor grow. On the other hand, the Kremlin has decisively reasserted control over regional executives, so that these are essentially beholden to the Kremlin and therefore quite likely to follow the Kremlin's orders. Now, if the Kremlin orders a regional boss to obtain a target percentage of the vote on its behalf in a national election, that boss could in principle still seek to curry favor with the Kremlin by manipulating beyond the target (and therefore contributing to excessive results at the national level). This is only possible, however, if the target set by the Kremlin is low enough – if the target is high, the regional executive may not even manage to meet it, much less to exceed it. There exist, in fact, cases where targets have not been met.

While this question is still an open one, there is good reason to believe that much of the responsibility for manipulation choices lies with the center – that is, with the government. For one thing, the Kremlin, because of Putin's efforts since 2000, now "wields a concentrated authority and keeps tight rein over regional cadres, which always defer to those at the top" (Levy, 2009). Moreover, as Wilson (2005) and Golosov (2006) document, the central government is quite hands-on when it comes to electoral strategy in general; it would be surprising, therefore, if this were not true specifically in regards to electoral manipulation. In fact, various analysts cite evidence supporting the notion that the central government is intimately involved in the electoral manipulations. First, Myagkov et al.'s analysis of election returns in Russian elections since 2004 strongly suggests that the geographical scope of the rigging has expanded under Putin beyond the few ethnic republics traditionally known for electoral manipulation, suggesting a well-organized and funded effort (2009, 100). Second, the government has consistently and explicitly thrown its weight behind the manipulators, suggesting complicity or, at the very least, implicit support for their actions. Borisova observes that "it seems clear that the agencies of the federal government are – at best – unwilling to come to grips with the scale of the fraud" (2000b). The head of the CEC in the 2000 election, Alexander Veshnyakov, in the face of hundreds of serious allegations of rigging, cynically announced that investigations had indeed found some fraud: "in Kaliningrad . . . four polling stations were each off in their vote counts by – drumroll, please – 15 votes" (Borisova 2000b). Similarly, instead of investigating allegations of manipulation in more recent elections under Putin, the current head of the CEC, Vladimir Churov, proclaimed that "there were no serious violations of the rules on election day" (cited in Myagkov et al. 2009, 137). Churov himself, a physicist by training, coauthored an article disputing the idea that the anomalies uncovered by Shpilkin in the 2007 and 2008 electoral data constituted evidence of electoral manipulation (Shpilkin, author's interview, 2010).[42] Third, the government has explicitly attacked initiatives to improve the quality of elections. For example, in 2008 the Kremlin shut down the European University of St. Petersburg, citing a fire risk, after it accepted a three-year grant from the European Union to develop a program that "instructed parties on how to ensure elections in Russia were not rigged" (Harding February 11, 2008).

Finally, there is evidence suggesting that the Kremlin directs the manipulation efforts from above. Putin's campaign staff for the 2000 election, for example, included top Kremlin officials, deputy police chiefs across the country, and top officials from the railway, tax, and agriculture ministries (OSCE 2000c, 2–3).[43] In her investigative report on that election, Borisova writes that "there are reasons to believe that Kremlin officials might have made clear, with not-always-subtle hints, that regional leaders were expected to deliver the Putin vote by hook or by crook" (2000b).[44] Central control only increased since then – Mebane and Kalinin write that "it appears that the entire regional state apparatus is now at the service of the party of power" (2009, 2). Even more explicitly, Alexander Kynev, an expert on Russian elections, asserts that the office of the President creates a *plan with specific targets* for the percentage of the vote in favor of each of the candidates on the ballot that each regional governor must obtain, and that sanctions accrue to those who fail to do so. In some instances, according to Kynev, the "results" of public opinion polls published by a government-supporting agency (FOM), reflect the plan's targets

---

[42] According to Shpilkin, Churov's article responded only to one of Shpilkin's analyses – the relationship between turnout and vote for United Russia. Churov argued that different regions have different electoral "cultures."

[43] Recall that Putin was acting president for a few months before the 2000 election, after Yeltsin resigned.

[44] As early as 1995, the then-Prime Minister Viktor Chernomyrdin "angrily and publicly berated governors for not delivering the vote" (Borisova 2000b).

(author's interview, May 6, 2010). Along similar lines, Mebane and Kalinin write that the control of regional executives by the Kremlin has rendered such executives "responsible for delivering '*recommended*' *electoral figures* to the Kremlin" (2009, 2; italics added).[45] As early as 2000, Fish locates the motive for excessive manipulation – manipulation that was not aimed at winning – in the Kremlin: the goal was to secure a strong victory for Putin by averting a second round of voting, even though there was little doubt that Putin would have won the second round (Fish 2005, 53). Thus, the evidence suggests that the central government has played a key role in the orchestration of excessive electoral manipulation in the Putin period, although the motives of regional executives may have contributed as well.

The Yeltsin years provide a counterfactual scenario that is helpful in understanding the motives for electoral manipulation in the Putin period. The existence of multiple centers of significant power and wealth under Yeltsin had clear consequences for incentives to manipulate elections. For one thing, the dispersion of electoral power under Yeltsin made for very tight races. The competitiveness of electoral politics under Yeltsin "was rooted, to a considerable extent, in incumbent weakness" (Levitsky and Way 2010, Ch. 5, loc. 9170). Yeltsin struggled to pass the 1993 constitutional referendum, and to win the concurrent legislative election, and according to many accounts he utilized substantial manipulation to eke out a victory. In the 1996 presidential election, for example, the leader of the Communist Party, Zyuganov, "emerged as a formidable opponent to the incumbent President Yeltsin" (Hesli 2003, 4). In the first round of voting, Zyuganov obtained 32 percent of the vote to Yeltsin's 35 percent. Yeltsin won the second round with 54 percent of the vote – a bare majority – with the help of extensive electoral manipulation (McFaul 1997; Myagkov et al. 2009). In other words, electoral manipulation under Yeltsin was in all likelihood aimed at winning the election at hand, and it was *marginal* – that is, it barely sufficed to win.

The perception that Yeltsin's regime was fragile shaped the choices of a wide range of political actors in ways that further undermined Yeltsin's strength. Almost throughout Yeltsin's tenure, his opponents had excellent chances: in the legislature, Yeltsin faced opposition majorities in both 1993 and 1995, and in the run-up to the 1996 presidential election, a reputable poll put Yeltsin's approval at less than 20 percent.[46] Yeltsin's weakness emboldened elites to challenge him, not only those affiliated with the opposition, but also those

---

[45] For a brief discussion of similar targets in Taiwan see Chapter 5, Section 5.4. On Indonesian elections, Anderson writes: "elections are carefully manipulated, and with some thermostatic sophistication: Golkar (the state party) won 62.9 percent of the vote in 1971, 62.1 percent in 1977, and about 64 percent in 1982" (1983, 490; Dan Slater pointed me to this cite, see Slater 2008).

[46] Data on presidential approval from VCIOM / Levada, reported in Treisman (2009, Figure 1). Shvetsova (2003) reports that one poll put Yeltsin's popularity at less than 5% right before the 1996 election.

who formerly supported him. For instance, various regional leaders and other influential elites such as Moscow Mayor Yuri Luzhkov threw their support behind Yevgeny Primakov's rival faction before the 1999 election (Shvetsova 2003, 218). The coalition Fatherland-All-Russia posed a serious electoral threat in the 1999 parliamentary election, which could well have cost Yeltsin and his associates the presidency in 2000 (Kryshtanovskaya and White 2009, 285). And in May of 1999 Yeltsin was almost impeached – a remarkable 283 legislators voting for impeachment (300 votes were required).

Alternative Explanations for Excessive Manipulation under Putin

I have argued that excessive electoral manipulation in Putin's Russia has been motivated by its indirect effects. I now consider three potential alternative explanations for excessive manipulation. The first one is that the Kremlin *was not aware of its own popularity*, and therefore the manipulation effort was aimed, from its viewpoint, at winning. This is quite unlikely, as reliable indicators of Putin's popularity, as well as pre-electoral public opinion polls, were available (Treisman 2009). In fact, experts decisively dismiss the possibility that the government might have been unaware about its excellent electoral chances (Myagkov et al. 2009, 135).

Potentially more plausible is the notion that the manipulation was aimed at obtaining a *two-thirds majority in parliament*. Of course, such an explanation could only account for the use of massive manipulation in legislative elections, for instance the one in 2007, and not in the presidential elections of 2000, 2004, and 2008. In the presidential elections, manipulation was by all lights excessive, as defined in previous chapters – that is, clearly not aimed at winning. Moreover, even in the 2007 election, United Russia obtained 15 more legislative seats than the 300 needed to amend the constitution or impeach the president (McFaul 2007) and, considering other pro-Kremlin parties (Fair Russia and the Liberal Democratic Party of Russia), the pro-Kremlin block controlled 393 out of the 450 total Duma seats.

A third alternative explanation is the notion that the government manipulated to *increase turnout*, and as an unintended consequence, very large margins of victory for Putin and his associates resulted. In fact, there is some evidence that the electoral manipulation was utilized to change turnout figures. Shpilkin, for example, finds that the distribution of turnout across precincts in the 2007 and 2008 elections had peaks at 60 percent, 70 percent, and 80 percent (author's interview, Moscow, May 2010).[47] Even those who have suggested that boosting turnout was a goal of manipulation, however, do not

---

[47] The peaks in the turnout distribution mean that there is a disproportionately large amount of precincts where turnout happens to be a round number – a highly unlikely occurrence. Mebane and Kalinin corroborate Shpilkin's finding and suggest that similar (although less-pronounced) peaks in turnout are discernible in the 2004 election.

take issue with the idea that increasing the proportion of the vote for the Kremlin candidates was also a goal of manipulation, and quite possibly the primary one.[48] Moreover, even if one granted that boosting turnout was the only, or the primary, goal of electoral manipulation under Putin – a proposition with no support in the literature – the question would be *why* the government might have sought higher turnout. In the first years of post-Soviet Russia, electoral rules required at least 50 percent turnout in a presidential election, and 25 percent in a legislative one, for the election to be valid. If the Kremlin manipulated elections to meet that threshold, one could say that it was manipulating *marginally* with respect to turnout (by extending the logic of the definition of marginal manipulation to the realm of turnout), and that large margins of victory ensued as unintended "collateral damage." There are serious problems with this idea. First, the turnout threshold for both presidential and legislative elections was abolished in 2006, and therefore it could not explain why the Kremlin might have sought a high turnout thereafter. Second, there is no obvious reason why boosting turnout figures must necessarily boost the proportion of the vote for the ruling party. There is evidence, in fact, that Russian elections have been manipulated both in ways that increase turnout figures, as well as in ways that decrease them. As Wilson (2005) and others have documented, the central government has made choices about which parties to prop up and which parties to undermine via the use of electoral manipulation.[49] Fish discusses specific instances where protocol falsifications involved both increasing Putin's total and decreasing Zyuganov's (Fish 2005, Ch.3). And journalists and observers have documented instances of ballot destruction. Therefore, the idea that large margins unwittingly followed from efforts to reach a turnout threshold is not very persuasive. Instead, it appears that, even in the realm of turnout, the logic of manipulation was one of "more than winning," and not one of "marginality." This idea rests on the observation that even when the winner obtains a large *proportion* of the vote, a small turnout can make it seem like only a small *absolute* number of people actually supported the winner. For example, if in a particular region United Russia received 45 percent of the vote and turnout was 33 percent, the actual proportion of the electorate supporting United Russia would amount to only 15 percent of the electorate. In fact, this precise critique was articulated about Mexican elections under the PRI by the eminent historian Daniel Cosío Villegas. Referring to the legislative election of 1970, he noted that the results for Mexico City:

... mathematically demonstrate that the PRI has been defeated in this election, because if the percentage of the vote obtained by its candidates is measured not with respect to

---

[48] e.g., Kynev, author's interview (2010); Buzin and Lubarev 2008, 184 (cited in Mebane and Kalinin 2009, 3).

[49] Some have alleged, for example, that the government manipulated Yabloko's and the Union of Right Forces' (SPS) vote total in the 2003 legislative election to deny them the requisite 5% for parliamentary representation.

the number of votes cast, but instead with respect to [the number of] registered voters, the conclusion is that the PRI is a minority party. In fact, it only reached 30% in district II, its maximum in [district] I with 42%, and its average across the twenty-four districts was 37%.

(*Proceso*, July 17, 1970)[50]

In other words, a low turnout could potentially undermine perceptions about the winner's electoral strength. To avert this danger, the manipulator can utilize electoral manipulation to obtain not only a large proportion of the vote, but also a large absolute number of votes. According to Shpilkin, in regions of Russia with a propensity for low turnout, even a large margin of victory could have made United Russia look unpopular (i.e., if the large margin was produced by a small number of votes), and this motivated the manipulation of turnout (author's interview, 2010).[51] Thus, turnout in Russia appears to have been manipulated not to meet some institutional turnout threshold, but rather to influence perceptions about the electoral strength of Putin and his team.[52] That such perceptions should matter (i.e., for their indirect effects) is precisely what I have argued in previous chapters.[53]

---

[50] Author's translation. Article reproduced in Cosío Villegas 1997, 386. In 1970 there were concurrent presidential and legislative elections.

[51] The concern with turnout is one of the ways in which the logic of excessive electoral manipulation connects with the practice of single-party elections, as discussed in Chapter 1.

[52] Kynev suggests an additional potential motive to manipulate turnout upward, in the regions, namely the fact that the number of representatives of a region to the national legislature depends on the number of votes obtained. Insofar as having more representatives improves the chances of maintaining or increasing the level of transfers from the center to the region, this provides incentives to manipulate not only the proportion, but also the absolute number of votes. This kind of incentive could be categorized as "marginal," as it is aimed at reaching a specific threshold (i.e., that associated with the maximum number of representatives that is feasibly attainable). But, three caveats are in order. First, it is only operative in legislative elections. Second, and more importantly, the incentives created by this mechanism, according to Kynev, are stronger for regions that receive net positive transfers from the center. Third, this mechanism itself generates incentives for excessive manipulation at the center. The reason for this is, as Kynev notes, the dominance of United Russia in the legislature means that this mechanism provides incentives to manipulate *specifically for United Russia* (Kynev, author's interview, 2010). In other words, perceptions about who will be in power – in this case, specifically about which party will dominate the legislature – shape incentives to manipulate. Therefore, one additional indirect effect of electoral manipulation (in any election) is to shape the incentives of certain regions to manipulate in legislative elections to increase the number of United Russia representatives of the region in the Duma (if there was uncertainty as to which party would dominate in the legislature, the incentives to manipulate would still exist, but they would not favor any specific party).

[53] Two clarifications are in order. First, turnout *figures* and actual voter participation are distinct concepts. I have argued that excessive/blatant manipulation can depress voter participation. In addition, electoral manipulation can be utilized to increase turnout figures (I discuss this distinction in detail in the study of Mexico in the next chapter). Second, it may be helpful to clarify that the idea of "turnout buying" (Nichter 2008) is distinct to the argument made here. Cox and Kousser (1981), Nichter and others have correctly argued that parties can bribe voters

Conclusion: Electoral Manipulation in Post-Soviet Russia

This case study documented patterns of electoral manipulation in post-Soviet Russia and explored the motives and mechanisms that have underpinned them (and continue to do so). It identified two broad patterns: first, under Yeltsin, electoral manipulation was marginal – that is, it was sufficient to win the election at hand but not to obtain a large margin. Second, since Putin became president, electoral manipulation has been excessive and blatant. The contrast between the Yeltsin and the Putin periods is striking. Whereas the use of electoral manipulation under Yeltsin barely allowed him to stay afloat, under Putin and Medvedev electoral manipulation has resulted in spectacular electoral results and effectively aligned political incentives in ways that contribute to his (and his associates') hold on power. Of course, electoral results are the product of a range of forces, motives, and efforts, and in any specific instance, a variety of factors will contribute to observed outcomes. What emerges from this case study is that the use of excessive and blatant manipulation in recent Russian elections is best understood as part of a broader effort by the group in office – Putin, his supporters, and the United Russia party – to consolidate and monopolize political power over the long run.

The findings of this case study connect with the theoretical discussion in the two preceding chapters. First, the distribution of power and resources in post-Soviet Russia rendered the potential payoff from excessive and blatant manipulation quite substantial throughout the post-Soviet period (although more so after Putin came to power). For one thing, the generally weak rule of law has meant that all post-Soviet governments have had considerable discretion in utilizing state resources to reward or punish citizens, politicians, and organizations according to arbitrary or partisan criteria. As discussed in Chapter 4, this implies that perceptions about who is likely to hold power strongly influence political behavior and, therefore, that the potential payoff to excessive manipulation is high – that is, that excessive/blatant manipulation could have substantial indirect effects.

However, consistent with Result 2 and Condition A in Chapter 5, the potential for indirect effects does not suffice for excessive/blatant manipulation to arise. In addition, one of the parties must have the capacity to implement electoral manipulation in such a manner.[54] In Russia, this was not the case during

---

to show up at the polls (if they are known supporters), or to stay at home (if they are known opponents). The underlying goal of such actions, however, is *to win the election being disputed*. In other words, their arguments elaborate the specific details of a particular form of electoral manipulation – variously referred to as vote buying, turnout buying, or abstention buying – assuming, with the prevailing wisdom, that the goal of the manipulation is to win the election at hand. In contrast, I am suggesting that manipulation could be utilized to boost overall turnout figures, not to win the election at hand or to meet a turnout threshold that would render the election valid, but for the indirect effects that are likely to ensue.

[54] In general, *some* incentives to manipulate excessively/blatantly might well exist in every electoral system – the theoretical claim (elaborated in Chapters 4 and 5) is that such incentives are

the Yeltsin years. Yeltsin's unpopularity and the strong political opposition that he faced made it virtually impossible for him to exploit electoral manipulation for purposes other than victory.[55] However, excessive electoral manipulation has become feasible in the Putin years, because of Russia's economic success, to Putin's success at increasing the Kremlin's power (underpinned by the economic windfall), and to Putin's popularity. It is possible that Yeltsin may have *wanted* to manipulate excessively (just like Kuchma, in his own words, wanted to do for Ukraine in 1999, without fully succeeding at it).[56] That said, there is every indication that incentives to manipulate excessively were greater under Putin and Medvedev than under Yeltsin – for one thing, the potential consequences for political and social actors of challenging the former were decidedly weightier than for the latter.

In the Russian case, excessive and blatant manipulation was utilized to influence multiple aspects of what I have termed the "political context" (Figure 4.2 in Chapter 4): among other things, such manipulation was used in the pursuit of oversized margins of victory, inflated turnout figures, nonsensical electoral outcomes such as high "support" for Putin in Chechnya, a reduction of vote totals for minor parties in legislative elections even when such parties would have attained at most a handful of seats (as some have argued Putin did to Yabloko and to the Union of Right Forces), and an inflated first-round vote to avert a runoff even when victory in the runoff would have been assured (as in the 2000 election). In so doing, excessive and blatant electoral manipulation yielded indirect effects that included the alignment of most political, business, and bureaucratic elites with the Kremlin, the elimination of internal and external challenges to the Kremlin from such elites (in contrast to the Yeltsin years), an increase in defections and problems for opposition parties, and the discouragement of opposition voters, among other things. Martin Wolf has written that the Kremlin's overarching goal under Putin is "not only to establish a monopoly of power but also to monopolise competition for it."[57]

The "increasing returns" nature of the feedback effects between the conditions that provide incentives to manipulate, on the one hand, and the effects of

stronger in situations where the rule of law is weak and the government has discretion to use state resources and power for partisan ends, and such resources and power are substantial in magnitude.

[55] As suggested previously, blatant manipulation was certainly possible in Yeltsin's time, but the strong opposition that Yeltsin faced likely meant that such blatancy did not come exclusively from the government's efforts at manipulation, but also from the efforts of its Communist opponents, and, crucially, that it did not suffice to convince the public that Yeltsin was electorally strong.

[56] As noted in Chapter 1. Some might argue that Yeltsin would not have wanted to manipulate elections excessively or otherwise seek to impose authoritarian-style rule, even if he had had the opportunity to do so (on the question of Yeltsin's democratic inclinations see Shevtsova 1997; Morozov 2000; Ghidadubli 2007).

[57] *Financial Times*, November 5, 2003, cited in Wilson (2005, 38).

manipulation, on the other, are worth highlighting: the fact that Yeltsin was barely able to win (e.g., to beat Zyuganov in 1996) even with extensive manipulation, only reinforced the perception that he could be beaten at the polls, which in turn increased the force of the political and electoral challenges that he subsequently faced (making it even more difficult to manipulate excessively). In contrast, the perception that Putin and his associates are electorally strong, that is, able to hold on to power – nurtured largely through their use of excessive and blatant electoral manipulation – in turn has increased the Kremlin's power and discretion in governing, and diminished the electoral challenges that Putin and his team have subsequently faced.

6.4 ZIMBABWE

The Distribution of Resources and Power in Zimbabwe

Over its century-long history, Zimbabwe – formerly Southern Rhodesia, Rhodesia, and Zimbabwe Rhodesia – has held twenty-nine legislative elections and four presidential elections. In what follows, I focus on national elections in independent Zimbabwe, beginning with the 1980 transitional legislative election provided for by the Lancaster House agreement that ended the liberation war. Subsequently, Zimbabwe held legislative elections (for the House of Assembly) in 1985, 1990, 1995, 2000, 2005, and 2008. In 1987, the government system was changed from parliamentary to presidential. Presidential elections were held in 1990, 1996, 2002, and 2008. In addition, a constitutional referendum was held in 2000. Information on electoral manipulation in Zimbabwe is not as plentiful as in Russia, but there is enough scholarly work to reconstruct a helpful picture. In this case study, I highlight somewhat different categories of indirect effects than in the Russian case – for example, I explore the effect of excessive manipulation on the political behavior of labor – and I utilize survey data to explore the effect of excessive and blatant manipulation on turnout. I contrast Zimbabwe and Russia at the end of this case study.

For the purpose of studying electoral manipulation, Zimbabwe's electoral history since 1980 can be divided into two periods, separated approximately by the turn of the millennium. In the first period, spanning 1980 to the late 1990s, Robert Mugabe and his party, the Zimbabwe African National Union – Patriotic Front (ZANU-PF, henceforth ZANU), were very popular and, by most accounts, could have easily won every election in a clean vote.[58] Nevertheless, they engaged in excessive and remarkably blatant electoral manipulation. This was reflected, for example, in Mugabe's margin of victory, which was 66 percent in 1990 and almost 88 percent in 1996. One could call this the

---

[58] There was some uncertainty ahead of the first, transitional, election of 1980. (I revisit this election later.)

period of "unbearable control of an indispensable, unopposable ruling party," to borrow a phrase from Christine Sylvester (1995).[59]

The second period (late-1990s until today) has been characterized by a dramatic shift in the distribution of power and resources – away from the central government. Inflation, joblessness, and a weak economy increasingly afflicted the middle class, workers, and ZANU's base – the poor and the peasants. As Mugabe's and ZANU's popularity and relative economic power eroded, a strong political opposition emerged, and Mugabe and his party faced very serious electoral challenges. In this period, electoral manipulation became essential for Mugabe and ZANU to continue winning elections, and electoral manipulation became marginal (albeit large-scale and brutal).[60] Therefore, in terms of timing, Zimbabwe is the mirror image of the Russian case, where an early period in which the incumbent party needed manipulation to merely hold on to power (and manipulation was marginal), was followed by one where its hold on power was solid and manipulation was excessive.

For the sake of clarity, I emphasize the distinction, drawn earlier in the book, between the scale of the manipulation, on the one hand, and the ensuing margin of victory, on the other. For purposes of this study, an election is said to be marginally manipulated if it is manipulated and results in a small margin of victory; an election is excessively manipulated if it is manipulated and yields a large margin of victory (for a more precise discussion see Chapter 3). Therefore, it is possible for an election to be *highly*, *violently*, and *brazenly* manipulated and nevertheless said to be *marginally* manipulated (i.e., if the resulting margin of victory is small). This is the meaning of the claim that elections in Zimbabwe after 2000 were marginally manipulated: although manipulation was perpetrated on a very large scale, indeed in all likelihood larger than in the pre-2000 period, margins of victory were small.[61]

How did background conditions shape incentives for electoral manipulation in Zimbabwe during the first period? During that period, background conditions in Zimbabwe rendered excessive manipulation feasible and high-payoff. The party in power enjoyed a disproportionate level of control over electorally relevant resources, faced weak constraints from the rule of law,

---

[59] I quote at greater length in a later section of this case study.

[60] Recall the distinction, from Chapter 3, between the scale of manipulation, on the one hand, and the ensuing margin of victory, on the other. In the latter period in Zimbabwe, electoral manipulation has, in all likelihood, intensified in extent and brutality in comparison with the former period, but it has nevertheless yielded relatively small margins of victory. Note that there is reason to believe that Mugabe and ZANU would have liked to continue to manipulate elections excessively in the second period, but feasibility constraints made this impossible (more on this further below).

[61] Similarly, while manipulation in the 1995 Zimbabwe election might have been undertaken on a smaller scale than in various other elections in that country, the fact that manipulation was nevertheless substantial *and* resulted in a large margin of victory render it *excessive* (more on this election later).

and enjoyed a high degree of freedom from external democratic pressures. First, the government inherited all the institutions of colonial control from Ian Smith's government, and chose to retain them virtually unaltered. These included the Central Intelligence Organization (CIO), the police, and the military, which was among Africa's largest. At independence, the Zimbabwean state was one of the strongest and most capable in Africa, with considerable surveillance and operational capabilities throughout the country. Weitzer writes that "[s]ince independence, repressive powers and political institutions have not been dismantled, and in some areas have been further strengthened" (1984, 530). Second, Mugabe and ZANU attained control of the state upon winning the 1980 transitional election, and swiftly utilized the state machinery to further accumulate political power, taking advantage of the fact that the government was only mildly constrained by the law.[62] Among other things, the government controlled parastatal corporations such as the Grain Marketing Board and the Agricultural Finance Corporation (Bratton 1987). Third, Mugabe's status as a hero of the liberation struggle granted him and ZANU a measure of leeway, domestically, regionally, and internationally, to engage in electoral abuses (as well as non-electoral ones) that in all likelihood had partisan motives. Fourth, there were few external democratic pressures on Mugabe's government.[63] These conditions rendered excessive and blatant electoral manipulation within reach. Moreover, the government had enormous discretion over a variety of policy instruments and benefits such as drought food relief (in the 1990s) – on which a large part of the population were strongly dependent – and the granting of business licenses; and it utilized such discretion according to partisan criteria (Brett 2005; Kriger 2005, 15–17, 22–24). This meant that choosing to support Mugabe's opposition could have serious consequences. Therefore, beliefs about the prospects that Mugabe and ZANU would remain in power importantly shaped citizens' and elites' political and electoral calculations and choices – as in Putin's Russia, there were strong incentives to "back the winner." Therefore, excessive and blatant manipulation had the potential to yield a substantial payoff, in terms of its indirect effects, to ZANU and Mugabe.

In the second period, ZANU and Mugabe's power was considerably diminished in comparison with the first period, but it remained substantial. Moreover, the rule of law in Zimbabwe, already weak in the first period, was battered further (Widner and Scher 2008, 249–254). Therefore, there is good reason to believe that Mugabe and ZANU would have *wanted* to continue to

---

[62] While the government had full control over the security apparatus, the courts, while biased in favor of ZANU, retained a measure of independence (see Makumbe 2002, 95; Widner and Scher 2008, 248).

[63] On the issue of leverage, see Levitsky and Way (2010, Ch. 6). They consider Zimbabwe a case of "high leverage," but also entertain the possibility that South Africa might have played the role of a "black knight" with respect to Zimbabwe, shielding it from Western pressures for democratization (308).

manipulate excessively in the second period, as they did in the first period, and that they would have benefitted from it. Mugabe had proven his willingness and his intention to manipulate excessively throughout the first period; what changed in the second period was that it was no longer feasible to do so. In Zimbabwe after the late 1990s, as in Yeltsin's Russia, the potential for a high payoff from excessive/blatant manipulation likely existed. The stumbling block in Zimbabwe was the feasibility of manipulating beyond the point needed to win.[64]

The reasons for the change or "transition" in Zimbabwe's political economy from the first to the second period are certainly interesting, and I devote some attention to these.[65] The purpose of this case study is not to explain that change, however, but to study the incentives to manipulate in each of the two periods. For these purposes, the change in relevant background conditions from one period to the other is appropriately viewed as largely exogenous, in the sense that background conditions in each of the periods are proximate causes of incentives to manipulate in that period, while the reverse is not true: if anything, excessive and blatant electoral manipulation in the first period might have *delayed* such changes, by strengthening the regime politically even as the economy foundered. By far, the most important factor behind the erosion of Mugabe, ZANU, and the government's central control of electoral and material resources was Zimbabwe's *steep economic decline.* I return to this issue later on. The key questions in this case study, then, are: why did Mugabe and ZANU manipulate elections extensively in the 1980s and 1990s if they were virtually certain to win without doing so? And, why did Mugabe and ZANU manipulate only marginally (if extensively and brutally) after the late 1990s? I focus on the first question for most of the case study, and briefly return to the second one at the end. In the next section, I document the fact of excessive and blatant manipulation in the first period, and in the section after that I explore the motivations behind such manipulation, with attention to its indirect effects.

Excessive and Blatant Electoral Manipulation in Zimbabwe

Mugabe's and ZANU's heroic role in the war of liberation, Zimbabwe's economic growth in the 1980s, and the government's pursuit of universal health and education policies made ZANU the clear favorite in every election until the late 1990s.[66] ZANU and Mugabe further consolidated control over the administration of elections, and over the political system in general, through

---

[64] One difference worth noting between the cases of Russia and Zimbabwe is that Mugabe proved himself *willing* to manipulate excessively (i.e., in the 1980s and early 1990s), while Yeltsin did not (perhaps because he did not have the opportunity to do so, or because he did not wish to).

[65] In the democratization literature, the term "transition" often denotes regime change, and/or movement in a democratic direction. I do not intend to convey such meanings here.

[66] This is compatible with the observation that *opposition* voters were disengaged (on which I discuss more later).

various constitutional amendments in the late 1980s.[67] Nevertheless, they substantially manipulated every election since independence. In 1980, ZANU obtained 63 percent of the vote and fifty-seven out of the eighty seats reserved for Africans. In 1985, it obtained 77 percent of the vote and sixty-four seats. In 1990, it obtained 80 percent of the vote and controlled 117 out of 120 seats.[68] In 1995, 81.4 percent and 118 out of the 120 contested seats. In the presidential elections of 1990 and 1996, Mugabe obtained, respectively, 83 percent and 92.7 percent of the vote. These spectacular (in fact, increasingly more spectacular) results reflect, among other things, the combined impact of Mugabe's and ZANU-PF's popularity, and the direct and indirect effects of their extensive efforts at electoral manipulation (which I document in the next subsection).

Of all the elections in the first period, the first, transitional election in 1980 was perhaps the only one where ZANU's victory was not a complete certainty.[69] Nevertheless, many observer groups agreed that the "will of the people" was a ZANU victory– in other words, that ZANU would have been the winner in a clean vote (Kriger 2005, 3). The election, however, was far from clean. In fact, it was marked by considerable voter intimidation, mainly on the part of ZANLA – the military arm of ZANU. Laakso reports, however, that although intimidation might have made a difference in some provinces, "much of the intimidation can be regarded as more or less neutral in terms of the final results" (2002, 330). In sum, the 1980 election was considerably manipulated, but even if it had not been, ZANU would still have been the rightful winner – that is, the 1980 election was an instance of excessive manipulation on the part of ZANU.[70] The manipulation was also blatant, partly because one of the main tools of manipulation was voter intimidation, which tends to be more public than some other forms of manipulation.[71]

---

[67] I describe some of these later.

[68] A series of constitutional reforms since 1987 changed the size of the legislature to 120 elected seats and 30 additional seats appointed by the president; it also ended the reservation of seats for whites.

[69] On the one hand, in a 1979 election, ZANU had not done especially well, but the election had been conducted with most of the country under martial law, and after calls for a boycott on the part of the liberation movements (Gregory 1980, 18–19). On the other hand, the political bargain leading to the 1979 election had not succeeded at ending the war, and Mugabe was widely regarded as having proved that he had the ability, if voted into office, to stop the war, therefore votes for ZANU were seen as votes for peace (Laakso 2002, 331). See also Herbst (1990, 2000).

[70] It is possible to argue that ZANU was not certain of victory in 1980, and therefore that electoral manipulation associated with that election (or, at least, some of the manipulation associated with that election) should be attributed to ZANU's uncertainty. This argument, however, could not be made about any subsequent election in the early period, throughout which ZANU victory was a given.

[71] In comparison, for instance, with ballot box stuffing, padding voter registration lists, or some forms of tampering with the vote count. See Chapter 1 for further discussion of this point.

ZANU was in an even stronger electoral position in the 1985 election, as its popularity was high and it now had access to the resources of the state apparatus for campaigning and electioneering. Nevertheless, ZANU again chose to engage in substantial electoral manipulation. The purpose of such manipulation was certainly not to win, because a ZANU victory was widely expected, but rather to stomp out opposition. The main opposition that Mugabe's government had faced in the 1980 election was from ZAPU, the political arm of the liberation movement associated with the country's Ndebele ethnic minority.[72] In the 1980 election, ZAPU had obtained 24 percent of the vote and twenty seats – a decent showing, but not one that threatened ZANU's hold on power. Nevertheless, between 1982 and 1987, the government engaged in massacres of Ndebele civilians and of ZAPU members, mainly in Matabeleland (Bratton and Masunungure 2008, 44). The purported motive was to quell attacks from dissident ex-ZIPRA guerrillas.[73] In reality, the government targeted not only the dissident guerrillas, but the full Ndebele minority and all of ZAPU, and made little effort to target the dissidents.[74] The government made a point of targeting areas of electoral contestation, such as the Midlands, where the vote had been divided with ZAPU in the 1980 election. In addition to these measures, the government pursued other strategies to increase its already overwhelming electoral advantage in the 1985 election. Villagers were intimidated into obtaining ZANU cards and voting for ZANU (Kriger 2005, 7–8). And Mugabe himself, in campaign speeches, repeatedly issued thinly veiled threats to those who would consider voting for the opposition. At a rally in Bulawayo, for example, Mugabe asked the audience: "Where will we be tomorrow? . . . Is it war or peace tomorrow? Let the people of Matabeleland decide this question" (Frankel, *Washington Post*, June 30, 1985).

Mugabe's and ZANU's electoral prospects continued to improve after the 1985 election. After that election, Mugabe simultaneously pressured and negotiated with the ZAPU leadership, leading to the Unity Accord in 1987. The Accord merged ZAPU into ZANU under the banner of ZANU, effectively eliminating (or "swallowing," as some called it) ZANU's strongest opponent. In addition, in 1987, the government passed a series of constitutional amendments that abolished the twenty house seats formerly reserved for whites, enlarged the size of the legislature, and instituted the office of the president. The president was given extensive powers that allowed him to rule practically without parliamentary approval (Makumbe and Compagnon 2000, 33–36). One consequence of this was a large degree of control by the president of electoral institutions and their staffing (Laakso 2002, 334). In view of all this, ZANU's victory in the 1990 election "was no surprise" (Laakso 2002, 336). The election, however, was manipulated by ZANU, largely through voter

---

[72] The Ndebele constituted 20% of the population.
[73] ZIPRA was the military arm of ZAPU.
[74] *Africa Watch* 1989, 16, cited in Laakso 2002, 331.

intimidation. A new opposition party, ZUM, had emerged before the 1990 election (partly consisting of disaffected former ZAPU members) and before the election numerous instances of harassment of ZUM supporters were reported, with the complicity of police, who either actively helped or looked the other way, and of the Central Intelligence Organization. Opposition voters were also harassed after the election (for instance, by the ZANU Women's League), on instructions from senior politicians (Kriger 2005, 19), probably with a view to deterring them from opposing ZANU in future contests.

Due in no small part to the sense of futility that past ZANU electoral behavior had produced among elites and citizens,[75] the 1995 legislative and 1996 presidential elections were the least contested in Zimbabwe's history (Laakso 2002, 337; Rich-Dorman 2005, 157). ZANU had virtually secured a majority of the legislative seats in 1995 even before the election was held because it was to run unopposed in 55 out of 120 (and it would control 30 additional appointed seats). Voters were discouraged and disengaged, and the main opposition candidates boycotted the 1996 presidential election. Nevertheless, in advance of these elections ZANU tampered with voter rolls, harassed opposition candidates, intimidated ordinary people, and stepped up the rhetoric of warning and threat. Makumbe and Compagnon found that, in the Harare South constituency, 41 percent of names on the voter rolls were not genuine (Makumbe and Compagnon 2000, 69–70). Changes in constituency delimitation were used to advantage ZANU, for instance by merging opposition districts within larger ZANU districts (Rich-Dorman 2005, 161). In Matabeleland, Mugabe told people to support ZANU if they wanted to keep the peace they had since 1987. Comparing ZANU to an elephant and the opposition to puppies, he said: "[t]he puppies could bark as long as they wanted provided they were far away. But the elephant would trample them if they got too near for comfort."[76]

In sum, despite Mugabe's and ZANU-PF's popularity, their access to state resources for campaigning, and their ability to shape electoral institutions and laws to their liking, they chose to pursue substantial electoral manipulation in every national election from 1980 to 1996. The result of ZANU's strategy was a string of overwhelming victories in blatantly manipulated elections. As Sylvester (1995, 411–412) put it: "[t]hese tactics seem excessive in a country where ZANU PF remains unchallenged, where it has never come close to losing a national election."

Keeping the Puppies Far Away: Motives for Excessive and Blatant Electoral Manipulation in Zimbabwe

Why did Mugabe and ZANU pursue such excessive tactics of manipulation? Consistent with the theory I developed in previous chapters, the evidence

---

[75] I provide more details on this point in the next subsection.

[76] *The Herald*, 6 April 1995, cited in Kriger 2005, 23.

suggests that Mugabe and ZANU pursued excessive and blatant electoral manipulation over the first two decades of independence, not to win, given that their victory was essentially guaranteed, but in the pursuit of a monopoly on political power. Mugabe's own metaphor aptly captures the idea: the goal of the "elephant" (i.e., ZANU) was not to beat another "elephant" (i.e., a comparably strong opposition) – none existed in Zimbabwe before the late 1990s – but to make sure that even "puppies" (i.e., weak opposition) refrained from seeking a small share of power. In the case of Zimbabwe, the motives of the ruling group were quite transparent. For one thing, they were clearly stated on numerous occasions by Mugabe himself. While campaigning for the 1995 election, for instance, Mugabe asked the public to give ZANU *"a massive 99.9 per cent vote to frighten away the fringe opposition"* (Makumbe and Compagnon 2000, 305).[77] This phrase succinctly sums up the logic motivating excessive and blatant manipulation: Mugabe does not speak of winning office, but rather of winning everything. And the rationale for doing so is to subsequently discourage any remaining opposition – therefore, this phrase captures the dynamic element of the argument that I have presented, where overwhelming victory today impacts political behavior tomorrow. Along similar lines, when campaigning at Shamva, "Mugabe said he wished to '*silence the opposition*' with an '*overwhelming and resounding victory*', even louder than the impact of the dynamite used in the local mines" (Kriger 2005, 23).

In Zimbabwe, thus, the logic of "more than winning" was not only put into practice, it was also openly articulated by those pursuing it. The goal of establishing a monopoly on power, voiced by Mugabe, was also an explicit element in ZANU's party platform. For example, Article 6 in the 1987 Unity Accord stated: "[w]e shall seek to establish a one-party state."[78] The idea of a one-party state was a major theme in the 1990 election campaign. In 1989, Mugabe stated that:

the united ZANU(PF) has the potential, given the commitment of its leadership and members, to develop into that sole party to which all Zimbabweans can and should lend their membership and support... any attempt to form any new political parties for the future is a long step backwards in the search for greater national unity and the transformation of society in favour of the people and, in particular, the peasant, the urban and farm workers, professionals and intellectuals.[79]

As this quote illustrates, the goal of a single-party state has historical and ideological roots in the liberation struggle, when different nationalist groups worked separately and sometimes clashed. Since then, ZANU and Mugabe have embraced, at least rhetorically, a Manichean viewpoint in which the

---

[77] Italics added.
[78] Bratton and Masunungure 2008, 45.
[79] Mugabe, Robert, 1989, "The Unity Accord: its promise for the future," in Canaan Banana, ed., *Turmoil and tenacity in Zimbabwe*, College Press, 354–355; cited in Laakso 2002, 334–335.

political world is "populated only by 'freedom fighters' and 'puppets' [of the West]" (Bratton and Masunungure 2008, 44). As one government propagandist put it, "the stampede for democracy should not undermine the gains of the liberation war."[80] In fact, the drive for single-party rule dated back to the pre-independence period (Sithole 1997, 129).[81]

ZANU's unabashed utilization of excessive and blatant electoral manipulation succeeded at discouraging and deactivating political opposition. Consider first Zimbabwe's *labor unions*. Soon after independence, the majority of Zimbabwe's trade unions coalesced into a single body, the Zimbabwe Confederation of Trade Unions (ZCTU). Initially, ZCTU had a close relationship with ZANU. Raftopoulos and Sachikonye (2001, 31) write that ZANU held the ZCTU in a "paternalist grip" since its founding in 1981. President Mugabe's brother, Albert, served as ZCTU's secretary general early on. It quickly became apparent, however, that the interests of government and of labor were not well-aligned, and they increasingly diverged over time. Nevertheless, labor only decided to take the quantum leap of entering electoral politics in 1999, after the background conditions had changed and ZANU's relative economic and political strength had declined significantly.[82]

On the one hand, the government had implemented a minimum wage and other worker protections, and it espoused a socialist and pro-worker rhetoric, actions that placed labor and the government on the same camp (Alexander 2000, 386; Brett 2005, 6). On the other hand, as early as 1987, workers were beginning to suffer from a high rate of unemployment and from inflation, and to oppose Mugabe's idea for "neoliberal" economic reform in the form of the IMF-backed Economic Structural Adjustment Program (ESAP). In the 1990s, the economic situation of workers continued to worsen, and the rift with the government to widen, as inflation rose, real wages declined, and wage and employment protections were reduced.

---

[80] Godfrey Chikowore, "Defending our heritage: armed struggle should serve as guiding spirit," *Herald* (Harare), 16 February 2002, quoted in Terrence Ranger "Historiography, patriotic history, and the history of the nation: the struggle over the past in Zimbabwe," University of Ghent, Annual Distinguished Lecture on Africa, 2003, 3; quoted in Bratton and Masunungure 2008, 44.

[81] Nevertheless, the drive to monopolize political power is unlikely to have stemmed exclusively from Zimbabwe's unique history – in fact, the idea of a single-party state was abandoned by 1991 (Sithole (1997) argues that the reason for this was the fact that ZAPU elites that had been "swallowed" by ZANU in the Unity Accord now made for some internal dissent within ZANU), several years before Mugabe's pronouncements about winning by 99.9% to frighten rivals, quoted earlier.

[82] Such a decline, of course, was in turn deepened by labor's decision to enter electoral politics in opposition to ZANU, as I relate later. Just like there exist positive feedbacks between the centralization of power and resources, on the one hand, and excessive and blatant manipulation, on the other (as the case of Putin's Russia illustrates; see also Chapter 5, especially Section 5.3), there exist positive feedbacks between the dispersion of power and resources and increased opposition electoral strength, as in Zimbabwe in the late 1990s and thereafter.

The possibility for labor to constitute itself into a political force existed for years,[83] as did the motive for pursuing such a course of action (as the previous paragraph illustrates). However, ZANU's electoral dominance, evident both in the size of its victories and in its determination to stomp out opposition wherever it was found, had fostered the perception that its hold on power was essentially unassailable, and that therefore acting against it was at best futile and at worst an invitation to retaliation by the government (Mugabe had repeatedly warned labor against directly entering electoral politics). Such a perception rendered labor reluctant to participate in electoral politics throughout the first period, even in the early 1990s when the rifts with the government were already quite substantial.[84]

The story of labor's relationship to electoral politics is echoed in that of *opposition politicians* and *political parties*, who, because of a growing sense of helplessness stemming from Mugabe's electoral dominance, and from the spectacle of ZANU's and its associates' systematic efforts to intimidate and bribe opposition politicians and voters, decided to boycott the 1996 presidential election, essentially handing Mugabe a victory even more overwhelming than any he had enjoyed before.[85] Laakso, for example, refers to the 1995 and 1996 elections as "elections without contest" (2002, 337).[86] More generally, opposition to ZANU from other political parties had been weak since 1990.[87] In the 1980s, *politicians inside the ruling party* were similarly "disciplined" by the dim prospects of success outside ZANU: ZANU experienced essentially no defections in the late 1980s, unlike many other political parties in the region

---

[83] See for instance Sylvester 1990, 397.

[84] While the literature tends to view organized labor in Zimbabwe as a natural ally of opposition parties, an alternative explanation for the behavior of labor in the 1990s is that the primary reason why ZCTU acted as the government's ally was the ideology of its leaders concerning the proper role of unionism (e.g., as a partner in development) and a certain wariness of opposition parties (see LeBas 2011).

[85] In a study of contemporary African elections, Lindberg (2006b) finds that opposition parties were substantially more likely to boycott "flawed" elections than "free and fair" ones (128). His database encompasses elections in Zimbabwe as well as in some other countries where excessive/blatant electoral manipulation likely underpinned deterrence dynamics analogous to those discussed here.

[86] Interestingly, the height of apathy and ZANU dominance coincided with the deepening of economic problems that was to quickly undermine ZANU's economic and political control (as discussed earlier in this case study) through the massive civil service strikes of 1996, the labor activism of 1997, and the formation of the Movement for Democratic Change (MDC) in 1999, and the defeat of Mugabe's constitutional referendum through the efforts of a coalition of civil society groups under the name of the National Constitutional Assembly in 2000.

[87] The weakness of opposition parties in the 1990s has various causes, in addition to the deterrent effect of ZANU electoral dominance and its use of blatant and excessive manipulation. According to Sithole, these parties suffered from "inept and divided leadership," and from infiltration by government intelligence services (Sithole 1997, 135). The quality of leadership, however, was in all likelihood partly determined by the perception that a successful political career outside ZANU was a near impossibility.

in the same time period.[88] The effect of the ZANU electoral quasi-monopoly on other social and political actors before the mid-1990s is well summed up by Sylvester:

This is a civil society in which there are relatively few party-autonomous public institutions to aggregate and articulate dissent to official power. ZANU PF is the centre of force into which disappears the independence of trade unions, opposition parties, and even citizen motivation for political contestation (1995, 408).[89]

Excessive and electoral manipulation affected not only the behavior of labor unions, middle class leaders, and opposition politicians and parties, but also that of citizens as *voters*. Initial enthusiasm among the electorate in the 1980 and 1985 elections, which had enormous turnouts, gave way to voter apathy as a feeling of futility set in among the public. Rich-Dorman writes that, between 1980 and 2000, "as the ruling party's domination of the electoral process increased, turn-out and participation decreased" (2005, 157). Laakso estimates turnout in 1980 at 90 percent, in 1985 at 85 percent, in 1990 at 56 percent, in 1995 at 54 percent, and in 1996 at 32 percent (2002, 333, 336–337, 339–340). In the 1990s, she writes, "apathy reflected cynicism and frustration," especially in urban areas – turnout in cities in 1996 was only 18 percent (2002, 341, 340).[90] Sylvester, writing in the mid-1990s, observes that:

the political climate can be such that the electorate perceives the government or ruling party as above the law; and rumours about security forces cheating on electoral rules suggest a perception that democracy is rigged in favour of ZANU PF. Also, using aggressive methods to get out the vote for a party that has already won, constitutes the political system as unbearably controlled by an indispensable, unopposable ruling party (1995, 412).

As a Harare worker, Tendai Masumbi, put it: "Why should I vote? It won't make any difference. Nothing will change" (Meldrum 1995). This kind of disposition on the part of voters can be further investigated using survey data. On the basis of data from a 1999 Afrobarometer survey of Zimbabwe's population, I estimate the relationship between respondents' perceptions about the quality of elections and their propensity to cast a vote. Of those who responded to the question about the honesty of elections, 60 percent said that elections were somewhat or very dishonest. This was by far (by more than 20 percentage

---

[88] Levitsky and Way (2010, Ch. 6, loc. 13495). On the logic of elite defections see Reuter and Gandhi (2010). According to Adrienne LeBas, up until 2000 ZANU was more fearful of internal splits and defections than of outside challenges, e.g., from labor (personal communication, March 2012).

[89] There was, however, some political competition and dissent within ZANU, and some ZANU politicians left the party to run as independents (only to be vigorously undermined by ZANU) (see Sithole 1997; Laakso 2002).

[90] Laakso also finds that in 1990, turnout in cities with no real political competition was much lower than in cities where there was competition (2002, 337).

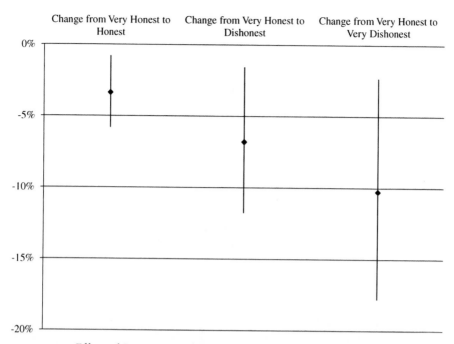

FIGURE 6.1. Effect of Perceptions about Electoral Honesty on Probability of Voting, Zimbabwe 1996 Presidential Election
Notes: Afrobarometer Round 1; 90% confidence intervals shown[91]

points) the largest proportion of those surveyed that believed elections to be unfair or dishonest in a set of similar surveys of African countries covering, in addition to Zimbabwe, Botswana, Ghana, Lesotho, Malawi, Mali, Namibia, Nigeria, South Africa, Tanzania, Uganda, and Zambia.[92]

Figure 6.1 displays the relationship between perceptions of electoral honesty and respondents' propensity to vote, controlling, through regression analysis, for education, age (and its square), and newspaper readership (a measure of interest in politics). Specifically, the figure shows the change in the propensity of an average respondent to cast a vote associated with a change in perceptions about the honesty of the election. As the figure indicates, a citizen who believes elections to be very dishonest is more than 10 percent less likely to vote than a similar citizen who believes them to be fully honest, once education, age, and political interest are accounted for.

In sum, the use of electoral manipulation by Mugabe and ZANU in the 1980s and most of the 1990s was not aimed at winning, judging both from ZANU's and Mugabe's explicit pronouncements and from the fact that their

[91] Probit regression, simulations conducted with Clarify (Tomz, Wittenberg, and King 2001).
[92] These are the countries included in Round 1 of Afrobarometer. For further details on the Afrobarometer data see Bratton, Mattes, and Gyimah-Boadi 2005.

popularity would have sufficed for them to win practically every election in that period. Instead, electoral manipulation was an important tool in the central government's strategy to silence, overwhelm, and eliminate opposition, to paraphrase Mugabe. With this goal in mind, Mugabe and ZANU sought not 50.1 percent of the vote, but 99.9 percent, and utilized their substantial central control over resources, over laws and regulations, and over the security forces to orchestrate excessive and blatant electoral manipulation.[93]

Marginal Electoral Manipulation in Post-2000 Zimbabwe

Initial improvements in the living standards of many Zimbabweans in the 1980s gave way, through the 1990s, to increasingly precarious economic conditions that eroded ZANU's political and economic strengths and resulted in a substantial redistribution of electorally relevant resources and power away from the central government. Mugabe retained control over the security apparatus of the state, but economic hardship substantially reduced the resources available to the government (Brett 2005, 14), the government's popularity declined sharply, and civil society became stronger (Sithole 1997).[94] Between 1980 and 1990, growth in per capita GDP averaged more than 4 percent per year, and inequality decreased as a result of social services and attention to the rural population (Brett 2005, 7). Beginning in the 1990s, however, economic mismanagement compounded with failed stabilization policies, in part encouraged by the International Monetary Fund, contributed to high inflation that eroded the real earnings of the middle class and trade unionists, as well as those of ZANU's bases of support – peasants and veterans of the liberation war – even as government officials enriched themselves through graft (Addison and Laakso 2003). By the mid-1990s, the real earnings of private sector workers in the formal economy were 75 percent of their 1990 levels, and those of the public sector were 61 percent of their 1990 level. Inflation further slashed real earnings by about half in the second half of the 1990s (Addison and Laakso 2003, 460–461).[95]

---

[93] I have argued that ZANU's behavior, and in particular its use of excessive electoral manipulation in pursuit of overwhelming victories, was strategically motivated. An alternative explanation is that it was ideologically motivated – that it was the "character" of the party, stemming from its military and/or Marxist origins, that drove its behavior. The internal diversity and dissent within ZANU, however, argue against the notion of a unified ideological outlook among ZANU politicians, while simultaneously underlining the plausibility of the strategic account (i.e., the use of excessive electoral manipulation with the goal of preventing defections and party splits). (I thank Adrienne LeBas for suggesting this alternative explanation.)

[94] For a sober look at the development of civil society in Africa see Bratton 1989 and 1994.

[95] Real incomes declined through a combination of policies that capped public sector wages, a weak labor market, and inflation. Over time the economic situation only continued to deteriorate – unemployment in 2005 was 80%, real GDP decreased by about half between 2000 and 2008, and Zimbabwe attained the world's highest rate of inflation and lowest rate of economic growth (Bratton and Masunungure 2008, 47).

Zimbabwe's economic troubles were severe and had important political consequences for the popularity of ZANU and for its political power. The decline was especially pronounced in the late 1990s, and the 1997–2000 period constituted a turning point. Liberation war veterans collectively threatened to abandon ZANU in the late 1990s, and, to retain their allegiance, the government provided them with pensions and other unaffordable benefits that, in turn, significantly worsened the fiscal deficit and the overall economic situation (Alexander 2000, 388). The government's decision to become involved in the Congo War was an additional significant drain on resources. Other social groups, such as labor, were taxed to pay for the veterans' benefits. The growing discontent spurred diverse civic groups and opposition parties to coalesce into an opposition party, the Movement for Democratic Change (MDC) led by Tsvangirai, that has since presented a formidable electoral challenge to ZANU. MDC had the support of labor as well as of "large numbers of students, professionals, whites, and businesspeople.... It was as if everyone opposed to Mugabe's continued tenure had joined MDC" (Makumbe 2002, 90).[96]

A sure indication of the decline in ZANU's popularity and political control was the fact that it suffered its first-ever defeat at the polls in the February 2000 constitutional referendum, largely as a result of the efforts of a coalition of civil society groups, the NCA. After 2000, the government was no longer able to manipulate excessively (although it may have desired to do so). Instead, the ZANU government found itself compelled to use every trick in the manipulator's hat to merely win elections. In the June 2000 parliamentary election, MDC won 47 percent of the vote and fifty-seven seats, versus 48.6 percent and sixty-two seats for ZANU – a vote margin of less than 2 percentage points.[97] As the 2002 presidential election approached, "nearly all analysts – including Mugabe's own supporters – were convinced that Mugabe stood no chance of winning a fair vote" (Makumbe 2002, 91). The Mugabe regime, aware that it was in danger of losing, went to great lengths to prevent such an outcome. It engaged in registration fraud, intimidation, ballot box stuffing, vote buying, and a variety of techniques of disenfranchisement. When all of this did not suffice, it allegedly tampered with the vote count (Makumbe 2002, 96–97). Mugabe obtained 56.2 percent and Tsvangirai 42 percent, by far the closest result in a presidential race since independence, and a clear indication of the tentative nature of Mugabe's hold on power. The March 2005 legislative election was manipulated through a variety of means. For many constituencies, official results "bore little resemblance to the totals and distributions of votes recorded by observers and party agents on the spot" (Bratton and

---

[96] For a sophisticated discussion of the rise of the MDC see LeBas 2011.

[97] The complete electoral results for elections in the first period are presented in the next subsection.

Masunungure 2006, 26; Zimbabwe Election Support Network 2005, 40–47).[98] ZANU obtained 59.6 percent of the vote and seventy-eight seats, MDC obtained 39.5 percent of the vote and forty-one seats, again a far cry from ZANU's typical electoral results in the 1980s and early 1990s.[99] By March of 2008, a public opinion poll indicated that only 20 percent of respondents intended to vote for Mugabe in the upcoming presidential election.[100] The first round of voting took place on March 29, 2008. It is beyond dispute that Mugabe lost the poll, and it is widely believed that his opponent, Tsvangirai, obtained an outright majority of the vote in the first round. The official first-round result was not announced for more than a month after the election, and it put Tsvangirai ahead of Mugabe, albeit without a majority, with 47.9 percent versus 43.2 percent of the vote. According to some reports, Mugabe intended to surrender power after learning that he had lost, but his security chiefs insisted that he remain in power (Timberg 2008, *Washington Post*, July 5).[101]

In sum, the second period was characterized by the rise of alternative centers of political power, a decline in the government's popularity, and a relative decrease in the state's economic and political might.[102] In turn, this made it impossible for the government to manipulate excessively, even as it rendered it imperative to manipulate to stay in office. In all likelihood, Mugabe would have

[98] As in previous elections, voter lists were inflated with "ghost voters," polling stations were disproportionately located in rural areas, and the electoral institutions were staffed with ZANU appointees (Bratton and Masunungure 2006, 26).

[99] In 2005, there were two elections – one in March for parliament (the House of Assembly), and a second one in November for the Senate, which was reintroduced having been previously abolished by the ZANU government in 1990. The November election was won by ZANU by a landslide, after the government's violent Operation Murambatsvina ("clear out the trash"), which violently displaced up to 700,000 city dwellers and was widely seen as retaliation against a perceived source of MDC support. The MDC called for a boycott of the senate election. Wellman (2010) argues that the operation was electorally motivated and, more generally, that slum policy constitutes a powerful tool of electoral manipulation. For a discussion of the relationship between increased political competition and violence in Zimbabwe, see LeBas (2006).

[100] Poll by the Mass Public Opinion Institute (MPOI), unpublished memo, March 12, 2008, reported in Bratton and Masunungure (2008, 55). (Masunungure directed the MPOI as of 2008.)

[101] This brief discussion of the 2008 election, focused on those aspects of it that are most relevant for purposes of the present study, does not convey the gravity of the events that surrounded it. After the first round, the regime embarked on a violent campaign of "electoral cleansing," killing, intimidating, and displacing MDC officials and supporters. These efforts targeted regions that had swung from ZANU toward MDC in the first round (Bratton and Masunungure 2008, 51–52; Robinson and Torvik 2009). The second-round result gave Mugabe 85.5% of the vote, implying that Tsvangirai received almost 1 million fewer votes than in the first round, out of a total of about 2.4 million valid votes.

[102] An additional factor in the relative weakening of the state was an increase in international scrutiny and "democratic" pressures, both from African nations and from the West, in part because of Mugabe's targeting of white farmers beginning in 2000.

wished to manipulate excessively even in the post-2000 period. The potential for indirect effects was still present – the government was still capable of rewarding and punishing political actors according to partisan criteria.[103] In other words, excessive electoral manipulation could probably still have yielded a potentially large payoff to the manipulator in the post-2000 period. But the implementation of such manipulation was no longer within the grasp of the government. Instead, the government utilized increasingly desperate and violent means to secure electoral victory where it was otherwise sure to lose.[104] As in the 1980s and 1990s, electoral manipulation in Zimbabwe after 2000 was one-sided and large-scale; but whereas it was excessive in the 1980s and 1990s, it was marginal after 2000.

6.5 CONCLUSION: PARALLELS AND DIFFERENCES

These case studies collectively exemplify the puzzle of excessive and blatant electoral manipulation, and show how a range of indirect effects resulted from such manipulation. They also indicate how incentives for excessive electoral manipulation resulted from the presence of the proximate background conditions theorized in Chapter 5 (Section 5.3). Loosely speaking, those conditions included an initial concentration of power and resources in the hands of the government, and a large measure of discretion in the use of government resources for partisan ends, in part stemming from a relatively weak rule of law and from the absence of strong external democratic pressures. The cases show that the concentration of power, resources, and discretion in the hands of the ruling party can stem from diverse sources. In Zimbabwe, the combination of a strong security apparatus inherited from the colonial government, and Mugabe and ZANU's status as liberators, underpinned such strength. In Russia, in contrast, Putin re-concentrated power largely on the basis of an economic bonanza based on rising oil and gas prices.

---

[103] It is not clear whether the potential payoff from excessive manipulation increased or decreased in the second period, in comparison with the 1980s and early 1990s. On the one hand, the economically weaker state had less to offer by way of payoffs and benefits. On the other hand, the economic crisis also affected the population, and the government still had full control over the CIO, the police, and the military.

[104] I emphasize again that the precise meaning with which the term "excessive" is utilized in this study can in some contexts diverge from the colloquial use of the word. Colloquially speaking, Mugabe's use of violent means to secure electoral victory could be called excessive – in the sense of "unacceptable," of something that crosses the line. As emphasized earlier, however, the large scale use of electoral manipulation – even of alarmingly violent manipulation – does not make it excessive in the sense in which the term was defined in earlier chapters (e.g., Chapters 1, 3, 4, and 5), if it does not suffice to significantly exceed the victory threshold. To be sure, electoral manipulation by ZANU was blatant throughout. Nevertheless, the tightness of the electoral races after 2000 meant the overall picture that emerged from post-2000 electoral results was that ZANU was electorally vulnerable.

In both Russia and Zimbabwe, the power and discretion of the ruling party, both in absolute terms and in relation to those of other social and political actors, experienced important shocks. In Russia, the shock – a steep rise in the international price of oil and gas – was positive and placed Putin in an initially advantageous position. Where Yeltsin manipulated to survive, Putin was now able to manipulate to enhance his position of power. In Zimbabwe, the shock was negative: an economic crisis, partly the result of pressures from international financial institutions and partly the outcome of mismanagement, broke down the ruling party's aura of invincibility and spurred its rivals to coalesce, eroding Mugabe's and ZANU's relative advantages and rendering excessive electoral manipulation no longer possible.[105]

These shocks divide the time period under study, for each of the cases, into two segments: a segment where the ruling party was clearly more powerful and resourceful than any other actor; and a segment where it faced one or more formidable rivals. But the temporal order of these two segments differed. In Russia, the period of ruling party power came second, while in Zimbabwe it came first. Nevertheless, in both cases the incentives and possibilities to manipulate elections – and, in consequence, the pattern of manipulation – responded accordingly. Under conditions of power and resource advantages, the ruling party manipulated excessively and blatantly, both in Zimbabwe and in Russia. In both cases, when the ruling party's advantages were smaller, manipulation barely sufficed to win.[106]

---

[105] This is not to say that the government in Zimbabwe ceased to have power, resources, and discretion; but merely that after 2000 they faced much stronger opposition than before.

[106] This is so even though both under Mugabe after 2000 and under Yeltsin, the *extent* of manipulation was substantial. The specific tactics of manipulation differed, with violence playing a more prominent role in Zimbabwe (see Chapter 1 for a discussion of the choice of tactics of manipulation).

7

Indirect Effects of Electoral Manipulation

Quantitative Evidence

This chapter continues the exploration of empirical implications of my theory. I present three pieces of analysis that speak to the indirect effects of electoral manipulation. In contrast with the case studies, the approach in the first two analyses is quantitative and the focus is on one specific kind of actor: the citizen as voter (while the case studies discussed indirect effects on a variety of actors). Part of the reason to zoom in on voters is simply data availability. I have been able to locate more information on voter behavior – specifically, on voter participation – than on the behavior of any other category of political or social actor. The first piece of analysis is based on survey data for more than sixty elections in several different countries, and it studies the relationship between perceptions about electoral manipulation and the propensity of an individual citizen to cast a vote. The analysis supports two empirical implications of the theory. First, a citizen who believes that elections are manipulated is less likely to cast a vote. Second, this effect is stronger for opposition supporters. The second piece of analysis also concerns the relationship of electoral manipulation and voter participation, but it is based on a different source of evidence. For this analysis, I utilize the fact that Mexico enacted deep electoral reform in the 1990s to construct a quasi-experimental estimate of the effect of electoral manipulation on aggregate voter participation at the state level. The main finding is that excessive electoral manipulation in Mexico before the 1990s substantially depressed voter participation rates. The first two pieces of analysis complement each other (as well as those from the case studies in the previous chapter) – they are based on different kinds of evidence and methods, and have different geographical and temporal coverage, yet arrive at similar conclusions.

Finally, the third analysis in the chapter tests one of the broadest empirical implications of the theory: if excessive electoral manipulation indeed has indirect benefits of the sort I have described, this is likely to impact duration in office. For this test, I utilize the original dataset described earlier in the book.

I find that excessive electoral manipulation is strongly associated with longer party duration in office, even after taking into account variation in electoral rules, the level of development, and the strength of the rule of law.

7.1 INDIRECT EFFECTS OF ELECTORAL MANIPULATION ON VOTER BEHAVIOR: EVIDENCE FROM SURVEYS

As suggested in previous chapters and illustrated in the case studies, the causal chain underlying the indirect effects of electoral manipulation runs through the "political context" (Figure 4.1 in Chapter 4). The political context is the set of circumstances under which social and political actors make political choices – bureaucrats choose whether to exert effort on behalf of the incumbent, politicians whether to run for office, businessmen and organizations whether to press for rents or policy concessions, voters whether to show up at the polls. The importance of the political context is that it contributes to shaping the beliefs of actors – for example, beliefs about the ruling party's grip on office, or about whether its opponents will actively challenge it. In turn, such beliefs influence behavior. In this section, I focus on a specific element of the political context as perceived by citizens, namely on citizens' perceptions about electoral manipulation. The mechanism for indirect effects that I have described suggests that citizens' political behavior will be sensitive to such perceptions. I specifically examine the following empirical implications of my arguments. First, for sympathizers of opposition parties, the perception that elections are likely to be manipulated will be associated with a lower propensity to vote.[1] Second, even when the data do not contain information on partisan sympathies, perceptions of electoral manipulation are likely to depress the average propensity to vote.[2] Third, these effects are more likely to be present where the relevant background conditions hold – loosely speaking, where the ruling party has considerable power, resources, and discretion.[3]

In this section, I analyze individual-level survey data for sixty-two elections in fifty-six countries between 1996 and 2002. Every survey contains a question that measures the respondent's *turnout behavior* – the dependent variable – and one that measures the respondent's *perceptions about electoral manipulation* – the independent variable. A handful of surveys also contain information about the respondent's partisanship. In addition, all surveys contain measures of control variables that are commonly used in analyses of turnout, including

---

[1] I discuss the reasons for this in Chapter 4. One reason is the existence of act-and-outcome-contingent payoffs. A second reason is that beliefs that the election outcome is predetermined can elicit expressive responses of discouragement and apathy.

[2] Suppose, for example, that opposition supporters are more sensitive than other citizens to beliefs about electoral manipulation. Then it is likely that, on average – that is, without conditioning on partisanship – beliefs about electoral manipulation correlate negatively with the probability of turnout.

[3] The relationship between background conditions and indirect effects is discussed in Chapters 4 and 5 (Section 5.3).

age, income, education, and political interest. The set of surveys includes every survey that I could find with measures of the independent and the dependent variables. The set includes countries in Africa, America, Asia, Western Europe, and Central and Eastern Europe, spanning a wide range of levels of institutional strength, social structure, and economic well-being (Nigeria, Peru, and Sweden, for example, are included in the set). All surveys are based on probability samples.

The analysis is straightforward. I estimate the effect of perceptions about electoral manipulation on the propensity to cast a vote using regression. I find that, on average, those individuals who perceive that the relevant election was, or will be, manipulated are less likely to vote. Moreover, in the Africa surveys, which contain information about partisanship, the effect of such perceptions on the likelihood of voting is driven by opposition supporters.[4]

Where possible, I exploit the properties of the data to probe the robustness of the findings. For example, a possible threat to inference is that the relationship between perceptions about electoral manipulation and turnout might be driven by "post-hoc justification" (i.e., if individuals who did not vote are more likely to respond that the election was manipulated to justify, ex-post-facto, the fact that they did not vote). To address this possibility, I estimate the relevant relationship in the subset of surveys that were conducted *before* the election took place, or between election rounds in multi-round elections. The finding holds up to this check.

A second potential issue is the possibility that the relationship between perceptions of electoral manipulation and turnout might be driven by an omitted variable. For example, cultural norms could lead "polite" individuals to feel compelled to say both that they voted and that they thought that the election was clean. To address this possibility, I estimate the analysis separately for individual countries. The fact that the result holds up in dozens of countries located in different regions and presenting wide variation in socioeconomic and institutional configurations renders this possibility less likely.[5] Finally, could the well-known propensity of individuals to over-report turnout in surveys represent a problem for this analysis? There is no obvious reason why this should be the case.[6] Ansolabehere and Persily (2008) study the

---

[4] The term "effect" implies causality. I will use causal language throughout the chapter for simplicity, and for consistency with the theory. As with any analysis of observational data, the possibility remains that the estimated relationships could reflect bias because of unobservable factors or other forms of simultaneity.

[5] I find that individuals who believe that elections were (or will be) manipulated are less likely to vote even in countries with the strongest democratic credentials. The proportion of respondents in such countries who actually believe that elections were manipulated is low, but those who hold such a belief have a lower propensity to turn out.

[6] One way in which over-reporting could cause bias is if the propensity to over-report was correlated with reported beliefs about electoral manipulation. I was not able to come up with a reasonable argument for why such a correlation might exist. Moreover, even if such a correlation existed, it is not clear whether it would strengthen or weaken the findings presented here.

relationship between turnout and beliefs about electoral manipulation using both self-reported turnout (past and future) and validated turnout data, and find that the relationship between the variables is virtually identical using all three turnout methods – in other words, turnout over-reporting did not affect the joint distribution of turnout and beliefs about electoral manipulation.[7]

A handful of studies have previously used survey data to address the relationship between electoral manipulation and turnout. In an early and influential study of Mexico, Domínguez and McCann (1996) show that Mexicans who believe elections to be fraudulent are less likely to vote.[8] Ansolabehere and Persily (2008) find that an individual's propensity to vote is uncorrelated with perceptions about election fraud in present-day United States. In this section, I bring a cross-national perspective to the issue, and I connect it to the theoretical arguments of the book.

Perceptions of Electoral Manipulation

I use data from three sources – Module 1 of the Comparative Study of Electoral Systems (CSES), Latinobarómetro (2000), and Round 1 of Afrobarometer. Within each group, the surveys can be pooled together or analyzed separately. The largest group consists of thirty-three surveys from Module 1 of the CSES, covering thirty-three elections in twenty-nine countries in the 1996–2002 period. An almost identical survey (in translation) was administered in every case, on nationally representative samples of citizens of voting age. There exist some differences in sampling procedures and in question design between surveys, but overall the study is designed so that the surveys can be pooled together. Surveys were completed through personal interviews, phone interviews and mailbacks.[9] Thirty-two of the surveys are for legislative elections, and one (Lithuania 1997) for a presidential election. On average, there are about 1,600 respondents per election. Most of the surveys were conducted after the election, but some were collected both before and after, and others between rounds of majoritarian elections. The survey question for perceptions about electoral manipulation is the following:

In some countries, people believe their elections are conducted fairly. In other countries, people believe their elections are conducted unfairly. Thinking of the last election in [country], where would you place it on this scale of one to five where ONE means

---

[7] See Ansolabehere and Persily 2008, Table 3 and Appendix D. Validated vote is based on government records, not on the respondent's answer to a survey question. They find no statistically significant relationship for any of their measures of turnout in the elections they study. (See Berent, Krosnick, and Lupia 2008 for a critique of both validated turnout records, and the idea that survey respondents over-report turnout.)

[8] I discuss survey-based findings for Mexico in the next section.

[9] Information on sampling frames or response rates is unfortunately not available; some of the survey houses provided weights (e.g., see Sapiro and Shively 2004).

that the last election was conducted fairly and FIVE means that the last election was conducted unfairly?

The Latinobarómetro set consists of identical surveys fielded in 2000 in Latin American countries, in Spanish. The question measuring perceptions about electoral manipulation is:

In some countries people think that elections are clean; in other countries people think that elections are not clean. Thinking about the last election, where would you place it on a 5-step scale, where 1 is clean and 5 is "not clean"?[10]

In the Afrobarometer set, the question about manipulation varies slightly from country to country, as does the list of possible answers.[11] The following question was asked in Namibia, Zambia, Zimbabwe, Botswana, Lesotho, Malawi, and South Africa.

On the whole, how would you rate the freeness and fairness of the last national election, held in [YEAR]?

Completely free and fair
Free and fair with some minor problems
On the whole, free and fair but with several major problems
Not free and fair
Don't know

The questions for Ghana, Mali, Tanzania, Nigeria, and Uganda are slightly different. The set of answers for those countries is:

Very dishonest
Somewhat honest
Quite honest
Very honest

For purposes of comparison, I assume that the "completely free and fair" category is equivalent to "very honest," and so on. Although all Afrobarometer surveys were administered between 1999 and 2001, the "last national election" year varied by country.

Table 7.1 displays the proportion of respondents who answered that the election was unfair, or not clean, or dishonest.[12] The table shows there is considerable variation in beliefs about electoral manipulation between countries

---

[10] Author's translation. The translation in Latinobarómetro's English-language documentation reads "rigged" instead of "not clean." The Spanish term is "no limpias." The CSES questionnaire in Spanish also uses the term "no limpias," which CSES translated into English as "unfair."

[11] For information on sampling procedures see Appendix B of Bratton et al. 2005.

[12] The numerator is the number of respondents choosing categories 4 or 5 in CSES and Latinobarómetro, "not free and fair" or "with major problems" in the first wording of the Afrobarometer question, and "very" or "somewhat" dishonest in the second wording of the Afrobarometer question. The survey for Zimbabwe (Afrobarometer) is the same as that used in the case study in Chapter 6.

TABLE 7.1. *Proportion of Respondents Perceiving Elections as Very or Somewhat Unfair, Dishonest, or Unclean*

CSES		Latinobarómetro		Afrobarometer	
Peru (2000)	54%	Paraguay	63%	Zimbabwe	60%
Thailand (2001)	37%	Ecuador	63%	Ghana	38%
Ukraine (1998)	35%	México	57%	Malawi	35%
South Korea (2000)	31%	Bolivia	56%	Lesotho	35%
Russia (1999)	28%	Colombia	54%	Mali	31%
Belarus (2001)	27%	Nicaragua	49%	South Africa	22%
Japan (1996)	27%	Perú	45%	Zambia	21%
Lithuania (1997)	26%	El Salvador	42%	Tanzania	18%
Mexico (1997)	23%	Brasil	41%	Nigeria	17%
Israel (1996)	20%	Honduras	35%	Namibia	12%
Russia (2000)	20%	Argentina	29%	Botswana	11%
Hong Kong (1998)	19%	Venezuela	25%	Uganda	8%
Hong Kong (2000)	17%	Guatemala	24%		
Mexico (2000)	17%	Costa Rica	21%		
Peru (2001)	14%	Uruguay	19%		
Taiwan (1996)	14%	Panamá	18%		
Slovenia (1996)	11%	Chile	17%		
Spain (1996)	11%				
Poland (1997)	10%				
United States (1996)	10%				
Romania (1996)	9%				
Spain (2000)	9%				
Portugal (2002)	7%				
New Zealand (1996)	7%				
Iceland (1999)	6%				
Canada (1997)	6%				
Hungary (1998)	5%				
Switzerland (1999)	5%				
Czech Republic (1996)	5%				
Sweden (1998)	4%				
United Kingdom (1997)	4%				
Norway (1997)	3%				
Denmark (1998)	2%				
Germany (1998)	2%				
Netherlands (1998)	2%				

Notes: CSES election year displayed in parentheses. Survey question for Latinobarómetro and Afrobarometer refers to the most recent national election at the time of the survey (see text for further details). Table displays proportion of respondents who chose either of the top two categories of "unfairness," "dishonesty," or "uncleanliness."

and elections. The variation roughly matches independent knowledge about the elections: Zimbabwe tops the Afrobarometer list (the figure refers to the 1996 presidential election, discussed previously), Chile and Costa Rica are near the bottom of the Latinobarómetro set, while countries with histories of gross electoral manipulation such as Mexico and Paraguay are near the top, and in the Scandinavian countries very few people believe that elections are unfair. This is true in general of "established" democracies. The availability of pairs of surveys at different points in time in the same country within the CSES set, as for Peru and Mexico, permits some additional validation of the idea that the information in the table is meaningful, because variation in average perceptions over time within each of these two countries correlates with independent information about what actually happened in each election. The pair of surveys conducted in Peru provides a nice contrast: the 2000 election, widely condemned as grossly manipulated by the ruling party, tops the CSES list, with more than half of those surveyed believing that the election was unfair. In contrast, the 2001 election – generally viewed as a clean election – is in the middle of the pack. Similarly, fewer Mexicans thought the 2000 election – the first time in seventy years that the ruling party lost the presidency – was unfair, in comparison with the 1997 Mexico survey.[13]

Looking across survey sets, the proportion of Mexicans who found the 1997 election to be unfair according to Latinobarómetro was much greater than the equivalent proportion in the CSES survey.[14] Various possible explanations for this come to mind. First, Mexican respondents could have had the 1994 presidential election in mind when answering the Latinobarómetro survey (because presidential elections traditionally mattered more in Mexico than legislative ones, and a presidential election was to take place relatively soon after the time when the survey was fielded). Second, it is possible that the delay between the time of the past election (1997) and the time of the survey (2000) meant that respondent perceptions changed, especially because Mexican electoral institutions were undergoing a process of rapid changes in the 1990s. Third, differences in question wording or sampling frame could be partly responsible.

Relationship between Perceptions of Manipulation and Turnout

To investigate the relationship between perceptions of electoral manipulation and turnout, I focus on two concepts. The "marginal effect" refers to the influence of beliefs about electoral manipulation on the probability that *an*

---

[13] The proportion of Russian respondents who perceived the election to be unfair was greater in 1999 than in 2000. The reason for this remains an open question. See Chapter 6 for further details on electoral manipulation in Russian elections.

[14] Because the Latinobarómetro survey was conducted several months before the 2000 election in Mexico, I assume that respondents would have had in mind the 1997 legislative election.

individual cast a vote.[15] The "total effect" captures the influence of beliefs about electoral manipulation on *aggregate* turnout in a country. In other words, the total effect of perceptions on turnout in a country reflects the cumulative marginal effects for each of the individuals in that country. To estimate the marginal effect of perceptions about manipulation, I regress self-reported turnout on such perceptions (with standard controls). I compute the total effect as the difference between two scenarios: one where every respondent in the country (or set of countries) believes that the election was fair/honest/clean, and one where every respondent holds the beliefs that they report in the survey. The total effect considers both the marginal effect of perceptions about electoral manipulation on the individual propensity to vote, and the distribution of such perceptions among respondents.

Table 7.2 displays the results of probit regressions on the pooled sample for each of the three sets of surveys, with heteroskedasticity-robust standard errors clustered by country. The analysis includes all the elections in Table 7.1 with the exception of Russia 2000 and Thailand 2001, for which the item on whether individuals cast a vote is missing or unusable.[16] Following common practice, I control for respondent education, gender, age, the square of age, income, and interest in politics.[17] All specifications include country dummies (these coefficients are not reported in the table). Two specifications are reported for the CSES; the first one omits the controls for income and political information, because list-wise deletion of cases with missing data on these items substantially reduces the number of elections and of observations. The principal message of the analysis reported in Table 7.2 is that the perception that the election was (or would be) unfair, dishonest, or unclean is associated with a statistically and substantively significant decrease in an individual's propensity to vote.

To obtain a sense for the magnitude of this effect, Table 7.3 shows the change in propensity to vote associated with the belief that the election was (or would be) substantially manipulated, compared with the counterfactual belief that the election was (or would be) free and fair.[18] The table provides point estimates as well as confidence intervals calculated via simulation, for a hypothetical average female respondent.[19] The perception that an election

---

[15] The word "marginal" here is used in its econometric sense, which is unrelated to the theoretical concept of "marginal manipulation."

[16] In the case of Russia, every respondent is coded as having voted, which could indicate a technical problem with the reporting of this item or an instance of gross over-reporting; in the case of Thailand the item was not fielded.

[17] For further information on the specific survey items used for each of the controls, please refer to the note below the Table.

[18] That is, a change in the response category from the "best" to the "worst," in the survey items given previously.

[19] All controls other than gender are set at their mean levels. The regressions used for Table 7.3 do not include country because the simulations software utilized, Clarify, cannot invert the matrix of regressors when these are included. Weights are also omitted (for those CSES surveys with weights) because Clarify does not support them (all simulations conducted with Clarify).

TABLE 7.2. *Regression of Individual Turnout on Perceptions of Electoral Manipulation*

Variable	CSES		Latinobarómetro	Afrobarometer	
	A	B	C	D	E (OLS)
Electoral Manipulation	−0.129***	−0.109***	−0.040***	−0.147***	−0.009
	0.00	0.00	0.00	0.00	0.19
Education	0.105***	0.101***	0.023***	0.041+	0.010
	0.00	0.00	0.00	0.11	0.20
Age	0.052***	0.045***	0.132***	0.103***	0.029***
	0.00	0.00	0.00	0.00	0.00
Age²	−0.000***	−0.000***	−0.001***	−0.001***	−0.000***
	0.00	0.00	0.00	0.00	0.00
Gender	−0.013	0.018	−0.020	−0.097	−0.020
	0.52	0.49	0.58	0.16	0.28
Income		0.039***	−0.048*	−0.006**	−0.002*
		0.00	0.05	0.05	0.06
Political Interest		0.256***	−0.097***	0.092	0.013
		0.00	0.00	0.19	0.43
Opposition Supporter					−0.177***
					0.00
Manip x Opposition					−0.023*
					0.06
Elec. Manip., Opposition (simple slope)					−0.031**
					0.01
Constant	1.372***	−0.767***	−1.214**	−2.478***	−0.013
	0.00	0.00	0.01	0.00	0.90
Country Dummies	Y	Y	Y	Y	Y
N	46783	26902	15314	18241	18392
Number of Elections	33	24	17	12	12

Notes: Models A–D are probit regression estimates, model E estimated by OLS, all with robust standard errors clustered by country; P-values shown below coefficients (*** P<0.01, ** P<0.05, * P<0.1, + P<0.15); coefficients of country dummy variables not shown; simple slope in model E calculated on the basis of regression parameters; regressions A and B use weights provided by survey houses; "Electoral Manipulation" refers to the questions about the fairness, honesty, and cleanliness of elections reproduced above in the text; "Income" refers to self-reported income quintile (*A2012*, CSES), self-reported frequency with which respondent goes without cash income (*povinc*, Afrobarometer; lower values indicate higher income), and interviewer's assessment of respondent's socioeconomic status (*s16 apreciación del nivel socioeconómico*, Latinobarómetro, lower values indicate higher income); "Political Interest" refers to a political information item that differs by survey (*A2023*, CSES), a dummy variable indicating high interest in politics (coded on the basis of *scint*, Afrobarometer), and self-reported attention to political news on TV (*p57st_a*, Latinobarómetro, lower values indicate higher attention levels; regression D controls for newspaper readership while regression E does not); "Education" refers to highest level completed (*A2003* in CSES, *educ* in Afrobarometer, and *s6 estudios realizados* in Latinobarómetro; response categories vary slightly). Unless otherwise specified in this note, higher values correspond to a higher level of electoral manipulation, more education, female gender, higher income, and higher political interest.

TABLE 7.3. *Marginal Effect of Perceptions of Electoral Manipulation on Probability of Voting*

	Point Estimate	Confidence Interval (90%)
CSES 1996–2002 (33 elections)	−10.3%	[−13.6%, −7.1%]
Afrobarometer 1999 (12 elections)	−11.0%	[−18.7%, −3.9%]
Latinobarómetro 2000 (17 elections)	−6.5%	[−11.6%, −1.3%]

Notes: Based on simulations for a female respondent with average values of all the other controls (see text for details).

is manipulated can reduce the probability that such a respondent will cast a vote by up to 11 percent. The average effect across the three sets of surveys, weighting by the number of elections, is a reduction in the probability of casting a vote of 9.4 percent. For the three sets of surveys, the results are highly robust to the omission of some or all controls, country dummies, weighting, and error clustering.

Figure 7.1 breaks down the marginal effect for counterfactual changes in beliefs about manipulation of different magnitudes, for the same average female respondent. The figure displays point estimates and simulation-generated confidence intervals for the CSES set of surveys; the rightmost item is equivalent to the CSES line in Table 7.3.[20]

I next estimate the effect of perceptions on turnout, election-by-election, to assess whether the timing of the survey in relation to the election might influence the findings. This would be the case, for example, if the relationship between perceptions about manipulation and the propensity to vote spuriously resulted from post-hoc justification by respondents who failed to cast a vote (and to justify it, expressed a negative opinion of the election by stating that it was unfair/dishonest/unclean). Table 7.4 displays the results for the CSES surveys.[21] Every survey was analyzed in a separate regression, using the set of controls in Column B of Table 7.2.[22] The table displays marginal effects and total effects; elections are sorted by total effect. The table indicates the timing

Marginal effects obtained by calculating the change in probability of voting associated with an infinitesimal change in perceptions about electoral manipulation, holding all other regressors at their means, on the model with weights and country dummies, are very similar. The CSES specification reported in Table 7.3 corresponds to the set of controls in regression A in Table 7.2 (with the exception of the country dummies), which maximizes sample size (the results using the larger set of controls, not shown, are slightly stronger). Omitting the country dummies slightly weakens the effect of electoral manipulation for the CSES and Afrobarometer sets (i.e., it makes it slightly smaller in absolute value), and slightly strengthens the effect for Latinobarómetro.

[20] Equivalent graphs for Afrobarometer and Latinobarómetro are similar (not shown).

[21] All Afrobarometer and Latinobarómetro surveys were conducted after the corresponding elections.

[22] The item on political interest is not available in all surveys. Marginal effects were generated from probit estimates by calculating the change in probability of voting associated with an infinitesimal change in perceptions about electoral manipulation, holding all other regressors

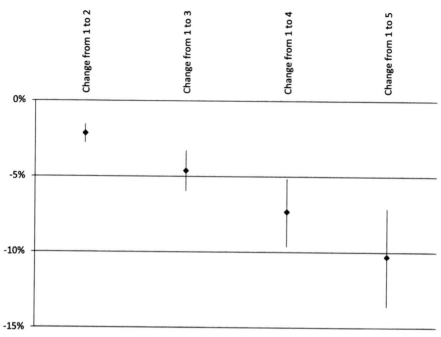

FIGURE 7.1. Effect of Perceptions of Electoral Fairness on Probability of Voting, CSES. *Notes:* Based on simulations for a female respondent with average values of all the other controls (see text for further details). Bars indicate 90% confidence intervals.

of the survey. When no timing is indicated, the survey was conducted after the election.

The marginal effect of perceptions of manipulation is statistically significant in twenty-three out of the thirty-three elections. The average marginal effect across the thirty-three country regressions of a change in the perceptions variable from 1 to 5 is a decrease in the probability of casting a vote of 8.5 percent. The timing of the survey does not change the size of the effects in any obvious way: considering only the five elections for which surveys were conducted before the election, the average effect is a decrease of 9.1 percent (and in four out of these five, the effect is negative and statistically significant), suggesting that post-hoc justification is unlikely to be driving the estimates.

The table also illustrates one way in which the marginal effects identified earlier matter in the aggregate, by indicating total effects in addition to marginal effects. To illustrate the substantive meaning of these two effects, consider the Ukraine 1998 election. If the average respondent switched from believing that the election was fully free and fair to believing that it was highly manipulated,

at their means. This method is slightly less precise than the simulations utilized for the pooled analysis, but it is simpler to implement.

TABLE 7.4. *Marginal and Total Effect of Perceptions of Electoral Fairness on Turnout, CSES*

Election	Marginal Effect (Change from 1 to 5)	Total Effect	P-Value	Timing of Survey
Ukraine (1998)	−19.2%	−9.5%	0.00	
South Korea (2000)	−10.0%	−5.1%	0.01	
Russia (1999)	−11.2%	−4.8%	0.00	Pre-election
Belarus (2001)	−12.8%	−4.4%	0.00	
Slovenia (1996)	−16.0%	−4.2%	0.00	
Portugal (2002)	−23.6%	−3.8%	0.00	
Hungary (1998)	−19.6%	−3.2%	0.00	Between rounds
Canada (1997)	−11.6%	−2.9%	0.00	
Poland (1997)	−12.4%	−2.9%	0.02	
Peru (2000)	−4.4%	−2.7%	0.01	
Mexico (1997)	−7.6%	−2.7%	0.06	
Switzerland (1999)	−23.6%	−2.6%	0.00	Between rounds
Spain (2000)	−13.6%	−2.6%	0.00	
United States (1996)	−11.6%	−2.6%	0.02	Pre-election
Czech Republic (1996)	−10.8%	−2.2%	0.00	Pre-election
Hong Kong (1998)	−5.2%	−2.0%	0.36	
New Zealand (1996)	−7.6%	−1.6%	0.07	
United Kingdom (1997)	−8.0%	−1.4%	0.06	
Spain (1996)	−6.0%	−1.1%	0.09	
Iceland (1999)	−6.4%	−1.0%	0.04	
Israel (1996)	−3.2%	−1.0%	0.21	
Netherlands (1998)	−10.0%	−1.0%	0.00	Pre-election
Lithuania (1997)	−2.4%	−0.9%	0.32	
Japan (1996)	−2.0%	−0.9%	0.63	Pre-election
Sweden (1998)	−6.4%	−0.7%	0.10	
Germany (1998)	−6.4%	−0.6%	0.03	
Peru (2001)	−2.4%	−0.6%	0.18	
Mexico (2000)	−1.2%	−0.3%	0.45	
Denmark (1998)	−4.8%	−0.2%	0.02	
Taiwan (1996)	−0.4%	−0.1%	0.87	
Norway (1997)	−0.4%	0.0%	0.95	
Hong Kong (2000)	0.0%	0.0%	1.00	
Romania (1996)	1.2%	0.2%	0.64	

Note: Based on CSES, Module 1. See text for further details.

the probability that she casts a vote would decrease by 19.5 percent – this is the marginal effect. Suppose now that everyone in Ukraine believed that the 1998 election had been fully free and fair. Then aggregate turnout in Ukraine in that election would have increased by 9.5 percent (this is the total effect). In contrast, in the 2001 election in Peru, perceptions about electoral manipulation were uncorrelated with individual and aggregate turnout (because the marginal effect is negative but it is not statistically significant at conventional levels).

Qualitatively, many of the findings are as expected: the total effect of perceptions of manipulation on aggregate turnout is quite small in the Scandinavian countries, and it is large in Russia, Ukraine, and Belarus. It is larger in Peru in 2000 than in 2001, and it is larger in Mexico in 1997 than in 2000 (moreover, only the 1997 effect is statistically significant). In countries with strong democratic institutions such as the United States and Switzerland, while marginal effects are of a non-negligible size, total effects are comparatively small because relatively few respondents believe elections to be unfair. How might one understand the finding that marginal effects are stronger (i.e., more negative) for Swiss and Portuguese respondents than for, say, Ukrainian ones? There are various ways to interpret the finding. First, in Switzerland and Portugal, the effect is driven by the very small proportion of the electorate who believes elections to be "unfair" (5 percent and 7 percent, respectively). These small portions of the electorate could hold idiosyncratic views that drive the effect. In contrast, more than a third of Ukrainian respondents believed the election to be unfair. Second, understandings of electoral "unfairness" are potentially correlated with the strength of democratic institutions. Electoral unfairness for a Ukrainian voter is likely to be much closer to this book's notion of electoral manipulation – voter intimidation, ballot box stuffing, tampering with the vote count, vote buying – than for a Swiss voter, for whom unfairness might refer to issues such as malapportionment (i.e., the degree to which allocations of legislative seats across parties correspond to the parties' respective vote shares).[23] If so, less stock should be placed on the findings for countries with the strongest democratic institutions (including some Latin American countries such as Costa Rica and Chile in the Latinobarómetro set). The central finding is robust to the exclusion of the wealthy democracies – the average marginal effect in the CSES set for countries other than wealthy democracies (i.e., those in Western Europe, the United States, Canada, and New Zealand) is a reduction in the propensity to cast a vote of 7.3 percent, quite close to the average of all individual-country marginal effects in the CSES set (8.5 percent).

The country-by-country results for the Latinobarómetro and Afrobarometer surveys are provided in Table 7.1A in this chapter's Appendix. Table 7.1A displays marginal and total effects for the Afrobarometer and Latinobarómetro sets of surveys. The survey items of interest in Afrobarometer are associated with elections in the late 1990s.[24] The country-by-country results from these

---

[23] For measures of malapportionment in Switzerland and Portugal, see Samuels and Snyder (2001).

[24] The item *parvot* asks whether the respondent cast a vote in the last election, referring to the election in 1999 for all countries except for Ghana (1996), Mali (1997), Tanzania (2000), Uganda (1996), and Zambia (1996). The item *prfele* is the question about the honesty of elections reproduced above in the text. That question was asked in reference to elections in

surveys also conform broadly to prior expectations: Nigeria, Zimbabwe, and Zambia all experienced major (in fact, excessive) electoral manipulation at some point in the 1990s, and, consistent with this, the marginal and total effects of perceptions about electoral manipulation on turnout are near the top of the table. The table is topped by Mali, which had an especially problematic legislative election in 1997 (Bratton 1998, 60). Ghana's 1996 election was largely free and fair, and the marginal and total effects for Ghana are accordingly small.[25]

Thus far, the analysis has shown that, on average, perceptions about electoral manipulation are associated with lower electoral participation in a relatively diverse set of elections. I now study whether the effect is driven by, or is stronger among, *opposition supporters*. I have suggested earlier in this section, and in earlier chapters, that perceptions about electoral manipulation could be associated with a lower propensity to vote among opposition supporters, particularly in settings where incumbents are disproportionately powerful. If this is true, marginal effects should be stronger for opposition supporters in the African cases with strong incumbents and, possibly, in the Latin American cases with a recent history of substantial electoral manipulation, where attitudes could have persisted even after electoral competition increased with democratization.

The Afrobarometer surveys include an item (*pidwin*) that asks respondents whether they identify with the ruling party, a losing party, or no party (neutrals). One issue with this question is that it is possible that opposition supporters may not feel comfortable expressing their partisan preference. This is especially likely where incumbents are powerful and are able to condition benefits on partisan preference and to harass opposition supporters, such as in Zimbabwe, Nigeria, and Zambia. Simply looking at the distribution of responses to this item strongly suggests that this is the case: while 41 percent of respondents in Ghana and 43 percent in Botswana identified with the losing party, only 6 percent did so in Zambia, 13 percent in Zimbabwe, and 15 percent in Nigeria. In contrast, the proportion of respondents who identified as neutral is very large in Zambia (64 percent), Zimbabwe (58 percent)

1999 in all countries except Ghana (1996), Mali (2000), Namibia (1996), Tanzania (2000), Uganda (1996), Zambia (1996), and Zimbabwe (1996). The year for these two items coincides in every case except for Mali, Namibia, and Zimbabwe. Mali is the only case for which the question about the honesty of elections refers to a later election than the question about voting.

25 Somewhat less clear-cut are the cases of Namibia and Malawi. Namibia's elections in the 1990s were relatively free of electoral manipulation (Bauer 2001, 46–48), and yet the marginal and total effects from the survey analysis are substantial in magnitude. This result could reflect frustration among opposition supporters with the ruling party's increasing electoral dominance, regional over-representation, and use of state resources to entrench itself. Malawi, in contrast, had a problematic 1999 election (there were issues with voter registration and intimidation), and yet it has small marginal and total effects. The fact that the 1994 election was cleaner than the one in 1999 might be partially responsible for this (Klees van Donge 1995).

and Nigeria (63 percent); in Ghana it is 33 percent, and in Botswana 24 percent. In light of this, I create an indicator variable taking the value of 0 for respondents who identify with the incumbent, and the value of 1 for those who identify with the losing party or are neutral. I then estimate the effect of beliefs about fairness on turnout, conditional on partisanship, on the pooled sample.

The regression results for the Afrobarometer analysis conditioning on partisanship are shown in Table 7.2 (Model E).[26] The marginal effect of perceptions about electoral manipulation on the probability of turnout of an incumbent supporter can be read directly from the coefficient on electoral manipulation. The effect is statistically indistinguishable from zero. In contrast, the marginal effect of perceptions of manipulation on the probability of turnout of an opposition supporter (including those who identified themselves as neutral) is negative and statistically significant. This marginal effect is given by the simple slope of electoral manipulation conditional on being an opposition supporter (shown in the table). The simple slope represents the effect on the probability of turnout of a one-unit change in perceptions about electoral manipulation. The magnitude of the effect implies that a supporter of the opposition whose confidence in the election wanes from very honest (4) to very dishonest (1) is less likely to cast a vote, by 9.4 percent. Therefore, almost the entire effect of electoral manipulation on turnout is driven by the effect on opposition supporters.[27]

The Latinobarómetro also contains a question about partisan preferences.[28] In this case, the marginal effect of perceptions about the cleanliness of the election on individual turnout remains negative, but fails to reach statistical significance when conditioning on partisanship.[29] In other words, the marginal effect of perceptions on individual turnout for either opposition supporters or government supporters is not statistically significant (it is worth noting that, as Table 7.1A shows, even before conditioning on partisanship, the marginal effect of perceptions on turnout reaches statistical significance only for seven out of seventeen countries in the Latinobarómetro set of surveys). To further investigate whether the overall effect of perceptions on turnout is driven by opposition supporters, I estimate the analysis (conditioning on partisanship) on the individual countries covered by Latinobarómetro. The marginal

---

[26] For simplicity of interpretation, I run a linear probability model.

[27] This is roughly comparable to the Afrobarometer point estimate in Table 7.2. (OLS and probit estimates of the marginal effect on the full sample without the interaction term are essentially identical.)

[28] The item is *p54st*, and it asks: "If elections were held this Sunday, which party would you vote for?" The possible responses are government, opposition, neither, and a few other standard options (e.g., don't know, don't vote).

[29] One possible reason for this is that the partisanship question may not have adequately identified opposition supporters, because of partisan turnover in the government. This possibility is less of an issue in the Afrobarometer sample.

effect of perceptions on turnout, conditional on partisanship, reaches statistical significance in three countries: Mexico, Paraguay, and Argentina.[30] In each case, the perception that elections are unclean significantly and substantially reduces individual turnout among opposition supporters, but not among incumbent supporters.[31] This finding fits well with the fact that Mexico and Paraguay have ample experience with excessive electoral manipulation in their recent histories, which could have contributed to shaping individuals' reactions to electoral manipulation in potentially lasting ways.[32]

In sum, the evidence studied in this section suggests that electoral manipulation, as perceived by citizens, has had an indirect effect on citizen electoral participation, on average reducing voter turnout. Moreover, the analysis that conditions on partisanship suggests that the electoral participation of opposition supporters is especially susceptible to discouragement, and it appears to drive the overall negative correlation between perceptions of electoral manipulation and voter turnout.

7.2 INDIRECT EFFECTS OF ELECTORAL MANIPULATION ON VOTER BEHAVIOR: EVIDENCE FROM MEXICO'S ELECTORAL REFORM

This section, as did the preceding one, explores the indirect effects of electoral manipulation on voter participation. In contrast with the survey analysis, the analysis here utilizes data for one country only – Mexico. Analytical leverage is obtained by comparing over-time changes across the different states of Mexico. The analysis here adds to the one in the previous section in various ways. First, it focuses on a previous step in the causal chain – on the actual use of electoral manipulation, not on actors' subsequent perceptions. Second, because the type of data and the analytical procedure differ from those in the survey analysis, the analysis here yields independent evidence on the relationship of interest. The research design exploits a unique historical circumstance: the Mexican electoral reforms of the 1990s that effectively ended an era of large-scale electoral manipulation by the ruling party, the PRI (I discuss the reforms presently). The effect of electoral manipulation on voter participation is identified by comparing how voter participation responded to the cleaning up of elections in the

---

[30] In the remaining countries, the marginal effect of perceptions conditional on partisanship does not reach statistical significance for opposition supporters nor for incumbent supporters.

[31] The marginal effect of a change in perception from "not clean" (5) to "clean" (1) on the likelihood of casting a vote in Argentina is −9.4 percent, in Mexico it is −15.6 percent, and in Paraguay it is −97 percent. Results based on linear probability models controlling for political interest, gender, age and its square, socioeconomic status, and education.

[32] Argentina also has a history of electoral manipulation. Brusco et al. (2004), for example, document widespread vote buying during the 2001 electoral campaign period on the basis of a survey covering three provinces (44 percent of respondents reported that parties distributed goods in their neighborhood during the campaign).

states of Mexico, which differed in their pre-reform levels of electoral manipulation. The central empirical finding is that, on average, excessive electoral manipulation by the PRI substantially reduced voter participation in Mexico in the decades before the electoral reforms of the 1990s. The findings support the idea that the PRI's notorious preoccupation with winning overwhelmingly (and with winning practically every office, every time) was motivated by the indirect effects that doing so promised to yield – on voters, as shown here, and on other political actors, as I have suggested in previous chapters.

The case of Mexico is important for a variety of reasons. First, as mentioned in the first chapter of this book, Mexico has played a prominent role in the study of authoritarian elections and electoral manipulation. Second, while the notion that electoral manipulation by the PRI depressed voter participation has previously been discussed in scholarship on Mexico, empirical investigations have only made use of a subset of the available evidence; in particular, existing analyses are all based on survey data and focus on elections one at a time.[33] While such evidence is of great value, the fact that Mexican electoral practices and institutions recently experienced change of historical proportions means that there exist additional, independent sources of information with the potential to yield additional insight on the workings of electoral manipulation, both in general and in the specific instance of Mexico. The analysis here does not focus on a specific election but instead explores a broader period of time that straddles the electoral reforms of the 1990s.

Research Design

The key idea is that different Mexican states displayed different average levels of electoral manipulation in the pre-reform period, but that all states have held similarly clean elections in the post-reform period (this claim refers to elections for national office). Insofar as electoral manipulation in the pre-reform period had indirect effects on voter participation, changes in turnout after reforms should reflect differences between states in the extent of such manipulation: voter turnout should have increased more (or decreased less) after the reform in those states where pre-reform electoral manipulation was greater.

This idea can be investigated empirically through a differences-in-differences design. To illustrate this, consider two states and suppose that in state A, elections displayed no electoral manipulation either before or after the reforms,

---

[33] Qualitative and survey analyses have supported this view. McCann and Domínguez (1998, 494–498) find that in the 1988, 1991, and 1994 elections, respondents who expected the elections to be fraudulent were less likely to cast a vote. Klesner and Lawson (2001, 37), Buendía and Somuano (2003) and Hiskey and Bowler (2005) also find a negative association between perceptions of manipulation for various elections under the PRI and a citizen's propensity to vote.

while in state B, elections were substantially manipulated before the reforms, but clean thereafter. In state A, turnout increases by 2 percent after the reforms, while in state B turnout increases by 4.5 percent. Then the indirect causal effect of electoral manipulation on voter turnout in state B is 2.5 percent – that is, the difference between the turnout changes in the two states. The turnout trend in state A serves as a counterfactual for the turnout trend in state B, in the hypothetical scenario that state B had had no manipulation either. Changes in turnout beyond those experienced by state A, then, are attributed to differences between the states in electoral manipulation. This idea can also be implemented in a regression framework, where it is possible to control for observable potential confounders.

Measured Turnout versus True Turnout

One challenge associated with implementing this strategy concerns the dependent variable, voter turnout. The question is whether measured turnout (or *turnout figures*) reflects *voter choices*, which is the theoretically relevant concept. The issue is that turnout figures reflect two processes that are simultaneously influenced by electoral manipulation, but could potentially drive such figures in different directions. On the one hand, electoral manipulation can mechanically influence turnout figures. For example, ballot box stuffing will make it seem as though more people cast ballots than actually did. On the other hand, electoral manipulation can have an indirect effect on the turnout choices of citizens. For example, citizens who perceive the PRI to be practically invincible – either because it is popular, or because it is unpopular but citizens who dislike it are unlikely to turn out at the polls, or because it can simply get away with cheating, to name a few possibilities – could be unlikely to cast a ballot. The problem is that these two effects work at cross purposes: one increases turnout figures, while the other reduces them. Therefore it is possible that the indirect effects of electoral manipulation, even if present, might not be discernible by comparing turnout figures before and after the reforms.

To put this issue in slightly more precise terms, I draw a further distinction between tactics of electoral manipulation that involve contact with the citizen (such as vote buying or voter intimidation) and those that do not (such as tampering with voter registration lists, stuffing ballot boxes, or altering the vote tallies). I define a citizen's *true turnout choice* as his/her choice to cast a vote of his/her own accord, considering all the available information about electoral manipulation, but in the absence of any electoral manipulation involving direct contact with him/her. *True turnout* is the sum total of citizens' true turnout choices thus defined. True turnout reflects citizens' free vote choices and it is, therefore, the quantity of interest for purposes of studying voter behavior (and the indirect effects of electoral manipulation). *Measured turnout*, or *turnout figures*, in contrast, reflects true turnout as well as all the distortions stemming from electoral manipulation, whether or not these involve direct contact with the citizens. In a fully clean election, measured turnout equals true turnout. But in the presence of electoral manipulation, true turnout is likely to differ from measured turnout.[34]

To address this issue, it is necessary to know how turnout figures were influenced by electoral manipulation in pre-reform Mexico. In the pre-reform period the PRI made ample use of tactics of electoral manipulation that inflated measured turnout, such as ballot box stuffing and bussing people around to vote multiple times (Klesner and Lawson 2001, 24). Nevertheless, for the most part, this was an issue in rural areas, not in urban ones (Molinar 1991). Part of the reason was the paucity of opposition oversight in rural areas (Molinar and Weldon 1988). Bezdek (1973), for example, finds that "rural ballot boxes are easier to stuff than urban ones."[35] Fox (1996, 190–191) reports that, in rural indigenous regions, both measured turnout and the proportion of the vote that went to the PRI in the 1988 election were remarkably high. He also reports that voter lists in thirty-five federal congressional districts contained up to 125 percent of the total number of adults counted in the census. In contrast, turnout figures in urban areas more closely reflected true turnout.

All of this suggests that, in the case of Mexico, there exists an opportunity to investigate the indirect effects of electoral manipulation on voter turnout (true turnout) by utilizing the rural/urban distinction. The preceding discussion has the following empirical implications. First, in the presence of indirect effects as theorized here, *measured turnout in urban areas should have increased after the reforms in proportion to pre-reform electoral manipulation* (because measured and true turnout are similar in urban areas). However, *in rural areas, there is no clear prediction as to the relationship between pre-reform levels of manipulation and post-reform changes in measured turnout*. The reason for this is that the cleaning up of elections should have had a downward effect on measured turnout (because of the reduction in or elimination of turnout-enhancing manipulation), as well as an upward effect (because of the increase in true turnout as citizens came to see elections as clean and became more willing to cast ballots). I emphasize that these statements are *relative to any overall baseline trend in turnout* because of factors unrelated to those considered here.[36]

---

[34] In their study of electoral manipulation in nineteenth century New York, Cox and Kousser (1981) speak about inflationary versus deflationary fraud: paying citizens to cast a vote inflates turnout, while paying them to stay at home on election day deflates turnout. According to the distinction I draw here, either of these practices would create a gap between true turnout (which should reflect participation choices in the absence of such payments or other forms of electoral manipulation) and measured turnout. For a more detailed discussion of these concepts see Simpser (2012).

[35] Cited in Davis and Coleman 1982, 592.

[36] There is evidence, for example, that turnout in Mexico has decreased in recent years across the board. Thus, it is possible to restate the first empirical implication in the text as: turnout figures in urban areas should have *either increased, or decreased less* in those states with greater levels of electoral manipulation, in relation to the turnout change in states with lower levels of electoral manipulation.

Data

I proxy electoral manipulation as the decrease in the proportion of the vote obtained by the PRI in the post-reform period, state-by-state. The idea is that the PRI's electoral performance before the electoral reforms of the 1990s was inflated by the use of electoral manipulation. After the reforms, however, national elections in all states were equally clean. Therefore, those states with the highest levels of electoral manipulation before the reforms would have experienced, after the reforms, a greater decline in the proportion of the vote going to the PRI.[37]

Mexican reforms to the electoral system began as early as 1977, but the crucial set of reforms came in the 1989–1996 period, and especially between 1993 and 1994. These reforms guaranteed the independence of Mexico's electoral management body, the *Instituto Federal Electoral* or IFE (Eisenstadt 2004, Alonso and Aziz Nassif 2005). As a result of these reforms, the IFE secured the backing of all major political parties and garnered considerable credibility in the public eye (Díaz-Santana 2002). The IFE oversaw national elections for executive and legislative offices, and in the legislative election of 1997 the PRI lost, for the first time in its history, the majority in the legislature. In 2000, it lost the presidency. In sum, the conduct of Mexican elections, and the public perceptions about their quality, experienced a dramatic shift as a result of the reforms of the 1990s. The pre-reform period was characterized by routine excessive and blatant manipulation of elections on the part of the PRI-government. This was true throughout the pre-reform period, and even at the apex of the PRI's popularity and power. On the basis of evidence from elections in the 1960s, for example, Marbry concludes that "electoral fraud is a widespread and persistent practice" (1974, 221–223).[38] In contrast, the

---

[37] State governments in Mexico, as well as citizens and other political and social actors, had reason to care about state-level electoral performance in national elections, as such performance had consequences for legislative representation and, more generally, it was presumably informative about the power of the rulers of the state. Accordingly, local electoral manipulation in national elections often received local attention. For example, electoral manipulation in the state of Baja California in 1973 in a national election became an important local issue (Padgett 1976). Note that data on electoral returns at lower levels of aggregation are not systematically available before the 1990s. Moreover, insofar as state-level dynamics drove choices about electoral manipulation, utilizing smaller units of analysis would only multiply the number of observations without describing substantial additional variation.

[38] Similarly, Cosío Villegas, writing in 1973, claims that especially in rural areas, "electoral fraud is practiced zealously, not in a half-baked manner" (1973, 396; my translation). And Durand Ponte documents that allegations of serious electoral fraud were leveled against the PRI regime in the presidential elections of 1940, 1942, and 1950 (1995, 67). The historical use of electoral manipulation by the PRI is de-emphasized in some of the recent scholarship. Magaloni (2006, 4–7) and Greene (2007, 7), for example, argue that the PRI resorted to fraud only when its sources of patronage had dried up and fraud was needed to win (Magaloni mentions that the PRI might also have used fraud to boost its vote share (5, fn.) but does not elaborate on the reasons for this). Schedler offers a different version of events: in reaction to democratizing

post-reform period has been characterized by much reduced levels of electoral manipulation in national elections.[39] While the electoral reforms have not completely eliminated all electoral manipulation, the pattern of manipulation has changed dramatically: instead of excessive manipulation perpetrated almost exclusively by the PRI, there is evidence that electoral manipulation in the post-reform period is both less extensive and more competitive, with multiple parties participating in it (Aparicio 2002). Moreover, practices such as ballot box stuffing, multiple voting, tampering with voter registration lists, and altering vote totals have been practically eliminated from national elections.[40]

Electoral data were culled from the *México Electoral* database (1972–2000) and the IFE (2003–2009). The variable for turnout represents the concept of *measured turnout* and it is equal to the total number of votes cast divided by the size of the electorate according to the voter list. The proportion of the PRI vote is the total number of valid votes cast for the PRI divided by the total number of valid votes cast. I operationalize the pre-reform period as 1972–1990 and the post-reform period as 1995–2009.

Average pre-reform turnout in national elections was 59 percent; post-reform, it was 56 percent. The PRI vote was 77 percent before the reform and 38 percent post-reform. The state-level data for these two variables are provided in Table 7.5. Variation in the decline of the PRI vote roughly comports with states' reputations for electoral manipulation and bad governance in the pre-reform period. For example, PRI support declined markedly in the post-reform period in Chiapas, Tabasco, and Quintana Roo. The decline was much milder in states with more "democratic" reputations, such as the Federal District and Baja California.[41]

Results

The empirical estimates that follow are based on the idea, discussed earlier, that in urban regions measured turnout reasonably reflects true turnout (while in rural regions it does not, because of the added complication that the tactics of electoral manipulation utilized by the PRI in rural areas inflated measured turnout). Accordingly, to implement the research design discussed earlier, I

---

pressures, the PRI first resorted to fraud in the 1980s, but as electoral reform progressed, it shifted to vote buying and intimidation (2002, 46). Earlier sources, in contrast, indicate that the PRI consistently made use of a variety of tactics from within the "menu of manipulation" throughout the pre-reform period, even though by all accounts its victory in national elections was guaranteed.

[39] This is true at least until the controversial presidential election of 2006, which was decided by a razor-thin margin of victory.

[40] Elections for subnational political office (state and municipality) do not depend on the national IFE and have not uniformly displayed the same degree of improvement. On subnational variation in democracy in Mexico, see Giraudy (2010) and Ibarra and Simpser (2012).

[41] The Pearson correlation coefficient between the PRI vote loss and the post-pre turnout change is -0.3 ($P<0.1$).

TABLE 7.5. *Variables for Mexico Analysis: Decline in PRI Vote and Turnout Change*

State	Decline in PRI Vote (percentage points)	Post-Pre Turnout Change (percentage points)
Baja California	28	−14.1
Jalisco	28	2.2
México	29	−10.9
Chihuahua	29	2.1
Coahuila	30	3.2
Sinaloa	31	5.2
Distrito Federal	32	−1.9
Nayarit	32	2.3
Tamaulipas	34	2.2
Nuevo León	35	4.1
Oaxaca	35	−4.2
Durango	36	1.4
Puebla	37	−8.1
Yucatán	38	−1.3
Aguascalientes	39	−0.9
Morelos	39	−0.3
Michoacán	40	−1.9
Hidalgo	41	−10.2
Veracruz	42	−5.2
Colima	42	15.0
Sonora	42	8.6
Guanajuato	43	2.7
Guerrero	43	−7.2
Tabasco	44	−2.1
Baja California Sur	46	−7.0
San Luis Potosí	47	0.6
Querétaro	48	0.3
Quintana Roo	48	−24.2
Campeche	48	−5.2
Zacatecas	49	−3.6
Tlaxcala	49	−15.5
Chiapas	49	−19.7

Notes: See text for a description of the data and sources.

focus on those states with above average levels of urbanization. I begin by ranking these states according to their respective levels of electoral manipulation in the pre-reform period. I denote those states ranked in the highest third as the treatment group, and those ranked in the lowest third as the control group. Thus, the treatment group consists of urban states with relatively high levels of electoral manipulation in the pre-reform period, while the control group consists of urban states with relatively low levels of manipulation in the pre-reform

TABLE 7.6. *Average State-Level Turnout Before and After the 1990s Electoral Reforms*

Variable:	Least Manipulated	Most Manipulated	Difference, Most − Least
Mean turnout, pre-reform	61.45%	61.44%	−0.01%
Mean turnout, post-reform	55.72%	60.28%	4.56%
Change in Mean Turnout	−5.73%	−1.16%	4.57%

Notes: See text for details.

period. The differences-in-differences estimate compares the pre-/post-reform changes in turnout of the treatment and the control groups.

Table 7.6 displays the average reported turnout for each group, by period, as well as the differences. The first and second lines show average turnout in the pre- and post-reform periods, respectively. The third line shows the post-/pre-reform difference in average turnout.

The first column of the table shows that turnout for the control group (i.e., the least manipulated) declined by 5.73 percent. In contrast, average turnout for the treatment group (most manipulated) declined by only 1.16 percent after the reforms.[42] The difference between these two, 4.57 percent, is the average effect of electoral manipulation on turnout – that is, the table suggests that electoral manipulation in the pre-reform period depressed true turnout by this amount. This difference has persisted even as general turnout levels in Mexico have fluctuated.[43]

As a robustness check, an alternative construction of the treatment and control groups – dividing urban states into two equal groups according to the level of electoral manipulation – yields a similar estimate (4.5 percent). In addition, a series of cross-sectional regressions of turnout on a treatment dummy in election years (every three years in between 1973 and 2009) paint a consistent picture, with coefficients for the pre-reform period averaging 0.7 percent, versus 5.9 percent in the post-reform period. This differences-in-differences estimate has the advantage of being straightforward, but it does not control for potential lurking variables and it does not fully utilize the available information on electoral manipulation and urbanization. Simpser (2012) presents a regression analysis utilizing data for all thirty-two Mexican states and controlling for a range of state characteristics that could potentially drive both electoral manipulation and turnout, including: economic factors (economic product per capita in levels and in changes, exports, and share in the extractive sector), socio-demographic traits (literacy, changes in fraction of rural population),

---

[42] In the years after the reforms, turnout in the formerly most-manipulated group of urban states increased in absolute terms (for example, considering the post-reform period as 1995–2000, average turnout in that group of states increased by 2.9%).

[43] General turnout in Mexico appears to be on the decline. (It is beyond the scope of the present analysis to account for general trends in turnout in Mexico in recent years.)

and electoral factors (competitiveness of electoral races).[44] The finding from that analysis is qualitatively similar: in the fully controlled regression, every percentage point added through electoral manipulation to the pre-reform PRI vote translates into a 2.2 percent decrease in true turnout in that period.

Conclusion: Indirect Effects of Electoral Manipulation in Mexico

Mexico before the 1990s presented the background conditions that my theory specifies as propitious for excessive and blatant manipulation: the PRI had considerable advantages over other parties in terms of resources for manipulation, and it essentially controlled all branches of government, including the judiciary and the electoral institutions. This rendered excessive and blatant manipulation well within reach for the PRI. The analysis in this section showed that the practice of excessive and blatant electoral manipulation by Mexico's ruling party before the electoral reforms of the 1990s in fact significantly reduced voter participation (by which I mean true turnout).

The research design utilizes the fact that the Mexican electoral reforms of the 1990s yielded a dramatic decrease in electoral manipulation, and essentially eliminated the practice of unilateral and excessive electoral manipulation by the PRI. A comparison of urban Mexican states with relatively high versus relatively low levels of pre-reform electoral manipulation suggests that such manipulation reduced voter participation (i.e., true turnout) in the pre-reform period. The analysis in this section does not distinguish turnout by partisanship. However, if, as the findings of the survey analysis in the preceding section of this chapter suggest, turnout among opposition supporters is more sensitive to excessive and blatant manipulation, then an *overall* effect on actual turnout could be taken to largely reflect an effect on the actual turnout *of opponents*. In sum, this section provides an additional piece of evidence consistent with the idea that electoral manipulation can be, and often is, sought for its indirect effects.

I proposed a conceptual distinction between *true turnout* – a potentially counterfactual notion corresponding to electoral participation choices free of coercion or bribery – and *measured turnout* or *turnout figures*. In the absence of electoral manipulation, these concepts of turnout correspond exactly. Electoral manipulation, however, will generally lead to divergence: measured turnout could be either higher (because of turnout-increasing electoral manipulation) or lower (because of the indirect effects of electoral manipulation on voter participation choices, or to the mechanical effects of turnout-decreasing electoral manipulation).

The possibility that electoral manipulation might either inflate or deflate turnout is of relevance to the application of election forensics techniques to

---

[44] That analysis also performs a variety of additional robustness checks (e.g., on the measure of electoral manipulation, the set of controls, and the grouping of elections into pre- and post-election periods).

detect or quantify electoral manipulation. In line with election forensics scholarship, my analysis suggests that turnout figures can be closely linked to electoral manipulation, and therefore such figures might be effectively used to document anomalous patterns that suggest electoral manipulation. Nevertheless, my analysis underlines the importance of understanding the nature of the relationship between electoral manipulation and turnout. Forensic analyses of elections are often predicated on the assumption that electoral manipulation has an inflationary effect on turnout. While this assumption is a reasonable one in certain contexts – such as in post-Soviet Russia, or in rural Mexico under the PRI in the pre-reform period – in general, the sign and magnitude of the effect of electoral manipulation on turnout are indeterminate, and will depend on the specific tactics of electoral manipulation utilized, as well as on the possible indirect effects of such manipulation on voter participation. Therefore, the application of turnout-based forensic electoral indicators ought to be informed by the context-specific ways in which electoral manipulation is likely to be related with the data on which such indicators are based.

7.3 ELECTORAL MANIPULATION AND THE LONGEVITY OF RULE

This section explores the empirical relationship between electoral manipulation and the length of tenure in office. The idea behind this analysis is that there is little reason to expect excessive electoral manipulation to influence its perpetrator's duration in office, other than by indirect effects. The reason for this is simply that the contribution of additional electoral manipulation to the probability of victory –that is, the direct effect of electoral manipulation – declines sharply as the running vote total moves further away from the victory threshold.[45] When the race is tight, electoral manipulation has the potential to significantly affect the probability of victory.[46] In contrast, once the victory threshold has been far surpassed by one of the parties, further manipulation will have little effect, if any, on a party's winning chances.

In cases such as Zimbabwe in the 1980s and 1990s, Russia since 2000, or Lukashenko's Belarus, incumbents were clear favorites, and therefore electoral manipulation by them could not increase in a discernible way their chances of winning elections through its direct effect on the vote totals. In fact, my data suggest that excessive electoral manipulation frequently occurs when incumbent parties have a considerable advantage.[47] Therefore, one would only expect

---

[45] As discussed in Chapter 5.

[46] That this is true even when manipulation is competitive and the manipulating parties' efforts partly or fully neutralize each other – the marginal contribution of a unit of manipulation to the probability of victory is largest whenever the vote total is in the vicinity of the winning threshold.

[47] My data contain information on pre-election polls for sixty-seven cases of excessive manipulation. Almost half of these (49%) occurred when the incumbent party had a considerable advantage – of at least 20% – according to pre-electoral public opinion polls. For a discussion of the poll data see Chapter 3. For this calculation I consider an election excessively manipulated

to find a relationship between excessive electoral manipulation and longevity in office if there was some link between the two other than the aforementioned direct effect. I have claimed that such a link exists, and collectively denoted its variants as "indirect effects." Therefore, evidence of a relationship in the data between excessive electoral manipulation and duration in office should increase confidence in the theory, and specifically in the existence and substantive importance of indirect effects.

Could such an empirical relationship – namely, between excessive electoral manipulation and the length of tenure in office – be produced in alternative ways that do not entail indirect effects? It is possible that a "third factor" might drive both a ruling party's longevity in office, and excessive electoral manipulation. Specifically, the traits that make it possible and desirable for incumbent parties to pursue excessive manipulation – centralized control over resources and political power, a certain level of independence from the rule of law and from international pressures – could also contribute to the party's longevity in office through means other than electoral manipulation. Empirically, this concern can be partially addressed by controlling for proxies of such potential third factors.

Empirical Analysis

In what follows, I utilize the country-level dataset introduced in Chapter 2 to study the relationship between electoral manipulation, marginal and excessive, and longevity in office. The unit of analysis is the "spell in office" for a ruling party. A spell in office is defined as a set of consecutive country-years during which the same party rules. The analysis is straightforward: I create variables to indicate the proportion of elections in the spell that displayed marginal manipulation, excessive manipulation, or either pattern of manipulation. I then use these to explain party duration in office, controlling for a range of potential confounders.

For empirical purposes, I call an election "excessively manipulated" if it was manipulated and the absolute margin of victory was at least 20 percent. An election is "marginally manipulated" if it was manipulated and the absolute margin of victory was less than 20 percent. The residual category is the set of elections that were not manipulated.[48] Table 7.7 displays the average length of the party spell in office, for each of three subsets of the data: spells that displayed no electoral manipulation at any point, spells that at some point

---

if medium or widespread manipulation took place and the absolute margin of victory was at least 20%.

[48] This approach, while not perfect, is simple and about as good as other, more complex possibilities. For example, one could use information about who manipulated the election and who won it, because an election where party A manipulates and party B wins by a large margin should not be defined as excessively manipulated. Such elections exist in the data (e.g., Zambia 1991), but they are rare.

TABLE 7.7. *Average Length of Party Tenure in Office by Pattern of Electoral Manipulation*

	Years	N
No Manipulation	5.49	55
Marginal Manipulation Only	5.44	78
Excessive Manipulation	9.09	116

Note: The unit is party spell in office.

displayed marginal manipulation but no excessive manipulation, and spells that at some point displayed excessive manipulation.

The table shows a strong association between excessive electoral manipulation and party duration in office.[49] While this finding is consistent with the hypothesis that excessive electoral manipulation causes longer duration in office, it is not possible to confidently infer causality on the basis of the cross tabulation only. To investigate the plausibility of a causal association more rigorously, I control for potential confounders – that is, for factors likely to be associated both with duration in office and with the use of excessive electoral manipulation. First, I control for the formal electoral rules. Electoral rules can influence the margins of victory, as well as incentives to manipulate (and therefore they can conceivably influence the likelihood of excessive manipulation). Such rules might also influence party duration in office. Specifically, I control for the type of electoral system (presidential, semi-presidential, or parliamentary), and for the method of selecting legislators (plurality versus proportional representation). I also control for the type of election (executive or legislative). The level of socioeconomic development could influence tenure in office via a variety of mechanisms, as well as possibilities and incentives for excessive electoral manipulation, as argued in previous chapters. For this reason I control for per capita GDP (logged). To proxy for the power of the government – which I have argued influences incentives and possibilities for excessive electoral manipulation, and could also drive duration in office – I control for the strength of the rule of law and for the strength of the bureaucracy.[50] To capture unobserved heterogeneity, I include region-specific effects.

[49] A difference of means test confirms that the figure for excessive manipulation is statistically greater than that for marginal manipulation (P<0.01). The figures for no manipulation and marginal manipulation are statistically indistinguishable.

[50] Information on formal electoral rules is drawn from the Database of Political Institutions Beck et al. 2001). Economic data is from the Penn World Tables. Data on bureaucratic quality and rule of law are from the International Country Risk Guide (ICRG); I use their measures of "Law and Order," and "Bureaucratic Quality." A stronger rule of law and higher bureaucratic quality correspond to higher values of these variables. For a discussion of the strengths and drawbacks of the ICRG data see Knack and Keefer 1995 and Treisman 2007.

I fit a parametric survival model, using the Weibull distribution and the accelerated-failure-time parametrization.[51] The results are presented in Table 7.8. I first investigate whether manipulated elections – regardless of the specific pattern of manipulation – have an effect on duration in office, without adding any controls (Model A).[52] The main explanatory variables are coded as follows. The variable for "marginal manipulation" represents the fraction of elections in the spell exhibiting marginal electoral manipulation. Similarly, the variable for "excessive manipulation" indicates the fraction of elections in the spell that were excessively manipulated. Finally, the variable for "any manipulation" gives the fraction of elections in the spell that exhibited electoral manipulation, irrespective of the margin of victory. All control variables are averages over the spell.

The first two models do not differentiate between marginal and excessive electoral manipulation. Instead, they only contain one variable for manipulation, "any manipulation." The uncontrolled regression, Model A, is provided as a baseline. It shows that electoral manipulation is associated with a longer party tenure in office. The coefficient on "any manipulation" is positive and statistically significant. Column A' displays the marginal effect in substantive terms: if all elections in a party spell were manipulated, the party in office would last, on average, 34 percent longer in office than if none were manipulated. Nevertheless, once the set of controls is added to the regression (Model B), the association between "any manipulation" and duration in office disappears entirely.

I next differentiate between excessive and marginal manipulation. Model C contains the two manipulation variables with no additional controls. Excessive electoral manipulation has a positive and statistically significant association with duration of a party in office. This result is highly robust to specification, as Model D, containing the full set of controls, suggests.[53] The marginal effect of excessive manipulation, based on Model D, is given in Column D': party duration is 48 percent longer in a spell in which all elections are excessively manipulated, in comparison with one where none are. As a robustness check, I recode the main explanatory variables in a way that takes into account not only the presence or absence of marginal or excessive electoral manipulation, but also the extent of the manipulation (using the 0–3 scale described in

[51] A substantial proportion of the spells in the data are ongoing – that is, their end date takes place after the last year in the dataset, an issue that is partly addressed by survival analysis. A semi-parametric model, such as the Cox proportional hazards model, would be appropriate in a longer panel.

[52] In discussing the results, I utilize causal language, with the caveat that, as mentioned previously, the analysis is based on observational data and therefore cannot fully pin down causality.

[53] The result holds up in a wide variety of specifications – e.g., controlling only for region, controlling for all covariates except for region, and controlling for GDP/cap but not for the rule of law or bureaucratic quality (these three variables are highly correlated).

TABLE 7.8. *Effect of Electoral Manipulation on Length of Party Tenure in Office*

Independent Variables	A	B	C	D	E	Marginal Effects A'	D'	E'
Any manipulation	0.29*	0				34%		
	.05	.98						
Excessive manipulation			0.86***	0.39*	0.70**		48%	101%
			.00	.07	.02			
Marginal manipulation			−0.27*	−0.22	0.18		−20%	20%
			.08	.20	.50			
Control Variables								
Region dummies:								
Middle East and North Africa		−0.23		0.3	0.25		35%	28%
		.24		.61	.68			
Latin America and Caribbean		0.11*		−1.07***	−1.04***		−66%	−65%
		.10		.00	.00			
Former Soviet Union		0.16		−0.80**	−0.94**		−55%	−61%
		.74		.05	.02			
Eastern Europe		−1.14***		−1.81***	−1.78***		−84%	−83%
		.00		.00	.00			
Asia		−0.86**		−1.05***	−1.08***		−65%	−66%
		.04		.00	.00			
Wealthy Nations		−1.79***		−2.26***	−2.14***		−90%	−88%
		.00		.00	.00			
Parliamentary system		0.15		0.30*	0.29*		35%	34%
		.40		.08	.10			

(continued)

233

TABLE 7.8 (continued)

Independent Variables	A	B	C	D	E	Marginal Effects A'	D'	E'
Relative portion of Lower House members elected by plurality		0.11* .10		0.06 .37	0.06 .38	6%	6%	6%
Proportion legislative elections		−0.23 .24		−0.27 .16	−0.27+ .15		−24%	−24%
Per capita GDP (log)		0.37*** .00		0.37*** .00	0.38*** .00		45%	46%
Rule of law		0.18** .01		0.14** .05	0.17** .02		15%	19%
Bureaucratic quality		−0.02 .87		0.06 .55	0.04 .70		6%	4%
Constant	2.17*** .00	−0.4 .64	2.16*** .00	−0.47 .60	−0.73 .38			
Number of Observations:	264	219	249	210	210			

Notes: First five columns display coefficients of Weibull survival model; P-values shown below coefficients; *** p<0.01, ** p<0.05, * p<0.1, + p<.15. Omitted manipulation category is "no manipulation"; omitted regional dummy is Sub-Saharan Africa. The three rightmost columns display exp(coefficient)-1*100%.

Chapter 2).[54] Model E uses these variables, and it is otherwise specified like Model D. Using this alternative measure does not qualitatively change the result, although it does strengthen the effect – as shown in Column E', excessive electoral manipulation essentially doubles party duration in office. The ratio of average durations in the raw data (Table 7.7) falls between the estimates from Models D and E. In sum, the regression analysis is consistent with the idea that excessive electoral manipulation increases party duration in office.[55]

Marginal electoral manipulation, in contrast, does not seem to be nearly as influential on party duration in office. In fact, in Models C and D, its coefficient is negative (although it is only statistically significant in Model C), suggesting that marginal manipulation on average reduces duration. In Model E, the coefficient on marginal manipulation is positive but statistically insignificant. One interpretation of these findings is that marginal electoral manipulation often fails to accomplish its goal, victory. This is the theoretical expectation in cases where the manipulation is competitive (Chapter 5); it is also consistent with prior empirical work (for instance, Lehoucq and Molina (2002) find that electoral manipulation in Costa Rica in the first half of the twentieth century, which followed the marginal pattern, rarely managed to change the outcome). The finding is also consistent with the idea that marginal electoral manipulation sometimes helps to win but other times provokes a popular backlash.[56]

The coefficient estimates on the control variables are of secondary interest to the task at hand, but nevertheless worth discussing. Ex ante theoretical expectations about the effect of the level of economic development on duration in office point in different directions. The level of economic development has been argued to have a positive effect on duration, no effect, or an effect the direction of which depends itself on the time in office.[57] In the analysis presented here, the level of economic development is associated with a longer party

---

[54] Specifically, these measures are created by multiplying, for every election, the dummy variables for marginal and excessive manipulation by the extent of manipulation in the election in question, and then averaging over the elections in a spell. (Recall that the extent of manipulation can vary somewhat independently from the degree to which it is marginal or excessive – e.g., there can be large-scale or small-scale marginal manipulation.)

[55] The results are robust to controlling for growth in GDP/cap (i.e., the average growth in the spell) in addition to the GDP/cap level. The effect of excessive electoral manipulation in Model D remains unchanged, while that in Model E remains strong, if slightly smaller (the coefficient is 0.67). The coefficient on marginal manipulation remains similar in magnitude and statistical significance. Growth in GDP/cap itself has a positive and statistically significant marginal effect on duration (the coefficient is 0.6–0.7).

[56] As discussed earlier in the book, one reason for this is that marginal electoral manipulation can be interpreted as a sign of vulnerability on the part of the manipulator. Excessive electoral manipulation, in contrast, is much less likely to elicit such a backlash, in part because it signals that the manipulator is strong.

[57] See, among many others, Powell and Whitten 1993; Cheibub and Przeworski 1999; and Chiozza and Goemans 2004. Some of the arguments and findings in the literature concern leaders, others governments.

duration in office, as is the rule of law. Bureaucratic quality has essentially no effect on duration (although it should be noted that GDP/cap, the rule of law, and bureaucratic quality are highly correlated). These effects hold across specifications. A parliamentary constitution appears to be associated with longer party duration in office, in relation to a presidential or semi-presidential one.[58] Neither the mode of electing legislators, nor the proportion of legislative elections, have statistically significant effects on party duration in office. Finally, the regional dummy variables capture effects on duration in relation to the omitted category, Sub-Saharan Africa. They suggest that, after accounting for the rest of the variables in the regression models, party duration in office is on average no different in the Middle East and North Africa, and appreciably lower in the wealthy nations, in Asia, and in Eastern Europe. The evidence for the former Soviet region and for Latin America is mixed across models, but it suggests a negative effect of region in comparison with Sub-Saharan Africa.

7.4 CONCLUSIONS

This chapter analyzed three kinds of evidence, all supportive of key theoretical propositions advanced in previous chapters. The first two sections zeroed in on one specific kind of indirect effect that played an important role in the case studies: the effect of excessive/blatant electoral manipulation on voter participation. On the basis of survey data, the first analysis showed that perceptions of electoral manipulation are strongly associated with a lower propensity to vote on average, and in particular with a lower propensity to vote for opposition supporters. By showing that this effect is at work in many countries in different parts of the world, the analysis highlights the generality of one of the mechanisms at the core of the theory. The analysis also quantified the effect that this individual-level effect could have on aggregate turnout, and suggested that the aggregate-turnout effects were greatest in countries where background conditions propitiate excessive manipulation. The analysis of the Mexican case lends further support to the theory, by using aggregate state-level data to estimate the relationship between excessive electoral manipulation by the PRI and voter participation. The analysis shows that excessive manipulation had a substantial (negative) indirect effect on voter participation.

The final section of the chapter examined a set of countries and elections even broader than that covered by the survey analysis in the first section, and showed that excessive electoral manipulation is associated with greater party longevity in office. Because excessive manipulation is virtually unrelated

---

[58] Prior work finds that parliamentary regimes last longer than presidential ones. Cheibub and Limongi (2002) review the theoretical arguments that have been offered to account for this, many of which are relevant to the question of party survival in office.

to the probability of winning, this finding suggests that excessive electoral manipulation must work its "magic" through means other than contributing to immediate victory in the election being contested – that is, through indirect effects such as those illustrated in Chapter 4 and in the case studies.

To be sure, there are limitations to the empirical exercise undertaken in this chapter and the previous one. As with all analyses based on observational data, the potential for unobserved confounders cannot be fully ruled out. Nevertheless, by considering a wide range of observable implications of the theory and its mechanisms, and assessing these in light of a variety of independent qualitative and quantitative sources of information, the analysis in these two chapters has provided solid evidence for the ideas presented earlier in the book, and displayed these ideas at work in a variety of time periods and geographical locations, as well as under different political and historical legacies, economic conditions, and formal and informal institutional settings.

APPENDIX

TABLE 7.1A. *Marginal and Total Effects of Perceptions of Electoral Manipulation on Turnout, Afrobarometer and Latinobarómetro*

Election	Marginal Effect (change from 4 to 1)	Total Effect	P-Value
Mali	−23.8%	−9.3%	0.00
Nigeria	−25.8%	−7.9%	0.00
Zimbabwe	−10.0%	−5.7%	0.04
Zambia	−21.2%	−5.6%	0.00
Namibia	−24.7%	−5.0%	0.00
South Africa	−16.2%	−4.6%	0.00
Lesotho	−7.8%	−2.9%	0.03
Uganda	−8.5%	−1.4%	0.00
Tanzania	−5.0%	−1.2%	0.02
Ghana	−1.4%	−0.6%	0.42
Botswana	−2.2%	−0.4%	0.74
Malawi	−0.5%	−0.2%	0.82
Mexico	−18.1%	−12.2%	0.00
Colombia	−15.6%	−10.0%	0.00
El Salvador	−15.3%	−8.6%	0.00
Costa Rica	−8.4%	−2.8%	0.06
Venezuela	−6.2%	−2.4%	0.11
Panama	−7.7%	−2.3%	0.00
Nicaragua	−3.7%	−2.1%	0.22
Honduras	−3.4%	−1.6%	0.47
Chile	−4.7%	−1.3%	0.15
Argentina	−3.0%	−1.2%	0.22
Uruguay	−0.6%	−0.2%	0.73
Guatemala	0.4%	0.1%	0.94
Paraguay	0.6%	0.4%	0.90
Peru	2.0%	1.1%	0.53
Bolivia	1.8%	1.2%	0.73
Brasil	3.7%	2.0%	0.35
Ecuador	4.8%	3.4%	0.08

Notes: Afrobarometer, Round 1 and Latinobarómetro, 2000. See text for further details.

8

Conclusion

This book set out as an inquiry into the causes of electoral manipulation. It documented unrecognized diversity in patterns of manipulation – specifically, it showed that excessively and blatantly perpetrated electoral manipulation is quite common – developed an original theory to explain such diversity, and showed the theory at work by analyzing evidence bearing on some of its main observable implications. At the heart of the argument is the idea that *electoral manipulation has informational properties.* By shaping information and expectations about the power and the prospects of political parties, electoral manipulation can decisively influence the behavior of a wide range of social and political actors. The informational properties of electoral manipulation increase what is at stake in choices about manipulation. Manipulating excessively and/or blatantly can convey or reinforce an image of strength, while failing to manipulate thus can project or reveal weakness. In turn, perceptions of party strength or weakness feed into the choices of political and social actors.

I termed the effects of electoral manipulation on actors' behavior via information-related mechanisms the indirect effects of electoral manipulation. The indirect effects of electoral manipulation have consequences that can be grouped into two major, overlapping categories: the electoral and the non-electoral. First, indirect effects matter for the manipulating party's (and, in consequence, other parties') future chances of holding power. In addition, indirect effects have consequences for the ability of the party in government to act as it prefers – extracting rents, steering policy, or changing laws, for example. In other words, one aspect of my theory consists of a dynamic account of incentives to manipulate elections – one that considers the effect of today's electoral manipulation on future elections. This part of the theory can be described, loosely speaking, as the claim that electoral manipulation is about *"more than winning today."* The second aspect of the theory concerns the effects of electoral manipulation on the manipulator's capacity and scope for acting (for example, on its bargaining power vis-à-vis other actors). This facet of the theory speaks to the consequences of electoral manipulation "*other than winning.*" The claim that electoral manipulation is not only about winning but also about conveying or obscuring information, together with the elaboration of the mechanisms linking such information with actors' behavior in areas of relevance to the manipulator (i.e., the elaboration of manipulation's indirect effects) constitute the theory of *more than winning* at the core of this book.

The theory of more than winning provides new grounds for understanding patterns of electoral manipulation that lie beyond the purview of traditional perspectives on the subject. In particular, it provides a parsimonious account for the seemingly extravagant and wasteful practice of excessive and blatant electoral manipulation: once electoral manipulation is seen not only as a means to win the election at hand, but also as a tool for influencing the behavior of the public – elites, citizens, bureaucrats, organizations, politicians, and others – excessive and blatant manipulation appears quite logical.

The cases and examples discussed throughout the book are drawn mostly from recent decades, but nothing in the logic of the argument precludes its application to earlier periods. Consider, for instance, the 1947 legislative election in Poland – a multiparty election that was thoroughly manipulated and won by the Communists with 80.1 percent of the vote, against 10.3 percent for the Peasants Party (Eley 2002, 300). The goal of the manipulation was, according to Wilson (2005, 13), not to win but rather to ensure that the Peasant Party lost by a large margin, thereby making it easier to subsequently force its leader to flee the country.

In addition to broadening the range of possible motives driving electoral manipulation, my analysis broadens the range of consequences to which manipulation might give rise. That electoral manipulation can change, or threaten to change, who wins is an important and widely appreciated fact. Less appreciated is the potential of manipulation to impact the configuration of power in deeper and longer-ranging ways – for example, through its role in the vicious circle whereby excessive and blatant electoral manipulation, on the one hand, and an unequal concentration of power and resources, on the other, mutually reinforce each other in what I have called an excessive/blatant electoral manipulation trap. The logic of excessive and blatant electoral manipulation, thus, points to a darker side of electoral politics. From a normative and a policy perspective, therefore, the analysis in this book suggests that excessive and blatant electoral manipulation ought to receive as much attention as the marginal variety routinely receives.

One area of practice where this last point applies is international election monitoring. This book's ideas simultaneously provide the basis for a critique of international election monitoring, and for making the case that it can have important positive effects beyond those usually ascribed to it. The critique stems from the fact that international election monitoring as currently practiced does not place enough emphasis on the indirect effects of electoral manipulation. Instead, it places great emphasis on its direct effects, specifically on the question of whether electoral manipulation in a particular election did or did not change who wins. This emphasis is apparent in the centrality that the notion of "the will of the people," as discussed earlier in the book, plays in many of the evaluations of elections by monitoring missions. An election is commonly said to reflect the "will of the people" if the candidate with majority support among the electorate – the one who would likely have won a clean vote – is the winner. For example, the European Union's assessment of the 1999 election in Nigeria concludes that, despite serious manipulation, "the result of the election . . . reflects the wishes of the Nigerian people" (European Union 1999). Regarding the 2004 recall referendum in Venezuela, the Carter Center writes that "the Aug. 15th vote clearly expressed the will of the Venezuelan electorate. Nonetheless, the recall referendum process suffered from numerous irregularities throughout the entire process" (Carter Center 2004).

The question of whether an electoral outcome reflects the majority's preference is certainly an important one. But, as this book has shown, electoral manipulation can have serious consequences even when the outcome does not subvert the "will of the people" – in particular, it can contribute to the over-time curtailment of political freedom and the entrenchment of authoritarian rule. To sharpen this critique of monitoring, I emphasize that international election monitors do in fact sometimes criticize questionable electoral practices on instances in which the will of the people was not subverted, but they stop short of indicating the possibility that such practices might give rise to indirect effects of the sort I have described. Consider, for example, the OSCE/ODIHR monitoring mission's assessment of the 2004 Russian election. On the one hand, the report criticizes various aspects of the conduct of the election; on the other, it mitigates the importance of such problems by indicating that Putin's popularity essentially guaranteed him victory (OSCE/ODIHR 2004). This book's arguments suggest a different perspective: despite the fact that Putin was popular, the shortcomings in the conduct of the election *in fact were* problematic, as documented in Chapter 6. The effects of Putin's excessive manipulation of the election on the subsequent behavior and choices of political parties and their backers, regional power brokers, bureaucrats, and voters are not highlighted in the report produced by the election monitoring mission. In light of this book's arguments, it becomes difficult to sustain that the use of excessive electoral manipulation in the 2004 election in Russia – which by all accounts did not subvert the will of the Russian people (because Putin would have likely won in a clean contest) – is less worrisome than, for example, the use of marginal electoral manipulation in the 1996 Russian election, which likely underpinned Yeltsin's victory and therefore subverted the people's will.

Nevertheless, this book's analysis also implies that international election monitoring as it is currently practiced has the potential to mitigate the indirect effects of manipulation, even when such effects are not explicitly acknowledged.[1] Insofar as monitoring renders it more difficult or costly to manipulate, it can potentially reduce the extent of manipulation, and therefore render excessive manipulation more difficult to attain. In turn, this can contribute to breaking the self-reinforcing feedbacks between excessive electoral manipulation and authoritarian power.[2] In other words, election monitoring has the potential to keep in check some of the most pernicious potential effects of electoral manipulation. This salutary role of monitoring would likely be reinforced if monitors emphasized excessive/blatant manipulation and the associated indirect effects as much as they have emphasized the importance of respecting the will of the people. In terms of policy, therefore, the implication is that monitoring assessments could be enhanced by incorporating an explicit awareness of the indirect effects of excessive and blatant electoral manipulation.[3] The preceding discussion, of course, applies not only to international election monitors but also to domestic ones.[4]

The logic of this critique extends as well to other kinds of efforts holding the potential to mitigate possibilities for excessive and blatant manipulation, such as certain kinds of institutional reform. A second policy area to which the present study connects, therefore, is that on "clean election reform" – institutional reform aimed at preventing electoral manipulation. A central concern in that policy debate and the related scholarly literature is the possibility that electoral reform, by adding safeguards to electoral procedures, might inadvertently make it more difficult for citizens to cast votes and therefore depress rates of voter participation. Schaffer (2008) has called such unintended negative effects "iatrogenic harm." Requiring voters to show positive identification at the polls is an example of a reform that has been argued to adversely impact rates of voter participation. Such reforms have been found to depress turnout in the Philippines, Venezuela, South Africa, and Taiwan, among other places (Schaffer 2002, 2008), and have been argued to have a similar effect in legal arguments in the United States by opponents of voter ID requirements (Ansolabehere and Persily 2008). There is disagreement, however, about whether electoral reform

---

[1] For empirical work on the potential for monitoring to reduce the extent of manipulation see Hyde (2007; 2011); Ichino and Schundeln 2012.

[2] Such feedbacks were discussed in Chapter 5, Section 5.3.

[3] On a practical level, it must be recognized that incorporating a concern with the indirect effects of manipulation may face the difficulty that such effects operate over time and sometimes can be more difficult to pinpoint than its direct effects. They may also be perceived as lying beyond the sphere of competence of election monitors. In this sense, research on the consequences of excessive and blatant manipulation has the potential to provide monitors with firmer analytical and empirical grounds on which to stand when incorporating indirect effects in their assessments. For a discussion of the possibilities and limitations of election monitoring see Carothers 1997; Simpser 2008; Kelley 2009; Hyde 2011; Simpser and Donno 2012.

[4] Little (2012) builds on the idea that electoral manipulation has information-related effects that permit a ruler to signal strength, to advance a different argument about election monitoring. He argues that election monitoring, by increasing the cost of electoral manipulation, reduces the equilibrium level of electoral manipulation needed by a ruler to signal a given level of strength.

helps or hinders voter participation (e.g., *Purcell v. Gonzalez*, 549 US 2006; Alvarez et al. 2008; Ansolabehere 2009; Erikson and Minnite 2009).

The arguments and evidence presented in this book speak to that debate in at least three ways. First, they suggest, consistent with one side of the debate, that electoral reform, insofar as it increases confidence in elections and mitigates the potential for indirect effects, can increase voter participation (simultaneously with any other effects that such reforms might have). Second, they describe conditions under which electoral manipulation could be expected to depress voter turnout. Importantly, while much of the debate on clean election reform has taken place in the United States, my arguments suggest that the potential for clean election reform to mitigate such indirect effects on voter turnout is even greater in developing countries.[5] Third, the arguments and evidence I presented underline the importance of clearly distinguishing between true rates of participation and official figures, since the latter could reflect the effects of electoral manipulation on participation. Failing to draw this distinction can lead to erroneous conclusions about the impact of election reform.[6]

Why, in sum, do parties and governments manipulate elections? I have argued and shown that there is substantially more at stake in manipulating elections than winning. Specifically, electoral manipulation can convey, reveal, or obscure information of relevance to the choices and behavior of bureaucrats, politicians, organizations, citizens, and other political and social actors. This simple idea is able to explain why electoral manipulation is frequently associated with overwhelming margins of victory, and why it is often perpetrated blatantly: beyond any possible contribution to the chances of victory in the election at hand, manipulating in this manner can convey an image of strength, while failing to do so can convey weakness. More generally, the analysis and evidence presented in this book suggest that there is much to be gained from understanding the role of information in elections and in the activities that surround them.

---

[5] See especially Chapters 5 and 6.

[6] As discussed in Chapter 7, it is possible for election reform to both increase actual turnout (e.g., by increasing voters' confidence and motivation to vote), and to simultaneously lead to a decrease in official turnout figures (by preventing certain forms of electoral manipulation that tend to inflate turnout figures, such as ballot stuffing or multiple voting).

References

Abdullaev, Nabi. 2008. "Medvedev won by curious numbers," *The Moscow Times*, April 14, Issue 3882, 1.

Abente, Diego. 1989. "Stronismo, post-Stronismo, and the prospects for democratization in Paraguay," Working Paper #119, March, Miami University, Oxford, Ohio.

Abente, Diego. 1995. "Paraguay," in Mainwaring, Scott and Timothy Scully, *Building democratic institutions: party systems in Latin America*, Oxford University Press.

Addison, Tony and Liisa Laakso. 2003. "The Political Economy of Zimbabwe's Descent into Conflict," *Journal of International Development*, 15(4): 457–470.

Adejumobi, S. 2000. "Elections in Africa: A fading shadow of democracy?" *International Political Science Review*, 21(1), 59–73.

Afrobarometer. "Summary of Results: Round 3.5 Afrobarometer Survey in Nigeria (2007)." www.afrobarometer.org. [Accessed 10 May 2009].

Alexander, Peter. 2000. "Zimbabwean Workers, the MDC & The 2000 Election," *Review of African Political Economy*, 27(85): 385–406.

Alonso, Jorge, and Alberto Aziz Nassif. 2005. *Campo Electoral, Espacios Autónomos y Redes: El Consejo General del IFE (1996-2005)*. Programa Interinstitucional de Investigación-Acción sobre Democracia, Sociedad Civil y Derechos Humanos, Mexico: CIESAS / Universidad Veracruzana.

Almond, Gabriel and Sidney Verba. 1963. *The Civic Culture*. Sage Publications.

Alonso, Paula. 1996. "Voting in Buenos Aires, Argentina, before 1912," in Posada-Carbó 1996, *Elections Before Democracy: The History of Elections in Europe and Latin America*. ILAS, University of London.

Alvarez, Michael, Thad Hall and Susan Hyde. 2008. *Election Fraud: Detecting and Deterring Electoral Manipulation*, Brookings.

Ames, Barry. 1970. "Bases of Support for Mexico's Dominant Party," *American Political Science Review*, 64(1): 153–167.

Anderson, Benedict R. 1983. "Old State, New Society: Indonesia's New Order in Comparative Historical Perspective," *Journal of Asian Studies*, 42(3): 477–496.

Anderson, Benedict R. 1996. "Elections and participation in three Southeast Asian countries," in Robert Taylor, *The politics of elections in Southeast Asia*, Cambridge University Press.

ANFREL (Asian Network for Free Elections). 2003. "Cambodia General Election 2003: Report of international observer missions, 15th May – 31st July 2003."

Ansari, Ali. Royal Institute of International Affairs, and University of St. Andrews. 2009. *Preliminary Analysis of the Voting Figures in Iran's 2009 Presidential Election*, Chatham House.

Ansolabehere, Stephen. 2009. "Effects of Identification Requirements on Voting: Evidence from the Experiences of Voters on Election Day," *Political Science & Politics*, 42(1): 127–130.

Ansolabehere, Stephen and Nathaniel Persily. 2008. "Vote Fraud in the Eye of the Beholder: The Role of Public Opinion in the Challenge to Voter Identification Requirements," *Harvard Law Review*, 121: 1737–1774.

Ansolabehere, Stephen and James M. Snyder, Jr. 2002. "The Incumbency Advantage in U.S. Elections: An Analysis of State and Federal Offices, 1942–2000," *Election Law Journal*, 1(3): 315–338.

Ansolabehere, Stephen, James M. Snyder, Jr. and Charles Stewart, III. 2000. "Old Voters, New Voters, and the Personal Vote: Using Redistricting to Measure the Incumbency Advantage," *American Journal of Political Science*, 44(1): 17–34.

Aparicio, Ricardo. 2002. "La magnitud de la manipulación del voto en las elecciones federales del año 2000," *Perfiles Latinoamericanos*, 20(June): 79–99.

Arditi, Benjamín. 1989. "Adiós a Stroessner: nuevos espacios, viejos problemas," *Nueva Sociedad*, 102(July-August): 24–32.

Arditi, Benjamín. 1990. "Elecciones y partidos en el Paraguay de la transición," *Revista Mexicana de Sociología*, 52(4): 83–98.

Arel, Dominique. 2001. "Kuchmagate and the demise of Ukraine's 'geopolitical bluff,'" *East European Constitutional Review*, 10(2–3): 54–59.

Argersinger, Peter. 1985. "New Perspectives on Election Fraud in the Gilded Age," *Political Science Quarterly*, 100(4): 669–687.

Arriola, Leonardo L. and Chelsea Johnson. 2012. "Election Violence in Democratizing States," mimeo, University of California at Berkeley, March 16.

Arrow, Kenneth. 1951. *Social Choice and Individual Values*. New York: Wiley.

Aslund, Anders. 2004. "Russia's economic transformation under Putin," *Eurasian Geography and Economics*, 45(6): 397–420.

Auyero, Javier. 2000. "The logic of clientelism in Argentina: an ethnographic account," *Latin America Research Review*, 35(3): 55–81.

Baker, Mark. 2005. "East: Why Do OSCE, CIS Observers Rarely Agree On Elections?" *Radio Free Europe / Radio Liberty*, April 12.

Baker, Peter. 2001. "Europe Denounces Election But Will Not Isolate Belarus," *The Washington Post*. September 10: A18.

Baland, Jean Marie and James Robinson. 2007. "How does vote buying shape the economy?" in Schaffer, Frederic Charles, ed. *Elections for Sale*. Lynne Rienner.

Balke, Nathan and Robert Gordon. 1989. "The Estimation of Prewar Gross National Product," *Journal of Political Economy*, 97(1): 38–92, February.

Barrington, Lowell W. and Erik S. Herron. 2004. "One Ukraine or many? Regionalism in Ukraine and its political consequences," *Nationalities Papers*, 32(1): 53–86.

Bartels, Larry. 1988. *Presidential Primaries and the Dynamics of Public Choice*. Princeton University Press.

Bauer, Gretchen. 2001. "Namibia in the first decade of independence: how democratic?" *Journal of Southern African Studies*, 27(1): 33–55.

BBC 2008, 30 January "Rivals in Kremlin Race."

Beaulieu, Emily. 2009. *Protesting the Contest: Election boycotts around the world 1990–2002*, PhD dissertation, University of California, San Diego.

Beaulieu, Emily, and Susan D. Hyde. 2009. "In the shadow of democracy promotion: Strategic manipulation, international observers, and election boycotts," *Comparative Political Studies*, 42(3), 392–415.

Beber, Bernd and Alexandra Scacco. 2009. "The Devil is in the Digits," *The Washington Post*, June 23.

Beck, Nathaniel. 2006. "Is causal-process observation an oxymoron?" *Political Analysis*, 14(3): 347–352.

Beck, Thorsten, George Clarke, Alberto Groff, Philip Keefer, and Patrick Walsh. 2001. "New tools in comparative political economy: The Database of Political Institutions," *World Bank Economic Review*, 15(1): 165–176.

Beissinger, Mark. 2007. "Structure and example in modular political phenomena: The diffusion of Bulldozer/Rose/Orange/Tulip revolutions," *Perspectives on Politics*, 5(02).

Bensel, Richard. 2004. *The American Ballot Box in the Mid Nineteenth Century*. Cambridge University Press.

Bensusán, Graciela. 1994. "Los sindicatos mexicanos y la legalidad laboral," *Revista Mexicana de Sociología*, 56(1): 45–78.

Berent, Matthew K., Jon A. Krosnick, and Arthur Lupia. 2011. "The Quality of Government Records and 'Over-estimation' of Registration and Turnout in Surveys: Lessons from the 2008 ANES Panel Study's Registration and Turnout Validation Exercises," Working Paper no. nes012554. August, Ann Arbor, MI, and Palo Alto, CA: American National Election Studies.

Bertrand, Marianne, Esther Duflo, and Sendhil Mullainathan. 2004. "How Much Should We Trust Differences-in-Differences Estimates?" *Quarterly Journal of Economics*, 119(1): 249–275.

Bezdek, Robert. 1973. "Electoral Opposition in Mexico," PhD dissertation, Ohio State University.

Birch, Sarah. 2000. "Interpreting the Regional Effect in Ukrainian Politics," *Europe-Asia Studies*, 52(6): 1017–1041.

Birch, Sarah. 2007. "Electoral Systems and Electoral Misconduct," *Comparative Political Studies*, 40(12): 1533–1556.

Birch, Sarah. 2012. *Electoral Malpractice*. Oxford University Press.

Bjornlund, Eric. 2004. *Beyond Free and Fair*. Woodrow Wilson Center Press.

Blaydes, Lisa. 2008. "Authoritarian elections and elite management: theory and evidence from Egypt," mimeo, Stanford University, April.

Blaydes, Lisa. 2010. *Elections and Distributive Politics in Mubarak's Egypt*. Cambridge University Press.

Bogaards, Matthijs. 2004. "Counting Parties and Identifying Dominant Party Systems in Africa," *European Journal of Political Research*, 43(2): 173–197.

Boix, Carles. 2003. *Democracy and Redistribution*, Cambridge University Press.

Boix, Carles and Susan Stokes. 2003. "Endogenous Democratization," *World Politics*, 55(4): 517–549.

Boix, Carles and Milan Svolik. 2007. "Non-tyrannical Autocracies," mimeo.

Boix, Carles and Milan Svolik. 2009. "The foundations of limited authoritarian government: institutions and power-sharing in dictatorships," mimeo.

Booth, John. 1998. *Costa Rica: quest for democracy*, Colorado: Westview Press.

Borisova, Yevgenia. 2000a. "And the winner is?" *Moscow Times*, September 9.

Borisova, Yevgenia. 2000b. "And the winner is? – Part II," *Moscow Times*, September 9.

Borisova, Yevgenia. 2000c. "And the winner is? – Part III," *Moscow Times*, September 9.

Borisova, Yevgenia. 2000d. "Baby boom or dead souls?" *thewalls.ru*, http://www.thewalls.ru/annals/suxx11.htm.

Box-Steffensmeier, Janet M. 1996. "A Dynamic Analysis of the Role of War Chests in Campaign Strategy," *American Journal of Political Science*, 40: 352–71.

Brady, Henry E. and David Collier, eds. 2004. *Rethinking Social Inquiry: diverse tools, shared standards*, Rowman and Littlefield Publishers, Inc.

Bratton, Michael. 1987. "The comrades and the countryside: the politics of agricultural policy in Zimbabwe," *World Politics*, 39(2): 174–202.

Bratton, Michael. 1989. "Beyond the state: civil society and associational life in Africa," *World Politics*, 41(3): 407–430.

Bratton, Michael. 1994. "Civil society and political transition in Africa," *Institute for Development Research Report*, 11(6).

Bratton, Michael. 1998. "Second elections in Africa," *Journal of Democracy*, 9(3): 51–66.

Bratton, Michael. 2007. "Formal and informal institutions in Africa," *Journal of Democracy*, 18(3): 96–110.

Bratton, Michael. 2008. "Vote Buying and Violence in Nigerian Election Campaigns." Afrobarometer: Working Paper No. 99, June.

Bratton, Michael and Eldred Masunungure. 2006. "Popular reactions to state repression: Operation Murambatsvina in Zimbabwe," *African Affairs*, 106: 21–45.

Bratton, Michael and Eldred Masunungure. 2008. "Zimbabwe's Long Agony," *Journal of Democracy*, 19(4): 41–55.

Bratton, Michael, Robert Mattes, and E. Gyimah-Boadi. 2005. *Public Opinion, Democracy, and Market Reform in Africa*, Cambridge University Press.

Bratton, Michael and Nicholas Van de Walle. 1997. *Democratic Experiments in Africa: Regime Transitions in Comparative Perspective*. Cambridge University Press.

Brehm, John and Scott Gates. 1993. "Donut Shops and Speed Traps: Evaluating Models of Supervision on Police Behavior," *American Journal of Political Science*, 37(2): 555–581.

Brehm, John and Scott Gates. 1997. *Working, Shirking, and Sabotage: Bureaucratic Response to a Democratic Public*, University of Michigan Press.

Brett, E. A. 2005. "From Corporatism to Liberalisation in Zimbabwe: Economic Policy Regimes and Political Crisis 1980-1997," Crisis States Programme Working Paper No. 58, London School of Economics.

Brownlee, Jason. 2007. *Authoritarianism in an age of democratization*, Cambridge University Press.

Bruhn, Kathleen and Kenneth Greene. 2007. "Elite Polarization meets Mass Moderation in Mexico's 2006 Elections," *PS: Political Science and Politics*, 40(1): 33–38.

Brusco, Valeria, Marcelo Nazareno and Susan Stokes. 2002. "Clientelism and Democracy: Evidence from Argentina," mimeo.

Brusco, Valeria, Marcelo Nazareno and Susan Stokes. 2004. "Vote buying in Argentina," *Latin American Research Review*, **39**(2): 66–88.

Brzezinski, Zbigniew. 2008. "Putin's choice," *The Washington Quarterly*, **31**(2): 95–116.

Buendía, Jorge and Fernanda Somuano. 2003. "Participación Electoral en Nuevas Democracias: La Elección Presidencial de 2000 en México," *Política y Gobierno*, **10**(2): 289–323.

Bulhakaŭ, Valer, ed., 2006. *The Geopolitical Place of Belarus in Europe and the World*. Warsaw: ELIPSA.

Bunce, Valerie. 2000. "Comparative democratization: big and bounded generalizations," *Comparative Political Studies*, **33**(6/7): 703–734.

Bunce, Valerie, Michael McFaul, and Kathryn Stoner-Weiss. 2010. *Democracy and Authoritarianism in the Postcommunist World*, Cambridge University Press.

Bunce, Valerie and Sharon Wolchik. 2010. "Defeating dictators: electoral change and stability in competitive authoritarian regimes," *World Politics*, **61**(1): 43–86.

Bunce, Valerie and Sharon Wolchik. 2010. "Defining and domesticating the electoral model: a comparison of Slovakia and Serbia," in Valerie Bunce et al. 2010. *Democracy and Authoritarianism in the Postcommunist World*, Cambridge University Press.

Burden, Barry. 2000. "Voter Turnout in the National Election Studies," *Political Analysis*, 8 (4): 398–398.

Burger, Ethan S. 2006. "The Divergence between Declaratory and Action Policy: U.S. Non-Recognition of the Results in the Belarusian March 2006 Presidential Election," in Valer Bulhakaŭ, ed., *The Geopolitical Place of Belarus in Europe and the World*. Warsaw: ELIPSA.

Calvo, Ernesto, and María Victoria Murillo. 2004. "Who delivers? Partisan clients in the Argentine electoral market," *American Journal of Political Science*, **48**(4): 742–757.

Camp, Roderic. 2004. "Citizen Attitudes toward Democracy and Vicente Fox's Victory in 2000," in Jorge Domínguez and Chappell Lawson, 2004, *Mexico's Pivotal Democratic Election*, Stanford University Press.

Campbell, Andrea. 2003. *How Policies make Citizens: Senior Political Activism and the American Welfare State*. Princeton University Press.

Campbell, Tracy. 2005. *Deliver the Vote: A History of Election Fraud, an American Political Tradition, 1742–2004*. New York: Carroll & Graf.

Candland, Christopher and Rudra Sil, eds. 2001. *The Politics of Labor in a Global Age: Continuity and Change in Late-Industrializing and Post-Socialist Economies*, Oxford University Press.

Cantú, Francisco and Sebastián Saiegh. 2011. "Fraudulent democracy? An analysis of Argentina's *Infamous Decade* using supervised machine learning," *Political Analysis*, **19**(4): 409–433.

Carbonell, José. 2002. *El Fin de las Certezas Autoritarias: Hacia la construcción de un nuevo sistema político y constitucional para México*, Mexico: Universidad Nacional Autónoma de México.

Card, David. 1992. "Using regional variation in wages to measure the effects of the federal minimum wage," *Industrial and Labor Relations Review*, **46**(1): 22–37.

Carey, John and, Matthew S. Shugart. 1995. "Incentives to Cultivate a Personal Vote: A Rank Ordering of Electoral Formulas," *Electoral Studies*, **14**(4): 417–439.

Carlsson, Hans and Eric van Damme. 1993. "Global games and equilibrium selection," *Econometrica*, **61**(5): 989–1018.

Carothers, Thomas. 1997. "Democracy without illusions," *Foreign Affairs*, **76**(1): 85–99.

Carothers, Thomas. 2000. "Struggling with Semi-Authoritarians," in Peter J. Burnell, ed., *Democracy assistance: international co-operation for democratization*, Frank Cass Publishers.

The Carter Center. 2004. "Executive summary of comprehensive report," Venezuela 2004 recall referendum, September 30.

The Carter Center and the National Democratic Institute. 1999. "Observing the 1998–99 Nigerian Elections: Final Report." Atlanta, GA and Washington, DC: Summer.

The Carter Center and the National Democratic Institute. 2002. "First Statement by the National Democratic Institute and The Carter Center on the Nigerian Electoral Process, 2003." Abuja, Nigeria: November 22.

Castañeda, Jorge G. 1999. *La Herencia. Arqueología de la Sucesión Presidencial en México*. México: Aguilar, Altea, Trejo, Alfaguara.

Chacón, Mario. 2009. "A theory of competitive authoritarian institutions and democratic transition," mimeo, Yale University, November.

Cheibub, José Antonio and Fernando Limongi. 2002. "Democratic institutions and regime survival: parliamentary and presidential democracies reconsidered," *Annual Review of Political Science*, 5: 151–179.

Cheibub, José Antonio and Adam Przeworski. 1999. "Democracy, elections, and accountability for economic outcomes," in Adam Przeworksi, Susan C. Stokes, and Bernard Manin, eds. *Democracy, Accountability, and Representation*, Cambridge: Cambridge University Press.

Chiozza, Giacomo and H. E. Goemans. 2004. "International Conflict and the Tenure of Leaders: Is War Still Ex Post Inefficient?," *American Journal of Political Science*, 48(3): 604–619.

Christensen, Raymond and Kyle Colvin. 2005. "Stealing Elections on Election Night: A Comparison of Statistical Evidence from Japan, Canada, and the United States," mimeo, prepared for the Annual Meeting of the American Political Science Association.

Christie, W. D. 1872. *The Ballot, and Corruption and Expenditure at Elections, A Collection of Essays and Addresses of Different Dates*. London: Macmillan and Co.

Cingranelli, David L. and David L. Richards. 2008. *The Cingranelli-Richards Human Rights Dataset Version 2008.03.12*. http://www.humanrightsdata.org

Cohen, Dara K., and Jessica Weeks. 2009. "Red herrings: non-state actors in the militarized interstate disputes dataset," unpublished manuscript presented at the International Studies Association annual meeting.

Collier, Paul and Pedro Vicente. 2011. "Violence, Bribery, and Fraud: the Political Economy of Elections in Sub-Saharan Africa," *Public Choice*, 153(1-2): 1–31.

Collier, Ruth Berins and David Collier. 1979. "Inducements vs. constraints: disaggregating 'corporatism,'" *American Political Science Review*, 73(4): 967–986.

Colton, Timothy J. and Michael McFaul. 2003. *Popular choice and managed democracy: the Russian elections of 1999 and 2000*, Washington, D.C.: Brookings Institution Press.

Comaroff, Jean and John L. Comaroff, eds. 2006. *Law and disorder in the postcolony*. University of Chicago Press.

Comaroff, John L. and Jean Comaroff, 2006. "Law and disorder in the postcolony: an introduction," in Jean Comaroff and John L. Comaroff, eds. *Law and disorder in the postcolony*. University of Chicago Press.

Commission on Security and Cooperation in Europe. 1995. "Armenia's Parliamentary Election and Constitutional Referendum, July 5 1995."

Comparative Study of Electoral Systems. 2001. Supplementary File Codebook, ICPSR 2683, June.

Cornelius, Wayne. 2002. "La Eficacia de la Compra y Coacción del Voto en las Elecciones Mexicanas de 2000," *Perfiles Latinoamericanos*, 20(June): 11–31.

Cornelius, Wayne. 2004. "Mobilized Voting in the 2000 Elections," in Jorge Domínguez and Chappell Lawson, eds., *Mexico's Pivotal Democratic Election: Candidates, Voters, and the Presidential Campaign of 2000*. Stanford University Press.

Corner, Paul. 2011. "The Plebiscites in Fascist Italy: National Unity and the Importance of the Appearance of Unity," in Ralph Jessen and Hedwig Richter, eds., *Voting for Hitler and Stalin: Elections under 20th-Century Dictatorships*, Frankfurt: Campus Verlag.

Cosío Villegas, Daniel. 1970. "La Derrota del PRI," 17 July, in Cosío Villegas, 1997, *Crítica del Poder*, Mexico: Clío / El Colegio Nacional.

Cosío Villegas, Daniel. 1973. "Lecciones a Montones," 21 July, in Cosío Villegas, 1997, *Crítica del Poder*, Mexico: Clío / El Colegio Nacional.

Cosío Villegas, Daniel. 1997. *Crítica del Poder: Obras Completas*. Mexico: Clío / El Colegio Nacional.

Cowen, Michael and Liisa Laakso, eds. 2002. *Multiparty Elections in Africa*, Oxford: James Currey, Ltd.

Cox, Gary. 1988. "Closeness and Turnout: A Methodological Note," *Journal of Politics*, 50(3): 768–775.

Cox, Gary. 1997. *Making Votes Count*. Cambridge University Press.

Cox, Gary. 1999a. "Electoral Rules and the Calculus of Mobilization," *Legislative Studies Quarterly*, 24: 387–420.

Cox, Gary. 1999b. "Electoral Rules and Electoral Coordination," *Annual Review of Political Science*, 2: 145–161.

Cox, Gary. 2009. "Authoritarian elections and leadership succession 1975–2004," mimeo, University of California, San Diego, June 17.

Cox, Gary and Morgan Kousser. 1981. "Turnout and Rural Corruption: New York as a Test Case," *American Journal of Political Science*, 25(4): 646–663.

Cox, Gary and Michael Munger. 1989. "Closeness, expenditures, and turnout in the 1982 U.S. House Elections," *American Political Science Review*, 83(1): 217–231.

Croissant, Aurel, Gabriele Bruns, and Marei John. 2002. *Electoral Politics in Southeast and East Asia*, Friedrich Ebert Stiftung.

Dahl, Robert A. 1956. *A Preface to Democratic Theory*. University of Chicago Press.

Dahl, Robert A. 1971. *Polyarchy: Participation and Opposition*. Yale University Press.

Dahlberg, Matz and Eva Johansson. 2002. "On the vote purchasing behavior of incumbent governments," *American Political Science Review*, 96(1): 27–40.

Dardé, Carlos. 1996. "Fraud and the Passivity of the Electorate in Spain, 1875–1923," in Posada-Carbó, 1996, *Elections Before Democracy: The History of Elections in Europe and Latin America*. ILAS, University of London.

Davis, Charles and Kenneth Coleman. 1982. "Electoral Change in the One-Party Dominant Mexican Polity, 1958–73: Evidence from Mexico City," *Journal of Developing Areas*, 16(4): 523–542.

Dekel, Eddie, Matthew O. Jackson, and Asher Wolinsky. 2008. "Vote Buying: General Elections," *Journal of Political Economy*, 116(2): 351–380.

del Pozo, Blanca Elena and Ricardo Aparicio. 2001. "Estudio sobre la participación ciudadana y las condiciones del voto libre y secreto en las elecciones federales del año 2000: Una aproximación a la magnitud de la inducción y coacción del voto," FLACSO and IFE, April draft.

Diamond, Larry. 1997. *Consolidating the Third Wave Democracies*, Johns Hopkins University Press.

Diamond, Larry. 2002. "Thinking About Hybrid Regimes," *Journal of Democracy*, 13(2): 21–35, April.

Diamond, Larry and Leonardo Morlino. 2004. "The Quality of Democracy," *Journal of Democracy*, 15(4): 20–31.

Díaz-Cayeros, Alberto, Federico Estévez, and Beatriz Magaloni. 2007. "Clientelism and Portfolio Diversification: A Model of Electoral Investment with Applications to Mexico," in Herbert Kistschelt and Steven Wilkinson, eds., *Patrons, Clients, and Policies: Patterns of Democratic Accountability and Political Competition*. Cambridge University Press.

Díaz-Santana, Héctor. 2001. "Estudio sobre la participación ciudadana y las condiciones del voto libre y secreto en las elecciones federales del año 2000. Informe final," FLACSO and IFE.

Díaz-Santana, Héctor. 2002. "El ejercicio de las instituciones electorales en la manipulación del voto en México," *Perfiles Latinoamericanos*, 20(June): 101–128.

Dixit, Avinash and John Londregan. 1996. "The determinants of success of special interests in redistributive politics," *Journal of Politics*, 58(4): 1132–1155.

Domínguez, Jorge and Chappell Lawson. 2004. *Mexico's Pivotal Democratic Election*, Stanford University Press.

Domínguez, Jorge and James McCann. 1996. *Democratizing Mexico: Public Opinion and Electoral Choices*. Johns Hopkins University Press.

Domínguez, Jorge and Alejandro Poiré, eds. 1999. *Toward Mexico's Democratization*. Routledge.

Donno, Daniela. 2009. "Monitoring Matters: Election Observation and Regional IGO Democracy Protection," mimeo, University of Pittsburgh.

Donno, Daniela and Nasos Roussias. 2009. "Cheating Pays: The Effect of Election Manipulation on Party Systems," Working Paper.

Downs, Anthony. 1957. *An Economic Theory of Democracy*, *The Journal of Political Economy*, 65(2): 135–150.

Duff, Brian, Michal Hanmer, Won-Ho Park and Ismail White. 2007. "Good Excuses: Understanding Who Votes With and Improved Turnout Question," *Public Opinion Quarterly*, 71(1): 67–90.

Dunning, Thad and Susan Stokes. 2007. "Persuasion vs. Mobilization," unpublished manuscript, Yale University.

Durand Ponte, Víctor Manuel. 1995. "La cultura política autoritaria en México," *Revista Mexicana de Sociología*, 57(3): 67–103.

Easter, Gerald M. 2008. "The Russian state in the time of Putin," *Post-Soviet Affairs*, 24(3): 199–230.

Eaton, Kent. 2004. "The link between political and fiscal decentralization in South America," in Alfred P. Montero and David J. Samuels, eds., *Decentralization and Democracy in Latin America*. Notre Dame, IN: University of Notre Dame Press.

Edlin, Aaron and Chris Shannon. 1988. "Strict Monotonicity in Comparative Statics," *Journal of Economic Theory*, 81: 201–219.

Egorov, Georgy, Sergei Guriev and Konstantin Sonin. 2009. "Why resource-poor dictators allow freer media: a theory and evidence from panel data," *American Political Science Review*, 103(4): 645–668.

Eisenstadt, Todd. 2002. "Measuring Electoral Court Failure in Democratizing Mexico," *International Political Science Review*, 21(1): 47–68.

Eisenstadt, Todd. 2004. *Courting Democracy in Mexico*. Cambridge University Press.

Eley, Geoff. 2002. *Foreign democracy: the history of the Left in Europe 1850–2000*, Oxford University Press.

Elklit, Jorgen and Palle Svensson. 1997. "What makes elections free and fair?" *Journal of Democracy*, 8(3): 32–46.

Enikopolov, Ruben, Vasily Korovkin, Maria Petrova, Konstantin Sonin, and Alexei Zakharov. Forthcoming. "Field Experiment Estimate of Electoral Fraud in Russian Parliamentary Elections," *Proceedings of the National Academy of Sciences*.

Erie, Steven P. 1988. *Rainbow's end: Irish-Americans and the dilemmas of urban machine politics, 1840–1985*, University of California Press.

Erikson, Robert and Lorraine Minnite. 2009. "Modeling Problems in the Voter Identification-Voter Turnout Debate," *Election Law Journal*, 8(2): 85–101.

Erikson, Robert S., and Thomas R. Palfrey. 2000. "Equilibria in campaign spending games: theory and data," *American Political Science Review*, 94(3): 595–609.

Fan, Simon C., Chen Lin, and Daniel Treisman. 2009. "Political decentralization and corruption: evidence from around the world," *Journal of Public Economics*, 93(1–2): 14–34.

Fearon, James D. 1999. "Electoral Accountability and the Control of Politicians: Selecting Good Types versus Sanctioning Poor Performance," in Przeworski et al, eds., *Democracy, Accountability, and Representation*, Cambridge University Press.

Fearon, James D. 2011. "Self-enforcing Democracy," *Quarterly Journal of Economics*, 126(4): 1661–1708.

Feddersen, Timothy and Alvaro Sandroni. 2006. "A Theory of Participation in Elections," *American Economic Review*, 96(4), 1271–1282.

Ferejohn, John. 1986. "Incumbent Performance and Electoral Control," *Public Choice* 50.

Ferejohn, John and Morris Fiorina. 1974. "The Paradox of not voting – A decision theoretic analysis," *American Political Science Review*, 68(2): 525–526.

Filmer, Deon and Lant Pritchett. 2001. "Estimating Wealth Effects without Expenditure Data or Tears: An Application to Educational Enrollments in States of India," *Demography*, 38(1): 115–132.

Fish, M. Steven 2005. *Democracy derailed in Russia: the failure of open politics*, Cambridge University Press.

FLACSO-IFE. 2000. *Estudio sobre la participación ciudadana y las condiciones del voto libre y secreto en las elecciones federales del año 2000*, Mexico, D.F.

Flintoff, Corey. 2006a. "Torn by Violence, Haiti Looks to Election with Hope," radio report, National Public Radio, February 6.

Flintoff, Corey. 2006b. "Haitians go to polls in national elections," radio report, National Public Radio, February 7.

Folke, Olle, Shigeo Hirano, and James M. Snyder Jr. 2011. "Patronage and elections in U.S. states," *American Political Science Review*, 105(3): 567–585.

Fox, Jonathan. 1994. "The difficult transition from clientelism to citizenship: Lessons from Mexico," *World Politics*, 46(2): 151–184.

Fox, Jonathan. 1996. "National Electoral Choices in Rural Mexico," in Laura Randall, ed., *The Reform of the Mexican Agrarian Reform*, Armonk: M. E. Sharpe.

Fox News. 2007. "International Observers say Russian Parliamentary Election Not Fair," Dec 3, http://www.foxnews.com/story/0,2933,314591,00.html

Frankel, Glenn. 1985. "Zimbabwe's ruling party seeks support in Matabeleland," *Washington Post*, First Section, A39, June 30.

Freedom House. 2012. "Methodology," *Freedom in the World 2012*, http://www.freedomhouse.org/report/freedom-world-2012/methodology

Freeland, Chrystia, John Thronhill, and Andrew Gowers. 1997. "Moscow's group of seven," *The Financial Times*, November.

Friedrich, Carl J. 1972. *The Pathology of Politics: Violence, Betrayal, Corruption, Secrecy and Propaganda*. New York: Harper and Row.

Fudenberg, Drew and David K. Levine. 1998. *The Theory of Learning in Games*, MIT Press.

Gaines, Brian. 1997. "Where to Count Parties," *Electoral Studies*, 16(1): 49–58.

Galeotti, Mark. 2012. The Power Vertical podcast, *Radio Free Europe*, January 5.

Gandhi, Jennifer. 2008. *Political institutions under dictatorship*, Cambridge University Press.

Gandhi, Jennifer and Ellen Lust-Okar. 2009. "Elections Under Authoritarianism," *Annual Review of Political Science*, 12: 403–422.

Gans-Morse, Jordan, Sebastian Mazzuca and Simeon Nichter. 2009. "Who Gets Bought? Vote Buying, Turnout Buying, and Other Strategies," Working Paper 09-0006, Weatherhead Center for International Affairs, Harvard University.

Geddes, Barbara. 2004. "Authoritarian Breakdown: Empirical Test of a Game Theoretic Argument," mimeo.

Geddes, Barbara. 2006. "Why parties and elections in authoritarian regimes?" mimeo, University of California, Los Angeles, March.

Gehlbach, Scott. 2010. "Reflections on Putin and the media," *Post-Soviet Affairs*, 26(1): 77–87.

Gehlbach, Scott and Alberto Simpser. 2011. "Electoral manipulation as bureaucratic control," mimeo, presented at the Midwest Political Science Association Annual Meeting, Chicago.

Gehlbach, Scott and Konstantin Sonin. 2009. "Government control of the media," mimeo, July 23, University of Wisconsin – Madison and New Economic School.

Gel'man, Vladimir. 2005. "Political opposition in Russia: is it becoming extinct?" *Russian Politics and Law*, 43(3): 25–50.

Gel'man, Vladimir. 2006. "From 'feckless pluralism' to 'dominant power politics'? The transformation of Russia's party system," *Democratization*, 13(4): 545–561.

Gel'man, Vladimir. 2008. "Party politics in Russia: from competition to hierarchy," *Europe-Asia Studies*, 60(6): 913–930.

Gel'man, Vladimir. 2009. "Subnational authoritarianism: Russia in comparative perspective," presented at the Annual Meeting of the American Political Science Association, Toronto, Canada, September 3–6.

George, Alexander L. and Andrew Bennett. 2004. *Case Studies and Theory Development in the Social Sciences*, Cambridge: Belfer Center for Science and International Affairs, Harvard University.

Gervasoni, Carlos. 2010. "A rentier theory of subnational regimes: fiscal federalism, democracy, and authoritarianism in the Argentine Provinces," *World Politics*, 62(2): 302–340.

Ghidadubli, R. G. 2007. "Boris Yeltsin's controversial legacy," *Economic and Political Weekly*, (May 19): 1818–1820.

Gibson, Edward. 1997. "The populist road to market reform: policy and electoral coalitions in Mexico and Argentina," *World Politics*, 49(3): 339–370.

Gibson, Edward L. 2005. "Boundary control: subnational authoritarianism in democratic countries," *World Politics*, 58(1): 101–132.

Gibson, Edward L. 2010. "Politics of the periphery: an introduction to subnational authoritarianism and democratization in Latin America," *Journal of Politics in Latin America*, 2: 3–12.

Gilison, Jerome M. 1968. "Soviet elections as a measure of dissent: the missing one percent," *American Political Science Review*, 62(3): 814–826.

Ginsburg, Tom and Tamir Moustafa, eds. 2008. *Rule by Law: the Politics of Courts in Authoritarian Regimes*, Cambridge: Cambridge University Press.

Giraudy, Agustina. 2009. "Subnational undemocratic regime continuity after democratization: Argentina and Mexico in comparative perspective." Paper presented at the 2009 Congress of the Latin American Studies Association, Rio de Janeiro, Brazil June 11–14, 2009.

Giraudy, Agustina. 2010. "The politics of subnational undemocratic regime reproduction in Argentina and Mexico," *Journal of Politics in Latin America*, 2: 53–84.

Golder, Matthew and Leonard Wantchekon. 2004. "Africa: dictatorial and democratic electoral systems since 1946," mimeo, August 17, prepared for Josep Colomer, ed., 2004, *Handbook of Electoral System Design*, Palgrave, mimeo, August 17.

Goldman, Wendy Z. 2007. *Terror and democracy in the age of Stalin: the social dynamics of repression*, Cambridge University Press.

Goldman, Wendy Z. 2011. "The Great Soviet Paradox: Elections and Terror in the Unions, 1937–1938," in Ralph Jessen and Hedwig Richter, eds., *Voting for Hitler and Stalin: Elections under 20th-Century Dictatorships*, Frankfurt: Campus Verlag.

Golosov, Grigorii V. 2006. "The structure of party alternatives and voter choice in Russia: evidence from the 2003–2004 regional legislative elections," *Party Politics*, 12(6): 707–725.

Gómez Tagle, Silvia. 2000. "De Política, Geografía y Elecciones," in Silvia Gómez Tagle y María Eugenia Valdés 2000.

Gómez Tagle, Silvia y María Eugenia Valdés, eds. 2000. *La Geografía del Poder y las Elecciones en México*, México: Instituto Federal Electoral.

Goodliffe, Jay. 2001. "The Effect of War Chests on Challenger Entry in U.S. House Elections," *American Journal of Political Science*, 45(4): 830–844.

Goodliffe, Jay. 2005. "When do War Chests Deter?" *Journal of Theoretical Politics*, 17(2): 249–277.

Gordon, Sanford C. and Dimitri Landa. 2009. "Do the Advantages of Incumbency Advantage Incumbents?" *Journal of Politics*, 71(4): 1481–1498.

Greene, Kenneth. 2007. *Why Dominant Parties Lose: Mexico's Democratization in Comparative Perspective*, Cambridge University Press.

Greene, Kenneth. 2010. "The political economy of authoritarian single-party dominance," *Comparative Political Studies*, 43(7): 807–834.

Gregory, Martyn. 1980. "The Zimbabwe election: the political and military implications," *Journal of Southern African Studies*, 7(1): 17–37.

Groseclose, Tim and James M. Snyder, Jr. 1996. "Buying Supermajorities," *American Political Science Review*, 90(2): 303–315.

Gross, Jan. 1986. "The First Soviet Sponsored Elections in Eastern Europe," *East European Politics & Societies*, 1(1): 4–29.

Gross, Jan T. 2002. *Revolution from abroad: the Soviet conquest of Poland's Western Ukraine and Western Belorussia*, Princeton University Press.

Haber, Stephen, Armando Razo and Noel Maurer. 2003. *The Politics of Property Rights: Political Instability, Credible Commitments, and Economic Growth in Mexico, 1876–1929*. Cambridge University Press.

Hadenius, Axel and Jan Teorell. 2007. "Pathways from authoritarianism," *Journal of Democracy*, 18(1): 143–157.

Hafner-Burton, Emilie Marie, Susan D. Hyde and Ryan Jablonski. 2012. "When Governments use Election Violence to stay in Power," unpublished manuscript.

Hale, Henry. 2003. "Explaining machine politics in Russia's regions: economy, ethnicity, and legacy," *Post-Soviet Affairs*, 19(3): 228–263.

Hale, Henry. 2005. "Regime cycles: democracy, autocracy, and revolution in post-Soviet Eurasia," *World Politics*, 58: 133–165.

Harding, Luke. 2008. "From Russia with fraud," *The Guardian*, April 20.

Harding, Luke. 2008. "Russian university that advised on election monitoring closed as fire risk," *The Guardian*, February 11.

Harsanyi, John and Reinhard Selten. 1988. *A general theory of equilibrium selection in games*, MIT Press.

Hartlyn, Jonathan and Jennifer McCoy. 2001. *Elections with 'adjectives' in contemporary Latin America: A comparative analysis*. Convention of the Latin American Studies Association.

Hartlyn, Jonathan and Jennifer McCoy. 2006. "Observer Paradoxes: How to Assess Electoral Manipulation," in Andreas Schedler, ed., *Electoral Authoritarianism: The Dynamics of Unfree Competition*.

Hausmann, Ricardo and Roberto Rigobón. 2004. "En busca del cisne negro: Análisis de la evidencia estadística sobre fraude electoral en Venezuela," mimeo.

Hayward, Susana. 2005. "Police stations attacked on the eve of Mexico elections," *The Mercury News*, February 6.

Heinemann, Frank. 2002. "Exchange-rate attack as a coordination game: theory and experimental evidence," *Oxford Review of Economic Policy*, 18: 479–494.

Heise, Julio. 1982. *Historia de Chile: el período parlamentario, 1861–1925*, Volume 2. Santiago de Chile: Editorial Universitaria.

Herbst, Jeffrey. 1990. *State Politics in Zimbabwe*, University of California Press.

Herbst, Jeffrey. 2000. *States and Power in Africa: Comparative Lessons in Authority and Control*, Princeton University Press.

Hersch, Philip L. and Gerald S. McDougall. 1994. "Campaign War Chests as a Barrier to Entry in Congressional Races," *Economic Inquiry*, 32: 630–641.

Hersh, Seymour. 1998. *The Dark Side of Camelot*, Little, Brown, and Company.

Hesli, Vicki. 2003. "Parliamentary and presidential elections in Russia: the political landscape in 1999 and 2000," in Hesli and Reisinger, eds. *The 1999–2000 elections in Russia: their impact and legacy*, Cambridge University Press.

Hesli, Vicki and William Reisinger, eds., 2003. *The 1999–2000 elections in Russia: their impact and legacy*, Cambridge University Press.

Heston, Alan, Robert Summers, and Bettina Aten. 2009. *Penn World Table Version 6*. Center for International Comparisons of Production, Income and Prices at the University of Pennsylvania.

Hicken, Allen. 2007. "How effective are institutional reforms?" in Charles Frederic Schaffer, ed., *Elections for Sale*, Lynne Rienner.

Hill, Ronald. 2002. "Belarus's Presidential Non-Election," *Journal of Communist Studies & Transition Politics*, 18(2): 126–138.

Hiskey, Jonathan and Shaun Bowler. 2005. "Local Context and Democratization in Mexico," *American Journal of Political Science*, 49(1): 57–71.

Hodess, Robin. 2004. "Introduction" to Transparency International *Global Corruption Report 2004*.

Holt, Michael F. 2008. *By One Vote: The Disputed Presidential Election of 1876*. Lawrence: University Press of Kansas.

Horowitz, Joel. 1999. "Bosses and clients: municipal employment in the Buenos Aires of the Radicals, 1916–30," *Journal of Latin American Studies*, 31(3): 617–644.

Howard, Mark Morjé and Philip G. Roessler. 2006. "Liberalizing electoral outcomes in competitive authoritarian regimes," *American Journal of Political Science*, 50(2): 365–381.

Hsieh, Chang-Tai, Edward Miguel, Daniel Ortega, and Francisco Rodríguez. 2009. "The price of political opposition: Evidence from Venezuela's Maisanta." NBER Working Paper.

Human Rights Watch. 1997. *Human rights in Zambia since the 1996 election*, July 1. Online report, http://www.hrw.org/reports/1997/zambia/.

Hyde, Susan D. 2006. *Observing Norms: Explaining the Causes and Consequences of Internationally Monitored Elections*, PhD dissertation, University of California, San Diego.

Hyde, Susan D. 2007. "The Observer Effect in International Politics: Evidence from a Natural Experiment," *World Politics*, 60(1): 37–63.

Hyde, Susan D. 2011. *The Pseudo-Democrat's Dilemma: Why Election Monitoring Became an International Norm*, Ithaca: Cornell University Press.

Hyde, Susan D. and Nikolay Marinov. 2008. "Does information facilitate self-enforcing democracy?" mimeo, Yale University.

Hyde, Susan D. and Nikolay Marinov. 2012. "Which Elections Can Be Lost?" *Political Analysis*, 20(2): 191–210.

Hyden, Goran and Colin Leys. 1972. "Elections and politics in single-party systems: the case of Kenya and Tanzania," *British Journal of Political Science*, 2(4): 389–420.

Ibarra, Juan Fernando, and Alberto Simpser. 2012. "The Political Origins of Subnational Authoritarianism," unpublished manuscript, CIDE and University of Chicago.

Ichino, Nahomi. 2006. "Voters and Thugs: Political Tournaments in Nigeria," unpublished manuscript.

Ichino, Nahomi and Matthias Schündeln. 2012. "Deterring or Displacing Electoral Irregularities? Spillover Effects of Observers in a Randomized Field Experiment in Ghana," *Journal of Politics*, 74(1): 292–307.

Ioffe, Grigory. 2008. *Understanding Belarus and how Western Foreign Policy Misses the Mark*. Lanham, Md.: Rowman & Littlefield.

Jason, Pini. 2003. "'Operation Earthquake' sweeps the polls," *New African*, 419: 28–29 (June).

Jensen, Richard J. 1971. *The Winning of the Midwest: Social and Political Conflict, 1888–1896*, Vol. 2. University of Chicago Press.

Jessen, Ralph and Hedwig Richter. 2011, "Non-competitive elections in 20th-century dictatorships: some questions and general considerations," in Ralph Jessen and

Hedwig Richter, eds., *Voting for Hitler and Stalin: Elections under 20th-Century Dictatorships*, Frankfurt: Campus Verlag.

Jessen, Ralph and Hedwig Richter, eds. 2011. *Voting for Hitler and Stalin: Elections under 20th-Century Dictatorships*, Frankfurt: Campus Verlag.

Joseph, Richard. 1997. "Democratization in Africa after 1989: Comparative and theoretical perspectives," *Comparative Politics*, 29(3): 363–382.

Kam, Cristopher. 2008. "The Market for Votes: Systematic Data on Electoral Corruption in the United Kingdom, 1808–85," presented at the Midwest Political Science Association, Chicago, April 3–6.

Karatnycky, Adrian. 2005. "Ukraine's Orange Revolution," *Foreign Affairs*, 84(2).

Karl, Terry Lynn. 1995. "The hybrid regimes of Central America," *Journal of Democracy*, 6(3): 72–86.

Kazakievic, Andrej. 2006. "Regional peculiarities in the context of Presidential Elections of 1994, 2001, and 2006," in Valer Bulhakaŭ, ed., *The Geopolitical Place of Belarus in Europe and the World*. Warsaw: ELIPSA.

Keefer, Philip. 2002. "DPI2000: Database of Political Institutions: Changes and Variable Definitions." March. The World Bank.

Keefer, Philip and David Stasavage. 2003. "The Limits of Delegation: Veto Players, Central Bank Independence and the Credibility of Monetary Policy," *American Political Science Review*, 97(3): 407–423.

Kelley, Judith. 2008. "Assessing the complex evolution of norms: the rise of international election monitoring," *International Organization*, 62(Spring): 221–255.

Kelley, Judith. 2012. *Monitoring Democracy: When International Election Observation Works, and Why it Often Fails*. Princeton University Press.

Kennedy, Ryan. 2006. "A Colorless Election: The 2005 Presidential Election in Kazakhstan, and What It Means for the Future of the Opposition," *Problems of Post-Communism*, 53(6).

Key, Valdimer Orlando. 1936. *The techniques of political graft in the United States*, PhD dissertation, University of Chicago.

King, Gary, Robert O. Keohane, and Sidney Verba. 1994. *Designing Social Inquiry: Scientific Inference in Qualitative Research*, Princeton University Press.

King, Gary, Michael Tomz, and Jason Wittenberg. 2000. "Making the Most of Statistical Analyses: Improving Interpretation and Presentation" *American Journal of Political Science*, 44(2): 347–361.

King, Ronald. 2001. "Counting the Votes: South Carolina's Stolen Election of 1876," *Journal of Interdisciplinary History*, 32(2): 169–191.

Kinzer, Stephen. 1993. "Ex-East German Leader Convicted Of Vote Fraud but Not Punished," *The New York Times*, May 28, "World" section.

Kitschelt, Herbert, Zdenka Mansfeldova, Radoslaw Markowski, and Gábor Tóka. 1999. *Post-Communist Party Systems: Competition, Representation, and Inter-Party Cooperation*, Cambridge: Cambridge University Press.

Kitschelt, Herbert and Steven Wilkinson, eds. 2007. *Patrons, Clients, and Politics: Patterns of Democratic Accountability and Political Competition*. Cambridge: Cambridge University Press.

Klees van Donge, Jan. 1995. "Kamuzu's Legacy: The Democratization of Malawi: Or Searching for the Rules of the Game in African Politics," *African Affairs*, 94(375): 227–257.

Klesner, Joseph. 1987. "Changing Patterns of Electoral Participation and Official Party Support," in Judith Gentleman, *Mexican Politics in Transition*, West View Press.

Klesner, Joseph. 1997. "The Enigma of Electoral Participation in Mexico: Electoral Reform, the Rise of Opposition Contestation, and Voter Turnout, 1967–1994," presented at the Annual Meeting of the Midwest Political Science Association, Chicago, April 10–12.

Klesner, Joseph. 2001. "The End of Mexico's One-Party Regime," *PS*, March, 107–114.

Klesner, Joseph and Chappell Lawson. 2001. "'Adios' to the PRI? Changing Voter Turnout in Mexico's Political Transition," *Mexican Studies*, 17(1): 17–39.

Knack, Stephen and Philip Keefer. 1995. "Institutions and economic performance: Cross country tests using alternative institutional measures," *Economics and Politics*, 7: 207–227.

Knight, Amy, 2010. "Forever Putin?" *New York Review of Books*, January 13.

Kobak, Dmitry, Sergei Shpilkin, and Maxim S. Pshenichnikov. 2012. "Statistical anomalies in the 2011-2012 Russian elections revealed by 2D correlation analysis," arXiv:1205.0741v2 [physics.soc-ph].

Kochin, Michael and Levis Kochin. 1998. "When is buying votes wrong?" *Public Choice*, 97.

Koshiw, JV. 2003. *Beheaded: the killing of a journalist*, England: Artemia Press.

Kriger, Norma. 2005. "ZANU (PF) Strategies in General Elections, 1980–2000: Discourse and Coercion," *African Affairs*, 104(414): 1–34.

Kryshtanovskaya, Olga and Steven White. 2005. "The Rise of the Russian business elite," *Communist and Post-Communist Studies*, 38: 293–307.

Kryshtanovskaya, Olga and Steven White. 2009. "The Sovietization of Russian politics," *Post-Soviet Affairs*, 23(4): 283–309.

Kunov, Andrei, Mikhail Myagkov, Alexei Sitnikov and Dmitry Shakin. 2005. "Putin's 'Party of Power' and the Declining Power of Parties in Russia," mimeo, The Foreign Policy Center.

Kuran, Timur. 1989. "Sparks and prairie fires: A theory of unanticipated political revolution," *Public Choice*, 61(1): 41–74.

Laakso, Liisa. 2002. "When elections are just a formality: rural-urban dynamics in the dominant-party system of Zimbabwe," in Michael Cowen and Liisa Laakso, eds., *Multiparty Elections in Africa*, Oxford: James Currey, Ltd., 324–345.

Laakso, Markku and Rein Taagepera. 1979. "'Effective' number of parties: a measure with application to West Europe," *Comparative Political Studies*, 12(1): 3–27.

LeBas, Adrienne. 2006. "Polarization as Craft: Party Formation and State Violence in Zimbabwe," *Comparative Politics*, 38(4): 419–438.

LeBas, Adrienne. 2011. *From Protest to Parties: Party-Building and Democratization in Africa*, Oxford: Oxford University Press.

Ledeneva, Alena. 2006. *How Russia Really Works: The Informal Practices That Shaped Post-Soviet Politics And Business*, Cornell University Press.

Ledyard, John. 1984. "The Pure theory of large 2-candidate elections" *Public Choice*, 44(1): 7–41.

Lehoucq, Fabrice. 2003. "Electoral Fraud: Causes, Types and Consequences," *Annual Review of Political Science*, 6: 233–256.

Lehoucq, Fabrice and Iván Molina. 2002. *Stuffing the Ballot Box: Fraud, Electoral Reform, and Democratization in Costa Rica*. Cambridge University Press.

Levitsky, Steven. 1999. "Fujimori and post-party politics in Peru," *Journal of Democracy*, 10(3): 78–92.

Levitsky, Steven. 2003. *Transforming Labor-Based Parties in Latin America: Argentine Peronism in Comparative Perspective*, Cambridge University Press.

Levitsky, Steven. 2007. "From populism to clientelism? The transformation of labor-based party linkages in Latin America" in Herbert Kitschelt and Steven Wilkinson, eds. *Patrons, Clients, and Politics: Patterns of Democratic Accountability and Political Competition*, Cambridge University Press.

Levitsky, Steven and Lucan Way. 2002. "The rise of competitive authoritarianism," *Journal of Democracy*, 13(2): 51–65, April.

Levitsky, Steven and Lucan Way. 2005. "International linkage and democratization," *Journal of Democracy*, 16(3), 20–34.

Levitsky, Steven and Lucan Way. 2009. *Competitive Authoritarianism: International Linkage, Organizational Power, and the Fate of Hybrid Regimes* [preliminary manuscript version of Levitsky and Way 2010], mimeo.

Levitsky, Steven and Lucan Way. 2010. *Competitive Authoritarianism: Hybrid Regimes After the Cold War* [Kindle version]. Cambridge University Press.

Levitt, Steven D. 2008. "Russian election fraud?" *The New York Times*, April 16, http://freakonomics.blogs.nytimes.com/2008/04/16/russian-election-fraud/.

Levy, Clifford. 2009. "Why Russians Ignore Ballot Fraud," *New York Times*, Week in Review, October 24.

Lewis, Paul. 1990. "Non-competitive elections and regime change: Poland 1989," *Parliamentary Affairs*, 43: 90–107.

Lewis, Peter M. 2003. "Nigeria: Elections in a Fragile Regime," *Journal of Democracy*, 14(3): 131.

Liddle, William. 1996. "A useful fiction: democratic legitimation in New Order Indonesia," in Robert Taylor, *The politics of elections in Southeast Asia*, Cambridge University Press.

Lieberman, Evan S. 2005. "Nested analysis as a mixed-method strategy for comparative research," *American Political Science Review*, 99(3): 435–452.

Lindberg, Staffan I. 2006a. *Democracy and Elections in Africa*, Johns Hopkins University Press.

Lindberg, Staffan I. 2006b. "Opposition parties and democratization in sub-Saharan Africa," *Journal of Contemporary African Studies*, 24(1): 123–138.

Linz, Juan. 2000. *Totalitarian and Authoritarian Regimes*. Lynne Rienner.

Linz, Juan, and Alfred Stepan. 1996. *Problems of Democratic Transition and Consolidation*. Johns Hopkins University Press.

Little, Andrew T. 2012. "Fraud and monitoring in noncompetitive elections," mimeo, New York University.

Lott, John. 2006. "Evidence of Voter Fraud and the Impact that Regulations to Reduce Fraud have on Voter Participation Rates," mimeo, August 18.

Lust-Okar, Ellen. 2005. *Structuring conflict in the Arab world: incumbents, opponents, and institutions*, Cambridge University Press.

Lust-Okar, Ellen. 2006. "Elections Under Authoritarianism: Preliminary Lessons from Jordan," *Democratization*, 13(3): 456–471.

Lyubarsky, Kronid and Aleksandr Sobyanin. 1995. "Scandal: FRAUD-3," *Current Digest of the Russian Press*, 47(18): 4–6.

Magaloni, Beatriz. 2006. *Voting for autocracy: hegemonic party survival and its demise in Mexico*, Cambridge University Press.

Magaloni, Beatriz. 2010. "The Game of Electoral Fraud and the Ousting of Authoritarian Rule," *American Journal of Political Science*, 54(3): 751–765.

Magaloni, Beatriz, Alberto Díaz-Cayeros, and Federico Estevez. 2007. "Clientelism and portfolio diversification: a model of electoral investment with applications to Mexico," in Herbert Kitschelt and Steven Wilkinson, eds. *Patrons, Clients, and Politics: Patterns of Democratic Accountability and Political Competition*, Cambridge University Press.

Mahoney, James and Gary Goertz. 2006. "A tale of two cultures: contrasting quantitative and qualitative research," *Political Analysis*, 14(3): 227–249.

Mainwaring, Scott and Timothy Scully. 1995. *Building democratic institutions: party systems in Latin America*, Oxford University Press.

Makumbe, John. 2002. "Zimbabwe's Hijacked Election," *Journal of Democracy*, 13(4): 87–101.

Makumbe, John and Daniel Compagnon. 2000. *Behind the Smokescreen: the Politics of Zimbabwe's 1995 General Elections*. University of Zimbabwe Publications Office.

Malesky, Edmund and Paul Schuler. 2006. "Nodding or needling: analyzing delegate responsiveness in an authoritarian parliament," *American Political Science Review*, 104(3): 482–502.

Mansfield, Edward, Helen Milner and Peter Rosendorff. 2000. "Free to Trade: Democracies, Autocracies and International Trade," *American Political Science Review* (June).

Marbry, Donald J. 1974. "Mexico's party deputy system: the first decade," *Journal of Interamerican Studies and World Affairs*, 16(2): 221–233.

March, Luke. 2006. "The contemporary Russian left after Communism: into the dustbin of history?" *Journal of Communist Studies and Transition Politics*, 22(4): 431–456.

Marples, David R. 2004. "The Prospects for Democracy in Belarus," *Problems of Post-Communism*, 51(1): 31–42.

Marples, David R. 2005. "Europe's Last Dictatorship: The Roots and Perspectives of Authoritarianism in 'White Russia,'" *Europe-Asia Studies*, 57(6): 895–908.

Marples, David R. 2006. "Color Revolutions: The Belarus Case," *Communist & Post-Communist Studies*, 39(3): 351–364.

Marples, David R. 2007. "Elections and Nation-Building in Belarus: A Comment on Ioffe," *Eurasian Geography & Economics*, 48(1): 59–67.

Marples, David R. 2008. "Is the Russia-Belarus Union Obsolete?" *Problems of Post-Communism*, 55(1): 25–35.

McCann, James and Jorge Domínguez. 1998. "Mexicans react to electoral fraud and political corruption: An assessment of public opinion and voting behavior," *Electoral Studies*, 17(4): 483–503.

McCormick, John P. 2006. "Contain the Wealthy and Patrol the Magistrates: Restoring Elite Accountability to Popular Government," *American Political Science Review*, 100(2): 147–163.

McCormick, John P. 2011. *Machiavellian Democracy*. Cambridge University Press.

McDonald, Michael. 2003. "On the Overreport Bias of the National Election Study Turnout Rate," *Political Analysis*, 11: 180–186.

McDonald, Ronald H. 1972. "Electoral fraud and regime controls in Latin America," *Western Political Quarterly*, 25(1): 81–93.

McFaul, Michael. 1997. *Russia's 1996 Presidential Election: The End of Polarized Politics*, Stanford: Hoover Institution Press.

McFaul, Michael. 2001. "Explaining party formation and nonformation in Russia: actors, institutions, and chance," *Comparative Political Studies*, 34(10): 1159–1187.

McFaul, Michael. 2007. "Putin's Plan," *The Wall Street Journal*, December 4.

McFaul, Michael and Kathryn Stoner-Weiss. 2008. "The myth of the authoritarian model: how Putin's crackdown holds Russia back," *Foreign Affairs*, 87(1): 68–84.

Mebane Jr, Walter R. 2006. "Election Forensics: The Second-Digit Benfords Law Test and Recent American Presidential Elections," presented at the Election Fraud Conference, Salt Lake City, September 29–30.

Mebane, Jr., Walter R. 2007. "Election Forensics: Statistics, Recounts and Fraud," mimeo, April 10.

Mebane, Jr., Walter R. 2008. "Election Forensics: Outlier and Digit Tests in America and Russia," presented at the American Electoral Process Conference, Center for the Study of Democratic Politics, Princeton University, May 1-3.

Mebane, Jr., Walter R. and Kiril Kalinin. 2009. "Comparative Election Fraud Detection," mimeo, August 7.

Mebane, Jr., Walter R., Jasjeet S. Sekhon, and Jonathan Wand. 2003. "Detecting and Correcting Election Irregularities," mimeo, October 9.

Medina, Luis. 2005. "The comparative statics of collective action: a pragmatic approach to games with multiple equilibria," *Rationality and Society*, 17(4): 423–452.

Medina, Luis. 2007. *A Unified Theory of Collective Action and Social Change*, University of Michigan Press.

Medina, Luis and Susan Stokes. 2002. "Clientelism as Political Monopoly," mimeo, University of Chicago.

Meldrum, Andrew. 1995. "Rubber-stamp parliament," *Africa Report*, May/June 40(3): 60–63.

Menes, Rebecca. 1998. "Paving Machines: Politics and the Provision of Public Infrastructure in American Cities during the Progressive Era, 1900–1910," mimeo.

Menes, Rebecca. 2006. "Limiting the reach of the grabbing hand: graft and growth in American cities, 1880 to 1930," in Edward Glaeser and Claudia Goldin, eds., *Corruption and Reform: Lessons from America's Economic History*, NBER and University of Chicago Press.

Merlevede, Bruno, Koen Schoors, and Bas Van Aarle. 2009. "Russia from bust to boom and back: oil price, Dutch disease and stabilisation fund," *Comparative Economic Studies*, June: 213–241.

Mill, John Stuart. 2008 [1859]. *Thoughts on Parliamentary Reform*, New York: Cosimo, Inc.

Milyo, Jeffrey and Timothy Groseclose. 1999. "The Electoral Effects of Incumbent Wealth," *Journal of Law and Economics*, 17: 699–722.

Minnite, Lori, and David Callahan. 2003. "Securing the Vote. An analysis of election fraud," *Dēmos: A Network for Ideas and Action*.

Minnite, Lorraine. 2009. "Finding election fraud – maybe," *Election Law Journal*, 8(3): 249–256.

Molina, Iván and Fabrice Lehoucq. 1999. "Political Competition and Electoral Fraud: A Latin American Case Study," *Journal of Interdisciplinary History*, 30(2): 199–234.

Molinar, Juan. 1985. "La Costumbre Electoral Mexicana," *Nexos*.

Molinar, Juan. 1991. "Counting the Number of Parties: An Alternative Index," *American Political Science Review*, 85(4): 1383–1391.

Molinar, Juan. 1991. *El Tiempo de la Legitimidad. Elecciones, autoritarismo y democracia en México*. Cal y Arena: México.

Molinar, Juan, and Leonardo Valdés. 1985. "Las elecciones de 1985 en el Distrito Federal," *Revista Mexicana de Sociología.*

Molinar, Juan and Jeffrey Weldon. 1988. "Elecciones de 1988 en Mexico: Crisis del Autoritarismo," *Revista Mexicana de Sociologia,* 52(4): 229–262.

Molinar, Juan and Jeffrey Weldon. 1994. "Electoral Determinants and Effects of PRONASOL," in Wayne Cornelius, Ann Craig and Jonathan Fox, eds., *Transforming State Society Relations in Mexico: The National Solidarity Strategy,* La Jolla: UCSD, Center for US-Mexican Studies.

Molinas, José, Anibal Pérez Liñán, and Sebastián Saiegh, with Ángela Montero. 2006. "Political institutions, policymaking processes and policy outcomes in Paraguay, 1954–2003," Inter-American Development Bank, Latin American Research Network, Working Paper #R-502, April.

Morozov, Petr. 2000. "Boris Yeltsin. Sketches for a Portrait," *Russian Social Science Review,* 41(1): 43–49.

Montero, Alfred P. and David J. Samuels. 2004. "The political determinants of decentralization in Latin America: causes and consequences," in Alfred P. Montero and David J. Samuels, eds., *Decentralization and Democracy in Latin America.* Notre Dame, IN: University of Notre Dame Press.

Morris, Roy. 2003. *Fraud of the Century : Rutherford B. Hayes, Samuel Tilden, and the Stolen Election of 1876.* New York: Simon & Schuster.

Morris, Stephen, and Hyun Song Shin. 1998. "Unique equilibrium in a model of self-fulfilling currency attacks," *American Economic Review,* 88(3): 587–597.

Morris, Stephen, and Hyun Song Shin. 2001. "Global games: theory and applications," mimeo, March.

Morton, Rebecca. 1991. "Groups in Rational Turnout Models," *American Journal of Political Science,* 35(3): 758–776.

Murillo, María Victoria. 2000. "From populism to neoliberalism: labor unions and market reforms in Latin America," *World Politics,* 52: 135–174.

Murillo, María Victoria. 2001a. *Labor Unions, Partisan Coalitions, and Market Reforms in Latin America,* Cambridge University Press.

Murillo, María Victoria. 2001b. "Partisan loyalty and union competition: macroeconomic adjustment and industrial restructuring in Mexico," in Christopher Candland and Rudra Sil, eds., *The Politics of Labor in a Global Age: Continuity and Change in Late-Industrializing and Post-Socialist Economies,* Oxford University Press.

Myagkov, Mikhail. 2003. "The 1999 Duma election in Russia: a step toward democracy or the elites' game?" in Hesli and Reisinger, eds., *The 1999–2000 elections in Russia: their impact and legacy,* Cambridge University Press.

Myagkov, Mikhail, & Peter Ordeshook. 2005. "The trail of votes in Ukraine's 1998, 1999, and 2002 elections," *Post-Soviet Affairs,* 21(1), 56–71.

Myagkov, Mikhail and Peter Ordeshook. 2008. "Russian elections: an oxymoron of democracy," mimeo, The National Council of Eurasian and East European Research.

Myagkov, Mikhail, Peter Ordeshook and Dmitry Shakin. 2005. "Fraud or Fairytales: Russia and Ukraine's Electoral Experience," *Post-Soviet Affairs,* 21(2): 91–131.

Myagkov, Mikhail, Peter Ordeshook and Dmitry Shakin. 2009. *The Forensics of Election Fraud: Russia and Ukraine.* Cambridge University Press.

Myerson, Roger. 2007. "The autocrat's credibility problem and foundations of the constitutional state," mimeo, University of Chicago, August.

Myerson, Roger. 2009. "Learning from Schelling's *Strategy of Conflict*," *Journal of Economic Literature*, 17(4): 1109–1125.

Myerson, Roger and Robert Weber. 1993. "A Theory of Voting Equilibria," *American Political Science Review*, 87(1): 102–114.

Mylonas, Harris and Nasos Roussias. 2008. "When do Votes Count? Regime Type, Electoral Conduct, and Political Competition in Africa," *Comparative Political Studies*, 41(11): 1466–1491.

National Democratic Institute for International Affairs. 1989. "The 1989 Paraguayan Elections: a Foundation for Democratic Change – International Delegation Report."

National Democratic Institute for International Affairs / The Carter Center. 1992. "The October 31 1991 national elections in Zambia."

Needler, Martin C. 1977. "The closeness of elections in Latin America," *Latin American Research Review*, 12(1): 115–122.

Nichter, Simeon. 2008. "Vote Buying or Turnout Buying? Machine Politics and the Secret Ballot," *American Political Science Review*, 102(1): 19–31.

Nickson, R. Andrew. 1988. "Tyranny and longevity: Stroessner's Paraguay," *Third World Quarterly*, 10(1): 237–259.

Nie, Norman, Jane Junn and Kenneth Stehlik-Barry. 1996. *Education and Democratic Citizenship in America*, University of Chicago Press.

Nyblade, Benjamin and Steven R. Reed. 2008. "Who Cheats? Who Loots? Political Competition and Corruption in Japan, 1947–1993," *American Journal of Political Science*, 52(4): 926–941.

O'Donnell, Guillermo and Philippe C. Schmitter. 1986. *Transitions from authoritarian rule: Tentative conclusions about uncertain democracies*. Johns Hopkins University Press.

O'Gorman, Frank. 1989. *Voters, Patrons and Parties: The Unreformed Electoral System of Hanoverian England, 1734–1832*, Oxford University Press.

Organization for Security and Co-operation in Europe / Office for Democratic Institutions and Human Rights. 1998. "Final Report: Republic of Armenia Presidential Elections," April 9.

Organization for Security and Co-operation in Europe / Office for Democratic Institutions and Human Rights. 2000a. "Kyrgyz Republic Presidential Elections," 29 October.

Organization for Security and Co-operation in Europe / Office for Democratic Institutions and Human Rights. 2000b. "Republic of Georgia – Presidential Election – 9 April 2000 – Final Report."

Organization for Security and Co-operation in Europe / Office for Democratic Institutions and Human Rights. 2000c. "Final Report: Russian Federation Presidential Election," 26 March.

Organization for Security and Co-operation in Europe / Office for Democratic Institutions and Human Rights. 2001. "Limited Election Observation Mission Final Report: Republic of Belarus Presidential Election," 9 September.

Organization for Security and Co-operation in Europe / Office for Democratic Institutions and Human Rights. 2003a. "Republic of Armenia – Presidential Election – 19 February and 5 March 2003 – Final Report."

Organization for Security and Co-operation in Europe / Office for Democratic Institutions and Human Rights. 2003b. "Georgia – Parliamentary Elections 2003 – 3-25 November – Post-Election Interim Report."

Organization for Security and Co-operation in Europe / Office for Democratic Institutions and Human Rights. 2004. "Final Report: Russian Federation Presidential Election," 14 March.

Organization for Security and Co-operation in Europe / Office for Democratic Institutions and Human Rights. 2005. "Election Observation Mission Final Report: Ukraine, Presidential Election," May 11.

Organization for Security and Co-operation in Europe / Office for Democratic Institutions and Human Rights. 2006. "Election Observation Mission Final Report: Republic of Kazakhstan, Presidential Election," February 21.

Ottaway, Marina. 2003. *Democracy Challenged: the rise of semi-authoritarianism*, Carnegie Endowment for International Peace.

Pacheco Ladrón de Guevara, Lourdes. 1993. "Geografía del Voto en Nayarit (1982–1991). Elecciones Federales y Municipales," in Gustavo Ernesto Emmerich, ed. *Votos y Mapas: Estudios de Geografía Electoral en México*, Toluca, Universidad Autónoma del Estado de México.

Padgett, Leon Vincent. 1976. *The Mexican Political System*, Houghton Mifflin.

Palfrey, Thomas, and Howard Rosenthal. 1985. "Voter Participation and Strategic Uncertainty," *American Political Science Review*, 79(1): 62–78.

Pastor, Manuel, and Carol Wise. 1997. "State policy, distribution and neoliberal reform in Mexico," *Journal of Latin American Studies*, 29(2): 419–456.

Pastor, Robert. 1999. "The Role of Electoral Administration in Democratic Transitions," *Democratization*, 6(4): 1–27 Winter.

Pempel, T. J., ed. 1990. *Uncommon democracies: the one-party dominant regimes*, Cornell University Press.

Peschard, Jacqueline. 1995. "Cambio y Continuidad en el Comportamiento Electoral del Distrito Federal, 1988–1994," PhD dissertation, El Colegio de Michoacán.

Philp, Mark. 1997. "Defining Political Corruption," *Political Studies*, XLV: 436–462.

Poiré, Alejandro. 1999. "Retrospective voting, partisanship and loyalty in presidential elections: 1994," in Domínguez and Poiré, 1999. *Toward Mexico's Democratization*. Routledge.

Political Risk Services. *International Country Risk Guide: A Business Guide to Political Risk for International Decisions*.

Posada-Carbó, Eduardo. 1996. *Elections Before Democracy: The History of Elections in Europe and Latin America*. ILAS, University of London.

Posada-Carbó, Eduardo. 2000. "Electoral Juggling: A Comparative History of the Corruption of Suffrage in Latin America, 1830–1930," *Journal of Latin American Studies*, 32: 611–644.

Posner, Daniel. 1995. "Malawi's New Dawn," *Journal of Democracy*, 6(1): 131–145.

Posner, Daniel. 2005. *Institutions and Ethnic Politics in Africa*, Cambridge University Press.

Powell Jr, Bingham G. and Guy Whitten. 1993. "A Cross-National Analysis of Economic Voting: Taking Account of the Political Context," *American Journal of Political Science*, 37(2): 391–414.

Powers, Nancy R. 1992. "The transition to democracy in Paraguay: problems and prospects, a rapporteur's report," Kellogg Working Paper #171, University of Notre Dame, January.

Przeworski, Adam. 1991. *Democracy and the Market*. Cambridge: Cambridge University Press.

Przeworski, Adam, Michael Alvarez, Jose Cheibub and Fernando Limongi. 2000. *Democracy and Development*. Cambridge University Press.

Przeworski, Adam and Jennifer Gandhi. 2001. "Cooperation, cooptation and rebellion under dictatorships," mimeo, New York University.

Przeworski, Adam and Jennifer Gandhi. 2006. "Cooperation, cooptation and rebellion under dictatorships," *Economics and Politics*, 18(1): 1–26.

Przeworski, Adam, Susan Stokes and Bernard Manin, eds. 1999. *Democracy, Accountability, and Representation*. Cambridge: Cambridge University Press.

Purcell v. Gonzalez, 127 S. Ct. 5, 7 (2006) (per curiam).

Raftopoulos, Brian and Lloyd Sachikonye. 2001. *Striking Back: the Labour Movement and the Post-Colonial State in Zimbabwe, 1980–2000*. Harare: Weaver Press.

Ramos Oranday, Rogelio. 1985. "Oposición y Abstencionismo en las Elecciones Presidenciales 1964–1982," in Pablo González Casanova, ed., *Las Elecciones en México. Evolución y Perspectiva*, Mexico: Siglo XXI.

Rauch, James and Peter Evans. 2000. "Bureaucratic Structure and Bureaucratic Performance in Less Developed Countries," *Journal of Public Economics*, 75(1): 49–71.

Rehnquist, William H. 2004. *Centennial Crisis : The Disputed Election of 1876*. 1st ed. New York: Alfred A. Knopf; Distributed by Random House.

Reuter, Ora John and Jennifer Gandhi. 2010. "Economic performance and elite defection from hegemonic parties," *British Journal of Political Science*, 41: 83–110.

Reyes del Campillo, Juan. 1993. "Guanajuato: Geografía Electoral," in Gustavo Ernesto Emmerich, ed. *Votos y Mapas: Estudios de Geografía Electoral en México*, Toluca, Universidad Autónoma del Estado de México.

Reynolds, John F. "A Symbiotic Relationship: Vote Fraud and Electoral Reform in the Gilded Age," *Social Science History*, 17.2 (1993): 227–251.

Rich-Dorman, Sarah. 2005. "Make Sure they Count Nicely this Time: The Politics of Elections and Election Observing in Zimbabwe," *Commonwealth and Comparative Politics*, 43(2): 155–177.

Riker, William and Peter Ordeshook. 1968. "A Theory of the Calculus of Voting," *American Political Science Review*, 62(1):25–42.

Robinson, James and Ragnar Torvik. 2009. "A Political Economy Theory of the Soft Budget Constraint," *European Economic Review*, 53(7): 786–798.

Rodrik, Dani. 2009. "Thew new development economics: we shall experiment, but what shall we learn?" in Jessica Cohen and William Easterly, eds., *What Works in Development Economics? Thinking Big and Thinking Small*, Washington, DC: Brookings Institution Press.

Rodríguez Araujo, Octavio y Álvaro Arreola. 1993. "Las Caras del Abstencionismo: Baja California, Chihuahua y Michoacán, 1974–1989," in Gustavo Ernesto Emmerich, ed. *Votos y Mapas: Estudios de Geografía Electoral en México*, Toluca, Universidad Autónoma del Estado de México.

Roemer, John. 2001. *Political Competition: Theory and Applications*, Harvard University Press.

Rosas, Guillermo and Kirk Hawkins. 2008. "Turncoats, True Believers and Turnout: Machine Politics in the Absence of Vote Monitoring," mimeo, February 29.

Rose, Richard. 2007. "The impact of president Putin on popular support for Russia's regime," *Post-Soviet Affairs*, 23(2): 97–117.

Rose, Richard and William Mishler. 2009. "How do Electors Respond to an 'Unfair' Election? The Experience of Russians," *Post-Soviet Affairs*, 25(2): 118–136.

Rosenstone, Steven and John Mark Hansen. 2002 [1993]. *Mobilization, Participation and American Democracy*, Longman.

Ross, Michael. 2004. "Does taxation lead to representation?" *British Journal of Political Science*, 34(2): 229–249.

Rutland, Peter. 2008. "Putin's economic record: is the oil boom sustainable?" mimeo.

Sakwa, Richard. 2009. *The quality of freedom: Khodorkovsky, Putin, and the Yukos Affair*, Oxford University Press.

Sakwa, Richard, and Martin Crouch. 1978. "Elections in communist Poland: an overview and reappraisal," *British Journal of Political Science*, 8(4): 403–424.

Salazar, Julián and Gustavo Ernesto Emmerich. 1993. "Ensayo de Geografía Electoral del Estado de México," in Gustavo Ernesto Emmerich, ed. *Votos y Mapas: Estudios de Geografía Electoral en México*, Toluca, Universidad Autónoma del Estado de México.

Samuels, David and Richard Snyder. 2001. "The Value of a Vote: Malapportionment in Comparative Perspective," *British Journal of Political Science*, 31(4): 651–671.

Sapiro, Virginia, and Shively, W. Philips. 2004. *ICPSR 2683 Comparative study of electoral systems, 1996–2001*, 4th ICPSR version, Inter-University Consortium for Political and Social Research, February.

Sartori, Giovanni. 1993. "Totalitarianism, model mania, and learning from error," *Journal of Theoretical Politics*, 5(1): 5–22.

Sartori, Giovanni. 1997. *Comparative constitutional engineering: An inquiry into structures, incentives, and outcomes*. Washington Square, N.Y.: New York University Press.

Sartori, Giovanni. 2005. *Parties and Party Systems: A Framework for Analysis*, ECPR Press (first published in 1976 by Cambridge University Press).

Schaffer, Frederic Charles. 2002. "Might Cleaning up Elections Keep People Away from the Polls? Historical and Comparative Perspectives," *International Political Science Review*, 23(1): 69–84.

Schaffer, Frederic Charles, ed., 2007. *Elections for Sale: The Causes and Consequences of Vote Buying*, Lynne Rienner.

Schaffer, Frederic Charles. 2008. *The Hidden Costs of Clean Election Reform*, Ateneo de Manila University Press.

Schaffer, Frederic Charles, and Andreas Schedler. 2005. "What is vote buying?" mimeo.

Schapiro, Leonard B. 1978. *The government and politics of the Soviet Union*, Vintage Books.

Schedler, Andreas. 2002. "The Menu of Manipulation," *Journal of Democracy*, 13(2): 36–50, April.

Schedler, Andreas. 2004. "El Voto Es Nuestro," *Revista Mexicana de Sociología*, 66(1): 57–97.

Schedler, Andreas, ed., 2006. *Electoral Authoritarianism: The Dynamics of Unfree Competition*, Lynne Rienner.

Scheiner, Ethan, 2006. "Democracy Without Competition in Japan: Opposition Failure in a One-Party Dominant State," Cambridge University Press.

Schelling, Thomas. 1960. *The Strategy of Conflict*, Harvard University Press.

Schuessler, Alexander. 2000. "Expressive Voting," *Rationality and Society*, 12(1): 87–119.

Scott, James. 1969. "Corruption, machine politics, and political change," *American Political Science Review*, 63(4): 1142–1158.

Scott, James. 1972. *Comparative Political Corruption*, Prentice-Hall.

Sekhon, Jasjeet. 2004. "Updating Voters: How voters act as if they are informed," Harvard University, mimeo, v.1.4.6.

Seligson, Mitchell A. 1996. "Cultura política en Paraguay: lineamientos de estudios de valores democráticos para el año 1996," mimeo, Vanderbilt University.

Sen, Amartya. 1999. "The Possibility of Social Choice," *American Economic Review*, 89(3): 349–378.

Shevtsova, Liliia. 1997. "Dilemmas of post-Communist society," *Sociological Research*, 36(5): 45–61.

Shpilkin, Sergey. 2008. "Analysis of Russian Elections," *Times Online*, April 18.

Shpilkin, Sergey. 2009. "Statistical study of Russian elections results (2007–2009)," *Troicky Variant*, 21(40): October 27.

Shvetsova, Olga. 2003. "Resolving the problem of preelection coordination: the 1999 parliamentary election as an elite presidential 'primary,'" in Hesli and Reisinger, eds., *The 1999–2000 elections in Russia: their impact and legacy*, Cambridge University Press.

Sil, Rudra. 2001. "Privatization, labor politics, and the firm in post-Soviet Russia: Non-market norms, market institutions and the Soviet legacy," in Christopher Candland and Rudra Sil, *The Politics of Labor in a Global Age*, Oxford University Press.

Silitski, Vitali. 2005. "Preempting Democracy: The Case of Belarus," *Journal of Democracy*, 16(4): 83–97.

Simpser, Alberto. 2003. "The manipulation of mass elections: fraud, expectations, and turnout," mimeo, Stanford University, November 12.

Simpser, Alberto. 2005. *Making Votes Not Count: Strategic Incentives for Electoral Corruption*, PhD dissertation, Stanford University.

Simpser, Alberto. 2008. "Unintended consequences of election monitoring," in Alvarez et al, *Election Fraud: Detecting and Deterring Electoral Manipulation*, Brookings.

Simpser, Alberto. 2011. "The political economy of electoral overinvestment," mimeo, University of Chicago.

Simpser, Alberto. 2012. "Does Electoral Manipulation Discourage Voter Turnout? Evidence from Mexico," *The Journal of Politics*, 74(3): 1–14.

Simpser, Alberto and Daniela Donno. 2012. "Can International Election Monitoring Harm Governance?," *The Journal of Politics*. 74(2): 501–513.

Sithole, Masipula. 1997. "Zimbabwe's Eroding Authoritarianism," *Journal of Democracy*, 8(1): 127–141.

Slater, Dan. 2003. "Iron Cage in an Iron Fist: Authoritarian Institutions and the Personalization of Power in Malaysia," *Comparative Politics*, 36(1): 81–101.

Slater, Dan. 2008. "Can Leviathan be Democratic? Competitive Elections, Robust Mass Politics, and State Infrastructural Power," *Studies in Comparative International Development*, 43(3–4): 252–272.

Slater, Dan and Erica Simmons. 2010. "Informative Regress: Critical Antecedents in Comparative Politics," *Comparative Political Studies*, 43: 931–968.

Smyth, Regina. 2006. *Candidate Strategies and Electoral Competition in the Russian Federation: Democracy without Foundation*, Cambridge: Cambridge University Press.

Snyder, James M. 1989. "Election Goals and the Allocation of Campaign Resources," *Econometrica*, 57(3): 637–660.

Sondrol, Paul A. 2007. "Paraguay: a semi-authoritarian regime?" *Armed Forces and Society*, 34(1): 46–66.

Spence, Michael. (1973). "Job Market Signaling," *Quarterly Journal of Economics*, 87(3): 355–374.

Spiegel Online. 2007. "Election observers unwelcome," November 16.

Stokes, Susan. 2005. "Perverse Accountability: A Formal Model of Machine Politics with Evidence from Argentina," *American Political Science Review*, 99(3): 315–325.

Stokes, Susan. 2007. "Is vote-buying undemocratic?" in Schaffer, 2007, *Elections for Sale.* Lynne Rienner.

Stokes, Susan, Thad Dunning, Marcelo Nazareno, and Valeria Brusco. 2011. *Buying votes: Distributive Politics under Democracies.* Yale University and the National University of Cordoba, Unpublished manuscript.

Stoner-Weiss, Kathryn. 2002. "Central governing incapacity and the weakness of political parties: Russian democracy in disarray," *Publius*, 32(2): 125–146.

Stoner-Weiss, Kathryn. 2006. *Resisting the State: Reform and Retrenchment in Post-Soviet Russia.* Cambridge University Press.

Sylvester, Christine. 1990. "Unities and Disunities in Zimbabwe's 1990 Election," *The Journal of Modern African Studies*, 28(03): 375–400.

Sylvester, Christine. 1995. "Whither Opposition in Zimbabwe?" *Journal of Modern African Studies*, 33: 403–423.

Szwarcberg, Mariela. 2009. *Making Local Democracy: Political Machines, Clientelism, and Social Networks in Latin America*, PhD dissertation, University of Chicago.

Tasker, Rodney and Shawn Crispin. 2001. "On an electoral collision course," *Far Eastern Economic Review*, January 11: 22–23.

Taylor, Jonathan. 2005. "Too Many Ties? An Empirical Analysis of the Venezuelan Referendum Counts," mimeo, Stanford University, November.

Taylor, Robert H. 1996a. *The politics of elections in Southeast Asia*, Cambridge University Press.

Taylor, Robert H. 1996b. "Elections and politics in Southeast Asia," in Robert Taylor, *The politics of elections in Southeast Asia*, Cambridge University Press.

Teehankee, Julio. 2002. "Electoral politics in the Philippines," in Aurel Croissant et al., *Electoral Politics in Southeast and East Asia*, Friedrich Ebert Stiftung.

Teorell, Jan. 2008. "Swedish electoral corruption in historical-comparative perspective: a research proposal," mimeo, presented at the Social Science History Association Meeting, Miami, October 23–26.

Thompson, Ginger. 2005. "Upset seen in vote in Southern Mexican state," *New York Times*, February 7.

Timberg, Craig. 2008. "Inside Mugabe's violent crackdown: notes, witnesses detail how campaign was conceived and executed by leader, aides," *Washington Post*, July 5, A01.

Tomz, Michael, Jason Wittenberg, and Gary King. 2001. *CLARIFY: Software for Interpreting and Presenting Statistical Results.* Version 2.0 Cambridge, MA: Harvard University, June 1. http://gking.harvard.edu.

Transparency International. 2004. *Global Corruption Report 2004.*

Treisman, Daniel. 2007. "What Have We Learned About the Causes of Corruption from Ten Years of Cross-National Empirical Research?," *Annual Review of Political Science*, 10: 211–244.

Treisman, Daniel. 2009. "Presidential popularity in a young democracy: Russia under Yeltsin and Putin," mimeo, University of California, Los Angeles.

Tucker, Joshua. 2007. "Enough! Electoral fraud, collective action problems, and post-Communist democratic revolutions," *Perspectives on Politics*, 5(3): 535–551.

Uzelac, Ana. 2001. "It's Lonely At the Top In Belarus," *The Moscow Times*, September 11.

Van de Walle, Nicholas. 2006. "Tipping games: when do opposition parties coalesce?," in Schedler, ed. *Electoral Authoritarianism: the Dynamics of Unfree Competition*. Lynne Rienner Publishers.

Vives, Xavier. 1999. *Oligopoly pricing: old ideas and new tools*. MIT Press.

Von Salzen, Claudia. 2004. "The state comes first for Vladimir Putin. Interview with Grigory Yavlinsky," Tagesspiegel, January 12, 2004.

Walton, John and Joyce A. Sween. 1971. "Urbanization, industrialization, and voting in Mexico: a longitudinal analysis of official and opposition support," *Social Science Quarterly*, 52(3): 721–745.

Wand, Jonathan, Kenneth Shotts, Jasjeet Sekhon, Walter Mebane, Jr., Michael Herron, and Henry Brady. 2001. "The Butterfly Did It: The Aberrant Vote for Buchanan in Palm Beach County, Florida," *American Political Science Review*, 95: 4.

Wang, Chin-Shou and Charles Kurzman. 2003. "Logistics: How to Buy Votes," mimeo, University of North Carolina at Chapel Hill, December 7.

Wang, Chin-Shou and Charles Kurzman. 2007. "Dilemmas of Electoral Clientelism: Taiwan 1993," *International Political Science Review*, 28(2): 225–245.

Ware, Alan. 1996. *Political parties and party systems*. Oxford University Press.

Way, Lucan. 2005a. "Kuchma's Failed Authoritarianism," *Journal of Democracy*, 16(2): 131–145.

Way, Lucan. 2005b. "Authoritarian State Building and the Sources of Regime Competitiveness in the Fourth Wave: The Cases of Belarus, Moldova, Russia, and Ukraine," *World Politics*, 57(2): 231–261.

Way, Lucan. 2006. "Authoritarian failure: how does state weakness strengthen electoral competition?" in Andreas Schedler, ed. *Electoral Authoritarianism: the Dynamics of Unfree Competition*. Lynne Rienner.

Weber Abramo, Claudio. 2004. "Vote buying in Brazil: less of a problem than believed?" in ch. 5, Transparency International *Global Corruption Report 2004*.

Wedeen, Lisa. 1998. "Acting 'As If': Symbolic Politics and Control in Syria," *Comparative Studies in Society and History*, 40(3): 503–523.

Wedeen, Lisa. 1999. *Ambiguities of Domination: Politics, Rhetoric, and Symbols in Contemporary Syria*, University of Chicago Press.

Wedeen, Lisa. 2008. *Peripheral visions. Politics, power and performance in Yemen*, University of Chicago Press.

Weil, David N., 2009, "Comment by David N. Weil," in Jessica Cohen and William Easterly, eds., *What Works in Development Economics? Thinking Big and Thinking Small*, Washington, DC: Brookings Institution Press.

Weingast, Barry. 1995. "The Economic Role of Political Institutions: Market-Preserving Federalism and Economic Development," *Journal of Law, Economics and Organization*, 11(1): 1–31.

Weingast, Barry. 1997. "The political foundations of democracy and the rule of law," *American Political Science Review*, 91(2): 245–263.

Weitzer, Ronald. 1984. "In search of regime security: Zimbabwe since independence," *Journal of Modern African Studies*, 22(4): 529–557.

Weitz-Shapiro, Rebecca. 2012. "What wins votes: why some politicians opt out of clientelism," *American Journal of Political Science*, 56(3): 568–583.

Wellman, Elizabeth Iams. 2010. "Elections and Evictions: Exploring the Political Calculus of Slum Demolitions," MA thesis, University of Chicago, June.

White, Gregory L., and Rob Barry. 2011. "Russia's dubious vote," *The Wall Street Journal*, December 28, A1

Whitmore, Brian. 2011. "The Decemberist Uprising," The Power Vertical blog, *Radio Free Europe*, December 8.

Whitmore, Brian. 2012. "The Medvedev Legacy," The Power Vertical blog, *Radio Free Europe*, January 25.

Widner, Jennifer and Daniel Scher. 2008. "Building judicial independence in semi-democracies: Uganda and Zimbabwe," in Tom Ginsburg and Tamir Moustafa, eds., *Rule by Law: the Politics of Courts in Authoritarian Regimes*, Cambridge: Cambridge University Press.

Wilson, Andrew. 2005. *Virtual politics: Faking democracy in the post-soviet world.* New Haven: Yale University Press.

Wilson, Andrew. 2006. "Belarus between 'Colored Revolution' and 'Counter-Revolutionary Technology,'" in Valer Bulhakaŭ, ed., *The Geopolitical Place of Belarus in Europe and the World*. Warsaw: ELIPSA.

Woldenberg, José. 1988. "Las Cifras y los Votos: Pistas para no irse con las Fintas," Cuadernos de Nexos, September. *Nexos*, Mexico.

Wurfel, David. 1963. "The Philippines," *Journal of Politics*, 25(4): 757–773, November.

Ziblatt, Daniel. 2009. "Shaping Democratic Practice and the Causes of Electoral Fraud: The Case of Nineteenth-Century Germany," *American Political Science Review*, 103(1): 1–21.

Zimbabwe Election Support Network. 2005. "Report on the Zimbabwe 2005 General Election, Final Copy," April.

Index